LEARNING TO TEACH GEOGRAPHY
IN THE SECONDARY SCHOOL

Praise for previous editions:

'This is a practical and visionary book, as well as being superbly optimistic. It has as much to offer the experienced teacher as the novice and could be used to reinvigorate geography departments everywhere. Practical activities and ideas are set within a carefully worked out, authoritative, conceptual framework.' – *The Times Educational Supplement*

'This is a modern, powerful, relevant and comprehensive work . . . a standard reference for many beginning teachers on geography initial teacher training courses.' – *Educational Review*

Learning to Teach Geography in the Secondary School has become the widely recommended textbook for student and new teachers of geography. It helps you acquire a deeper understanding of the role, purpose and potential of geography within the secondary curriculum, and provides the practical skills needed to design, teach and evaluate stimulating and challenging lessons.

It is grounded in the notion of social justice and the idea that all students are entitled to a high-quality geography education. The very practical dimension provides you with support structures through which you can begin to develop your own philosophy of teaching, and debate key questions about the nature and purpose of the subject in school.

Fully revised and updated in light of extensive changes to the curriculum, as well as to initial teacher education, the new edition considers the current debates around what we mean by geographical knowledge, and what's involved in studying at Masters level. Key chapters explore the fundamentals of teaching and learning geography:

- Why we teach and what to teach
- Understanding and planning the curriculum
- Effective pedagogy
- Assessment
- Developing and using resources
- Fieldwork and outdoor learning
- Values in school geography
- Professional development

Intended as a core textbook and written with university and school-based initial teacher education in mind, *Learning to Teach Geography in the Secondary School* is essential reading for all those who aspire to become effective, reflective teachers.

Mary Biddulph is Lecturer in Geography Education, School of Education at the University of Nottingham, UK.

David Lambert is Professor of Geography Education at the Faculty of Culture and Pedagogy, Institute of Education, University College London, UK.

David Balderstone is a School Improvement Partner and Associate Headteacher in Milton Keynes, UK.

LEARNING TO TEACH SUBJECTS IN THE SECONDARY SCHOOL SERIES

Series Editors: Susan Capel and Marilyn Leask

Designed for all students learning to teach in secondary schools, and particularly those on school-based initial teacher training courses, the books in this series complement *Learning to Teach in the Secondary School* and its companion, *Starting to Teach in the Secondary School*. Each book in the series applies underpinning theory and addresses practical issues to support student teachers in school and in the training institution in learning how to teach a particular subject.

LEARNING TO TEACH GEOGRAPHY IN THE SECONDARY SCHOOL

A companion to school experience

Third edition

Mary Biddulph,
David Lambert and David Balderstone

Routledge
Taylor & Francis Group

LONDON AND NEW YORK

Third edition published 2015
by Routledge
2 Park Square, Milton Park, Abingdon, Oxon OX14 4RN

and by Routledge
711 Third Avenue, New York, NY 10017

Routledge is an imprint of the Taylor & Francis Group, an informa business

First edition published 2002 by RoutledgeFalmer
Second edition published 2010 by Routledge

British Library Cataloguing in Publication Data
A catalogue record for this book is available from the British Library

Library of Congress Cataloging in Publication Data
Biddulph, Mary.
Learning to teach geography in the secondary school : a companion to school experience / Mary Biddulph, David Lambert and David Balderstone. – Third edition.
pages cm
Includes bibliographical references.
1. Geography–Study and teaching (Secondary). I. Lambert, David, 1952- II. Balderstone, David. III. Title.
G73.L345 2015
910.71′2–dc23
2014043191

ISBN: 978-1-138-77943-3 (hbk)
ISBN: 978-1-138-77944-0 (pbk)
ISBN: 978-1-315-77127-4 (ebk)

Typeset in Interstate
by Swales & Willis Ltd, Exeter, Devon, UK

CONTENTS

ILLUSTRATIONS

FIGURES

TABLES

TASKS

BOXES

ACKNOWLEDGEMENTS

Acknowledgements are gratefully expressed for material from the following publications:

Andrew Turney and Eve Jakeways, Field Studies Council, Brockhole.

Fien, J. and Slater, F. (1981) 'Four Strategies for Values Education in Geography'. *Geographical Education* 4, 1: 39–52.

Rawling, E. (2001) *Changing the Subject: The Impact of National Policy on School Geography 1980–2000*, Geographical Association: Sheffield

Taylor, E. (2009) *GTIP Think Piece – Concepts in Geography*. Sheffield: Geographical Association. Available at: www.geography.org.uk/gtip/thinkpieces/concepts/ [accessed 25 April 14].

Roberts, M. (2013) *Geography Through Enquiry: Approaches to Teaching and Learning in the Secondary School*. Sheffield: Geographical Association.

Roberts, M. (1986) 'Talking, Reading and Writing'. In D. Boardman (ed.) *Handbook for Geography Teachers*. Sheffield: Geographical Association, pp. 68–78.

Waters, A. (1995) 'Differentiation and classroom practice', *Teaching Geography*, 20, 2: 81–84.

Leat, D. and Chandler, S. (1996) 'Using Concept Mapping in Geography Teaching', *Teaching Geography*, 21, 3: 108–12.

Enright, N., Flook, A. and Habgood, C. (2006) 'Gifted Young Geographers'. In D. Balderstone (ed.) *Secondary Geography Handbook*. Sheffield: Geographical Association, pp. 368–83.

O'Connor, P. (2007) 'Progressive GIS', *Teaching Geography*, 32, 3: 147–50.

Jones, M. and Ryecraft, P. (2007) 'Animated Discussions in Geography', *Teaching Geography*, 32, 2: 93–96.

Holmes, D. and Walker, M. (2006) 'Planning Geographical Fieldwork'. In D. Balderstone (ed.) *Secondary Geography Handbook*. Sheffield: Geographical Association, pp. 210–225.

Robinson, R. and Serf, J. (eds) (1997) *Global Geography: Learning through Development Education at Key Stage 3*. Sheffield: Geographical Association/Birmingham Development Education Centre.

Material on page 300 is reproduced from *The Challenge of Globalisation: A Handbook for Teachers of 11-16 Year Olds*, 2003 with the permission of Oxfam GB, Oxfam House, John Smith Drive, Cowley, Oxford OX4 2JY, UK www.oxfam.org.uk/education. Oxfam GB does not necessarily endorse any text or activities that accompany the materials.'

Introduction

> I have learnt that geography is all around, and geography affects us all. Me, I'm geography, the building's part of geography, everything is geography. It's not just about Jamaica's there, Africa's there, Britain's there . . . it's about us as a community.
>
> (15-year-old geography student)

The quote above is from a 15-year-old geography student, at the end of a year-long curriculum development project about young people's geographies. What this student expresses here is how learning geography has helped him to appreciate that understanding the world requires more of him than merely knowing a list of places. Learning geography has helped him to see connections between himself and others and also appreciate the geographical significance of the world around him. It seems to us that geography has opened his eyes to the world as an object of thought.

This book has been written for beginning teachers of geography, those individuals who want to help this student and others like him develop a love for learning geography. In writing this book, we make several assumptions about you, the reader. We assume that you have decided to become a geography teacher in a secondary school, because you want to achieve something fairly specific in relation to young people's educational opportunities. In order to realise this ambition, we assume that you are a geographer with a deep interest in the subject and a desire to continue learning geography. We also assume that you probably have a geography degree or a degree in a related field and so have a good academic grounding in the principle theories and practices that are part and parcel of being 'a geographer'. Our third assumption is that you like and respect young people and that you want them to enjoy the benefits that accrue from a high-quality geographical education. These are all important starting points for learning to teach geography, but we would stress the overarching idea that as a geography teacher you are committed to your own learning as well as that of your pupils.

As this book demonstrates, the landscape of education is in a constant state of change as educational theory, educational policy and classroom practice slip and slide between different and often competing discourses. As a beginning teacher, it is easy to become so entrenched in the day-to-day of teaching it can become relatively easy to allow the 'bigger' educational debates to pass you by: 'What have they got to do with me?' is a disposition that can prevail when you are very busy learning to teach. However, we argue very clearly here that there is a relationship between the macro level of educational debate and decision-making and the micro-level of teaching and classrooms – decisions made elsewhere in seemingly distant corridors of power impact on what you teach and how you teach it. What we are trying to achieve in this book is to help you understand this relationship in order that you can engage critically with it. School geography is not what it was in the past and will change further during your own teaching career. You are part of this community of practice we can call 'geography education' and we encourage you to have agency and exert influence – in your own classroom to begin with but potentially among your colleagues and beyond, using networks such as the Geographical Association (GA).

Thus, you will quickly realise that like academic geography, school geography does not stand still. You will need to dedicate time and energy to developing your own subject knowledge if you are to engage and inspire your pupils. We are not talking here about simply plugging any knowledge 'gaps': this is a somewhat reductionist notion of what we mean by subject knowledge development. We argue that it as your responsibility to both develop your understanding of what we mean by knowledge in school geography and what it means to 'think geographically' as well as develop your subject knowledge for teaching. In our view this is essential to ensure geography, as experienced by pupils, remains dynamic, relevant and interesting. At the same time, we would reassure you that as a new entrant to the profession you also bring with you new and unique perspectives on the discipline – these new geographies, drawn from the academic frontier, when appropriately transformed for secondary pupils, have much to offer the geography curriculum in schools.

In attending to what we believe are important aspects in learning to teach geography, we are very clear that regardless of your capabilities as a geographer, you must be able to also connect with the young people you teach in order to help them access key ideas in the discipline. Thus, when making teaching decisions, your pupils need to be at the forefront of your thinking: who they are, what makes them tick, what they find difficult/easy/interesting and so on are crucial elements in the choices you make and the actions you engage in. No technique or approach can be excluded; you need to be able to draw from as wide a teaching repertoire as possible to meet the needs of different pupils. And please remember, the pupils you will meet are an enormously diverse population – which is why in considering pupils' needs we reject crude categories such as 'high ability' or 'low ability' as ways of labelling pupils. These terms have slipped too easily in the lexicon of teaching and learning, only serving to mask individual pupils' learning aptitudes.

A further important principle for us is that the teaching profession is necessarily a 'broad church'. It is important for pupils that their teachers are from a range of contexts and traditions (but who share the goal of providing high-quality geographical education). Good geography teachers are not born. We can learn how to become effective – but at the same time there is no such thing as a 'typical geography teacher' – no hard and fast 'rules' that govern what we must do and no personality traits that one must possess to be 'good'. But there *are* fundamental principles that underpin good teaching in geography and it is these we have tried to elaborate on, debate and explore in this book. We hope that the complex mix of intellectual and practical activity that characterises teachers' work comes through, and that the issues and ideas discussed here will inspire you in developing both your critical understanding of what it means to teach geography and in your practical pursuits of helping pupils to learn.

We have been determined that this text is not a 'tips for teachers' text (there are plenty of those available elsewhere). What we advocate here is a form of intellectual engagement ensuring that theory underpins practice in realistic ways. This form of engagement is important as you learn to teach for several reasons. First, understanding the change processes in education helps you to make informed decisions about your practice because you have a *critical* understanding of the issues at hand. Second, an imported part of your professional responsibility is to participate in the processes that often drive educational change, for example the consultations that preceded changes to the National Curriculum in 2013, and the substantial changes to GCSE subject criteria and A-level subject content in 2014 (for first teaching in 2016). To do this effectively means that you need a well-informed basis from which to draw. Finally, most initial teacher education (ITE) courses are now Master's level courses and it is a requirement of this level of study that you demonstrate your understanding of the theory-policy-practice relationship. 'Tips' can get you out of an immediate classroom dilemma, but in the long term you need the support of something more theoretically informed, more rigorous and ultimately more meaningful if you are to sustain high-quality classroom practice.

A final thought before we begin – a text such as this does not come to life of its own accord. This is the third edition of this particular book. We have had the sound foundations of the first and second editions to build on. Having said this, this edition has grown out of a considerable team effort and has also drawn heavily on the ideas and contributions of colleagues in the geography education community – their research and writing has made the development of this text possible. We are also all, in different ways, indebted to our school and university colleagues, past and present, for their support and encouragement. In particular colleagues at the School of Education, University of Nottingham and colleagues at the University College London Institute of Education have played a crucial part in developing our thinking; their expertise, energy and enthusiasm has over the years provided inspiration.

In many ways, our biggest debt is to the several generations of student teachers we have known, and who have successfully worked and continue to work in geography departments all over the country. Learning to become a geography teacher is hard work and can be physically, emotionally and mentally exhausting. Many student teachers have commented that preparing to become a geography teacher was the most challenging thing they had ever done. Many of these have now become school leaders. They have a dynamic view of the subject and its pedagogy and constantly question what is worth teaching. Our ongoing working relationships with these teachers, not least through the meetings, journals and conferences of the Geographical Association, leave us feeling very optimistic for the future of school geography.

We have ostensibly written this book for beginning teachers of geography, but we have really written it for pupils, who rely on their geography teacher to help them understand the complex interactions of the physical and human world and in doing so establish some sort of order in what Bonnett (2008) describes as a 'seemingly chaotic world' (p.6). So while you, the new geography teacher, may be our focus, our long-term sights are set squarely on the contribution high-quality geography lessons make to young people's educational experience and their developing capabilities.

Mary Biddulph, David Lambert and David Balderstone

1 Why teach geography and what to teach in geography

> In our working lives as geography teachers we should never forget or abandon those ideals which draw us to the job in the first place. School geography has the potential to develop young people's understanding of their 'place' in the world and so help form their identity.
>
> (Huckle 1997: 241)

Introduction

This chapter aims to put contemporary geographical education in England and Wales into a broad context. It briefly considers the changing relationship between school and academic geography and also examines what might be our rationale for including geography in the school curriculum in the first place. In particular it opens up the debate about 'what to teach' arguing that effective school geography is more than mere facts, but requires sustained engagement with what is known as 'powerful knowledge'.

By the end of this chapter, you should be able to:

- consider what is geography's distinctive contribution to the school curriculum
- contribute to the professional debates concerning the nature of geography in the school
- understand the changing relationship between school and academic geography and connect your own academic interests with development in the school curriculum
- understand the knowledge debate and how this impinges on the kinds of geographical knowledges that are taught in schools
- locate school geography in England within a wider discourse about school geography internationally.

The purpose of learning geography – 'thinking geographically'

> The function of geography in school is to train future citizens to imagine accurately the conditions of the great world stage and so to help them to think sanely about political and social problems in the world around.
>
> (Fairgrieve 1926: 18)

This statement, published just eight years after the end of the First World War (and only seven years before Hitler came to power in Germany), still has contemporary significance. The only thing, arguably, that Fairgrieve might add today is the word 'environmental' (and possibly 'economic') to the list of global issues. The statement expresses a goal – perhaps the overriding goal – for geography in education; it helps remind us why we are teaching geography and not something else. Also, the words chosen are significant: Fairgrieve could have used the word 'understand', but he preferred to write 'imagine'; why?

The purpose of this section is to examine the aims, or goals, of geography in education. A number of debates are explored which help identify the ways in which geography can be justified as a curriculum subject. In particular, we tackle the tension (picked up again elsewhere in this book) between school geography being tailored to serve the 'needs of pupils' on the one hand, and school geography being shaped by developments in 'the discipline' (i.e. in Higher Education) on the other.

The study of geography as an academic discipline in Britain is a relatively recent phenomenon (since roughly the latter part of the nineteenth century). Although the vocabulary of geography (i.e. place names) had been present in schools since before that time, the study of geography in education (coupled to the systematic training of geography teachers) is an even more recent enterprise: Fairgrieve's 1926 book is a useful landmark. But it is also worth noting that some prestigious schools did not even teach it as recently as the 1960s, and occasionally geography is still openly attacked for somehow failing to box to the same intellectual 'weight' as related subjects such as history. The subjects are, of course, different, and we shall spend no time in this book 'defending' geography from its perceived deficiencies – we take it as read that you are as convinced as we are of the value of the study of geography, not least because you have chosen to teach it. However, it is important for those involved in teaching geography to be clear about its purpose and to be knowledgeable about its position in the education system. This brings us to the key question posed by the Nuffield Review of 14–19 Education Training for England and Wales:

> What counts as an educated young person in this day and age?

For those committed to ensuring that all young people receive a 'broad and balanced education, it seems astonishing that geography would not have a role to play in the educational endeavour. Could a young person be described as 'educated' *without* knowledge understanding of our (human) relationship with each other and the physical world? We think not, yet there are others, some in positions of power and authority, who either do not understand geography's potential as an educational resource or who have a very narrow view of what constitutes 'geography'. It is a popular, almost comic representation, that to learn geography means to merely memorise facts about the world, only to then regurgitate them at opportune moments such as in a pub quiz or when completing the weekend crossword.

To counteract this naivety and challenge the popular mythology described above, Peter Jackson (2006) argues that 'thinking geographically' provides a clear and coherent rationale for the value of learning geography in school. The point being that thinking geographically is about how we develop in pupils a particular geographical way of seeing the world that is distinct from 'thinking historically' or 'thinking scientifically'. Lambert (2004) expresses school geography as something akin to a language. In the case of geography, the content (rivers, cities, mountains, etc.) comprises its vocabulary, that is, the detail we use to frame our engagement with the subject, whereas concepts such as space, place, scale, environment, comprise its grammar, that is, the structures that frame the detail and help us to make sense of it. The point here is that while content is important, content alone is not enough; it is the concepts that frame and give purpose to school geography because understanding concepts allows pupils to apply their geographical knowledge and understanding to new, challenging and controversial ideas, wherever they may be – not just in school.

Jackson argues that four pairs of very distinct geographical concepts provide a starting point for developing pupils' geographical thinking:

- space and place
- scale and connection
- proximity and distance
- relational thinking.

However, he accepts that geographers could quite easily explore different concepts or groups of concepts that would equally, but differently help pupils to think geographically (see Chapter 3 on Planning for further discussion on working with concepts).

The Geographical Association's Manifesto entitled *A Different View* (2009) picks up the theme of 'thinking geographically' and considers how this very powerful idea helps pupils make sense of the world:

> An essential educational outcome of learning geography is to be able to apply knowledge and conceptual understanding to new settings: that is, to 'think geographically' about the changing world.

> (p. 9)

Box 1.1 Thinking geographically

Thinking geographically – using the big ideas to organise the information – enables children and young people to develop an understanding of:

- The physical world: the land, water, air and ecological system; landscapes; and the processes that bring them about and change them.
- Human environments: societies, communities and the human processes involved in understanding work, home, consumption and leisure – and how places are made.
- Interdependence: crucially, linking the physical world and human environments and understanding the concept of sustainable development.
- Place and space: recognising similarities and differences across the world and developing knowledge and understanding of location, interconnectedness and spatial patterns.
- Scale: the 'zoom lens' through which the subject matter is 'seen', and the significance of local, regional, national, international and global perspectives.
- Young people's lives: using their own images, experiences, meanings and questions; reaching out' to children and young people as active agents in their education.

(*Source*: Geographical Association, 2009: 11.
www.geography.org.uk/adifferentview)

While 'thinking geographically' provides a powerful argument for a high-quality geography education for all, the views of pupils themselves add significant weight to this. In 2009 Ipsos Mori completed a poll for the Geographical Association, asking 11–14-year-olds what issues they felt it was important that they learnt about in school (www.geography.org.uk/resources/adifferentview/worldissuessurvey/#top. [accessed 10 August 2014]). The headlines from the poll include:

- Young people see Crime and anti-social behaviour as the most important issue affecting either their local area or the world generally, followed by Economy and jobs. War and terrorism, Poverty and hunger, and Environment and climate change are also seen as more important issues globally.
- Crime and the Environment are the subjects that young people are most likely to have learnt about/discussed at school.
- Geography is the subject in which young people have most often learnt about/discussed these issues at school, and the one in which they most commonly expect to do so.
- The great majority think it is important to learn about issues affecting different parts of the world, particularly how the world they live in may change.
- Most young people think that not enough time is spent learning about the wider world in school.

In addition, over 90 per cent think it is important to learn about where things like food, energy and water come from, and to learn about how their world may change in the future. Pupils identified geography as the main subject for learning about these things. Pupils do see the point of learning geography!

Task 1.1 A rationale for teaching geography

1 Read Peter Jackson's article 'Thinking Geographically' (2006: 199–204).
2 In what ways does the idea of *'Thinking Geographically'* provide a rational for teaching geography in schools?
3 Read the Geographical Association's 'Manifesto'.
  Use both the article, the Manifesto and your own thoughts and ideas, and set about the task of structuring a rationale for teaching school geography that could be published on a school's website for parents and prospective pupils to read – what is the essential message you wish to communicate about the purpose of learning geography?
4 It will also be important to talk to a group of pupils about their thoughts on the value of learning geography. Before you do this, be sure to follow your school's procedures regarding gaining permission to talk with pupils.
5 Compare your rationale with those of other student colleagues or even colleagues in school.
6 When in a school for a teaching placement, begin to think of ways in which the curriculum pupils are learning is helping them to think geographically. This will be an idea to come back to later.

Note: These readings can be found on the GA's website: www.geography.org.uk/adifferentview

---

Despite the messages of the Manifesto, the power of the argument for thinking geographically and the findings of the Ipsos Mori poll, young people's opportunity for a geography education has been seriously undermined in recent times by a range of national and more localised policy initiatives that have marginalised the subject in the school curriculum:

- The relentless focus on numeracy and literacy at the expense of subject teaching.
- The skewed curriculum in Key Stage 3 whereby some schools have focused on more generic curricular (learning to learn, skill-based, competency-base curricular; see Chapter 2).
- The reduction in teaching time for geography at Key Stage 3 with some schools now teaching a two-year curriculum at Key Stage 3 rather than a three-year curriculum, as was originally intended. This means that some pupils have no further engagement with geography, as a school discipline, after the age of 12–13 years.
- The rise of multiple-award bearing courses post-14, such as vocational courses, which used to carry up to four GCSE equivalent qualifications as opposed to one GCSE qualification on GCSE geography courses.
- The expansion of the academies program whereby research from the University of Birmingham clearly indicates that in some academies no geography was being taught at all (see Chapter 3 for more on this).

- The view, by some commentators, that geography as a school subject carried tradition-
  alist overtones and as such is irrelevant to young people growing up in a twenty-first-
  century interconnected globalised world.

(Lambert 2004)

These kinds of manoeuvres and initiatives mean that geography has to have a very powerful case in order to secure its place in the school curriculum. We are not arguing here for an adver-tising campaign for geography. We are arguing that such positioning is not necessary when it is clear to pupils, parents and senior managers that geography is making a worthwhile contribu-tion to pupils' broader educational experience. In recent times, what constitutes 'broader educa-tional experience' and 'worthwhile' has come under some serious scrutiny as curriculum reviews have caused us to think hard about what pupils should learn in a national education system. The election of the Coalition government in 2010 resulted in swift and radical changes to the school curriculum, including the geography curriculum (see Chapter 2), and one of the most sig-nificant messages emanating from these changes was that in any curriculum overhaul 'subject knowledge' would preside over more generic interpretations of the school curriculum. In the next section we discuss what 'subject knowledge' might mean in school geography and question the sometimes very limited and therefore limiting views of knowledge in the school curriculum.

The knotty question of what to teach in school geography

'Knowledge' and the elements of learning

The 'elements of learning' is a phrase that emerged in the heyday of the quasi-independent Her Majesty's Inspectorate (HMI) of schools – that is, before the invention of Ofsted in 1992, when inspection became less collegial and more an instrument of the state. In discussion documents about the curriculum, many of which still repay reading today (HMI 1986), HMI distinguished knowledge from understanding, as well as from skills and values. It became *de rigueur* to describe lessons in terms of the elements of learning that were being prioritised. Over a sequence of lessons, teachers were encouraged to plan for a balance between them.

Today the distinctions made between the four elements of learning are less clear cut. True, GCSE specifications have assessment objectives which are classified in similar terms: knowl-edge, understanding and skills. *Values*, however, seem to have less priority in official docu-ments – particularly galling to some geographers as it is recognised that the values people hold towards, say, fossil fuel production, or technology, govern to a greater or lesser degree how these aspects of the geography of a place, theme or issue are understood: fracking is not controversial in Texas to anything like the degree to which it is controversial in Sussex, for example, and this in itself is an interesting geography. The human beliefs and values people hold are a variable that helps how we understand the earth and its human occupation.

Skills on the other hand have become ubiquitous in recent years, to the extent that skills sometime appears to be a catch-all for learning and the outcomes of education. Thus, employers and politicians speak about the twenty-first-century skills that children need to be 'given' and the importance of learning life skills – and of learning to learn. It is almost like skills sound more mod-ern, and more useful, than knowledge and understanding. The temptation to go along with this is great in the age of the internet when (it seems) all knowledge is freely available through your laptop, phone or tablet. But if this is the implication, it needs to be resisted. There is no doubt at all that the skills of doing, finding out, making, and applying are vital: but they are reduced to being almost meaningless (literally) without a knowledge (or knowledge making) context. That is, knowledge rather than information. This is why we say that teachers are, above all, in the knowledge business – and geography teachers are in the geographical knowledge business.

Notice, once again, that we say *knowledge*. Some may prefer that we say understanding. Or at least take the two together, as conceptually distinct but related entities like salt and pepper or fish and chips. Knowledge and understanding are indeed conceptually distinct according to Trevor Bennetts (2005), who has written with clarity about the importance of teaching being concerned with progressing students' understanding (see p 42 in this book). He argues that understanding is far more than an accumulation of knowledge. Who can doubt that? But when we talk about a knowledgeable person, don't we assume that they understand what they are presumed to know about? If they do not, they are simply parrots not people – and parrots do not have knowledge in any meaningful sense (if you are interested in the philosophy here, then it is derived from Brandom and his 'inferentialism': reading Derry (2014) would be a good place to start).

One of the unfortunate side effects of distinguishing knowledge from understanding, in GCSE assessment criteria for example, has been that it has tended to downplay knowledge. It puts knowledge and understanding in a relationship with each other that appears to be hierarchical, so that knowledge is considered to be 'low level' in comparison to understanding. At worst, this has been manifest in some teachers turning away from knowledge altogether, denying that they are in the knowledge business and instead focusing on 'learning skills'. Ultimately, such teachers prefer to categorise themselves as facilitators of learning rather than teachers. To us, this is an abrogation of responsibility: children deserve respect, and to be respectful of children we should offer to teach them (and we think that children should be taught geography and how to think geographically).

To us, knowledge is the main heading. There are sub-headings that fit beneath this, and we would include all the remaining elements of learning: the values, skills and understanding that contribute to, and/or can illustrate, the acquisition and development of geographical knowledge. It (almost) goes without saying that by acquisition of knowledge we have in mind something far more extensive than a list of 'facts'. Knowledge is alive: it needs to be engaged with, argued about, contested and sometimes struggled with in order to comprehend and be able to apply it. We are in the knowledge business and this is the main reason that teaching geography is so exciting: what could be more important than teaching young people more about the earth and its systems, its diverse peoples and places and the changing relationships that exist between human beings and 'nature'?

Think about geographical knowledge

Knowledge is tricky material. Epistemology, the theory of knowledge, can quickly take us to some deep and forbidding waters: for example, how do we know what we know? Is what 'we' know the same as what others know? Is all knowledge of equal value, or is some knowledge better than others? Well, to become a teacher you don't have to become a philosopher too. So we can leave some of these enormous questions for another day. However, if we really do think that teachers are in the knowledge business, then we do have to engage in a theoretical discussion, if only to help clarify what it is we think we are doing as teachers. It is our professional identity at stake and our professional responsibility to do this – otherwise, we settle for being mere technicians implementing what (we think) Ofsted, or 'the government' wants. Teachers must grasp more leadership and initiative than this, for there is a sense in which the policy makers do not know what they want!

Thus, the Minister of State for Schools may announce that (s)he wants more 'rigour' and a curriculum based on the 'core knowledge' of academic subjects (this is indeed what the 2010–2015 Coalition government has insisted). As geography specialists, we should welcome this. However, plenty of reservations were expressed, partly because assumptions were made about what this meant – not helped by a former Schools Minister saying that 'all eleven-year-olds should know the rivers of England'. What does that mean? Left up to him, geography lessons may well have turned into round after round of learning lists of countries of Africa, capital cities of Asia and so on and so on. Fortunately, he was only the Schools Minister. Decisions about what to teach and how to teach are, or should be, left to teachers who draw from a range of professional knowledge, including knowledge of geography: what it is, its subject matters and its procedures.

Fortunately, there are plenty of useful and readily accessible contributions to this theoretical debate (such as Firth 2011, 2013; Lambert and Morgan 2010; Lambert and Young 2014; Morgan 2013; Roberts 2014; Standish 2013).

The questions we think do need to be addressed are:

- What constitutes geographical knowledge?
- How do we select what to teach?

To get you thinking about this, we ask you to read the context of Box 2. This is taken from the Geographical Association's National Curriculum pages.

Box 1.2 Selecting the geographical knowledge to teach

The central aim of the geography curriculum is to guide teachers in the selection of what to teach. This should be worthwhile, suitably challenging and above all motivating and interesting to pupils.

It is helpful to distinguish three forms of geographical knowledge. In selecting what to teach all three are important. Moreover, they intersect and are mutually dependent: they cannot be taught in isolation of each other, but all should be taught.

'Core knowledge' [Kn1]:

This refers to the subject as it resides in the popular imagination:

> If geography is the 'world subject' its core knowledge is gleaned and created from the information communicated in globes and atlases. Much of this amounts to geographical context, and in this sense can be distinguished from the main contents of the curriculum. It is not low level or trivial material but it can become so if taught badly, e.g. as an end in itself.

The GA, in its 2009 manifesto, likens learning geography to learning a 'language'. Using this metaphor, the idea of 'vocabulary' captures the role of 'core knowledge'. It may be thought of as extensive world knowledge, in itself fairly superficial yet enabling.

'Conceptual content knowledge' [Kn2]:

Sometimes referred to as concepts or generalisations, and the key to developing understanding:

> This may be seen as the main content of the geography curriculum. Key concepts and generalisations in geography show how geography contributes to pupils' acquisition and development of 'powerful knowledge'*. Using the language metaphor, the concepts of geography are like its 'grammar'. It may also be thought of as more intensive world knowledge, taking in the realm of processes, different perspectives and of values.

*According to Michael Young to acquire 'powerful knowledge' is the main point of going to school: It 'provides a reliable basis for moving beyond particulars and therefore beyond one's own experience' (Young 2008). Young's ideas (he is not a geographer) have been challenged and refined by Margaret Roberts (2014).

'Procedural knowledge' [Kn3]:

Thinking geographically is a distinctive procedure and includes using a wide range of skills:

> The teacher can model this by example, but it is also learned through exposure to, and direct experience of, high-quality geographical enquiry which might include decision-making or problem-solving scenarios. There are two characteristics of geographical approaches, or a geographic orientation, to making sense of the world that are particularly striking to note:
>
> a   The recognition of the significance of place and unique context.
> b   The adoption of a relational (or sometimes, 'holistic') approach to enquiries (e.g. taking account of both physical and human factors; or the links between local phenomena and wider global processes).

Learning geography requires pupils to engage mentally with questions about people, society, environment and the planet. This means they identify, assimilate, analyse and communicate data of various kinds, and learn the skills to do so productively. This will often entail using information technology – manipulating maps, diagrams, graphs and images (sometimes referred to collectively as 'graphicacy') – structured talk and debate and writing for a variety of audiences.

Task 1.2 Applying a knowledge taxonomy to school geography

Read the contents of Box 1.2.

1   With reference to a mainstream geography topic such as 'energy' or 'migration', can you apply this taxonomy of knowledge? Is it helpful in suggesting to you a balance of 'what to teach' in geography lessons tackling such topics?
2   Can you make links between Kn 1, 2 and 3 and the so-called 'elements of learning' (and/or GCSE assessment objectives)?

Knowledge and understanding: the importance of reasoning and making meaning

Geo-graphy (literally, 'Earth-writing') is the ancient but never-ending task of describing and making sense of the world. Doing geography in school inducts young people into this process in a way that takes them beyond only their day-to-day encounters. A vast quantity of information about the world is available at our fingertips through television and the internet, but making sense of this geographically requires disciplined acquisition and application of Kn1, Kn2 and Kn3.

The place of 'core knowledge' (Kn1) in school geography has perplexed generations of geography teachers. Responding to times gone by, when school geography was repetitive, burdensome on the memory and dull (an image that has cast a long shadow in the popular imagination of what geography is – as we have just seen in the case of a recent Schools Minister), geography teachers have wanted to shrug off a poor image in which bored pupils had to reel off list after list of place names, products and what we might call today trivia (this is inert information 'learned' simply because it appears on the list).

However, core knowledge (Kn1) is not trivial. For information to become knowledge, we have to give it meaning. In geography, this very often comes from the links and relationships we make between individual bits of information. When 'core knowledge' is built up this way, it is enabling. It enables us to make links and comparison and to develop and refine our inner geographical imaginations. It provides a locational framework or geographical context.

We can take this argument even further. Maybe there is nothing intrinsically geographical about place names or rivers or mountains. It is how we study these – geographically – that gives them geographical and explanatory meaning. For instance, using the question sequence: What? Where? Why there? How? Developing procedural knowledge [Kn3] is key to making geographical meaning because it entails a growing realisation of the disciplinary practices that create, interpret and use geographical knowledge. In schools we have, over the years, come to refer to this as 'enquiry learning' (see Chapter 3 of this book) and Margaret Roberts in particular has helped us deepen our understanding of what this means in geography classrooms (Roberts 2003, 2013). Though the enquiry approach has acquired varied forms and has many facets, at its heart lies the deceptively simple idea that pupils identify, gather and process data in order to draw conclusions, contribute to discussions and/or ask new questions. In doing so, they extend and deepen their understanding of phenomena, and their understanding of the world is taken far beyond their own direct experience.

Is geographical knowledge powerful knowledge?

A possible source of minor confusion with 'core knowledge' (or what we have called Kn1) is that the term is often associated with the American educationist E. D. Hirsch. Hirschian ideas of 'cultural literacy' appear behind the notion of 'core knowledge' and his so-called core knowledge sequence (Hirsch 1987, 2011) – or facts that every American 'needs to know'. Hirsch's ideas have now been imported to the UK via Civitas (www.coreknowledge.org.uk/aboutck.php). However, in geography it is interesting to note that in the 2011 Ofsted report on the subject's health in schools, it explicitly states a definition of 'core knowledge' (2011: 4) as principally the locational, world geographical knowledge that it might be reasonably expected that pupils be taught (and which Ofsted have found is often lacking).

As we have argued, such core knowledge (or 'Kn1') has its place but not in the old, discredited gazetteer context of bygone days – that is, as if countries, capitals, capes and bays were the full extent of geographical knowledge and the end point of learning geography. Partly because of the felt need to create a distance from this unambitious and restricted, but enduring popular view of geography, many new geography teachers appear sometimes to underplay the importance of 'Kn1': atlases are not used frequently enough and the teaching of case studies is sometimes 'careless' of the significance of locational context within a wider global narrative.

The notion of 'powerful knowledge' (Young 2008) may be helpful for identifying what really counts as knowledge in school geography: it offers a useful counterpoint to core knowledge. It embraces what are considered to be the substantive conceptual contents of geography ('Kn2') and the main procedures and processes of doing geography or being geographical ('Kn3'). It also opens up an important discussion about what is presumed to be the main purposes of the studying the subject in school. For convenience, we summarise the characteristics of powerful knowledge in Box 1.3.

Box 1.3 Powerful Knowledge (PK)

PK refers to the knowledge that children and young people are unlikely to acquire at home, TV, the internet or in the workplace.

PK is knowledge that they will need if they are to become active and informed citizens and workers in the complex modern world, sometimes called the 'knowledge society'.

PK is characterised by these features. It is often, but not always:

- evidence-based
- abstract and theoretical (conceptual)
- part of a system of thought
- dynamic, evolving, changing – but reliable ('testable' and open to challenge)
- sometimes counter-intuitive
- existent outside the direct experience of the teacher and the learner
- discipline-based (or at least in domains that are not arbitrary).

Perhaps the key point to acknowledge, which is implied by the final two bullet points in the table, is that powerful knowledge – whether in the sciences, history, engineering, the arts or geography – is created in specialist disciplinary communities. All knowledge is socially constructed, but powerful knowledge has particular qualities that arise from the academic communities that produce (and continually revise) it. The significance of disciplinary knowledge, according to Basil Bernstein (2000) is that it enables individuals and societies to think the 'unthinkable' and the 'yet-to-be-thought' rather than be content with received wisdom, common sense or habitual practices.

Young and Muller (2010) position powerful knowledge development as one of the central purposes of school, and they helpfully distinguish between three alternative curriculum 'futures' in relation to knowledge.

- Future 1 (F1) Subject boundaries are fixed and maintained through tradition and vested interests. Here, subject knowledge is for the select few, considered to be a desirable end in itself. This is under-socialised knowledge, or knowledge as 'given' (and maybe what was in the Schools Minster's head).
- Future 2 (F2) Subject boundaries are relaxed or removed entirely. Generic outcomes, such as 'learning skills', become the principal aim. Content selections are flexible and often driven by concerns of immediacy or 'relevance'. Subject boundaries are arbitrary; this is over-socialised knowledge.
- Future 3 (F3) Disciplinary boundaries are recognised and maintained but also crossed for the creation and acquisition of new knowledge. This sees subject knowledge as dynamic and forward looking, not fixed and backward looking. Knowledge is not fixed or given (as in F1), nor entirely arbitrary (as in F2). Students are introduced to the 'epistemic rules' and procedures of the subject discipline.

Thus, Young and Muller (2010) present a 'social realist' theory of knowledge (discussed in the context of geography by Roger Firth 2011a, 2011b). An F1 curriculum represents an under-socialised theory of knowledge which in effect requires teachers simply to 'deliver' the content: this can be equated with a traditional grammar school delivery conception of school. In contrast, F2 is over-socialised, which in effect denies that knowledge has any objective 'reality' that is not socially constructed. So, F1 assumes knowledge as given and, unless students can be persuaded to 'defer gratification', such knowledge is seen as irrelevant and boring and is often rejected. In contrast, F2 can be superficially attractive, responding to students' 'everyday experience', but is no shortcut to educational success: it may fail to provide access to the real, reliable knowledge needed by students to access life opportunities. Young and Muller's proposal for F3, which is provide access to powerful knowledge in the school curriculum for all, is therefore based on greater social justice. For us, it presents an argument for deeper thought about the role of the subject. Young and Lambert (2014) explore Future Three in a full-length book which includes a chapter on geography. F3 should cause us to interrogate the conceptual frameworks of subject (e.g. see Lambert and Morgan 2010). F3 knowledge is seen as bounded (that it is made within a disciplinary epistemic framework) but also dynamic and changing.

In conclusion, we advocate an F3 approach to thinking about geography in the school curriculum. This requires taking on the proposition that geography is powerful knowledge, which in turn means that we teach a judicious mix of Kn1, 2 and 3.

Universities and their relationship with school geography

As discussed above, part of the argument in support of F3 knowledge is that it acknowledges the disciplinary nature of knowledge and the role of the communities of practice in producing new knowledge. Firth (2013) writes about the need for 'a stronger and more mutually supportive relationship between higher education and school geography' (2013: 72) if the kinds of knowledge discussed above are to impact on the school curriculum in ways that teachers can access and use. Charles Rawding also has written at length on the importance of teachers' engagement with 'The Changing Nature of Geography' (Rawding 2013).

At one time, school geography was heavily influenced by the work going on in universities. The regional paradigm, which so dominated the work in universities pre-1964, percolated into schools relatively uncontested, via examination syllabuses set by the universities. School geography was characterised by a 'capes-and-bays' approach to teaching where content was learned by rote and building pupils' geographical understanding was unheard of. Against a backdrop of rapid global technological advancements and significant societal changes in terms of new national economic needs, increased social mobility and the need for a more educated workforce, the school–university relationship shifted gear. The Schools Council was responsible for fostering developments in curriculum and assessment and a key characteristic of this remit became greater working relationships between schools and the academy. As university geography turned away from early twentieth-century regionalism and looked towards quantitative approaches, modelling and theory building, these developments gradually filtered into the school curriculum via the curriculum development projects of the day, new examination specifications and geography textbooks. However, as Butt and Collins (2013) remind us, this was not a 'golden age' of school–university relations. Relatively few teachers enjoyed first-hand experience of the expertise of university geographers, and, they argue, even those who did were perceived as being very much the junior partners' (Rawling 1996, cited in Butt and Collins 2013: 295). Having said this, one essential idea to take on board here is that, for the first time, teachers were at the heart of making the geography curriculum: they were engaged, with universities and other education professionals, in a collaborative endeavour where the subject, teachers professional expertise and their knowledge and understanding of pupils' needs and interests combined to develop the school geography curriculum.

The school–university relationship started to decay from the mid-1970s (see Butt and Collins 2013, for more), but the introduction of the National Curriculum in 1988 left the view of both teachers and the universities (while some were consulted over curriculum content), marginalised. The timing of this fracturing is interesting as around this time the universities themselves started to find that new accountability systems, designed to 'measure' research quality, were starting to bite: the pressure was on to develop world-class research, leaving little or no time to engage with school-based activity.

> One consequence [of the national curriculum] was that the curriculum links between school and university geography were severed; at a time when university geography was taking a new turn to the left with developments in cultural geography (Jackson 1989) school geography was being forced to turn to the right.
>
> (Biddulph 2013)

There have been several revisions of the National Curriculum since 1988, each comprising a more manageable framework for teachers to work with. The 2007 curriculum in particular, structured around concepts rather than content, once again meant that teachers were (more or less) in the curriculum driving seat. However, centralisation had taken its toll on the school–university relationship and building bridges between schools and the academy became limited to specific projects (e.g. the Young Peoples' Geographies Project), conferences and events, or the work of specific organisations such as the International Geographic Union (IGU) The Royal Geographical Society (RGS) and the Geographical Association (GA). However, as Morgan (2008), writing about cultural geography reminds us:

> there are potential problems when ideas from cultural geography are picked up and translated into classroom activities without a clear understanding of the intellectual contexts in which those ideas were developed and the pedagogical contexts in which they are implemented.
>
> (p. 22)

What Morgan is expressing here is a view echoed by Butt and Collins, namely that we need to bear in mind that the work of universities and schools is necessarily very different and while school geography can be informed by developments in the discipline, and the discussion about 'knowledge' above reminds us of the significance of this, not all university geographies can be appropriated or are appropriate for the school curriculum. Elsewhere, Castree, Fuller and Lambert (2007) have used the metaphor of a border to describe the very real divide between university and pre-university geography. They urge geographers to broaden the scope of 'cross-border' involvement in order to avert what they see as a potential crisis of geographical literacy in wider society (2007: 132).

Interestingly, the call for some degree of 'cross-border' involvement has been answered by the Coalition government, who in the 2010 White Paper *The Importance of Teaching* announced that in their proposals to review A-level examinations, they would require Ofqual (the Office of Qualifications and Examinations) and the awarding bodies to engage the involvement of university subject departments in the review process. An A-level Content Advisory Board was established in 2014, consisting mainly of university academics. This set out the parameters for Awarding Bodies to write new A level of specifications. This appears to be a sensible move, with certain messages about the government's perceptions of what A-levels are for:

> A-levels are a crucial way that universities select candidates for their courses, so it is important that these qualifications meet the needs of higher education institutions.
>
> (p. 49)

While we would agree that A-levels (and indeed all examinations) are rigorous, the involvement of universities in this way could either be a way of ensuring continuity between school and university study, or it might be an attempt to manipulate the sector in order to legitimise new education policy. The extent to which universities are 'heard' remains to be seen.

Your 'passion' as a geographer

Having raised some issues relating to the school university divide, we now want you to consider your own passion for and expertise in geography and begin to think about the extent to which your geographical knowledge, as experienced in universities, can contribute to the geography as learned in schools.

Task 1.3 Fantastic geographies

If geography is a diverse discipline and a powerful educational resource, then what other aspects of geography would you like to see included in the school geography curriculum? Are some of these geographies more appropriate for certain age groups than others? Boxes 1.4 and 1.5 show two examples of 'Fantastic geographies' completed by PGCE students from the University of Nottingham. The two examples below are starting points for these students' thinking about ways of connecting their experiences of university geography with aspects of the school geography curriculum.

Box 1.4 Identity

Literature on identity seems to be notorious for its complexity and abstraction,...! Nonetheless, identity is the touchstone in cultural geography and the subject that I enjoyed the most at university that is ostensibly absent from pretty much all school geography lessons. The class investigated local, national and transnational scales of identity, and the complex and conflicting ways in which these 'layers' interact and intertwine, as well as gaining an appreciation of how identities are constructed, displayed and contested in the communities that we all manoeuvre through in our daily lives.

(Adams 2014)

Box 1.5 Lakes

For my 'fantastic geographies', I decided to develop a introductory module about lake ecosystems. Lakes play a significant role in the hydrological cycle. They support very complex ecological structures as well as a significant proportion of the human population globally.

This scheme of work began by separating lakes from the hydrological cycle, and comparing them to other water bodies, drawing out their differences, for example the fact they are static water bodies. Then we considered the formation and internal structure of a lake, as a basis to look at the different habitats in a lake, developing a full understanding of the lake ecosystem.

Then we took a more human approach, looking at how humans threaten lakes and their ecosystems; eutrophication and mis-management of fishing, through a case study of Lake Victoria. Students then do a research projected entitled 'Adopt a Lake' where they 'discover' a world lake. They need to describe the geomorphological elements of the lake and catchment, as well as discussing the threats and management of these, commenting upon their success.

(Howe 2014)

Task 1.3 *(continued)*

We now want you to consider:

1   What is your fantastic geography?
2   Why is this fantastic geography for you?
3   What are the origins of this fantastic geography?
4   Why do you think it is important for pupils to study this fantastic geography?

   To answer these questions, you first need to return to the *geography* literature you will have read when you studied this type of geography at university. Why is it necessary to do this? We believe that it is important, if we are to truly build pupils' geographical understanding, that they and you need to be clear where geographical ideas have come from – what are their theoretical roots and what are the debates that surround your chosen example? Before you go any further, write one side of A4 summarising the main ideas in your chosen area of geography. This will then form the basis for your thinking and subsequent planning.

5   In what ways is this 'fantastic geography' different from the types of geographies you have seen in school to date?
6   Devise a short sequence of up to five lessons for a Key Stage group, of your fantastic geography. Identify:

   - the geographical questions you might want pupils to explore
   - the geographical content
   - possible sources of information
   - possible teaching and learning strategies.

Negotiate with your mentor to teach your 'fantastic geography'. Evaluate your teaching – what did your pupils learn?

(Acknowledgement: We are grateful to PGCE geography students and Mary Biddulph and Dr Roger Firth from the University of Nottingham for permission to use this activity from their Geography PGCE course.)

School geography in an international context

This final section of Chapter 1 invites you to now consider where school geography in England and Wales might be situated in relation to broader international contexts. Much is written in the press and elsewhere about where England is situated in international comparison tables such as PISA (Program for International Student Assessment, funded by the OECD). This next section does no such thing. Rather, we want you to understand something of the broader debates in geography education in order to locate the professional context in which you are working.

   Just as education is an international phenomenon, so too is geography education. However, neither of these is expressed in a uniform manner across the world; they take different forms in different national policy settings. And as geographers know better than most, the uniqueness of locality does not imply that places can only be understood as singularities. Thus, although school geography may look different between countries, it is nonetheless important and useful to look across these divergences and focus on the overarching strengths of engaging children and young people with geographical knowledge and enquiry in their formal schooling. But although there are general processes at work, for instance resulting in broad general agreement across the world about the value of universal primary and secondary education, there are local disagreements about the finer details. There is in other words a geography of geography education!

This includes whether geography is actually present or not in the school curriculum. It is interesting to note in this context that the British government's expert group advising on National Curriculum reform in 2010 showed that most 'high performing' education jurisdictions, like Finland, Singapore, Ontario (Canada) and Victoria (Australia) do indeed include geography in the curriculum (DfE 2011). However, despite this, it is very well documented that internationally the place of geography in the school curriculum is frequently under pressure. Whether from 'new' subjects such as psychology, or from cross-curriculum concerns such as education for sustainable development and citizenship, or simply from the perceived need by policy makers to provide more curriculum space for economically 'useful' subjects such as science, technology, engineering and mathematics (the so-called STEM subjects), the place of geography often appears vulnerable.

So how does school geography vary between international contexts? In comparing school geography in the USA with its counterpart in the UK, we are struck with two important initial observations. The first is that it is necessary to be cautious when making any generalisations across these nations: the USA has a federal system and although there are excellent national standards (NCGE 2014) the curriculum is decided locally, state by state; similarly, within the UK there are significant differences between the status and contents of geography between the nations of England, Scotland, Wales and Northern Ireland. Having said that, it is possible to make the general observation that in the USA geography is positioned within the social studies, while in the UK school geography is usually thought of as a discrete subject, albeit broadly speaking within the 'humanities' (although the separate subject identity has been weakened in recent years in Scotland's more integrated and skills led 'curriculum for excellence', it has been actually reinforced in England in the 2014 National Curriculum). The dominance of social studies in the USA matters; in the USA, school geography has often failed to develop substantially beyond low-level description – in effect, providing the base map and contextual information to underpin the study of history and civics. Furthermore, it rarely addresses what the UK would recognise as physical geography – this being syphoned away and taught as earth science. In the UK, the humanities label notwithstanding, there is a deep regard for the wholeness of geographical study, and the subject's potential as a bridge between the human and physical sciences (although it has to be said, in passing, that until recently there has been a perceived weakening of physical geography in schools, a point being addressed in the reform of GCSE and A-levels in England).

Thus teaching geography in the USA and the UK is different, for there are different traditions and assumptions. It is different again in other countries. In Finland, for example, geography teachers are usually also teachers of biology, reflecting the close link that exists in Finland between studies of people and the environment (geography) and their biological settings. Teaching geography is somewhat more 'science' based than in the USA – or the UK for that matter: teaching geography in Finland is within a different tradition and the subject has a distinctive identity.

The question of whether or not geography's (and geography teachers') self-identify as a 'science' (or as 'scientists') is a significant consideration for in all these countries, and indeed around the world, there are mounting pressures on teachers of geography in schools to embrace digital technologies of various kinds and especially GIS technologies. This is not in itself a problem: digital technologies pervade our everyday lives! However, in some countries, and the USA would be a leading example, such pressures are associated with moves to express geography as the 'spatial science' – even speculating that GIS technologies in the modern world are now so important that geography should become classified on a par with the STEM subjects. This is highly unlikely ever to happen because although most geographers and geography teachers may use various applications of GIS (again, as we all do in our everyday lives) they are not often the designers and makers of these technologies: geography does not own GIS, and GIS does not belong to geography. However, the suggestion opens up crucial and very interesting debates about the nature of geographical knowledge and skills – and geography's value as a subject in school education. We can expect that debates such as this play out differently in different countries depending on local traditions, and the identity of geography as a school subject and academic discipline.

The International Geographical Union Commission on Geographical Education attempts to monitor trends in geographical education around the world and how the subject has evolved over time (see for example Haubrich 2006). In her overview of one attempt to survey the issues and challenges facing school geography around the world, Eleanor Rawling (2004) observed a number of features worth noting, including:

- geography's uncertain place in the school curriculum, particularly at primary level;
- decline in the opportunities for high-quality teacher education in geography, with a concomitant decline in the number of specialist teachers of geography;
- problems arising from the growth of assessment and performance-led systems, often at the expense of curriculum development;
- the need to ensure that geography is involved in technological developments (internet, multimedia, GIS);
- the need to address the public image of the subject, such that the public, students and policy makers recognised its potential as a school subject.

If we believe that the earth as an object of study, and people's relationship with the earth as an object of thought, are seen as important in their own right, and therefore fundamental components of the school curriculum, then this list gives pause for thought. While Rod Gerber's (2001) previous survey of geography in 31 countries led him to a 'cautious optimism' about geography's place in the school curriculum, Rawling's (2004) assessment is less sanguine – stressing the need to 'recognise the real threats to the subject' and to be prepared to 'take immediate action within our own communities' (p. 169). Recurrent among the perceived threats to geography (which remain true to the present day) are the enduring pressures to 'integrate' studies (particularly in the humanities and social studies), the rise of vocational education (which tends to ask what 'use' is geography) and the tendency towards more 'skill- based' (rather than 'subject-based') education in schools.

Summary and key points

Subjects are better understood as the distinctive means to desirable ends. They can be thought of as stimulating and useful resources that can be organised in such a way as to stir curiosity and motivate worthwhile learning. The learning is described and directed by carefully selected educational goals. The selection is based on what we think education is for, what kind of experiences and encounters students should have and where we think the subject resource can take us. Thus:

- What concepts can be grown and developed within this subject?
- What knowledge can be acquired and in what way is it known, and is useful to know?
- Which skills can be developed and refined with this subject?
- How can the subject help us make sense of the world and engage with it more intelligently?

If subjects are simply seen as the container or vehicle for 'delivering' authorised content, and they often are seen exactly in these terms, then it is not surprising that many pupils respond appropriately and sometimes with contempt. Geography is a fantastic subject with extraordinary educational potential for informing future citizens. Geography not only helps pupils understand the savage power and differentiated impact of natural hazards but also the challenges in coping with the aftermath. It challenges pupils with 'real world' issues from the local and often nearby, to the global and sometimes distant. The subject is rich in multimodal information and communication skills, and can induct pupils into the £20 billion GIS industry that underpins almost all economic activity in the modern world.

Like most subjects, geography is difficult to teach well if you are not sure about what it offers and where it can take you (Lambert 2004, 2005). Relatively few teachers have a meaningful relationship with the subject that involves a connection to what has been happening in the wider discipline during the last 20 years. Also, relatively few teachers have the space or time to engage creatively with the subject through asking fundamental questions about what is worth knowing. Relatively few would even recognise this as part of their job, and yet it is arguably the most significant element of being a teacher, to make an interesting, worthwhile and relevant school geography experience for young people. The purpose or value, therefore, of doing geography may indeed lie in the subject matter itself (Lambert 2004: 82).

This chapter has tried to encourage debate on these variables and your engagement with these early in your career and will enable you to locate other aspects of what it means to teach geography within these broader perspectives. Your views will change, be challenged and at times you may well feel confused , but the wise teacher 'does not bid you enter the house of his [sic] wisdom, but rather leads you to the threshold of your own mind' (Gibran 1926: 67; cited in Edwards 1996: 222). Or, as one student teacher wrote, 'My teaching philosophy is based on the words of Proust: "the real voyage of discovery does not consist in seeking new landscapes, but in having new eyes"' (Walford and Haggett 1995: 12). What you will find in this book is material to inform your response to key questions about teaching geography. They are questions which you are well advised to return to from time to time.

Further reading

Firth, R. (2013) 'What constitutes knowledge in geography'. In D. Lambert and M. Jones (eds) *Debates in Geography Education*, London: Routledge.
This chapter provides a very helpful critical overview of some of the key debates an questions relating to subject knowledge and the school geography curriculum.

Morgan, J. (2011) *Teaching Secondary Geography as if the Planet Matters*. London: Routledge.
In this book, John Morgan articulates careful and considered arguments for why teachers (and especially beginning teachers) need to stay focused on how geographies are consistently made and remade and the need for both teachers and learners to remain vigilant of this. This book will help you to remain critically engaged with the discipline of geography as you continue to understand the significance of this for the school curriculum.

2 The geography curriculum

Introduction

> The starting point for curriculum design in geography should be a rigorous and defensible version of the subject matter to be taught in the light of teachers' knowledge and understanding of the pupils they teach.
>
> (Morgan and Lambert 2005: 95)

The quote above is unambiguous in calling on geography teachers to engage with some significant questions about the curriculum:

1   What are we teaching? – How do we decide what to teach (after all we cannot teach 'everything' in geography)? How can we be assured that our content selection is appropriate? What do we have to teach, in what depth, and how?
2   Why are we teaching it? – What is the purpose of what we are teaching? What are we trying to achieve in terms of broader educational purposes?
3   Who are we teaching it to? – What are our pupils needs and interests? What do they find difficult? How can we connect the geography we teach to the life experience of our pupils?
4   How do we know they are learning and making progress?

In posing these questions, we seek to engage you in curriculum thinking without which pupils' actual experience of geography (the contents and activities of geography lessons) will be left deficient in a number of ways. Curriculum thinking takes you beyond the level of the competently planned lesson and imaginatively prepared resources (although both are important) into the realms of questions about education. As Lambert asks:

> Is education primarily to serve the needs of society and economy (providing skilful and employable people for the world of work in the global market place), or is it mainly to provide worthwhile experiences and knowledge to help individuals 'live sanely in the world' . . . Or has education to serve both these purposes and more besides?
>
> (Lambert 2003: 59)

Set against a backdrop of wider debates about the purpose of education, the question 'What is a geography curriculum for?' is an important question to pursue – what exactly is/should/

could be geography's contribution to the school curriculum and what ways does learning geography contribute to Kelly's concept of an educational curriculum for a democratic society? (see below)

In this chapter, we open up for debate several key questions concerning the school geography curriculum, including:

- What do we mean by a 'curriculum'?
- What external influences shape the curriculum?
- What different curriculum models persist?
- What is the relationship between the curriculum and pupils' opportunities to make progress in their geographical learning?

In posing these questions we are, in some ways, looking ahead to when you are have developed some professional skills, gained some classroom experience and have started to question the content and approach to your subject. We would argue that the degree to which the principles of curriculum development are understood and can be applied is one indicator of a teacher's graduation from basic practical competence to being a reflective and proficient teacher.

By the end of this chapter, you should be able to:

- appreciate different approaches to curriculum planning and development and the messages each conveys about the kinds of geographies pupils learn
- understand the historical context of the school geography curriculum – a curriculum timeline
- understand the links between the school geography curriculum and the broader purposes of education
- appreciate the different levels of curriculum decision-making and your professional role or responsibility
- understand the significance of the idea of 'curriculum-making' in your professional practice
- understand the significance of the idea of progression in relation to our understanding of the curriculum.

What is a curriculum?

Curriculum, as a term, has many different incarnations within the context of education. Kelly (2009) discusses the idea of an *educational* curriculum (his emphasis) namely a curriculum that is 'justifiable in educational terms' (p. 7). What he means by this is that in a democratic society the curriculum should be concerned with promoting democratic freedoms such as:

> freedom and independence of thought, social and political empowerment, respect for the freedom of others, of an acceptance of variety of opinion, and of the enrichment of life of every individual in that society regardless of class, race of creed.

(p. 8)

A curriculum based on such principles is, he argues, likely to be truly educational. He goes on to carefully map out different notions of 'curriculum', referring to the distinction between the 'planned and received' curriculum, providing a sharp reminder of the difference between what we *think* we are teaching, and what pupils actually learn. Oates (2011) provides a helpful working definition for us to consider:

> The curriculum – taught and untaught – represents the totality of the experience of the child within schooling (aims, content, pedagogy, assessment). It includes unassessed and uncertificated elements – including opportunities to acquire vital 'personal' and 'social' capitals. A national curriculum cannot specify and control all elements of the 'real' curriculum – and will run into terrible difficulty if it attempts so to do.
>
> (p. 133)

This definition provides us with a conceptual framework around which we can begin to think about pupils and what they learn. It tells us in very direct terms that the 'curriculum' is not merely the laid-down content to be 'delivered' by teachers. In Oates's definition, words like 'experience', 'personal and social capital' imply something much more significant, including the positioning of pupils at the heart of leaning. This definition also reinforces the notion that the curriculum is not just about what happens in classrooms; it implies that important distinctions need to be drawn between the taught and untaught curriculum, between the visible and the hidden curriculum, between a national curriculum and the school curriculum, and most significantly between an educational curriculum and a curriculum that fails to serve such a purpose. The reference above to a national curriculum will be considered later in this chapter, but it is worth noting here that Oates, Kelly and even the 2014 National Curriculum Orders for the school curriculum (DfE 2014) draw a clear distinction between the National Curriculum and the school curriculum – they are not the same thing:

> The school curriculum comprises all learning and other experiences that each school plans for its pupils. The national curriculum forms one part of the school curriculum.
>
> (DfE 2014: Section 2.2)

Much of the above takes a macro view of the curriculum. But layered into these debates is also the notion of a subject-based curriculum, which Rawling has shown has been the dominant curriculum structure in terms of the formal curriculum in English education for over a century (2001: 19). Geography has been a contributor to this subject-based curriculum in secondary schools since the late nineteenth century (and long before that in primary schools). Taught via textbooks with emotive titles such as *The World-Wide Geographies, Book IV* by Jasper H. Stembridge or *A Tour of the Motherland: A First Geography of the British Isles* (author unknown), geographical learning was presented within a regional framework reinforcing notions of imperialism and colonialism, through an approach of barely disguised environmental determinism.

The discussion that follows serves to demonstrate the ways in which the school curriculum, including the geography curriculum, has been subject to a range of different influences that have had and continue to have profound effects on the kind of geography curriculum, national and otherwise, that teachers end up teaching. In embarking on an exploration of the relationship between wider societal influences and the curriculum, we consider the ways the aims of school geography have changed over time and what this has meant for Kelly's 'educational curriculum'.

1. Ideology

In her 2001 book entitled *Changing the Subject: The Impact of National Policy on School Geography 1980-2000*, Eleanor Rawling gives a detailed and authoritative account of the debates that raged leading up to and following from the implementation of the first National Curriculum for geography in 1991, and its subsequent incarnations in 1995 and 2000. An important element in her discussion is a clear summary of the impact that ideological traditions had on both curriculum and pedagogy. We would argue that interrogating these different traditions will enable you to identify the influence each has had and will continue to have on the school geography curriculum.

Task 2.1 Ideological traditions and politics

Study Figure 2.1, which summarises ideological traditions and the role of politics in school geography.

1   In small groups, discuss what appears to be the dominant ideological tradition informing the current school curriculum. Ask yourselves why you think this? What is informing your opinion here?
2   How does this tradition present itself in the current National Curriculum Orders for geography? Again, ask yourselves why you think this; what is in the contents of the Orders that leads you to your conclusions?
3   In what ways does this tradition become apparent in the way geography is taught in schools you have been in, or can you detect other influences? How do teachers talk about teaching and learning? What kind of language do they use? What kinds of teaching strategies do they use and why? What kind of ideological tradition might school practice reflect and is it the same as that embodied in the National Curriculum document?

On reflection, how does teaching geography now compare to the types of geography you learned in school and the ways you were taught? Having begun to consider the significance of ideology and politics, how do you now think ideology possibly influenced your own geography education?

---

2. Aims and purposes

As Rawling (2001) reminds us, the first National Curriculum for geography in England and Wales, implemented under a Conservative government in 1991, was virtually aims free. There was no overriding sense of educational purpose and the rationale for including specific

Ideological tradition	Characteristics	Impact on school geography in England
Utilitarian/informational	• education primarily aimed at 'getting a job' and 'earning a living' • a focus on useful information and basic skills	• nineteenth-century emphasis on locational knowledge ('capes and bays') and on useful knowledge about the countries of the world • the 1991 GNC reinstated an emphasis on maps, locational knowledge and world geography
Cultural restorationism (as promoted by the New Right in English policy making in the 1980s and 1990s	• restoring traditional areas of knowledge and skills (cultural heritage) • providing pupils with a set package of knowledge and skills which will enable them to fit well-defined places in society and the workplace	• economic and regional geography related to Britain's early twentieth-century empire and trading links • the 1991 GNC seemed to stress factual information and to focus on the geography of Britain in a relatively unchanging world
Liberal humanist (also called classical humanist)	• worthwhile knowledge as a preparation for life; the passing on of a cultural heritage from one generation to the next • emphasis on rigour, big ideas and theories, and intellectual challenge	• the development of geography as an academic discipline in the 1950s and 1960s and the resulting higher status accorded to the subject in schools • stress on scientific methods, theories and quantitative techniques in the 'new geography' of the 1960s and 1970s
Progressive educational (also called child-centered)	• focusing on self development or bringing to maturity the individual child/pupil • using academic subjects as the medium for developing skills, attitudes, values and learning styles which will help them become autonomous individuals	• the geography curriculum development projects of the 1970s and 1980s (Geography for Young School Leaver, Bristol Project, Geography 16–19) • emphasis on enquiry, active learning and development of skills, attitudes and values through geography • child-centred primary education 1960s–1970s • 'thinking skills' (late 1990s)
Reconstructionist (also called radical)	• education as an agent for changing society, so an emphasis on encouraging pupils to challenge existing knowledge and approaches • less interest in academic disciplines, more focus on issues and socially critical pedagogy	• geography's involvement with e.g. environmental education, peace education, global education in the 1970s–1980s • the current interest by the New Labour government in sustainable development education and citizenship seems to offer opportunities for reconstructionism, but may only be a relatively utilitarian reaction to changing societal concerns
Vocationalist or industrial trainer (Note: in some ways this cuts across all the other traditions)	• Provide pupils with knowledge and skills required for work • or use workplace and work-related issues as a stimulus for learning skills/abilities • or use work-related issues for questioning status quo	• the Geography, Schools, Industry Project (GA sponsored, 1983–91) used work-related contexts in a progressive way for curriculum change and active learning. More recently, government-promoted careers education, work-related initiatives and key skills have been more utilitarian in character (skills for work).

Figure 2.1 Ideological traditions and their impact on school geography

(Source: Rawling 2001: 32)

subjects under the remit of a 'national curriculum' was unclear. Organisations, such as the Geographical Association and the Royal Geographical Society, both of whom campaigned hard for geography to be included as one of the ten National Curriculum subjects in 1991, acknowledged the challenge of planning a curriculum where both the journey and the destination were unclear. Operating in something of a curriculum fog, geography teachers had to focus on trying to turn a long list of content (183 'statements of content to be taught') into coherent and meaningful learning experiences for their pupils without any clear sense of where they were trying to get to? There was no clear rational for the content that was included (because of the lack of aims) and the fact that the content was extensive in nature clearly communicated a particular view of teaching, namely that it was the role of teachers to 'deliver' the pre-prescribed content via a transmission pedagogy, into the empty heads of children. The 1991 National Curriculum was, argues Lambert (2003), 'an authoritarian experiment in curriculum control, and of course it failed' (p. 166).

Why did it fail? Geography teachers' responses to this content-heavy curriculum were variable. In some cases it seemed that teachers chose to 'relinquish[ed] curriculum planning and development at a school level to text book writers', choosing to purchase complete sets of texts that would do the curriculum thinking for them (Lambert 2004: 78). However, others very clearly took the details of the Order and somehow made it work. Margaret Roberts' (2005) research into geography teachers' response to the National Curriculum reveals that the imposition of the National Curriculum from above resulted, in some cases, in limited change on the ground. Many teachers retained in some form the kind of geography curriculum that reflected their beliefs about what a 'good' geography education should comprise; it seems that even when the overwhelming message to teachers was that they were merely 'deliverers' of a centrally prescribed body of knowledge, they, in some cases unintentionally, and in others deliberately, usurped the ideological messages of the day and did what they thought was right. The consequence for the 'national' bit of the National Curriculum was that there were as many interpretations of national prescription as there were schools.

Subsequent National Curriculum revisions sought to address the 'aims' problem, and the bodies responsible for consulting on and developing subject-specific curricular such as the School Curriculum and Assessment Authority (SCAA), later to be the Qualifications and Curriculum Authority (QCA), were keen to ensure that individual subjects had a clearer direction of travel than that embodied in the 1991 Orders. The 1995, 2000 and 2007 Orders each had an 'importance' statement expressing the contribution of geography to young people's education. These revisions articulated more clearly than ever before a relationship between a national education system and its role in contributing to longer-term societal aspirations.

For the 2000 curriculum, the aims and detailed elaborations of their meanings were published in the *Handbook* for teachers:

a   The curriculum should aim to provide opportunities for all pupils to learn and achieve.
b   The school curriculum should aim to promote pupils' spiritual, moral, social and cultural development and prepare all pupils for the opportunities, responsibilities and experiences of life (DfE 1999).

What the aims above provided was a much clearer sense of a direction of travel for a national education system and therefore the school curriculum. There was now some sense of what education was trying to achieve. The details of the aims, as outlined in the *Handbook*, pay particular attention to the personal qualities an education system might want to develop in young people, acknowledging the significance of the relationship between a national system of education and the needs and aspirations of society. What the National Curriculum was now trying to achieve, probably for the first time, was to articulate this relationship and represent the educational opportunities necessary to create the kind of society we aspired to at the start of the twenty-first century.

What did all of this this mean for the school geography curriculum? White (2004) notes that 'unlike some other subjects, most of geography's aims in the 2000 curriculum Orders closely match the overall aims statements' (p. 11). However, he also criticises the geography curriculum for lack of attention to cultural issues, opting instead to prioritise 'intra-subject material to do with geographical enquiry and skills' rather than attend to the potential of geography to help young people understand themselves and others in the world (p. 11). This, he argued, left school geography disconnected from the experiences and perspectives of the children who teachers were trying to educate. Others would disagree. Roberts (2003) and Lambert (2004) both contend that by the time the National Curriculum was revised in 2000 the focus for curriculum planning and development had shifted and teachers now had more control over what and how they taught: the connections between young people's cultural worlds and the school subject, connections that White felt were missing from statutory documents, could be bridged by teachers via the curriculum choices they now could make.

The 2007 National Curriculum revision for geography occurred against a backdrop of developments in the wider social discourse around, not just the educational needs, but also the broader social and emotional needs of young people. This discourse was prompted by a public inquiry, held in 2003, into the death of 8-year-old Victoria Climbie, which found that, at all levels, education, health care and social services failed this little girl because of the separation and segregation of the services involved with her care. In the light of these findings, the then Labour government published a Green Paper entitled 'Every Child Matters' followed in 2004 by the Children Act.

The outcome for education was that the 2007 curriculum revision would explicitly support the broader goals of Every Child Matters. The National Curriculum (all subjects) now had the express purpose to enable children and young people to become:

- successful learners who enjoy learning, make progress and achieve
- confident individuals who are able to live safe, healthy and fulfilling lives
- responsible citizens who make a positive contribution to society.

These aims are significantly different from those of 2000 and were reflected in increasing demands for greater professional accountability through the measurement of educational outcomes; the shift in ideology from that of the New Right to a more reconstructionist view of education under New Labour was cut through with a more utilitarian discourse around basic skills, and the development of competencies. While a subject-based national curriculum was technically in place, this became superseded by a new and powerful discourse to do with generic learning strategies, 'learning to learn' and competencies – *what* children learn seemed to be less important (Biddulph 2013).

The election of a new coalition government led by a Conservative/Liberal democrat coalition in 2010 marked an 'about-turn' in education policy. The emphasis on children's emotional well-being, so evident in the 2007 revision, was dropped in favour of what appeared to be more 'traditional' education priorities, including a return to 'subject knowledge'. A curriculum review was announced and, by 2014, a new National Curriculum comprising a new set of aims and new subject Orders arrived in schools. GCSE and A-level examinations were also under review at the same time.

Box 2.1 The aims of the school curriculum in England

The national curriculum provides pupils with an introduction to the *essential knowledge* they need to be educated citizens. It introduces pupils *to the best that has been thought and said*, and helps engender an *appreciation of human creativity and achievement*.

The National Curriculum is *just one element in the education of every child*. There is time and space in the school day and in each week, term and year to range beyond the national curriculum specifications. The national curriculum provides an outline of *core knowledge* around which teachers can develop exciting and stimulating lessons to promote the development of pupils' knowledge, understanding and skills as part of the wider school curriculum.

(*Source*: DfE 2014: Sections 3.1. and 3.2;
Italics are our emphasis)

On initial reading, you might feel that there is little that is troublesome in these aims, yet if we examine them more closely, some significant questions start to emerge. We focus on just two:

1   *essential knowledge/core knowledge* – what does this mean? Who decides what comprises the 'essential' or 'core' knowledge that young people should learn? Where are such ideas from? (See Chapter 1 for a discussion on this.)
2   *The best that has been thought.* What *is* the best that has been thought? Who decides this? What is the place of the individual pupil and his/her ideas, thoughts and perspectives in such aims?

On a daily basis, when busy in school, it is difficult to think about aims and what they mean – they are on the distant horizon and *appear* to be of little consequence. However, as we can already see 'aims' are complex – while 'no aims' means no sense of direction, the aims that we are given have a significant impact on what gets taught in schools – including in geography.

In addition to curriculum aims, at the start of the 2007 National Curriculum for geography there was a clear statement of geography's 'importance' to pupils' learning. The 2014 National Curriculum has a 'purpose statement'. The difference is significant. The 'importance' statement captured something of geography's distinctive contribution to young people's educational experience. Does the 'purpose statement' communicate different messages?

Task 2.2 Evaluating the purpose of learning geography

The statements below (Box 2.2) are the 2007 'importance' statement for geography and the 2014 'purpose' statement, both of which articulate different, but significant ideas about what learning geography should achieve for young people.

Read each statement carefully.

1 On a copy of each, highlight/underline terms or phrases which you agree are *essential* in capturing *why* young people should learn geography.
2 Now highlight/underline any elements which you feel are less than essential – ask yourself why you think this.
3 Are there any ideas you have about the value of learning geography that you feel are missing from either of these statements? Write them down and consider why you think these are important to you, why might they be missing from either of these statements.
4 It is worth noting the difference, even in the title of such statements – 'importance' versus 'purpose' – what do different terms tell us about different views of learning geography?
5 What ideals about learning geography does each statement reveal? Which of the two statements do you think is more useful to teachers and why?
6 Having analysed each of the statements and considered what you feel might be missing from each of these, try to write your own statement detailing the value of learning geography for young people. Perhaps, if you are currently in a school, consider what such a statement for *your school* and *your context* would need to comprise.
7 Compare the three different statements and consider what values underpin each one.

Box 2.2 The importance of geography

Importance statement 2007

The study of geography stimulates an interest in and a sense of wonder about places. It helps young people make sense of a complex and dynamically changing world. It explains where places are, how places and landscapes are formed, how people and their environment interact, and how a diverse range of economies, societies and environments are interconnected. It builds on pupils' own experiences to investigate places at all scales, from the personal to the global.

Geographical enquiry encourages questioning, investigation and critical thinking about issues affecting the world and people's lives, now and in the future. Fieldwork is an essential element of this. Pupils learn to think spatially and use maps, visual images and new technologies, including geographical information systems (GIS), to obtain, present and analyse information. Geography inspires pupils to become global citizens by exploring their own place in the world, their values and their responsibilities to other people, to the environment and to the sustainability of the planet.

(*Source*: DfCSF 2007: 3)

Box 2.3 The purpose of study

Purpose statement 2014

A high-quality geography education should inspire in pupils a curiosity and fascination about the world and its people that will remain with them for the rest of their lives. Teaching should equip pupils with knowledge about diverse places, people, resources and natural and human environments, together with a deep understanding of the earth's key physical and human processes. As pupils progress, their growing knowledge about the world should help them to deepen their understanding of the interaction between physical and human processes, and of the formation and use of landscapes and environments. Geographical knowledge, understanding and skills provide the frameworks and approaches that explain how the earth's features at different scales are shaped, interconnected and change over time.

(*Source*: DfE 2014, available online at https://www.gov.uk/government/publications/national-curriculum-in-england-geography)

In addition to the 'purpose statement', the 2014 National Curriculum for geography also comprises a specific set of subject aims. The 'purpose statement' and the 'aims' fulfil distinctly different roles. The purpose statement provides a justification for 'why learn geography?' whereas the aims are more specific statements about geography's distinctive contribution to the school curriculum. The aims link back to notions of 'thinking geographically' as discussed in Chapter 1, as they lay out the geographical concepts and skills that children will learn, the understanding and application of which will enable them to apply their geographical understanding to new contexts, beyond the confines of school. Kinder (2013), talking about the then draft orders for geography, comments that in fact the geography National Curriculum is not really a curriculum at all, but more a minimum set of criteria on which teachers build their own curriculum. You may have a view on this.

Task 2.3 The National Curriculum for geography: aims

The National Curriculum for geography aims to ensure that all pupils:

- develop contextual knowledge of the location of globally significant places – both terrestrial and marine – including their defining physical and human characteristics and how these provide a geographical context for understanding the actions of processes;
- understand the processes that give rise to key physical and human geographical features of the world, how these are interdependent and how they bring about spatial variation and change over time;
- are competent in the geographical skills needed to: collect, analyse and communicate with a range of data gathered through experiences of fieldwork that deepen their understanding of geographical processes;
- interpret a range of sources of geographical information, including maps, diagrams, globes, aerial photographs and Geographical Information Systems (GIS);
- communicate geographical information in a variety of ways, including through maps, numerical and quantitative skills and writing at length.

(Available at: https://www.gov.uk/government/publications/national-curriculum-in-england-geography

---

Box 2.4 Examining broader educational aims and subject specific aims

It is, at this stage worth considering, what, if any, is the relationship between the stated aims of education and the stated aims of the geography curriculum, and asking to what extent either will serve to support Kelly's earlier notion of an 'educational curriculum for a democratic society'. It is worth asking yourself how and in what ways do any of these aims play out in practical ways in the geography curriculum in your school and do they reflect the purpose of learning geography? Do pupils see this purpose? What, if anything do they have to say about the contribution of geography to their learning?

Curriculum models

Curriculum theory is a relatively new field of education enquiry which really took hold in school geography following the publication of Norman Graves's definitive text *Curriculum Planning in Geography* (1979). Graves details the changes and challenges facing curriculum thinking in geography in the era leading up to the eventual arrival of the National Curriculum in 1988. The model in Figure 2.2 summarises the different scales at which curriculum planning has to operate (see also Chapter 3):

Graves's model reminds us that the curriculum is dynamic and that the scales of planning interact with each other. While there appears to be some sort of planning hierarchy, the model reinforces the significance of a feedback mechanism (element 6 in the diagram) on other levels of planning (elements 2–5 on the diagram) and also the notion that the geography curriculum is subject to a range of influences, not least research in geography (element 2a) and other factors such as whole school activity, educational research and local situational variables (elements 5a–c). It could be argued that some of these elements, as well as influencing each other, are also likely to conflict with each other too. The model has been criticised because it presents a very rational approach to curriculum planning and development, which at whatever scale you are working – national, local or classroom – it is not. As we have seen already, the curriculum is a very messy entity because of the multiple variables that influence, shape and disrupt it.

Having considered the curriculum in broad terms, we now turn our attention to different models of curriculum which are underpinned by particular ideological traditions and philosophies. The models under consideration here are drawn from the work of Smith (2000) and Kelly (2009). Each has significant implications for both what gets taught in schools and how it is taught:

1   The cultural transmission model
2   The objectives led model – curriculum as product
3   The process/praxis model.

1. The cultural transmission model

The cultural transmission model in many respects represents a stereotypical view of Victorian schools, classrooms, teaching and learning. It can appear to be an authoritarian model where

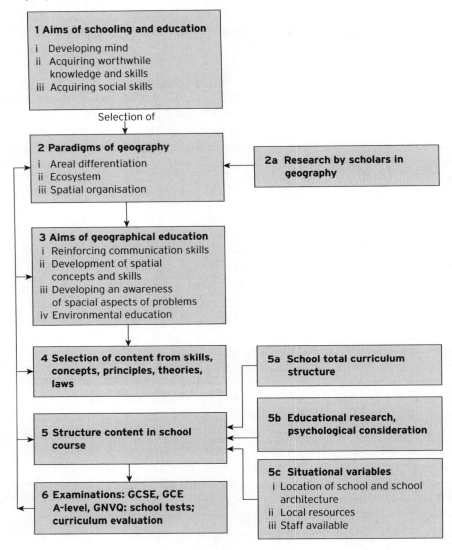

Figure 2.2 Graves's model for curriculum planning in geography at the general level

(*Source*: Graves 1979: 43)

the teacher is the subject 'expert' who, quite literally, 'tells' pupils what to think. Geographical knowledge is seen as incontestable and unproblematic (longest rivers, highest mountains, capital cities). Firth (2013) describes this as an 'absolutist' view of knowledge, namely knowledge that is 'external, fixed, universal and certain' (p. 64), but as Marsden (1997, cited in Lambert and Morgan 2010) reminds us, the curriculum content is 'not a collection of facts, but a state of the art conceptual framework for the subject' (p. 47).

This 'collection of facts' model is problematic because it represents geography as an inert field of enquiry rendering the knowledge base of the discipline fixed in a moment in time (Lambert 2004, cited in Biddulph 2013). However, as geographers, we like to feel that our subject is dynamic, responsive to changes in the human and physical environments, influential in helping us make sense of a complex world and that it is, quite literally, 'all around us'. Thus, by definition, a 'transmission' model undermines all we hold dear about geography. For teachers, such a curriculum model marginalises their subject expertise and positions them as 'deliverers' of a pre-determined 'fact-based' curriculum, rather than as subject experts working within the 'state of the art conceptual framework' (Marsden 1995: 67) in order to plan and make a relevant and current school geography curriculum (see Biddulph 2014).

2. The product model

The 'product' model, where the curriculum is framed around a series of measurable pre-determined objectives, represents a very different view of education from that of the cultural transmission model. This model is rooted in twentieth-century notions of industrial production (inputs – processes – outputs) and represents a technical-rational view of curriculum planning: precise learning objectives are identified, taught to pupils and the outcomes are then measured in order to make judgements about learning. It represents a very instrumental view of education with the underpinning assumptions that learning is linear and that assessment processes can make accurate and reliable judgements about learning outcomes.

This model is prolific in the UK and other countries around the world, possibly because it is relatively simplistic in design and execution – it leaves nothing to chance. It is also 'hot on measurability' (Smith 2000, cited in Biddulph 2014) so more than meets the growing demand from senior managers in schools and school inspection processes for 'data' that allegedly demonstrates a school's success. Graves's model (above) has been likened to this model of curriculum.

This model is not just problematic *per se*; it is also problematic for geography:

> the casualty in this model is the subject as experienced by pupils. Broken down into increasingly smaller and smaller units the tendency is to focus only on the parts and not the whole, and prioritise small detail over the broader and more significant conceptual understanding. Such fragmentation means that the 'big picture' of the discipline is lost for pupils and the idea of education is reduced to schooling.
>
> (Biddulph 2014: 7)

What is being argued here is that the increased fragmentation of the subject reduces the educative potential of geography; if the subject's conceptual framework is dismantled into smaller and smaller bits and pieces, namely objectives, then the curriculum loses its potential to enable pupils to 'think geographically'.

3. The process/praxis model

This model is rooted in a developmental view of education, whereby attending to the cognitive development of young people is but one element in the educational experience. It is a model underpinned by what some might negatively see as progressive ideology (Michael Gove, cited in *The Guardian* 2008), but which for others is a model that is more attentive to the professional responsibilities of teachers to 'teach' and is more mindful of the role that pupils play in mediating the curriculum. This engagement, by teachers and pupils, means that this model not about teachers delivering a package of content, or pupils storing facts to be measured at a later date, but is a curriculum model requiring careful critical engagement by both teachers and pupils in what and how to learn. The educationalist Lawrence Stenhouse, director of the Schools Council Humanities Project and a proponent of the process model, argued in the 1970s and 1980s that a truly educational curriculum is to be founded on broadly democratic principles whereby pupils' views and perspectives were integral to the curriculum experience (Stenhouse 1975). These principles, such as 'equality, autonomy, fairness', and 'collective human well-being and emancipation' (Smith 2000, cited in Biddulph 2014: 8) are not regarded as an end point to work towards, they inform every step of pupils' and teachers' curriculum experience – they are ever-present. What does such a model look like in practice and what does it mean for school geography?

In many respects the Geographical Association's notion of 'curriculum making' (2009) is school geography's contribution to the idea of a process curriculum – but with a difference! The model (see Figure 2.3) presents what Lambert and Morgan (2010) call 'three pillars of curriculum-making':

1   Pupils' experiences: their curiosities, interest, experiences and spatial encounters, which are very different to those of adults.
2   Teaching/pedagogy: teachers draw on their knowledge and understanding of the subject and their professional understanding of teaching to support pupils' learning geography.
3   Geography the subject: the subject discipline is the 'resource' around which learning occurs.

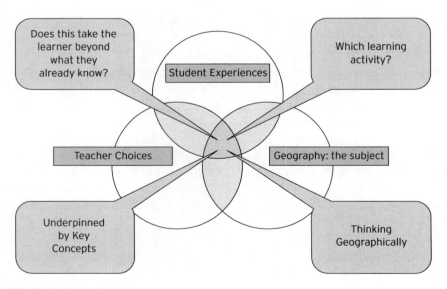

Figure 2.3 Curriculum-making

(*Source*: The Geographical Association, *A Different View: A Manifesto for School Geography*, 2009)

Their argument is that the concept of 'curriculum-making' ensures that three essential elements, pupils, teachers and the subject are in balance with each other; each plays an equally significant role in the curriculum process and over-emphasising one at the expense of another renders the process curriculum unbalanced. For example, too much attention to pupils' experiences, at the expense of the subject, will undoubtedly fail to take pupils anywhere new in their learning and so will fail to develop their capacity to think geographically. Too much emphasis on subject at the expense of attention to pedagogy or pupils' needs and interests will fail to engage pupils because of inappropriate teaching practices.

While the model is akin to the process model as defined by Smith and others, it differs because of the emphasis it places on the subject discipline. The model in some ways addresses criticisms that some child-centred curricula focus too much on classroom activities at the expense of subject learning; here, the subject plays an equal part in the curriculum process. Lambert and Morgan (2010) describe curriculum-making as 'the in-between work' that teachers have to do in terms of mediating, say, a scheme of work and the pedagogical processes they select to teach. The principles that underpin this model and which are geography specific include:

- commitment to a critical engagement with geographical ideas: pupils and teachers thinking geographically;
- commitment to subject relevance for pupils in a given context;
- the use of pedagogical practices and resources that foster critical engagement with the discipline;
- the opportunity to learn geography that takes account of the needs and interests of pupils, but which takes them beyond what they already know.

However, and like the other models, this model is also not unproblematic. Firstly, it is in many ways the antithesis of a heavily prescriptive outcomes-driven model because it is dependent on a much more enquiring approach to teaching and learning where outcomes are less than predictable (see the section on geographical enquiry in Chapter 3). This lack of predictability could be more risky for teachers; the very fact that the curriculum is seen as a process means that it requires teachers to be *responsive* to and mindful of the unintended, the unpredictable and the unimagined ways that pupils' minds work – we do not always know where things are going. Because of this lack of predictability, curriculum-making is heavily dependent on the quality of teachers as both geographers and as professionals; high-quality geography teachers are crucial to the curriculum-making model because without subject expertise it is much more difficult for a teacher to deal productively with the unpredictable (see Smith 2000). We would argue that if pupils are to experience a high-quality geographical education, they should be taught by well-qualified geography teachers who are both knowledgeable and passionate about their subject and knowledgeable and passionate about teaching. Such pre-conditions off-set any potential issues with the process model for the curriculum.

The final model, the praxis model, is in some ways a development of the process model, but has intentions beyond educating pupils into the ways and means of geographical meaning-making. This model, while drawing on the practice and principles of the process model, is underpinned by a very clear articulation of the intentions it serves, namely critical engagement that takes pupils beyond the immediate and that equips them with ideas and ideals of social justice, fairness and therefore emancipation, of themselves and others. While this might seem to some as over-ambitious in intention, and for others inappropriate as a curriculum model, nonetheless the praxis model, linked to ideas of critical pedagogy (see Chapter 4), is committed to not just educating young people for their own sake, but in doing so enabling their freedom of thought and action.

What does a praxis curriculum look like? Lambert and Morgan (2011) writing about development education in school geography, while not specifically advocating a praxis curriculum, provide some important insights into what teachers might consider. Their argument is that, in the context of development education, much of what pupils are taught in school geography is treated as unproblematic and incontested. For example, take the concept of 'development' – rather than being taught as a political and ideological construct derived from of multiple meanings that are socially and historically situated, they argue that the tendency is to assume

> that there can be agreement on what development is, and that having more development is better than having less. With this agreement in mind, the focus is on closing the 'gap', adjusting the imbalance and 'helping' countries develop. The effect of this is to redefine the issue of development as one of 'problem-solving' rather than 'problem-posing', and the solutions to be considered are all concerned with modifying or reforming the existing (global) system rather than posing the question of whether that system may itself generate the 'development gap'.
>
> (p. 21)

In a praxis-orientated geography curriculum, teachers and pupils would, together, critique both the term and their assumptions about its meaning. Dialogue would be at the heart of the learning process, but the underpinning principles would be for pupils to question the origins of ideas, rooted in the discipline, and interrogate the power structures that sustain them. This kind of teaching and learning calls for a more critical pedagogy where pupils and teachers question authorised wisdom and in doing so are equipped to both understand more deeply, for example, 'development' and, in appreciating global inequalities, feel motivated to act.

This model too has its downsides, not least its incompatibility with a prescribed centralised curriculum, as well as its incompatibility with the current examination and accountability systems. It is also dependent on the quality of teachers, both in terms of their constant engagement with the philosophical ideas that shape and reshape the discipline, and also their commitment to the ideals of praxis. Some would argue that this is not the role of school geography or indeed education. Lambert and Morgan (2011) cite the ideas of Alex Standish claiming that one perspective might be that:

> teaching about global issues in geography has become more concerned with promulgating particular moralistic values rather than learning geographical knowledge.
>
> (p. 13)

Task 2.4 Evaluating curriculum models

Having considered the different curriculum models, it is worth now considering how these ideas play out in schools.

- In the school where you are teaching, how does the geography department present its KS3 geography curriculum? How is the subject broken down into manageable units and how do these units connect together? What is the sequence in which pupils study them?
- Closely examine one unit and consider the following questions:

  1 What are the intentions of the unit in terms of what pupils will learn?
  2 How is it framed – around objectives or geographical questions (or bits of both)?
  3 Drawing on the descriptions and discussions about curriculum models above, what kind of model does your department seem to be adopting? Why do you think this is so (possibly discuss this with the head of department)?
  4 In what ways might the idea of 'curriculum-making' be in evidence in the planning of the curriculum? Do teachers understand the term?

John Morgan (2010) highlights the tensions and contradictions that exist for teachers in the different ways that the curriculum is conceptualised. He argues that the dominant curriculum discourse is that of 'curriculum-as-fact', but that other constructions, curriculum-as-value (where geographical knowledge is taught as contingent and perspectival), and curriculum-as-ideology (where the geographical knowledge taught represents certain interests and marginalises others) have also prevailed. He goes on to make a case for a fourth conceptualisation – curriculum-as-text, whereby rather than teaching knowledge, geography teachers are teaching what he calls 'preferred discourses' (p. 29).

> An example would be accounts of gentrification which are couched in terms of lifestyle choices and voluntarism, with no attention to the economic conditions that create low rents in certain parts of inner cities.
>
> (p. 29)

This typology of approaches to the curriculum illustrates the curriculum tensions that teachers experience. With education systems framed by 'economic codes', the dominance of the curriculum-as-fact conception is, argues Morgan, at odds with the postmodern culture in which teachers and pupil live their lives. What he is suggesting is that the curriculum is subject to pressures and constraints within and beyond schools, namely economy and culture.

You have to consider whether or not you agree with Morgan.

(For the full text see Morgan, J. (2010), in D. Lambert and D. Balderstone (eds) *Learning to Teach Geography in the Secondary School*. 2nd Edition, London: Routledge)

Progression

In this chapter (and indeed this book), we propose that the idea of 'curriculum' is one of the most significant concepts in education because it focuses our attention on *what* we think it is worthwhile and important to teach young people. But what exactly should we select to teach about the earth as the home of mankind is a tricky question with no ready-made and clear-cut answer. To help us, two other concepts are also crucial:

1   Pedagogy (see Chapter 4) – how we choose to teach the ideas and other material we consider worth teaching – is also crucial, which is why we spend so much time in this book discussing teaching technique as well as curriculum matters.
2   Assessment – how we go about judging the performance of the students we teach – is important too. As we see in Chapter 8, assessment can serve many different purposes, but fundamentally it is concerned with evaluating whether students have grasped the subject matter: our assessments enable us to judge what they understand and are able to do as a result of their geography lessons.

If we imagine curriculum, pedagogy and assessment to be the signature concepts underpinning your professional identity as a teacher (that is, it is in these aspects that you acquire and develop specialist professional knowledge enabling you to talk about your work at a high level with other professionals), then close behind is the idea of 'progression'. The following quote clearly shows why:

> The idea of progression is implicit in any discussion of the nature of learning we hope students will engage in. If we did not hope that students should, in some sense, progress we would have no foundation on which to construct a curriculum or to embark on the act of teaching.
>
> (Daugherty 1996: 195)

In this section we briefly discuss the way to *position* the idea of progression in relation to curriculum, pedagogy and assessment. In many respects, it is far from clear what *kind* of idea is the idea of progression! Is it a broad-brush idea, best understood as a general principle? Or is it a fined grained and more technical idea requiring lots of detail about precise learning pathways and sequences? Quite a lot of research from the fields of mathematics and science education, seeking empirical evidence for 'learning progressions' in specific topics, might propel us to the latter view. It offers the promise of telling us the building blocks, and how to sequence material so as to teach it in the most efficient manner. Trevor Bennetts (2005) pointed out that

> the idea of progression is especially applicable to advances in the quality of students' learning, it can also be applied to the design of courses which are intended to bring about such advances. Much of the treatment of progression in the educational literature is about how best to structure courses to enable students to advance their learning in an orderly way.
>
> (pp. 157–158)

However, we are cautious about this. For one thing, geography is not the same kind of subject as physics of mathematics – it does not have the same kind of verticality or linearity as those subjects. But even in the sciences, it is far from clear how helpful it is in practice to lay down the law that progression can be tracked in detail in a way that applies in the same way to all students. It is for this reason that Bennetts also pointed out that:

> The idea of progression becomes increasingly important over longer time-scales, during which students' developing capabilities are affected by maturation processes, as well as by experience. Probably the most widely accepted principle underpinning planning for progression is that there should be a reasonable match between the demands of the curriculum and the capabilities of students; and that teachers' objectives, expectations and strategies should, therefore, take account of the ways in which students' capabilities develop . . .
>
> (p. 158)

> Expressed in this simple form, it could be claimed that the idea of progression equates with the intuitive, common sense approach adopted by many teachers, who draw upon their professional experience to pitch their lessons at appropriate levels. Difficulties begin to emerge when attempts are made to define progression in understanding in more precise ways, and to measure the extent to which it is being achieved.
>
> (p. 159)

We agree with Bennetts' words entirely: difficulties certainly do emerge when we are pushed into making precise 'measurements' of progress as Chapter 8 shows, where we recount the brief history of the coming and the going of National Curriculum 'levels'. Such pressure – to measure progress – is ever present, however, as it seems so utterly common sense to accept that progression has to be planned for and monitored and that the only effective way of doing the latter is by the use of assessment.

When the National Curriculum levels were abolished in 2014, it caused consternation in some quarters for it looked like the idea of progression had been abolished at the same time. Of course, this was not the case: what was abolished was the notion that we should allocate a 'level' of progress according to a predetermined set of criteria to every child. Abolition set us free from the crude and sometimes limiting sense of a ladder of progress. It enabled us to focus on the assessment of understanding and ask ourselves:

- Has this student grasped what I was intending to teach?

Progression, then, is not best thought of as a technical and detailed 'ladder' underpinned with precise criteria with which to measure it. This is what the philosopher Andrew Davis (1998) has described as an empirical fallacy, or as we would describe it 'the search for the Holy Grail': the search for robust empirical grounds for measuring precise steps of progress will be frustrating and endless, and, ironically, less than robust. Instead, he argues, it is better to focus conceptually on what we expect – or perhaps aspire for – our students to learn. We tend to agree, and as with Trevor Bennetts (2005: 167) we would invest professional energy into designing good classroom activities (which are in themselves assessment opportunities) that enable students to deepen and broaden their knowledge, understanding and skills. He suggests that assessment can be based on tasks that require students to, for example:

- outline the meaning of specific ideas and illustrate their application (usually in given locational contexts);
- describe or explain the links and relationships between ideas, e.g. within a given generalisation or model such as a demographic transition model or a model of landscape change;
- demonstrate or evaluate the usefulness of a specific conceptual construct such as 'central business district' or 'least cost location';
- interpret experience or information by applying relevant ideas, such as 'distance decay' on commuting patterns;
- apply cognitive skills to the search for meaning (i.e. tasks which require students to go beyond recall in demonstrating their understanding), such as imagining alternative future land use change on the high street.

Individual students will perform in different ways in relation to such tasks and for most there will be reasonably clear ways in which they may be able to develop their responses further – for example, and depending on the particular tasks, using a greater range of variables, or using comparative statistics, or achieving greater precision in explaining a process – to 'make progress'.

Summary

In this chapter, we have asked you to begin to do some hard thinking about the school geography curriculum. You can see from the discussion here that the curriculum is not a straightforward unproblematic entity and that while when you start teaching you may be more concerned with the day to day of lesson planning, at some stage you will have to consider your relationship with the curriculum. As Lambert reminds us:

> What is worth teaching and why. Only when we have worked out an answer to this does the question 'how shall I try to do this' make any sense. To treat the subject as the vehicle for a pedagogical adventure is, morally, education without a heart.
>
> (Lambert 2004)

Your professional values come into play here – what kind of geography you feel pupils should learn and the ways you believe they should learn it become rooted in the kind of curriculum your create. In thinking about different types of curricula, it is important to return to the knowledge question we considered in Chapter 1. We say this because knowledge, curriculum, pedagogy and assessment, while discussed distinctively in the chapters of this book, eventually will need you to knit them together.

Further reading

Lambert, D. and Morgan, J. (2010) 'What does it mean to be a teacher of geography'. In *Teaching Geography 11-18: A Conceptual Approach*, Maidenhead: Open University Press.
A very useful chapter in laying out some of the challenges of what it means to be a geography teacher. It will help you start to frame you relationship with what it describes as two big ideas - geography and education.

Biddulph, M. (2014) 'What kind of curriculum do we really want?' *Teaching Geography* 39, 1: 6-9.
This article raises some important questions about the nature of the school geography curriculum and the implications of different approaches to curriculum theory for the kinds of geographies we teach. It develops some of the ideas presented in this chapter.

3   Planning

The schools that had a good or outstanding geography curriculum had thought carefully about creating a more relevant curriculum at Key Stage 3 with a greater emphasis on topical concerns such as sustainability, globalisation, interdependence, poverty and wealth, as well as a fieldwork programme which showed clearly how students should progress in terms of their geographical skills. In these schools, the numbers of students choosing geography at GCSE and A level were being maintained, or even increasing. This reflected the fact that students were prepared to study a subject which they saw as relevant and with which they could engage.

(Ofsted 2011: 32)

Introduction

Chapter 2 considered the complex debates about what a geography curriculum actually is. However, one of the main tasks of being a teacher is to plan a geography curriculum that will engage, excite and challenge pupils to think about the world in which they live. This chapter is about planning a geography curriculum and how this relates to other aspects of planning such as lesson planning, planning for differentiation, and lesson evaluation – the cyclical process of practical planning. There is no intention here to separate theoretical discussions about the geography curriculum from the practical planning issues, in fact quite the opposite. This chapter draws in the wider curriculum debates presented in Chapter 2 and sets about the task of considering what they mean for the day-to-day work of teachers.

While we consider what constitutes high-quality planning in school geography, we do so with certain assumptions in mind. Although teachers have to work with statutory requirements such as the National Curriculum, as well as a certain level of prescription from exam boards, the principle underpinning this chapter is about planning an interesting, relevant and challenging school *geography*. We acknowledge that this needs to take account of prescription, but prescription does not need to drive decisions about what and how to teach – this is the responsibility of teachers.

By the end of this chapter you should:

- have an understanding of the relationship between curriculum planning and lesson planning in school geography
- know and understand the different dimensions to effective planning at a school level
- appreciate the relationships between wider curriculum debates and how these impact on the practicalities of planning for teaching
- understand the relationship between geography, the discipline and the geography you plan to teach.

Planning a geography curriculum: some issues to attend to

It is tempting when you first learn to teach to become engrossed in the mechanics of teaching individual lessons: 'I have Y7 tomorrow afternoon and I have to teach them about types of volcanoes – what am I going to *do* with them?' is a fairly reasonable reflection of the kind of conversation early career teachers have with themselves and each other. Such a question presumes that the decision about what to teach has already been made elsewhere and that all you have to do is plan some interesting activities to fill an hour-long lesson. However, before you can get to the point of activity design, you have to attend to matters of curriculum content, namely, what geography do you want your pupils to learn?

Decisions about what to teach are influenced by many different and often overlapping factors. In any consideration of the 'what' question, it is essential that you return to broad educational aims and purposes – what do you hope to achieve for pupils when you teach geography? What do you hope pupils will come to value and understand as a consequence of your curriculum and teaching? It also worth revisiting the 'purpose' statement for National Curriculum geography (see Chapter 2) as well as the aims and objectives of the examination specifications you will be teaching. What do these tell you about the longer term intentions your school's geography curriculum, and what, if any, is the relationship between KS3, GCSE and A level aims and purposes?

While all of this 'thinking about' and 'revisiting' might seem somewhat detached from the practicalities of planning, the reality is that without recourse to these broader purposes, your curriculum, at a school level, will become somewhat purposeless: undertaking this kind of thinking will, in the long run, serve to underpin your practical long-term, medium-term and day-to-day planning.

Planning a geography curriculum

As well as considering the aims of the curriculum, it is also important to revisit the 'big ideas', the concepts that underpin geography as a discipline. So what are concepts and what is their role in planning? Colman (2001, cited in Taylor 2009) defines a concept as 'A mental representation, idea or thought corresponding to a specific entity or class, which may be either concrete or abstract' (go to www.geography.org.uk/gtip/thinkpieces/concepts/). Commentators agree that concepts are categories of objects or ideas that have something in common which come about from the way in which we classify their attributes, name them and put them into a 'growing filing system' to recall and use in future communication with others:

> So basically, a concept is a classifier, something that helps us make sense of a very complex world. Our shared concepts help us communicate, so if someone says 'farm' we have a basic idea what they're talking about, even if our idea 'farm' might be a bit different to theirs.
>
> (Taylor 2009)

While identifying key concepts helps you to explore your own thoughts around what it means to 'think geographically' (see Chapter 1) and to consider how you might articulate geographical concepts in your school, they are nonetheless at a significant level of abstraction from teaching – you cannot plan and teach a topic on 'place', but you will teach about places to enable pupils to gradually, over time, come to develop a complex understanding of the concept, place. Concepts themselves need classifying and breaking down in order to make them manageable as planning tools. Vygotsky (1962, cited in Roberts 2013) distinguished between spontaneous and scientific concepts with the former derived for our everyday experiences of the world , and the latter derived from disciplines. Gagne (1965) and Roberts (2013) distinguish between simple, descriptive 'concepts by observation' (concrete concepts), namely those derived from things we experience through our senses such as 'road' or 'park', and the more complex organising 'concepts by definition' (abstract concepts) which are representations in our 'minds as words related to ideas' such as trade or interdependence (p. 82).

The complexity of concrete concepts depends upon how difficult they are to experience or whether understanding of another concept is required. For example, understanding trade patterns or carbon footprints will support pupils in developing their understanding of interdependence – interdependence is too complex to simply teach as a stand-alone concept. The complexity of abstract concepts is influenced by the number of variables involved in the defined relationships. This is an important distinction to make as it implies that the former (concrete) may be learned through a process of discovery whereas the latter (abstract), must be taught in some direct manner.

Another way of classifying concepts would be to organise them into a hierarchy. The higher-level concepts would be the more general organising concepts such as spatial interaction or inequality. These would be followed by more specific concepts. The majority of nouns, with the exception of particular people, places or events, are concepts. However, adding an adjective or combining two concepts creates what are termed 'compound concepts'. For example, river and pollution are concepts but river pollution is also a concept which is different from its component concepts.

If concepts help us to organise our ideas and are a means of communicating these ideas to others, then what might be concepts which frame geography? The table below lists concepts different geographers have identified as being important:

Table 3.1 Some suggested sets of concepts for geography

Leat (1998)	Geography Advisors' and Inspectors' Network (2002)	Rowley and Lewis (2003)
Cause and effect **Classification** **Decision-making** **Development** **Inequality** **Location** **Planning** **Systems**	Bias Causation Change Conflict Development Distribution Futures Inequality Interdependence Landscape Scale Location Perception Region Environment Uncertainty	Describing and classifying Diversity and wilderness Patterns and boundaries Places Maps and communication Sacredness and beauty
Holloway et al. (2003)	Jackson (2006)	UK 2008 Key Stage 3 Curriculum (QCA 2007)
Space Time Place Scale Social formations Physical systems Landscape and environment	Space and place Scale and connection Proximity and distance Relational thinking	Place Space Scale Interdependence Physical and human processes Environmental interaction and sustainable development Cultural understanding and diversity

Source: Taylor, E. (2009) *GTIP Think Piece - Concepts in Geography.* Geographical Association

As the table suggests, there is debate over what might be *the* organising concepts in the discipline, and some would argue that certain concepts in the lists, while relevant to geography are not necessarily distinctively geographical; they apply to other disciplines too. It is worth asking yourself why these differences occur – for what reasons is the list identified by Leat different to that identified by Jackson? Liz Taylor suggests returning to the original publications to clarify the ways in which different geographers interpret geographical concepts and for what purpose.

The concepts in geography are the essence the subject, they provide the underlying structure for the discipline and are central to its understanding. Growing familiarity with these concepts will help pupils to understand what it means to think geographically – a disposition to think critically and creatively about people and places using geographic information.

If we agree that concepts are central to how we understand geography as a discipline, they remain important curriculum decision-making tools in the face of any curriculum prescription from central government. For example, learning about 'Russia' (as prescribed in the 2014 National Curriculum for England) could either comprise a list of cities, rivers, mountains and coastlines (geographical facts), or learning about Russia could be embedded in lessons about:

- climate change and international trade as new shipping routes emerge between the north Atlantic and the north Pacific;
- environmental and sustainability issues surrounding the Sochi Winter Olympics;
- the political geographies of Russia's much contested boarders.

We are not arguing that knowing cites, rivers and so on is unimportant, the section on 'knowledge' in Chapter 1 reminds us of the significance of different types of knowledge. What we are saying is that such content alone is not good enough in meeting the needs of broad educational purposes. In summary, despite curriculum prescription, planning what to teach and the selection of content is dependent on thinking geographically; that is, with concepts. If anything, lack of prescribed concepts in a statutory framework makes it even more important that geography teachers ask themselves 'What are the concepts that frame our school's geography curriculum?'

In the context of curriculum planning, Taylor (2009) considers the idea of substantive and second-order concepts as a means of organising your curriculum thinking (see Table 3.2). She describes substantive concepts as the substantive content of geography. For example,

Table 3.2 Taylor's second-order concepts for curriculum planning

Interaction	**Change**
Interaction is closely linked to change as geographers want to find out how things are linked together and how one aspect affects another. It is relevant to both physical and human geography and the interaction between the two.	Change is crucial as a driver within both human and physical geography. Managing change is a key aspect of geography – learning from past change (for example coastal erosion or city morphology) and predicting and managing future change (such as migratory patterns or resource supply and availability). Time (a dimension of change) could be seen as important to geography as space and place, as past, present and future changes are part of geography's field of enquiry.
Perception and representation	**Diversity**
Perception and representation consider how people think about the world and how they communicate that thinking to others. At school level, this has been explored in ideas of sense of place and also in geographies of tourism and development. How the world is represented to us through, for example, news programmes, films, social media, affects how we perceive the world and how we act within it, this, in turn affects the lives of others.	Diversity means more than just cultural diversity because it focuses on the complexities of the world: places and environments are diverse between and within themselves. Diversity in, for example, quality of life within or between countries may lead to concerns about inequality. This in turn could lead to consideration of potential conflict between groups or/and lead to consideration of resource allocation to redress social inequalities.

Source: Adapted from Taylor, E. (2009) *GTIP Think Piece – Concepts in Geography.* Geographical Association

concepts such as field, power, meander or city, while of a different order to one another, are nonetheless all concepts we can identify in geography. Whereas second-order concepts are the ideas you can use to organise the content. Taylor identifies the second-order concepts for geography as diversity, change, interaction, and perception and representation.

What Taylor advocates is that:

> second order concepts are the ideas used to organise the content and to shape questions within a discipline. The intersection of substantive content and second order concepts is where the discipline of geography is created. Being applicable across all the content areas, second order concepts are thus likely to be a much smaller group.
>
> (Taylor 2009)

Taylor goes on to explain how, through the lens of specific second-order concepts, learning substantive concepts can be planned for in a more focused way. For example, when teaching about flooding on the Somerset Levels, *what* you plan to teach is very different when planned from the perspective of *'change'* (which would consider flooding patterns over time, impact on landscapes and how to accommodate the inevitability of rising water levels in the future) to that planned through the lens of *'perception and representation'* (which would consider the floods from multiple perspectives such as media representation of flood events, pupils' perceptions of these events and what 'experts' have to say about the social and environmental consequences of flood management). It is not the intention here to suggest that second-order concepts are used in isolation, but that *individually* second-order concepts support the selection of substantive concepts for teaching and learning, and that *collectively* they constitute an overarching practical planning tool, but one that is grounded in geography rather than more generic notions of learning.

In particular, Taylor suggests that this kind of approach supports planning geographical enquiries. However, just as is the case with the concept lists for geography, so too you have to question whether or not you agree that Taylor's second-order concepts provide a viable planning framework – are there other potential second-order concepts that geography teachers should consider?

Table 3.3 Planning with second-order concepts: *example: flooding on the Somerset Levels*

Diversity	Change	Interaction	Perception and representation
Causes and consequences of flooding in different regions of the UK Consequences on physical and human landscape of the Levels	Flooding and the physical landscape of the Levels Flooding and the human landscape of the Levels Past flood events and their social, economic and environmental	Weather and the local environment	Media representations Expert representation (environment agency, professors of hydrology)

Task 3.1 Concepts

A

1   Look carefully at Taylor's concept lists. For each group (National Curriculum, Leat, Rowley and Lewis and so on), consider what are the different messages each communicates about geography as a discipline and why these differences are significant. What are the implications of these differences for your own understanding of thinking geographically?

2   Now write a list of what you feel might be the organising concepts for school geography – you don't have to rely on the ideas presented here – there may be other concepts or combinations of concepts not here that you feel are important enough to include. Compare your ideas with others, justifying decisions you have made.

3   If you are based in a school, then discuss with other geography teachers how they use concepts to plan the school's geography curriculum.

B

1   Select a topic from the list below:

   • The impacts of river flooding on an urban area
   • Inner city regeneration
   • Global food consumption
   • Factors affecting agricultural land use
   • Inter-relationships between the different components of ecosystems
   • Health inequalities in the UK.

2   Now use Taylor's second-order concepts (see Table 3.2 and Table 3.3 as an exemplar) to identify the different substantive concepts you would teach. Consider which substantive concepts are more difficult than others to learn? Is there a hierarchy of substantive concepts in your list? Are some concepts more appropriate for different age groups – KS3, GCSE or A-level?

Planning a geography curriculum: the practicalities

What kind of planner are you?

Having clarified the significance of geographical concepts in curriculum thinking, we now need to consider how to enact some of this thinking in order to create the kind of geography curriculum that will serve broader educational purposes.

Rawling (2008) states that, before you can proceed with detailed planning, you need to consider what kind of curriculum planner you are. She presents a continuum of 'planning attitudes' ranging from cautious, to balanced, through to progressive and then adventurous. The cautious planner tends to stay with what he/she knows works and has a somewhat guarded approach to curriculum change whereas the balanced planner tends to 'cherry pick' new content leaving 'tried and tested' schemes in place. The adventurous planner tends to see curriculum change as an opportunity for review and innovation and is constantly on the look-out for ways to draw more radical ideas about the subject into the curriculum.

Each 'planning attitude' has its relative strengths and weaknesses. The adventurous planner may well sometimes lose sight of statutory requirements and blur the subject boundaries to such an extent that pupils don't always see what they are learning as geography. The cautious planner, while providing a secure curriculum basis from which student can learn, may well miss opportunities to broaden pupils' geographical understanding of current events. It is worth considering the planning approach adopted by teachers you work with – where on the planning spectrum might you place a department in which you have taught and why? Where would you place yourself and why? Research tells us that despite changes 'imposed from the top', teachers' attitudes to the curriculum are highly significant in shaping the geography curriculum in school (see Roberts 1995).

Linked to the notion of 'planner-types' are two other important curriculum ideas: curriculum planning and curriculum development. Graves (1979), Rawling (2007), Biddulph (2013) all agree that planning and development, though connected, are also distinct from each other and are not to be confused.

Curriculum planning: Planning takes account of important educational ideas such as progression, differentiation and assessment. When planning, you make decisions about the sequence in which you will teach particular units of study across all key stages; you also make decisions about the sequence of lessons within a particular scheme – considering the most logical order for pupils to learn about, for example, how coastlines change. Such decisions, while seemingly pragmatic are actually quite sophisticated because they require knowledge and understanding of conceptual complexity, how young people learn as well as curriculum requirements.

Planning takes place at a range of scales: (see Box 3.1).

Box 3.1 Levels of curriculum planning

- *Planning at a national scale:* linked to the broad aims of a national education system identifying aims, procedures and assessment requirements.
- *Planning at a school level:* where teachers, generally working in departmental teams, plan a curriculum specific to the needs of their pupils in their school. At this level, planning has to take account of pupils' contexts and also their needs and interests, how to develop pupils' geographical understanding (progression), the resources available to the department, staffing and subject expertise among teachers, time available for teaching. At this level, assessment is both internal to the school in the form of both formative and summative assessment, as well as external based on national requirements and qualification acquisition.
- *Planning at a classroom level:* normally associated with practical lesson preparation (see Chapter 4), individual teachers still need to keep careful watch over the medium term to ensure subject coherence, i.e., does it all hang together in a relatively logical way?, and progression in learning. Teachers have different degrees of freedom over the curriculum and pedagogic choices they make, depending on the school they are working in – some schools are insistent that pupils' curriculum experiences are the same across the department, others allow teachers significant degrees of freedom to decide how and what they teach, but generally within a broad framework of subject expectations.

Curriculum development: Development is the process of curriculum review, innovation and change. In your school, you may be part of a teaching team that regularly carries out some form of curriculum audit, reviews the content and process of the curriculum, identifies content areas in need of change and considers ways in which the current curriculum can be taken into new territories of geographical learning. Progression, differentiation and assessment are also elements of curriculum development.

Ultimately, any curriculum development, such as introducing a new topic on urban change in the light of a new housing proposal in your local area, will have to be 'planned', but a planned curriculum is not necessarily one that is in a process of development; indeed, a planned curriculum may meet statutory requirements but suffer from being relatively stagnant through lack of development and innovation.

Long-term planning: having an overview

It is important to have some sort of overview of how the curriculum fits together across all key stages to ensure both curriculum coherence and to avoid excessive repetition of curriculum content. For example, in some schools pupils seem to study rivers at almost all key stages! It could be argued that 'the spiral curriculum (Bruner 1960, 1996), whereby pupils have opportunities to revisit key ideas, concepts and process in order to deepen their understanding as they mature is the rationale for this, and careful long-term planning will ensure that this is the case. However, for pupils, such repetition – if not planned for carefully and thoughtfully – can have the effect of narrowing their understanding of what geography actually is, and merely demotivate them as they tire of 'studying the same old thing'.

Creating a curriculum overview can take many forms. You may take a fairly logical approach to the process and map out the main themes and concepts you want to teach year by year, ensuring pupils study a range of places, at a range of scales and drawing on a

	Autumn 1	Autumn 2	Spring 1	Spring 2	Summer 1	Summer 2
Y7	What's my Place?	Why is a place like it is?	What's going on in Britain?	What's going on in Tanzania??	Why's the weather the weather ?	Why's it so hot? Why's it so cold?
Y8	What's made the Peak District?	Where do we work?	Can we keep the lights on?	Where does all the water go?	Why is there so much conflict?	What's going on in China?
Y9	What's happening at the seaside?	What's happening in the mountains?	How is the earth made and remade?	Is the climate changing?	Can we feed the planet?	Where's my stuff from?

Figure 3.1 Overview of a hypothetical Key Stage 3 curriculum

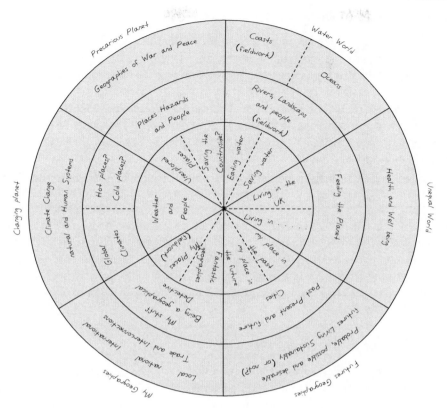

Figure 3.2 Circular model for curriculum planning: an example

(*Source:* Royal geographical Society. Available at www.geography.org.uk/secondary)

range of geographical skills (see Figure 3.1). Another approach is the 'planning circle' from the Royal Geographical Society (see Figure 3.2). The example here illustrates how one school decided to organise its curriculum - as you can see the decision has been taken about a set of concepts around which the teachers wish to frame their KS3 curriculum, they have then selected the content to support conceptual learning. This diagram enables you to see not just what you have decided to teach but communicates a more direct relationship between concepts and content.

Both models, linear and circular, enable schools to maintain a general overview of the geography curriculum, making curriculum changes as they deem fit without sacrificing the overall coherence of the curriculum. When you first start working in a geography department, it is important to gain an overview of the whole curriculum so that when you start teaching you have sense of your own, and therefore your pupils', direction of travel.

Planning schemes of work

A curriculum overview, such as those presented in Figures 3.1 and Figures 3.2, provided the basis for planning more detailed schemes of work. It is schemes of work that provide the rationale and framework for developing pupils' educational experiences in geography.

Schemes of work articulate the educational goals of a course and suggest strategies for achieving them. An individual scheme of work outlines the subject content to be covered, the resources available, and the teaching strategies and learning activities that determine the nature of this educational experience for the pupils.

Although a scheme of work is a planning tool, it should also be a *working* document, summarising teachers' thinking about a course, providing a structure and offering guidelines for more detailed lesson planning. Sometimes, especially when a teaching team comprises a number of non-geography specialists, schemes of work can become very prescriptive – almost a straitjacket from which no teacher is allowed to deviate. While in some respects this is understandable, a scheme of work should actually be flexible, allowing individual teachers to interpret the subject and how to teach it in ways they deem appropriate for their classes. All schemes of work should be reviewed on a regular basis so that improvements can be made where necessary.

How should schemes of work be planned?

There are available (on the web and in texts on teaching) a wide range of grids and structures you could use to help you to plan your schemes of work. However, no one structure, as such, is the right way to plan, but schemes of work have a key role to play in ensuring continuity and progression in pupils' learning in geography.

Some structures are more useful than others in capturing the level of detail required to ensure that pupils make progress in their geographical understanding. Also, because the curriculum can be framed in different ways, you will need to use different models for different units of work: some emphasise questioning and the enquiry process, and others concentrate on the product of learning.

A useful way of planning a scheme of work is to develop a planning grid or chart which identifies all the elements that need to be considered. The goals will provide a clear indication of the overall educational purposes of the course including the aims, which are general statements about the direction of learning intended and the priorities within a course. The learning objectives will show the more specific goals of the course indicating the geographical knowledge, understanding, skills and attitudes through which the aims are realised.

Box 3.2 is a possible outline you could begin to develop.

Box 3.2 The features of a scheme of work

Year group					Time/Number of lessons
Title of unit/these					
Syllabus/subject content/programme of rationale Indicate the significance of the geographical knowledge and understanding that pupils will develop. This is to be expressed in terms of the geographical significance of the knowledge, rather than as it relates directly to pupils lives.			**Cross-curricular elements** Indicate how the unit may contribute to any cross-curricular themes, dimensions or competences. Are there any links with work in other subjects?		
Key questions	**Learning objectives, key ideas and generalisations**	**Learning activities, teaching strategies**	**Skills**	**Resources**	**Assessment opportunities and evidence**
Use key questions to structure the learning objectives and to provide a sequence to the learning through an enquiry approach.	Identify learning objectives. These may relate to an examination specification or the National Curriculum Programme of Study. Aim for a balanced coverage of knowledge, understanding and attitudes/values.	Use a variety of learning activities and teaching strategies. Activities should be designed to investigate the key questions and develop the learning objectives identified.	Which geographical skills will be developed or used in the learning activities? Also indicate any other general learning skills that may be developed.	Use a variety of resources to support learning and to provide interesting and motivating learning experiences.	Indicate possible learning outcomes that could provide evidence of pupils' attainment in geography. What do you want pupils to produce? How do these relate to assessment criteria? Match assessment tasks to learning objectives. Try to balance the assessment of knowledge, understanding, skills and attitudes/values. Be selective – you don't have to assess everything!

In general terms the geographical content of a scheme should be stated in terms of the places, themes, topics and issues which have been selected for study. The selection of this content will be influenced by the requirements of the National Curriculum Programme of Study or examination specification. The content of specific lessons is indicated in the statement of key ideas or concepts. Key questions arising from these ideas can then be used as a structure for the learning in lessons. The sequence of these key ideas and questions needs to be planned carefully as it will have a significant influence on the way pupils make progress through a particular course of study. If the sequence is not well-conceived and fails to gradually build pupils' geographical understanding, it may be that geography teachers themselves become responsible for reinforcing misconceptions rather than challenging them, and for confusing pupils rather than educating them.

 A scheme of work should include a range of learning activities and teaching strategies (see Chapter 4). It should also take into account, in general terms, the range of pupils' learning needs and abilities, providing an indication of how learning will be differentiated.

Planning learning activities and teaching strategies will also require you to plan how you will assess pupils' achievements and progress in geography. Again, the aim is to use a variety of assessment methods and to consider carefully how, when and in what context you use formative assessment approaches, and where you situate summative assessment opportunities. (See Chapter 8 on assessment.)

Although a scheme of work may often be produced by an individual teacher, a collaborative approach to planning can be of great value to a geography department. The discussion that accompanies this approach to planning tends to bring assumptions to the surface which can then be questioned and reflected upon. It can encourage teachers to focus on important curricular issues with consideration being given to criteria for the selection of content, learning activities and teaching strategies.

A scheme of work can provide support for non-specialist teachers, learning support teachers and staff responsible for broader curricular policies and decisions within a school. Schemes of work will provide information about the geography curriculum in a school for senior staff and governors as well as advisers and inspectors. They can also facilitate valuable dialogue with teaching colleagues in other schools, for example, as part of the process of cross-phase liaison. As from 2014, it is also a statutory requirement that all maintained schools in England, that are required to teach the National Curriculum, publish their curriculum online for parents and others to access (Department for Education 2013).

It should be remembered that geography courses make an important contribution to the whole curriculum experience for pupils in a school. Learning and undertaking activities in geography should contribute to achievement of the overall curriculum aims for all young people. Schemes of work are therefore helpful when reviewing the overall breadth and balance of the curriculum. You should give some attention to cross-curricular links by considering how the work that pupils will be doing in geography will fit in with work that they undertake in other subjects. Geography can make a contribution to and draw from curriculum areas such as history, the creative arts, English, and even modern foreign languages (see Coyle et al. 2010, for more on teaching geography through the medium of a modern foreign language).

The 2007 review of the secondary curriculum stressed the importance of meeting a range of different national agendas such as the Every Child Matters agenda (see Chapter 2) and the development of generic personal, learning and thinking skills. There were also messages about teaching and learning from other initiatives such as the National Strategies in numeracy and literacy to consider. The 2014 National Curriculum makes no such references. However, it does, as do examination specifications, place emphasis on the responsibilities of all curriculum areas to plan, teach and support pupils' literacy and numeracy development. This is explored in more detail in Chapter 4, but it is important in any consideration of curriculum planning that you attend to how your curriculum will contribute to these aspects of pupils' learning.

In a similar vein, the National Curriculum in England and Wales, the Northern Ireland National Curriculum and the Curriculum for Excellence in Scotland all make specific reference to 'inclusion' as a key curriculum principle, requiring teachers to plan and teach in ways that enable *all* pupils to access geography, regardless of their cognitive capacity, their language skills or their socio-economic context. Inclusion, however, is not just about the activities you plan and how you take account of the more generic capabilities of your pupils. Inclusion is also about your interpretation of curriculum content; the choices you make about the geographies you include and the sequence in which you teach them so that pupils can begin to make sense of often abstract and sometimes seemingly irrelevant ideas.

While all of the above may seem like yet more confusing layers of responsibilities, Rawling (2007) provides some sensible advice here, distinguishing between:

- those things which you must address because they are statutory and immediately and directly relevant to you;
- those things which are only advisory but represent relevant official advice and so should certainly be considered and checked;
- those things which are non-official advice and guidance, some of which may be very helpful and some of which may not, but which can all be used at your own discretion.

You could perhaps add to this:

- those things that *you* judge to be important to your pupils in your school; exercising professional judgement is crucial to effective curriculum planning.

Planning for geographical enquiry

I think of enquiry not simply as a set of skills but as an approach to teaching and learning geography. I think it is important that when students are learning geography through enquiry, they extend their geographical knowledge and understanding at the same time as they learn skills, both skills specific to geography and generic skills used in other subjects.

(Roberts 2013: 8)

Enquiry learning usually refers to situations where pupils are actively enquiring into issues, questions or problems. When using the enquiry process to plan a scheme of work, key questions and learning activities need to be developed which relate to the different stages of this process. In this section, we will consider three different models for planning your curriculum around geographical enquiry:

1   Margaret Roberts' framework for learning through enquiry
2   Liz Taylor's planning model using second-order concepts
3   Eleanor Rawling's route for geographical enquiry.

Geographical enquiry has long been a feature of geographical education. It was embedded in the work of the School Council's geography projects of the 1970s and 1980s and in the geography National Curriculum since its second publication in 1995. The enquiry process has influenced the development of a number of GCSE and GCE AS/A2-level examination specifications, with enquiry questions often used to provide a structure to the content. Different examination styles, such as the use of decision-making papers, further encouraged the development of enquiry approaches, assessing pupils' ability to apply their geographical knowledge and understanding to the analysis of particular geographical issues and questions. Pupils could also be actively engaged in the enquiry process through fieldwork investigations required by some external examinations. Enquiry was prominent in the 2007 National Curriculum, and yet in the 2014 version, while it is a requirement in other subjects – notably in history, science, and mathematics – it is conspicuous by its absence in geography. However, enquiry is a key feature in the 2014 GCSE National Criteria for Geography, which includes problem-solving and fieldwork (DfE 2014). While not specifically mentioned in the draft subject content criteria for geography A-level (DfE), nonetheless enquiry processes are writ large in the annex: *Quantitative skills in geographical contexts*.

While it receives no specific mention in the 2014 geography Orders in England, this in no way means that geographical enquiry is redundant as an approach to planning geographical learning. As this book continually reminds you, decisions about what and how to teach must be underpinned by what you believe to be important for young people's geographical education and cannot be driven by statutory requirements alone.

As indicated above, enquiry is by no means exclusive to geography. What makes an enquiry 'geographical' is what is being investigated and the kinds of questions being asked (Roberts 2003, 2013). For us, its importance as an approach to learning geography can be justified in relation to the purposes of education and in relation to how knowledge is constructed. Enquiry emphasises a student-centred approach to learning that involves pupils in making sense of new information and in constructing geographical knowledge. Roberts (2003, 2007, 2013) suggests four essential aspects of geographical enquiry that need to be considered when planning both schemes of work and individual lessons:

- Enquiry is question driven: teachers spark curiosity, creating a 'need to know'.
- Enquiry is supported by evidence: teachers supports students' use of sources of geographical information as evidence.
- Enquiry requires thinking geographically: teachers provide opportunities for students to make sense and exercise reasoning.
- Enquiry is reflective: teachers provide opportunities for students and themselves to reflect on learning; students build their critical capacities through reflection.

(Roberts 2013: 9)

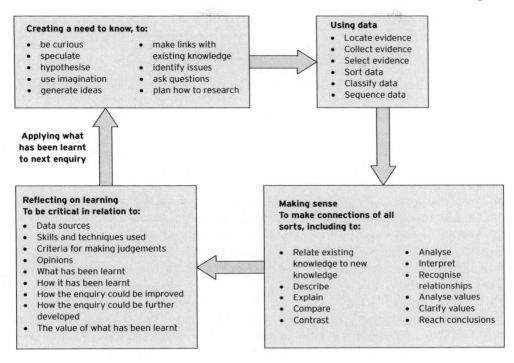

Figure 3.3 A framework for learning through enquiry

(*Source*: Roberts 2003: 44)

Roberts' diagram of geographical enquiry (see Figure 3.3) appears to suggest a fairly logical approach to enquiry planning, implying that the starting point is generally 'creating a need to know', and that an enquiry flows from there. However, she also suggests (see Roberts 2013) that, if you imagine the diagram with the arrows removed, then an enquiry could 'start' at any stage of the process; 'reflecting on their learning' could lead pupils and/ or you, their teacher, to create geographical questions which are rigorous and have some intrigue about them, which could then be the spark for a new round of geographical enquiry – an enquiry doesn't , as such, have to 'start at the beginning'.

As the diagram suggests, it is important that pupils can take ownership of geographical questions – creating a need to know supports this sense of ownership as pupils are, for example, presented with a problem, an image, a piece of text that raises their curiosity and encourages *them* to 'ask questions'. What is important in creating 'a need to know' is, argues Roberts, not so much an engaging resource to kick-start pupils thinking, but what she refers to as 'stance', meaning how teachers' *attitude* to their subject influences whether or not pupils engage with the ideas and issues you want them to explore. For Roberts (2013), stance is characterised by seven 'qualities':

- expressing uncertainty or doubt
- expressing a sense of puzzlement
- expressing a sense of wonder or amazement

- indicating the hypothetical nature of knowledge
- speculating about information rather than presenting it simply as 'fact'
- expecting students to think about something for themselves
- conveying an interest in what is being studied.

(Roberts 2013: 35)

Think about your own teachers, those who captured your interest and who may well be your professional role models – how did they engage your interest and how did they communicate their own enthusiasm for teaching? What seemed to be their 'stance' and how did it influence you?

Any geographical enquiry needs data that can be used as evidence in the investigation providing pupils with opportunities to use and develop a range of enquiry skills. Here, data doesn't necessarily mean 'numbers' – data can be maps, graphs, data tables, text, images, part of a film, a painting, an artefact and so on, and is likely to be a combination of these; data is sources of evidence that pupils engage with in order to begin to search for answers/solutions to their geographical questions. Pupils use information collected from this data to develop understanding and construct geographical knowledge. Pupils need to make sense of what they are learning, to see relationships between different bits of information, to make connections and relate it to what they already know. Roberts (2013) also argues that geography teachers need to adopt an approach that encourages critical reflective thinking throughout the enquiry process that enables pupils to 'go meta' (Bruner 1996) by helping them to become more aware of their own thought processes. Durbin (date unknown) suggests that the model also allows for some creative working; creating a need to know can utilise all sorts of creative and imaginative sources, encouraging pupils to respond in creative ways in terms of the work that they produce.

Taylor's work on concepts (see pages 49–51) also supports curriculum planning centred around enquiry; her argument being that the second-order concepts – diversity, change, interaction, and perception and representation – support more focused curriculum planning including the creation of 'pithy' geographical questions from which enquiry work can grow. The model in Figure 3.3 suggests a very different approach to enquiry planning. In stating questions to pursue and broad outcomes to achieve, this model frees teachers up to bring their own ideas and teaching approaches into the enquiry process. However, such a model is dependent on a teacher's capacity to 'think geographically' and could prove highly problematic for non-specialists to work with without a significant degree of subject support.

A third possible geographical enquiry framework is represented in the model entitled 'The route to enquiry' (see Figure 3.5). When investigating an issue, question or problem in geography, a sequence of questions can be used to guide pupils through a series of stages.

Any study of people-environment issues, questions or problems will inevitably involve some consideration of the significance of attitudes and values in influencing decisions taken about the environment and in giving rise to conflict between groups and individuals (Naish et al. 1987). The route for geographical enquiry therefore incorporates values enquiry. This provides opportunities for values analysis and values clarification (see Chapter 9). It should also provide a framework within which pupils can develop and justify their own values and responses.

Finally, the influence of the enquiry process has important implications for planning teaching and learning in geography. Roberts (2013) suggests that there are a number of important questions that need to be considered by teachers in order to plan a scheme of work around geographical enquiry. It is also useful to reflect on these issues and questions when using enquiry approaches to plan lessons.

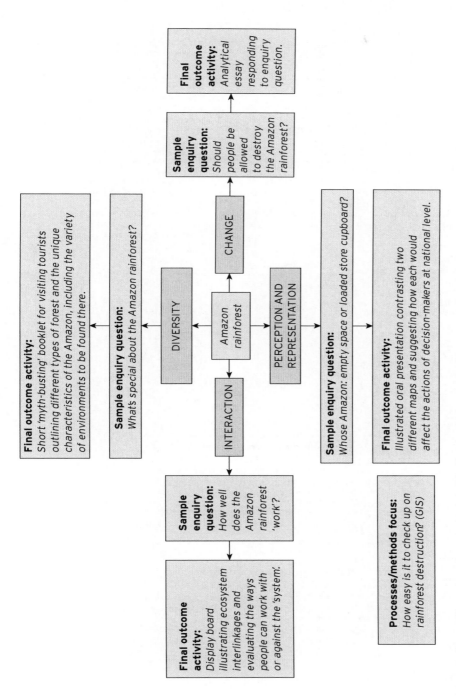

Final outcome activity:
Short 'myth-busting' booklet for visiting tourists outlining different types of forest and the unique characteristics of the Amazon, including the variety of environments to be found there.

Sample enquiry question:
What's special about the Amazon rainforest?

DIVERSITY

Final outcome activity:
Display board illustrating ecosystem interlinkages and evaluating the ways people can work with or against the 'system'.

Sample enquiry question:
How well does the Amazon rainforest 'work'?

INTERACTION

Amazon rainforest

CHANGE

Sample enquiry question:
Should people be allowed to destroy the Amazon rainforest?

Final outcome activity:
Analytical essay responding to enquiry question.

PERCEPTION AND REPRESENTATION

Sample enquiry question:
Whose Amazon: empty space or loaded store cupboard?

Final outcome activity:
Illustrated oral presentation contrasting two different maps and suggesting how each would affect the actions of decision-makers at national level.

Processes/methods focus:
How easy is it to check up on rainforest destruction? (GIS)

Figure 3.4 Pathways through an Amazon topic led by the organising concepts

(*Source:* Taylor 2008)

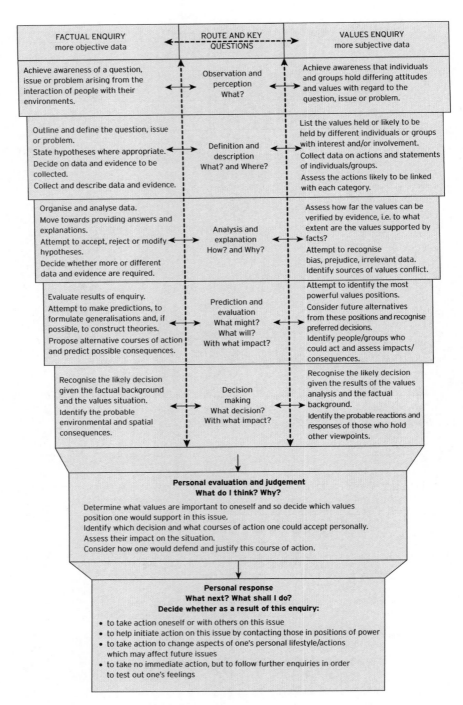

FACTUAL ENQUIRY more objective data	ROUTE AND KEY QUESTIONS	VALUES ENQUIRY more subjective data
Achieve awareness of a question, issue or problem arising from the interaction of people with their environments.	Observation and perception What?	Achieve awareness that individuals and groups hold differing attitudes and values with regard to the question, issue or problem.
Outline and define the question, issue or problem. State hypotheses where appropriate. Decide on data and evidence to be collected. Collect and describe data and evidence.	Definition and description What? and Where?	List the values held or likely to be held by different individuals or groups with interest and/or involvement. Collect data on actions and statements of individuals/groups. Assess the actions likely to be linked with each category.
Organise and analyse data. Move towards providing answers and explanations. Attempt to accept, reject or modify hypotheses. Decide whether more or different data and evidence are required.	Analysis and explanation How? and Why?	Assess how far the values can be verified by evidence, i.e. to what extent are the values supported by facts? Attempt to recognise bias, prejudice, irrelevant data. Identify sources of values conflict.
Evaluate results of enquiry. Attempt to make predictions, to formulate generalisations and, if possible, to construct theories. Propose alternative courses of action and predict possible consequences.	Prediction and evaluation What might? What will? With what impact?	Attempt to identify the most powerful values positions. Consider future alternatives from these positions and recognise preferred decisions. Identify people/groups who could act and assess impacts/consequences.
Recognise the likely decision given the factual background and the values situation. Identify the probable environmental and spatial consequences.	Decision making What decision? With what impact?	Recognise the likely decision given the results of the values analysis and the factual background. Identify the probable reactions and responses of those who hold other viewpoints.

Personal evaluation and judgement
What do I think? Why?

Determine what values are important to oneself and so decide which values position one would support in this issue.
Identify which decision and what courses of action one could accept personally.
Assess their impact on the situation.
Consider how one would defend and justify this course of action.

Personal response
What next? What shall I do?
Decide whether as a result of this enquiry:

- to take action oneself or with others on this issue
- to help initiate action on this issue by contacting those in positions of power
- to take action to change aspects of one's personal lifestyle/actions which may affect future issues
- to take no immediate action, but to follow further enquiries in order to test out one's feelings

Figure 3.5 The route for geographical enquiry

(*Source*: Rawling 2007)

Box 3.3 Things to consider when planning an enquiry-based scheme of work

- What is the nature of the geographical content of this scheme of work? What are the main concepts we want pupils to understand? What place-based examples will we use?

- What are pupils likely to already know – either from geography or from other curriculum areas or in relation to generic skills such as literacy and numeracy? How will this scheme take them beyond what they already know?

- What key questions need to be asked to enable pupils to engage with this area of subject matter? What are possible subsidiary questions and how will they be created – teacher-led or student-generated? How can teaching and learning activities be devised to encourage pupils to ask their own questions?

- How is the enquiry to be structured and managed – teacher-led or student-led? How much autonomy will pupils have in both framing and conducting the enquiry? What type of support will they need, depending on how the enquiry is framed?

- What resources are needed to enable pupils to conduct the enquiry questions?How are these resources selected and collected? How can pupils independently search for sources? What support will pupils need to examine sources critically and analytically?

- What geographical techniques and procedures could be used to answer the enquiry questions? How can these techniques and procedures be incorporated into pupils' activities? What range of activities will be used? Web-based research? Data manipulation? Photograph analysis, text analysis? And so on.

- How will pupils be organised – groups, pairs, individually? What will be the balance of different ways of working across the scheme? How will support teachers be briefed and deployed?

- What will be the outcome of the enquiry in terms of what the pupils 'produce' – presentation? Newspaper report? Video-diary? Storyboard? How will pupils' learning be assessed; what will be the assessment criteria and how will they be used – by teachers and pupils? What opportunities will there be for formative assessment *during* the enquiry and for student reflection? How will the processes in which the pupils are engaged be evaluated during and after lessons? How can what has been learned from the evaluation be built into subsequent lessons and units of work?

(Adapted from Roberts 2013: 195–196)

Ferretti (2013) summarises the significance of geographical enquiry:

> An enquiry approach to geography starts with an engaging and worthwhile question about a real issue, something which intrigues learners and inspires them to find out more. It leads them to use different kinds of information and skills to find answer and construct their own knowledge. It helps them to evaluate information and to emphasise and respect the views of others. It is a very powerful way in which young people can understand contentious issues and develop their geographical knowledge.

(p. 113)

Task 3.2 Evaluating schemes of work

These two activities are designed to encourage you to look critically at schemes of work you will be using.

1   Select one scheme of work currently used by a school you are working in. Use the following questions to help you to evaluate the scheme:

   • Is the purpose of the scheme clear – why is this geographical knowledge significant?
   • What are the main concepts and geographical skills that the pupils are expected to develop? Are they developing these in a progressive way?
   • How does the scheme take account of the need to develop pupils' generic numeracy, literacy and IT skills?
   • Is the scheme framed by objectives or enquiry questions and are these framed appropriately?
   • Are the suggested learning activities varied and appropriate in fulfilling the intentions as expressed in objectives/enquiry questions?
   • What will pupils be producing as a consequence of the activities and how will these outcomes be used formatively?
   • How will pupils' attainment be judged at the end of the scheme?
   • How does scheme of work 'measure up' in terms of providing a coherent plan form pupils' geographical learning? Justify your thinking.

2   Select an aspect of the curriculum you will be expected to teach. Plan a series of 2–3 lessons using Margaret Robert's model for planning geographical enquiry. When the lessons have been planned and resources have been developed, again evaluate planning using the questions in '1' above to help you.

Evaluate both schemes having considered the curriculum discussion about different principles of curriculum design discussed in Chapter 2.

Making the geography curriculum happen: using 'curriculum artefacts'

One of the most rewarding and enjoyable aspects of teaching geography is the potential for being creative. All teachers have this potential, but geography appears to us to have some particular qualities that set it apart. For instance, the world is always changing before our very eyes: new countries are born, cities grow, trade relations between countries develop – and of course floods occur, volcanoes erupt and landslips happen, both large and small. Thus the task of geography, to 'write the world', is never done.

Furthermore, we have learned in modern geography that to imagine the subject as a transparent 'window' on the world is inadequate. In geography we take the earth as an object of our thought, but we now understand that what we see and study depends on who we are and what we think we are looking for – our gaze is not neutral. Geographers have a perspectival or relational understanding of the world and this is exciting to develop with young people, and it sometimes requires ingenious teaching.

With these thoughts in mind, it is perhaps quite salutary to reflect on how the adoption of standard, rational procedures and practices that form the professional toolkits of lesson planning and planning schemes of work can sometimes work against us. So, if we always start with our aims and objectives; if we always adopt a predictable lesson structure (such as the 'three-part lesson'); if we always provide 'formative assessment' moments to identify targets or 'progress'; if we are always concerned to be 'pacey' and to accelerate learning – then we risk flattening out our geography lessons into something less than they could be.

Developing 'curriculum artefacts' represents an alternative way to thinking about preparing sequences of lessons. Rather than starting with the topics and the aims, we start with an artefact of some description. This could be: a picture or collection of pictures, a poem, a selected excerpt of literature or film or music, a video clip, an animation – anything that can be studied as a source of information or data. In this list, we are of course doing nothing more than pointing out that the teaching and learning resources in geography are (should be) highly varied. However, we are making a distinction between a teaching and learning 'resource' and what we are calling a 'curriculum artefact'. The best artefacts are textured and multi-layered: in other words, they can stand scrutiny and repeated examination. And we make them into curriculum artefacts by investing them with special significance.

The final point in the previous paragraph is key. The curriculum artefact becomes yours! You invest it with special meaning. You do this as a geography specialist who can see the potential wrapped up in the artefact – as a source of data and inspiration to think about a topic or idea in a way that will provide the platform for developing a deeper understanding of it. It is highly unlikely that the artefact will be the sole resource used in a sequence of lessons, but it will be the key or signature material that drives the sequence: as such, it may be referred to frequently as a kind of reference point.

If we refer back to Margaret Roberts' useful characterisation of the enquiry approach to teaching and learning geography (see Figure 3.3), we could imagine a powerful curriculum artefact fulfilling several functions. It could, for example, contain mystery that fires a 'need to know'. It may also be rich in data that can be identified, recorded and analysed by the pupils. Thus, it is almost certainly the case that activities will need to be devised to help pupils engage mentally with the artefact. Further data and material resources may need to be gathered to ensure that the artefact's true potential is realised by the pupils.

Before illustrating this approach with an example (which you can easily 'make your own'), we should just emphasise the reason why we insist on calling the signature resource a 'curriculum artefact'. There are two reasons:

1   It is hard to imagine how a teacher can invest 'special significance' to the video clip, song, story (or whatever has been selected) without applying curriculum thinking to it. By this we mean thinking that is guided by a clear sense of educational goals and purposes. The selected artefact is not simply stuff to be learnt or copied; neither is it simply illustrative of an event or occurrence or feature. It has been selected because

you can see its potential to provide a powerful platform for deepening understanding of a geographical idea or theme.

2   To make a true 'curriculum artefact' from an ordinary 'teaching resource' requires the application of curriculum-making principles such as shown in Figure 2.3 (see Chapter 2). Thus, you are working within the broad context of your subject discipline. You are taking account of, and holding in balance the competing priorities of subject, student and pedagogic technique. Developing a curriculum artefact is curriculum-making in practice.

Bearing all this in mind, it is worth stressing that we are not advocating that every lesson should – or even can – be based on a curriculum artefact. These take time to develop. As we remark in the section on selecting and using textbooks, the approach modelled in this section is best thought of as augmenting more standard 'day-to-day' teaching. But think: if you develop just two curriculum artefacts per term, you will have a dozen in two years. If they are good, they will be usable across age groups and you will constantly want to refine and develop their use. If you work as part of a geography team, you will be exchanging your artefacts with your colleagues.

Box 3.4 Example of a curriculum artefact: international migration

This curriculum artefact is an Irish folk song, composed of a series of letters telling the story of nineteenth-century Irish migration to the UK and the USA as a consequences of the potato famine . For geographers, the song charts the story of one family's experiences of the mass migration at that time.

Pupils will require some contextual information such as the causes and consequences of the potato famine, and also additional data such as population data, in order to make sense of the lyrics of the song.

The process:

1   Set the scene – using atlases, pupils need to find Ireland, the UK and the USA. They need to establish some sense of distance and perhaps have a conversation about how we travel between these places today – time, mode of transport and so on.
2   Play pupils the song and the accompanying video. It may be useful to play it twice – first without lyrics and then with the lyrics (all available on the GA website).
3   Gather some first impressions about the content of the song – ask pupils to devise a set of their own questions, stimulated by the song.
4   Give pupils images and text telling the story of the potato famine (focus on causes and consequences).
5   Working in pairs, pupils will now need a simple outline map of the world showing the British Isles, the Atlantic Ocean, and the USA. On the map, and with the song playing again, pupils use the lyrics to 'plot' the song, using symbols only – it may be helpful to discuss appropriate symbols with the group before they start.
6   Completing the maps will focus pupils' attention on the details of the words as they start to 'map the story'.
7   Having completed their story map, pupils will need plenty of time to discuss what the story reveals.

Key points you could tease out:

- The potato famine was a main push factor.
- Employment opportunities elsewhere (USA and UK) were major pull factors.
- Much of the work for migrants was dangerous – e.g. building the railways.
- Relationships were maintained, but only through letters (compare this with communication opportunities today).
- Some migrants (Michael in the song) did make money and did/do return home.
- Family fragmentation is part of the migrant experience, then and now.
- There is a gender and age dimension in the song – the sister/parents did not leave. Is this true today?

8   Having considered a historical migration, it would now be possible to develop pupils conceptual understanding by studying a more contemporary/different migration such as Eastern European migration to the UK (economic migration) or forced migration such as migration as a consequence of war or political oppression.

(*Source*: Adapted from the Geographical Association website.
Song, lyrics and ideas available at: www.geography.org.uk/
cpdevents/curriculum/curriculummaking/artefact/#14155
[accessed 13 August 2013])

We can see from this example that the curriculum artefact is more than a teaching resource – it can be used as an articulation of set of ideas and thus become a continual reference point for further teaching. For example, when studying a more contemporary example of migration, pupils can be reminded of Michael's story or the experiences of parents left behind – the artefact threads through the sequence of lessons, and the map can be the basis for building new and different migration stories.

Task 3.3 Planning to use curriculum artefacts

Find something that you feel could be a curriculum artefact – song, picture, artefact of some sort, film clip. Whatever you feel is special enough in geographical terms of be used thoughtfully to help pupil understand complex geographical concepts. A starting point for planning with artefacts remains the geography you want pupils to learn.

1   Think about how you will introduce/use the artefact and plan carefully where you might reuse it/the ideas it represents.
2   Consider what additional information might be needed by the pupils to access the main ideas.
3   What teaching/learning resources will you need to prepare?
4   How will you judge pupils' learning – what do you want them to produce (maybe their own song/painting/artefact) to illustrate their new geographical understanding?

Share your ideas with other student colleagues in order to evaluate your ideas and develop/refine them. Be prepared to try out your ideas in your teaching.

Planning lessons

Common advice given to beginning teachers about the importance of lesson planning:

> Don't step into a geography classroom to teach unless you are clear about what you intend to teach, how you intend to teach it and why you intend to teach it!

Often student teachers comment that they rarely see experienced teachers using a lesson plan. This may be the case, but experienced teachers generally already possess a mental framework for their lessons which has become internalised as a result of several years of teaching experience. However, you need to remember that they were, at one point in their career, where you are now; they too had to plan their lessons, and even now, some experienced teachers, when trying to teach a new idea or use a set of activities new to them, will still write a formal lesson plan.

As a student teacher, you are required to produce explicit written plans for your teaching. While this is, to a certain extent, linked to prescribed professional 'competencies', more importantly high-quality lesson planning enables you to teach high-quality geography lessons; thinking carefully about the planning process and understanding the principles that underpin a 'good plan' is crucial to your professional development. It may seem odd, but high-quality thinking and planning *before* a lesson helps reduce the amount of thinking that we have to do *during* lessons so we can concentrate on managing the lesson, directing pupils' learning and responding to their learning needs. Lesson planning is not formulaic and there is no one set model or framework that is prescribed as being better than another. However, there are certain principles that underpin effective planning. Indeed, over time, you will develop a format for your plans that reflects and best suits your approach to lesson planning – in many respects, lesson planning is both a matter of professional responsibility and personal preferences.

In this section, we discuss in some detail the features of a lesson plan and the relative purpose of each feature. Slater (1986) likens a lesson to a 'planned performance', where learning takes place within 'distinct episodes' which are linked together allowing the plot to gradually unfold. Lesson resources (textbooks, computers, artefacts) are the 'props' and the physical space of the classroom is the set. Planning may even involve a degree of rehearsal! Effective planning requires you to think carefully about the geographical nature of the content of a lesson and how the content and concepts you want pupils to learn link to bigger concepts in the wider discipline. The content of your plans will, to a great extent, be informed by the specific scheme of work you are working from.

At a simple level we can see that lesson planning is, in fact, a cyclical process whereby each step in the planning and teaching process informs your next steps. Lesson plans and their evaluations are important records of the teaching and learning that has taken place; they could be regarded as an important source of 'data' that you can then use to inform future teaching and learning.

Features of a lesson plan

In this section we will look in some detail at the different component part of lesson plans. We will consider two different planning principles: planning using objectives and planning for geographical enquiry. At this stage in your career, there are certain fundamental features

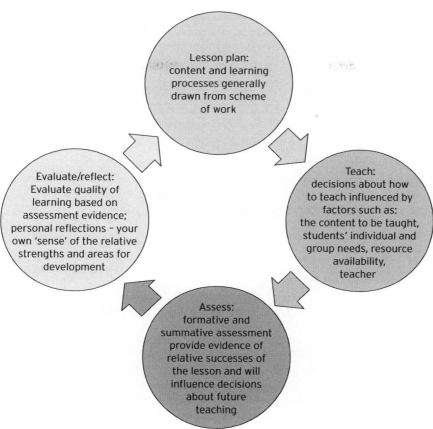

Figure 3.6 Lesson planning as a cyclical process

of a lesson plan that we suggest you adhere to, as shown in in Table 3.4 and while Table 3.5 suggests a slightly different model of planning, both can be used flexibly and in response to how you approach planning, which inevitably will evolve with experience.

Rationale

There should be a clear rationale for the geography you are teaching. It is worth asking yourself: Why are geographers interested in this topic/field of enquiry, and how is this geographical knowledge used in the real world? For example, when teaching 'coastal erosion', we could explain to pupils that they need to learn about coasts because it is a requirement of a GCSE or an A-level specification. However, we would argue that such a rationale is not good enough and that in order to see value in their geographical learning, pupils need to understand what makes geographical knowledge significant. Returning to the 'coasts' example, expert knowledge of coastal erosion enables local authorities, local communities, charitable organisations such as the National Trust and so on to make decisions about where best to locate coastal defences, how such defences affect other areas of the coastline and where best not to interfere with coastal processes and let nature take its course. While we do not advocate a utilitarian view of geographical knowledge, for pupils to have some sense of the contribution geographical knowledge makes to real social and environmental issues may serve to give the school subject real purpose. This level of thinking and rationalisation requires you to draw on both your knowledge of the discipline and your knowledge of teaching and learning in order to ensure that pupils see purpose in the geography they are learning.

Aims

Lesson plans need a broad statement of the geographical learning to take place in a lesson, or possibly over a couple of lessons. An individual lesson aim, linked to a scheme of work, provides a clear sense of direction for your planning and teaching and as such should not be too vague. Ask yourself: What do I want pupils to have learned by the end of this lesson/ sequence of lessons?

Aim: To understand how 'virtual water' contributes to fresh water consumption at a range of scales

As an enquiry question, this statement of intended learning might become:
How much water do we 'eat' in the world?

The 'aims' statement is broad enough for you and your pupils to bring a degree of interpretation and personal expertise/interest to the lesson, but clear enough to focus planning and teaching – we know what this lesson is trying to achieve in terms of pupils' geographical learning. It is likely that the enquiry question is more engaging and more likely to capture pupils' curiosity from the outset, but it will still need suitable resources to build on pupils curiosity in meaningful ways. What is important is that whatever the framing of your lesson – enquiry or outcomes – the direction of travel needs to be in a language that pupils can understand.

Objectives

Initially, student teachers often find it difficult to distinguish between aims and objectives. Objectives are the small steps in understanding needed to help pupils achieve the aim. In the example above, in order for pupils to understand the concept of virtual water and how it relates to global fresh water consumption, you are likely to have steps in their understanding such as:

1   To understand the difference between 'small' water and 'big' water.
2   To analyse water content of foods we consume.
3   To calculate our own 'water footprint'.
4   To evaluate global imports and exports of water through food.

(*Data source*: Read Professor Tony Allen's excellent and accessible text *Virtual Water: Tackling the Threat to our Planet's Most Precious Resource*. Published by I.B Tauris in 2011).

What has happened here is we have taken the 'big concept' of virtual water in the aim and in the objectives, broken it down into more manageable concepts for pupils to understand.

A word of warning at this stage: if objectives are too prescriptive and therefore restrictive, then it becomes impossible for pupils to bring anything of their own ideas and understanding into a lesson; objectives just become a 'tick-list' for teachers and school managers to draw spurious conclusions about 'learning' at the end of a lesson (see Chapter 8 on Assessment for further discussion). If objectives are too vague, then generally the lesson will lack direction.

Task 3.4 is intended to help you to develop your ability to specify learning objectives.

The learning objectives are related to specific subject content, determined by the scheme of work. This subject content should then be in elaborated in the main text of the lesson plan, ensuring links between the geographical concepts and skills you want pupils to learn and various strategies you intend to put into practice to enable them to learn these concepts and skills. The lesson may also include links to other areas of learning, not necessarily prescribed by statutory frameworks but deemed important by the school/department or other aspects of the curriculum such as personal, social and health education (PSHE) or other subjects.

Your plan should contain information about the context of the lesson. It may include details about the composition of the group (its size, gender balance and ability range) as well as background information about prior learning and action points brought forward from previous lessons.

Differentiation

The *differentiation* section may contain information about certain pupils and their learning needs as well as an indication of the strategies to be used to support particular pupils. Where learning support assistants or teachers are available, you should plan for to their role in the lesson so that the valuable support they provide can be used effectively.

Planning and preparation

Planning and preparation are closely related. Consideration should be given to the preparation of the room (layout, location of equipment, diagrams/information/questions on the board) and how resources will be organised. This section on the plan is a useful *aide memoire*, ensuring that you have all the resources you need before you start teaching, thus supporting your orderly management of the lesson: there is nothing worse than not having enough A4 paper or forgetting the atlases when you have already started your lesson.

Geographical content

Too often, lesson plan seem to say little about the 'geography' to be learned other than in objectives statements. Roberts (2010) notes that many student teachers attend to the management aspect of their lesson – organisation of resources, student groupings and so on, but the geographical content can either be light or non-existent. Roberts suggests the following:

Table 3.4 The features of a lesson plan

Date: _____	Lesson: _____	Time: _____
Class: _____	Room: _____	

Title of lesson

Rationale:
A statement about the geographical significance of the lesson.

Lesson's aims:
State clearly the overall purpose of the lesson – what you are hoping to achieve.

Learning objectives
These represent your specific intentions for pupils' learning. Write clear statements of the geographical learning of the lessons in terms of what you expect pupils will know and understand, be able to do and the values/attitudes you wish them to consider by the end of the lesson.

Subject content: National Curriculum/ specification Links Indicate which aspects of the National Curriculum Programme of Study or the examination syllabus are being taught and learned in this lesson.	**Cross-curricular** Indicate any links that there may be with the content of other subjects. What other aspects of learning may be evident? Could the lesson contribute other curriculum ideas such as citizenship? How will this lesson develop numeracy/literacy/ICT skills?
Resources What resources will be needed for this lesson – materials and equipment? Use this as a checklist to support your preparation.	**Advance preparation (room and equipment)** Does the room need to be prepared for the activities that you have planned (grouping and seating arrangements)? Does any equipment need to be set up? Is the data projector working? Do you need your own lap-top?
Differentiation How do you plan to address particular pupils' learning needs – specific adaptations of resources and strategies, extension/enrichment activities? How will learning support assistants be used?	**Action points** What are the links with learning that has taken place in previous lessons? Also indicate any issues that you need to follow up from previous lessons with this group (pupils, learning, or classroom management).

Time	Geographical learning	Teaching and learning strategies/actions
Indicate how much time you are planning to allow for each activity. This will help you to monitor the pace of activities in the lesson.	Detail the geographical learning that will be taking place at each stage of the lesson. Record here geographical	• Describe here the nature of teaching and learning activities that will support geographical learning. What are you/ the students doing at each stage of the lesson? • Consider how you will you introduce activities?

concepts and content to be learned, skills to be used and questions to be considered. This column is a means of ensuring that your planning is clear about the geographical content that will enable students to achieve the objectives or address the enquiry questions. This is where you map out progress in geographical understanding.	• Use key words as prompts for expla-nations, demonstrations or for any exposition. • How will the resources be distributed and used? • What specific questions do you want to ask at key points in the lesson? How will you monitor, manage and conclude activities? • How and at what points will you judge students' learning during the lesson?

Assessment opportunities

Consider the potential outcomes from the learning activities and tasks. What evidence of geographical understanding might be provided by these tasks? You can add to this section after the lesson as a result of monitoring the learning that has taken place during the lesson.

Evaluation of learning	Evaluation of teaching
Comment on the learning that has taken place. Refer back to the learning objectives. How successful were the learning activities in achieving the aims and objectives? Comment on pupils' progress, competence, motivation and interest in learning. How appropriate were the activities in meeting the learning needs of particular pupils?	Your reflections on the effectiveness of the teaching strategies used in the lesson. Focus on the clarity of your explanations and exposition. What strategies, actions or interventions were effective when managing activities or monitoring pupils' learning? How successful were particular classroom management strategies? Be objective and realistic. Try not to be too self-critical.

Action points

What issues need to be followed up? This might include concepts or generalisations that need to be reinforced, skill or viewpoints that need to be clarified. It could also include issues relating to your own professional development such as classroom management or ways in which you monitor or support learning.

Table 3.5 Lesson planning framework: Year 10, the characteristics of different natural ecosystems

Date: _____ Yr10_____	Lesson: _____ Room: _____	Time: _____	Class: ____

Title of lesson: The characteristics of different natural ecosystems

Lesson's aims:
To examine the characteristic features of different natural ecosystems in the world.
To examine relationships between climate and vegetation.

Learning objectives:
To know the main global climatic zones.
To know the characteristic features of the main natural ecosystems in the world.
To understand how climate influences vegetation.
To interpret climatic data and thematic atlas maps (climate and vegetation).

Subject content: National Curriculum/syllabus links	Cross-curricular links/themes/competences
Simple recognition of the existence and variety of major world biomes (global scale ecosystems) related to climate graphs and vegetation zones.	Environmental education (*about* the environment - nature of ecosystems) Science/biology - global vegetation zones.

Resources	Advance preparation (room and equipment)
Atlases. Sheets with summary of natural ecosystems table and film clips, pictures from wildlife and geographical magazines, world map outlines.	YouTube film ready to play.

Differentiation	Action points
Mainly by support. John and Liz have problems identifying information from thematic maps. The summary table should provide a suitable structure.	Make links with Key Stage 3 study of the characteristics and distribution of one type of vegetation (tropical rainforest) and its relationship with climate, soil and human activities.

Learning activities/tasks	Time	Teaching strategies/actions
Identifying links with previous learning. Recap KS3 study of tropical rainforests.	5	**Introduction** What are the differences between the amount and types of vegetation in the Arctic, in a tropical rainforest and a desert? What are the reasons for these differences?

Learning activities/tasks	Time	Teaching strategies/actions
Use atlas maps to mark the following lines of latitude on to a world map outline: Equator (0) Arctic Circle (66.5 N) Antarctic Circle (66.5 S) Tropic of Cancer (23.5 N) Tropic of Capricorn (23.5 S) Then label the climatic zones - tropical, Temperature, Polar. Identify characteristics of natural ecosystems shown in Disney clips.	15	Explain activity 1 - Identifying global climatic zones (monitor the pace of the activity and check atlas skills).

Learning activities/tasks	Time	Teaching strategies/actions

Find the 20 E longitude meridian and mark it on the map. Also mark the following points along this line – 5 N, 10 N, 23.5 N, 40 N, 52 N, 65 N, 70 N. Use climate and vegetation maps to complete the summary table.	10	Show video clips from Disney films and ask pupils to identify the characteristic features of:
		
		• Jungle Book
		  Tropical rainforest
		• Aladdin Desert
		• Lion King
		  Savanna grassland
		• Bambi
		  Temperate woodland
		Check the location of the longitude meridian and places marked.

		Use one example to illustrate how the table should be completed. Ask pupils to search out and collect pictures of different ecosystems (and vegetation) for the display in the next lesson. Debrief the lesson's objectives using 'Assessment for Learning' matching activity in groups.

Assessment opportunities, objectives and evidence
Use of atlas skills and interpretation of thematic maps. Written homework after next lesson to assess pupils' understanding of the relationship between climate and vegetation and their recall of knowledge about the characteristic features of global ecosystems.

Evaluation of learning		Evaluation of teaching
Good recall of previous learning from KS3 about climate and vegetation in tropical rainforests. All the pupils managed to identify the climatic zones successfully. Most of the weaker pupils experienced difficulties in interpreting the thematic atlas maps when completing the summary table. The table helped to structure learning successfully.		Timing of the initial activities was about right but the table took longer to complete mainly because of the difficulties in interpreting climatic maps. The use of the Disney clips was extremely effective – interesting and motivating – the characteristics were clear. Perhaps use PowerPoint slides of the world map and ecosystems table to demonstrate and support explanation of tasks.

Action points
Complete the Global Ecosystems table and name the ecosystems. Examine the influence of climate upon vegetation using examples from the table. Begin work on displays of global ecosystems showing climatic data, vegetation and world distributions.

Lesson plans could include:

- additional headings which focus on geography.
- What is being investigated?
- What geographical data is being used?
- What are the big ideas underpinning this lesson?
- How is this lesson developing students' geography?

(Roberts 2010: 113)

The planning outline in Table 3.4 has a distinct section for detailing the geographical learning at each stage of the lesson. While Table 3.5. has a different structure, the geographical content of each lesson is still clear. When you start planning, it is worth taking a highlighter pen to your plan and highlighting where you have outlined the geographical content – you might be surprised by the relative brevity of the detail. If this is the case, then this lack of subject detail needs attending to.

Learning activities

It is desirable for lessons to include a variety of activities to support geographical thinking and help maintain motivation. In the lessons shown in Table 3.5, the teacher uses questioning to draw pupils' attention to the key features of the environments and highlight links with previous learning about one of the ecosystems studied in Key Stage 3. This also helps the teacher to emphasise the relevant vocabulary used to describe the ecosystems being investigated in the main activity of the lesson.

Ofsted (2011) have commented on the significance of this 'scene setting' phase of a lesson and have observed that in lessons judged by them to be 'satisfactory' or weak that:

> In many cases, the activity at the start of the lesson had little relevance to the main task; it added little to the students' learning and used up precious time.
>
> (p. 26)

This message applies to all phases of a lesson – engaging pupils in 'activity' for the sake of it, whether at the start, middle or end of the lesson makes no contribution to pupils' geographical learning. Planning needs to reflect the relationship between geographical content, learning activities and student motivation.

Time management

Time management is a crucial part of planning. You will need to make realistic judgements about how much time pupils will spend on different activities in order to learn the geography you want them to learn. Too much time spent on one activity will have a significant knock-on effect into other parts of your lesson. However, timing is also a matter of judgement, and it may be that during a lesson you decide 'in the moment' to extend pupils' working time on an activity in order to ensure that their understanding of a specific concept is secure; ploughing on makes little sense if pupils' do not have sufficient understanding to help them tackle a new set of ideas.

Assessment

Although located towards the end of our lesson planning framework, assessment should not be an afterthought. It is an integral part of the process of successful teaching and learning. Assessing learning and the principles of formative assessment are discussed further in Chapter 8; however, when planning lessons, it is helpful to indicate where assessment opportunities might arise during a lesson as what you find out will enable you to make judgements about next steps in learning.

Many schools impose a lesson format on teachers, including the need to have a 'plenary' at the end of a lesson in order to review pupils' learning. All well and good, except the process of reviewing learning and judging attainment requires time, structure and purpose and cannot be effective in a five-minute 'quick-quiz' or a 'post-it note' activity at the end of a lesson; judging pupils' progress within and between lessons is much more complex than this.

Evaluation and reflection

Sandwiched between the end of one lesson and the start of planning for the next sits lesson evaluation and reflection. The purpose of reflecting on your teaching and evaluating pupils learning is to enable you to make thoughtful, thought-through decisions about what happens in your next lesson.

The planning framework in Figure 3.4 suggests one approach to reflection and evaluation; there are many others from which you can draw. The evaluation part of this process needs to consider the quality of geographical learning; you need to have a conversation with yourself

---

Task 3.4 Writing learning objectives

The aim of this activity is to provide you with an opportunity to practise writing 'learning objectives'.

1   Read the two-lesson descriptions, then write what you think are likely to be appropriate 'learning objectives' for these lessons. Think about the balance between knowledge and understanding, geographical skills, and values and attitudes.
2   In a similar vein, read the lesson descriptions and decide whether or not it is possible to express the learning of the lesson in terms of one or two enquiry questions. If so, what would these be? Think about in what ways the purpose of a lesson changes if framed by objectives or an enquiry question.

Lesson 1

This is a Year 7 lesson during the pupils' first term at the school. The teacher is aiming to build upon the pupils' knowledge and understanding about different types of rock and the ways in which they can be classified from Key Stage 2. The pupils are working in groups of four (mainly due to the resources available). Each group has a box containing samples of about five different types of rock.

The introduction to the lesson involves the pupils suggesting the ways that the different properties of rocks might be assessed. There is also a brief recap of the ways in which rock types are classified (igneous, sedimentary and metamorphic).

(continued)

(continued)

The main tasks in the lesson involve the pupils assessing and describing the main properties of their rock samples. Individually, they record this information on a printed rock identification/classification sheet and include an annotated sketch of each sample. The teacher monitors the pupils' progress, checking the outcomes.

In the final third of the lesson, the teacher shows some slides of different landscapes in Britain associated with each rock type and distributes an activity sheet 'Rock around Britain'. The pupils have a list of well-known landscape features and rock types. Using atlases (physical geography and geology maps), the pupils have to match the labels of the rock type and landscape to the correct location on the map.

Lesson 2

Year 10 pupils have been studying Changing Economic Activities and are examining the changing location of industry in Britain. The lesson begins with the teacher questioning the pupils to develop a brief recap of factors influencing the location of particular industries that they have studied.

Working in pairs, the pupils are given copies of a wide range of adverts and promotional literature designed to attract new businesses or industries to different places in Britain. The pupils are initially encouraged to find the location of these places in an atlas. The teacher uses a couple of examples to draw pupils' attention to the locational factors that are emphasised in the adverts and the images of the places that are promoted in the adverts (through both the illustrations and the written information). The pupils record the relevant information that they have identified for each place in a table under appropriate headings such as accessibility, environmental factors, available services, proximity to markets, government aid/grants and so on.

The lesson concludes with a discussion about the relative importance of the factors identified and about the images that each of the places is trying to promote. A homework exercise requires the pupils to design and produce a similar promotional advert for a local industrial estate/business park that they surveyed as part of a fieldwork visit.

about the extent to which the pupils have learned what you intended, the quality of that learning (in terms of depth of understanding, rather than how well they behaved) and identify any misconceptions, confusions or gaps in conceptual understanding that need addressing.

So far we have considered the different components of planning a geography lesson in some depth. It should be clear from this discussion that there are important links between the different aspects of the planning process. For example, there should be a close relationship between the learning activities, the intended geographical learning and the learning needs of the pupils. These will in turn influence the preparation and use of resources as well as the different levels of support you will give to pupils at different phases of a lesson. Careful planning of the component parts must also consider how these parts connect to each other – ultimately, lessons need to be seen as a whole.

Task 3.5 Observing and planning lessons

These activities examine the relationship between planning and what happens in a classroom. The assumption is, as stated earlier, that effective planning brings about successful learning. To this end, one of our principal tasks as a teacher is to design learning activities and teaching strategies that help pupils to achieve various intended learning outcomes.

A

A useful task to undertake when observing an experienced teacher teaching a lesson is to try to develop a written plan for the lesson that you are observing. Familiarise yourself with the main features of a lesson plan that are described earlier in this chapter and then use a copy of the lesson planning framework (Figure 3.4) to record the features of the lesson that you are observing.

Try to focus on the following aspects:

1 Is it possible to identify distinctive episodes in the lesson? How long do they last?
2 What are the learning activities and teaching strategies that comprise these episodes?
3 How does the teacher manage, monitor and conclude these lesson episodes? (Where appropriate, write down any key words that would help you as prompts if you were to teach this lesson.)
4 Is it possible to identify a coherent structure to the sequence of these lesson episodes?
5 What learning processes are evident in the lesson (i.e. what skills will the pupils be using)? Do you focus on what they learn or what they did not learn?
6 What are the learning objectives for this lesson? How are they revealed? (These learning objectives may be shared with the pupils at the start of the lesson, during activities, or by way of conclusion. Alternatively, they may be self-evident in the activities and strategies that you observe.)
7 How does the teacher know whether these learning objectives have been achieved during the lesson?
8 Are any links made with previous or future learning?
   What strategies are used to support differentiation in the lesson? (These may include specific resources, tasks or activities, the use of a learning support assistant, feedback or support from the teacher, and variations in the pace and depth of learning.)

Discussion: Discuss this plan and what you have observed with the teacher of the lesson or your tutor. The discussion should focus on the relationship between planning and what happens in the classroom (teaching and learning). The questions indicated above may be helpful to this discussion. Record any reflections the teacher shares with you on the success of the lesson in the lesson evaluation section of the plan!

(continued)

(continued)

B

At some stage you have to actually plan a lesson, but is can help to practise first. Select one of the two lessons outlined above and, on a lesson proforma, plan the lesson in some detail and reflect on the process of writing a lesson plan:

1   How long did it take you?
2   What additional information would you need to write a more detailed plan?
3   Consider how you represent the geography you want pupils to learn. If you were teaching this lesson, is your own knowledge secure enough to support pupils?
4   What resources are you likely to need to teach the lesson?
5   Are assessment processes clear?

Ultimately, can you imagine yourself teaching this lesson?

A lesson contains discrete 'episodes' or 'scenes' based around individual activities and strategies which, when 'knitted' together, ensure that a lesson is coherent in terms of both the geographical learning taking place – that is, pupils make progress as the lesson unfolds (see Chapter 2 and Chapter 8 for further discussion on 'Progression', and also discussions later in this chapter), and how the activities relate to each other. Often a poor lesson plan is characterised by a lack of clarity in terms of the geographical learning you expect to take place, inappropriate structure and activities which take pupils nowhere and are either too centred on the teacher (too much inappropriate teacher talk) or too centred on pupil activity (the pedagogic adventure), both at the expense of pupils' learning. Maintaining an appropriate balance between the role of the teacher and the work that pupils need to undertake in order to learn some geography is difficult to maintain, takes practice and is rooted in effective planning.

Planning for geographical enquiry: a different concept of lesson planning

It is unlikely that all the outcomes of learning can be predetermined. There is often learning taking place in a classroom that is unpredictable and unintended. Also, if we recognise that individual pupils have different aptitudes and learning needs, it can be difficult (and undesirable) to determine in too fine-grained a way common objectives for all pupils (see Chapter 8 on Assessment).

Earlier in this chapter, the discussion about curriculum planning identified geographical enquiry as an alternative to the objectives-led model of curriculum planning. A key principle in geographical enquiry is that learning is a process engaging both teachers and pupils. The enquiry approach emphasises the importance of both teachers and pupils asking questions, with pupils actively involved in the learning processes in order to answer these questions (Rawling 2007; Naish *et al.* 1987). Just as curriculum planning can be framed around geographical enquiry, so too can lesson planning.

An enquiry-based approach to learning in geography involves following a meaningful sequence of enquiry questions when investigating any geographical issue or problem (see Figure 3.3). This route for enquiry provides a framework within which teachers can organise learning 'pathways' in geography. Key questions can be particularly useful when planning lessons where it is difficult to predetermine more precise learning objectives.

Key questions would comprise:

What? – observation and perception
What and where? – definition and description
How and why? – analysis and explanation
What might happen? – evaluation, prediction and decision-making
What impact?
What decision?
What do I think? – personal evaluation and personal response
Why?
What will I do next?

(Rawling 2007: 44)

While the list above provides some sense of the nature if geographical questions, the reality is that asking 'good questions' is difficult. At a curriculum planning level, Roberts (2013) suggests the development of 'key questions' from which you can then draw 'more manageable questions which reflect the structure of what is being studied. Drawing on the work of historian M. Riley (2000), Roberts suggests asking yourself the following:

Does each of your enquiry questions:

- Capture the imagination of your pupils?

- Place an aspect of historical [geographical] thinking, concepts or process at the forefront of pupils minds?

- Result in a tangible, lively, substantial, enjoyable 'outcome' activity (i.e at the end of the lesson sequence) through which pupils can genuinely answer the enquiry question?

(p. 29)

At both a curriculum-planning and lesson-planning level, you need to avoid simple 'yes' and 'no' answers to questions, that is, closed questions. You also need to avoid those that require descriptive answers only, such as 'What is it like to live in a shanty town?' Questions such as this may require pupils to synthesise information from different sources, which in itself requires a degree of skill, but in actuality the only answer it really invites is one of description. What might be a better question? Perhaps 'Is Kibera a good place to live?' What makes this better? 'Kibera' is a real place and so already the question takes on some significance. It also allows pupils to build on any prior knowledge they may have of shanty towns, but it also invites them rethink their perceptions and both take account of and also look beyond the economic model of development, often prevalent in school geography's approach to studying

---

Task 3.6 Devising questions in geography

For this activity, you need to find a small number of articles about geography issues from newspapers or geographical journals.

1   Identify the geographical issues that are reported in these articles.
2   Write a series of key questions that could be used to help pupils to investigate these geographical issues. Try to put these questions into a logical sequence so that they could be used to structure an enquiry for pupils.
3   Identify some key ideas and geographical concepts that could be linked to these key questions. These ideas and concepts could be the likely learning outcomes of a geographical enquiry that focuses on the questions that you have devised.
4   What would be the best way to plan such a lesson. Try either an adapted version of the lesson planning framework in Tables 3.4 or 3.5 to support this process or devise your own planning approach.
5   Discuss with other colleagues your ideas and explore any challenges you have had to deal with in this planning process.

---

certain places. Pupils have to start to consider how, in the midst of economic poverty people still live their lives, go to school, have aspirations, feel part of a community and so on; the question invites pupils to 'think otherwise' about a particular place and in doings so reconsider what we mean by 'quality of life' – the concept becomes more complex. Asking rigorous, appropriate and challenging questions is dependent on your own knowledge and understanding of geography – because it appears more open to pupils' responses, it would be easy to assume that geographical enquiry is so open ended that 'anything goes' – this is not the case.

Planning for differentiation in teaching and learning

One of the fundamental challenges facing teachers when setting out to plan for successful learning is how to meet the different needs of pupils. The need to improve differentiation has been a key issue in the drive to raise standards in education for a long time. Within geography education, it has been identified as a key issue in OFSTED's review of its inspection findings, reporting the need for more challenge in geography for higher-attaining pupils, particularly in Key Stages 3 and 4:

> Too often, teaching is directed at pupils of average ability. Lessons which are highly structured or too teacher-directed limit the opportunities for independent enquiry and extended writing. Yet higher attainers and others can flourish in an environment of research, discussion, collaboration and initiative.
>
> (Ofsted 2008: 22)

Differentiation is a planned process of intervention in the classroom, designed to maximise learning potential based on individual needs. There are differences in all classes. These differences may be in the amount of work that pupils complete, in their ability to work independently or collaboratively, or in specific learning skills such as reading, writing or listening and so on. Differentiation is not about simply allowing these differences to show themselves, it is a planned process meaning that teachers need to do something intentionally to support specific pupils. This is often in the form of a dialogue between teachers and individual pupils about progress.

Curriculum planning and planning individual lessons provides teachers with a great deal of scope for responding to differentiation issues. However, differentiation is a subtle art that reflects you knowledge and understanding of geography, of learning and of the young people sitting in front of you. It is not a simplistic instrumental way of managing pupils, and it needs to be approached in a flexible way, as unplanned and unexpected outcomes can have benefits for the learner. For example, pupils might do better than expected or, alternatively, they might just drop below the expectations you have of them because the work is beyond their scope at this particular stage in their development. As teachers, we are continually adjusting our expectations of what pupils can achieve as we monitor and assess their progress in learning.

We discuss differentiation in teaching in more detail in Chapter 4.

Planning for continuity and progression in pupils' learning in geography

In Chapter 2 we discussed in some detail the significance of the idea of progression in curriculum thinking. In this section we revisit progression as a means of exposing some of the issues you will need to consider when planning a curriculum that enable pupils to make progress in their geographical learning. There are two ideas that go hand in hand here:

- continuity
- progression.

Continuity

Continuity refers to the way the curriculum is structured to ensure that breadth and depth is developed and to provide opportunities to widen pupils' understanding. This often involves revisiting ideas, knowledge and skills in different contexts to reinforce learning through a 'spiral curriculum' (Bruner 1960).

Geography courses in secondary schools should build on pupils' experience of and learning in geography from Key Stage 2 in primary schools. We should also be able to identify continuity between courses within a school, that is, between Key Stage 3 and GCSE. This suggests that there are certain significant features of geographical education that will be evident throughout a pupil's experience of geography in school. These might include aspects of content or particular types of learning activity. Bennetts (1995) summarises continuity in the following way:

The idea of continuity suggests the persistence of significant features of geographical education as pupils move through the school system. Such features could include aspects of content, particular types of learning activity or common assumptions about the subject. With strong continuity, it is possible to design courses which enable pupils to build upon their previous experience and learning; and, thereby, help them to acquire knowledge and develop their understanding, skills and competencies in a structured way. Continuity of provision and approach can be looked for both within and between schools.

(p. 75)

Progression

Progression refers to the routes or threads are planned so that pupils' learning advances in a systematic way as they return to different elements of their geographical education. The progressive development of concepts (revisiting, reinforcing and refining, rather than repeating) conforms with Bruner's idea of a spiral curriculum. This development is influenced by the ways in which pupils mature as well as by their educational experiences. Progression in geography for 5-16-year-olds should involve the following:

- An increase in the breadth of studies. There should be a gradual extension of content to include different places, new landscapes, a variety of geographical conditions and a range of human activities.
- An increasing depth of study associated with pupils' growing capacity to deal with complexities and abstractions. As pupils mature intellectually, they are able to make sense of more complex situations, to cope with more demanding information, to take account of more intricate webs of inter-relationships and to undertake more complicated tasks.
- An increase in the spatial scale of what is studied. There should be a growth in pupils' ability to take account of greater complexities and to make use of general ideas, which enables them to undertake successful geographical studies of larger areas.
- A continuing development of skills to include the use of specific techniques and more general strategies of enquiry matched to pupils' developing cognitive abilities.
- Increasing opportunity for pupils to examine social, economic, political and environmental issues. Older pupils should not only be more skilled at evaluating evidence and the consequences of alternative causes of action, but should develop greater appreciation and understanding of the influence of people's beliefs, attitudes and values.

(Bennetts 1995, 2005)

Your own subject knowledge of geography as an academic discipline will be a major source of ideas and understanding when planning for progression. It helps you identify aspects of a theme that are worthy of study and select geographical concepts, theories and models that are relevant to the study of this theme. It will help you analyse what is involved in understanding particular ideas and relationships in geography. Below is an example of how we might think about progression in one aspect of geographical learning - weather.

Box 3.5 Weather: an example of continuity and progression in geographical learning

Key Stage 2

Pupils might study how weather varies between places and over time, by examining the influence of site conditions, seasonal weather patterns and weather conditions in different parts of the world.

Key Stage 3

The focus is on the differences between weather and climate and on reasons for the spatial variations in aspects of weather and climate.

GCSE

Pupils would be expected to develop a broader geographical perspective and to examine the processes in greater depth:

- the measurement of weather conditions and the use of these measurements to identify variations in weather patterns and distinctive climatic regions;
- the influence of different types of atmospheric systems on weather and climate in different parts of the world;
- the ways in which weather and climate affect people's activities;
- the ways in which human activity can indirectly change weather and climate.

A-level

There is likely to be some continuity in the ideas and sub-themes from GCSE. The challenge for the teacher, therefore, would be to introduce pupils to new content and to extend them more intellectually. For example, factors influencing atmospheric circulation (the earth's heat budget, global surface and upper wind circulation, including cells, Rosby waves, jet streams and fronts) and the resulting global patterns of pressure precipitation and temperature could be studied. More complex ideas about the causes of condensation and precipitation would be considered, including the importance of lapse rates and different conditions of atmospheric stability.

Pupils might be expected to develop a more detailed understanding of atmospheric systems and the characteristics of the weather associated with these systems. This would probably include the ability to interpret synoptic charts and satellite photographs. The concept of microclimates could be studied, including the formation of fogs and local winds as well as the development of urban microclimates. A more detailed interpretation of theories about the impact of human activity on global weather and long-term climatic change would be expected.

Task 3.7 Reviewing schemes of work: identifying evidence of continuity and progression in planning for teaching and learning

A Progress in geography within Key Stage 3

Familiarise yourself with the view of progression outlined in Chapter 2 and above.

Review the Key Stage 3 schemes of work for Years 7–9 for a school you are working in to find out the extent to which this view of progression is reflected in one school's planning. Which issues have and have not been overtly addressed in this planning? You might find it useful to revisit the discussion about concepts in geography earlier in this chapter in order to think carefully about progression in pupils' conceptual learning.

Does the planned curriculum allow for:

- increasing the breadth of study
- increasing the depth of study
- increasing the spatial scale of study
- developing geographical skills
- developing enquiry skills and strategies (and pupils' understanding of enquiry)
- increasing opportunity to examine geographical issues and relevant attitudes and values.

Identify aspects of progression that could benefit from further development. Your tutor might be able to suggest some of the aspects that could be considered. It should be remembered that schemes of work benefit from review and are not intended to be 'tablets of stone'.

B Continuity in pupils' learning

Select a specific geographical theme – rivers, settlement, development – and consider what evidence there is that continuity has been planned into your school's geography curriculum.

As a group of student teachers, select one theme and, in broad terms, plan how that theme will evolve between KS2–KS3–GCSE–A level. Use the weather exemplar above as a model.

Summary and key points

We have covered a lot of ground in this chapter exploring different layers of planning, from the national level down to the classroom level, as well as considering different approaches to both curriculum and lesson planning, highlighting the importance of progression and continuity in the planning process. The detail here is designed to support your thinking in terms of getting to grips, not just with the mechanics of planning, but with professional principles that underpin the planning process. Attending to principles is important, because without some adherence to these principles, your teaching will lack purpose and direction and is likely to slide into what Lambert (2004) describes as a highly active and sometime entertaining, but ultimately unfulfilling 'pedogogic adventure' (p. 83).

Further reading

Roberts, M. (2013) *Geography through Enquiry: Approaches to Teaching and Learning in the Secondary School*, Sheffield: Geographical Association

Taylor, L. (2013) 'What do we know about concept formation and making progress in learning geography'. In D. Lambert and M. Jones (eds) *Debates in Geography Education*, London: Routledge.

4 Pedagogy

Pedagogy is the act of teaching together with its attendant discourse. It is what one needs to know, and the skills one needs to command, in order to make and justify the many different kinds of decisions of which teaching is constituted.

(Alexander 2004: 11)

Introduction

'What shall I teach 9Y tomorrow?', 'How do I teach 10S about glacial troughs?' These are the kinds of very real and pragmatic questions that teachers constantly grapple with, and as you start your teaching career you will be asking yourself similar kinds of questions on a day-to-day basis; the 'what' and 'how' of teaching is a professional preoccupation! However, while such questions may seem straightforward enough (you just have to look at the curriculum to decide what to teach and look on the departmental intranet system under 'lesson plans' to decide how to teach, right?), we would argue that to approach teaching and learning in this way is too simplistic and devalues the professional responsibilities that go with 'what' and 'how' decisions. In matters of teaching and learning, you need to be thinking about pedagogy, and what this means for teaching and learning in geography.

By the end of this chapter, you should be able to:

- understand the importance of using a range of teaching styles
- understand the principles that underpin the effective use of different teaching strategies
- develop a repertoire of teaching styles and strategies that you can use successfully to bring about pupil learning in geography.

What is pedagogy?

Often in schools we hear pedagogy mistakenly used as a technical term for teaching strategies, but let us be clear, it is not just about teaching strategies. In 2007, The DfES, defined pedagogy as:

the act of teaching, and the rationale that supports the actions that teachers take. It is what teachers need to know and the range of skills that teachers need to use in order to make effective teaching decisions.

(DfES 2007: 1, cited in Ferretti 2013: 104)

Watkins and Mortimore (1999) argue that it is a mistake to consider pedagogy as only being concerned with the act of teaching; this, they argue, is 'didactics'. They contend that while it is a much contested term, pedagogy is also concerned with learning and so they define pedagogy as 'any conscious activity of once person designed to enhance the learning of another' (p. 3). Immediately this tells us that teaching is not just a technical-rational activity centred on filling in a lesson plan, and mechanistically and unthinkingly implementing certain pre-ordained lesson structures and assessment processes. Hallam and Ireson (1999: 71) define a 'pedagogy for secondary education' as comprising:

1   consideration of the aims of education and the values that underpin teaching;
2   knowledge of theories of theories of learning;
3   knowledge of different conceptions of teaching;
4   knowledge of models of teaching and learning and of the dynamic interaction between student characteristics, the characteristics of the learning environment, task demand, the process of learning and teaching and different kinds of learning;
5   understanding of how these can be operationalised in the classroom;
6   knowledge and skills of evaluating practice, research and theory in relation to education.

Alexander's definition of pedagogy, in the opening of this chapter, expands on this definition when he refers to the *attendant discourse* that underpins decisions you make about what and how to teach. By attendant discourse, he is referring to the inter-related factors that help to shape decisions we make about teaching and learning.

In Figure 4.1, the inner circle comprises those domains that reflect the immediacy of teachers' work. This work is, however, always influenced by the context in which it takes place, represented here by the domains in the adjacent circle. However, it is the domains in the outer circle that provide day-to-day teaching with a broader sense of purpose. As Alexander explains:

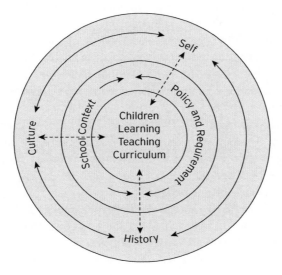

Figure 4.1 Concentric representation of pedagogical influences
(*Source*: adapted from Alexander 2004: 12)

Where the first four domains enable teaching and the next two formalise and legitimate it, the last three locate it − and children themselves − in time, place and the social world, and anchor it firmly to the questions of human identity and social purpose without which teaching makes little sense. They mark the transition from teaching to education.

(Alexander 2004: 12)

Alexander's framework is important in reminding us that an important part of 'learning to teach geography' involves developing, what is described as your pedagogic knowledge. An evolution of this concept is Lee Shulman's notion of 'pedagogic content knowledge' (PCK), namely 'subject matter *for teaching*' (Shulman 1986, cited in Brooks 2006: 6). Shulman argued that separating subject knowledge and pedagogy was in fact unhelpful in guiding teachers to a better understanding their everyday work. What teachers needed was to understand the ways that subject and pedagogy intersected and thus how each shaped an informed the other; it is this intersection, argues Shulman, that better represents how the subject (in this case geography) is adapted and re-presented for teaching. Shulman proposed six key elements of pedagogical content knowledge:

1   knowledge of representations of the subject
2   pupils' pre-conceptions, conceptions and misconceptions of the subject
3   general pedagogical knowledge
4   curriculum knowledge
5   context-specific knowledge
6   knowledge of the purposes of education.

There are clear similarities between Alexander and Shulman's conceptions of the complexities of teachers work. However, emphasising the intersection of subject and pedagogy helps us to locate the subject within broader conceptions of teaching.

There are no short-cuts to acquiring knowledge about teaching and learning. Initially this knowledge will be developed from your observation of experienced classroom practitioners at work, advice from mentors and other teachers, and reflections on your own experiences of practical teaching. Part of this will involve acquiring a language for talking about geography teaching. However, once the initial frameworks have been established and you become more autonomous, you will, as a reflective practitioner, make more sense of your own teaching and increase your pedagogic content knowledge in a more independent way.

The implication here is that learning to teach involves personal professional growth marked by a growing awareness of the complexity of classroom processes and how you can interpret and influence these. There is also usually a significant shift in focus from a concern with your own performance towards greater consideration of what Tony Fisher describes as a 'complex interplay of three specific types of knowledge' (1998: 32): knowledge about learners, knowledge about geography and pedagogic knowledge.

Central to the development of a geography teacher's pedagogic knowledge is the need to build up a broad repertoire of teaching styles and strategies. David Leat describes geography as 'an enormously eclectic borrower' with geographers being 'inclined to play fast and loose in applying ideas and techniques' (Leat and McAleavy 1998: 113). Receptiveness to ideas about different approaches and a willingness to be flexible, imaginative and take risks can only enhance one's pedagogic knowledge. It also puts us in a better position to promote the intellectual development of pupils and respond to recent concerns about the lack of challenge in many geography lessons.

While this chapter seeks to introduce you to teaching styles and strategies that can be used to bring about geographical learning, it is not intended as a 'manual' of techniques for teaching. In order to be an effective geography teacher, there are principles you will need to interpret which you can then apply in practice. Likewise, the integral processes of planning, teaching and reflection (that is, practice) will enable you to better understand the real significance of the principles of effective teaching

A matter of style and strategy

With education currently being the focus of much discussion and debate, we could be forgiven for believing that teaching is anything *but* a personal activity. In the late 1990s/early 2000s, attention shifted from specifying what should be taught in schools towards attempts to influence how it should be taught. In searching for ways to raise 'standards', it was often suggested that certain methods of teaching were more appropriate than others. National initiatives such as the National Numeracy Strategy (DfES 2000) and the National Literacy strategy (DfES 2001) along with the Key Stage 3 National Strategy (of which geography was but one subject) (DfES 2002) set out particular approaches to planning and teaching, which, while not compulsory, were bound up, often in schools' own accountability agendas, but also the school inspection process. Described by Alexander (2004) as 'a pedagogy of compliance' (p. 12), the methods of teaching advocated in the strategies comprised a narrow range of over-generalised alternatives, were evidence-light and ignored important considerations such as learners' needs, teaching contexts, and in particular, what pupils were learning – geography.

The term 'teaching style' is used to describe the way in which geography is taught. It has a very important influence on the educational experience of pupils because it affects how they learn geography. Your teaching style is determined by your 'behaviour' (demeanour and the way in which you relate to pupils) and the 'strategy' that you choose to bring about the learning intended (McCormick and Leask 2005).

Although you may feel that certain teaching styles and strategies might be more appropriate for you, given your personality and philosophy about teaching, it is important that you develop a repertoire of different styles and strategies. This is because you need to consider the characteristics and needs of the pupils (their attitudes, abilities and preferred learning styles) and the intended learning outcomes, as well as your own preferred ways of teaching. You should draw upon your pedagogic knowledge about how teachers teach and how pupils learn. You can consider how your personal qualities and approach to classroom management influence the way that you teach. The nature of the learning environment (classroom appearance and layout), the size of the class and the availability of appropriate learning resources also have a significant influence on the decisions that you make.

Some of the terms that are used to describe different ways of teaching are not always helpful. Terms such as didactic, teacher-directed, whole-class, experiential and practical are vague and open to misinterpretation. At best they are only general descriptions, and at worst they are completely wrong.

For example, terms like 'progressive' and 'traditional' teaching styles are value-laden and stereotypical extremes. One view of progressive teaching might be that it is enquiry-based, child-centred, concerned with problem-solving and as such is forward looking and good. Another might be that it is trendy and lacking intellectual substance. Traditional teaching may be seen as being old-fashioned, autocratic, and lacking creative opportunities or as being reliable and effective at maintaining academic standards. Didactics, generally associated with the traditional 'chalk and talk' transition model of teaching in England, in Europe takes on a very different meaning as the term generally refers to what we in the UK would understand to be scholarly and taught knowledge.

In the past, research has focused on the relationship between different styles of teaching and the effectiveness of pupil learning. This often tends to lead to more value being placed on one style than another because it is believed to be more effective or, as Roberts also suggests, because it relates more to the researchers' 'particular educational aims and philosophy' (Roberts 1996: 235). This can be seen in the work of the Schools Council geography projects, which from the 1970s advocated and valued particular styles of teaching. The 14–18 Bristol Project, a geography development project focusing on the needs of high-attaining pupils, promoted a more interactionist style of teaching geography. Influenced through a process of school-based curriculum development, greater emphasis was placed on the significance of values in decision-making and on the deeper learning processes inherent in the interactionist model.

It will not take you long to realise that there is often a gap between the rhetoric or ideals espoused about teaching styles and what actually happens in the classroom. Pragmatism and an understanding of particular school contexts and cultures lead teachers to adapt their teaching styles and strategies. This should not, however, be taken to its extreme, leading to the false belief that you cannot use a particular style or strategy with the pupils in a particular school (see Morgan 2010).

To learn about teaching styles and strategies, it is important for you to analyse and engage critically with your own practice. To do this, Roberts (1996, 2006) has introduced a different framework for looking at style and strategy (see Table 4.1). By carefully studying this framework, it is possible to imagine what geography lessons consistent with particular styles of teaching and learning might be like.

In the closed style of teaching, the teacher controls the selection of content and the way it is presented to the learners. This content is presented as 'authoritative knowledge' to be learnt by the pupils. The teacher also decides how this content or 'data' is to be investigated and analysed by prescribing the procedures to be followed. The pupils follow instructions presented in textbooks and worksheets or through whole-class teaching. The learning outcomes or key ideas and generalisations are predetermined by the teacher to be accepted by the pupils as valid conclusions.

A framed style is guided by more explicit geographical questions. Even though the teacher still decides the focus of the geographical study or enquiry, pupils are encouraged to generate their own questions. Presenting pupils with questions or problems to be solved, or decisions to be made creates what Roberts describes as a 'need to know' among these

Table 4.1 A framework for looking at styles of teaching and learning in geography

Stage of teaching and learning	Closed	Framed	Negotiated
Questions	Questions not explicit or questions remain the teacher's questions.	Questions explicit, activities planned to make pupils ask questions.	Pupils decide what they want to investigate under guidance from teacher.
Data	Data selected by teacher, presented as authoritative, not to be challenged.	Variety of data selected by teacher, presented as evidence to be interpreted.	Pupils are helped to find their own data from sources in and out of school.
Interpretation	Teacher decides what is to be done with data, pupils follow instructions.	Methods of interpretation are open to discussion and choice.	Pupils choose methods of analysis and interpretation in consultation with teacher.
Conclusions	Key ideas presented, generalisations are predicted, not open to debate.	Pupils reach conclusions from data, different interpretations are expected.	Pupils reach own conclusions and evaluate them.
Summary	The teacher controls the knowledge by making all decisions about data, activities, conclusions. Pupils are not expected to challenge what is presented.	The teacher inducts pupils into ways in which geographical knowledge is constructed, so that they are enabled to use these ways to construct knowledge themselves. Pupils are made aware of choices and are encouraged to be critical.	Pupils are enabled by the teacher to investigate questions of concern and interest to themselves.

(*Source:* Roberts 1996: 240 and 2006: 96)

pupils. The resources and content are still selected by the teacher but they are more usually presented as 'evidence' to be interpreted and evaluated.

In the framed style, the teacher helps the pupils understand the processes and techniques involved in geographical enquiry. Evaluation is important as pupils need to understand the strengths and limitations of different sources of information and techniques for presenting or analysing these data. Conflicting information or viewpoints will need to be explored and it will be possible for pupils to come to different conclusions when examining this information.

In a negotiated style of teaching and learning, the teacher will identify the general theme to be studied but the pupils will generate the questions that will guide their enquiry either individually or in groups. These questions will be negotiated with the teacher, who will also provide guidance about the methods and sequence of enquiry as well as about the suitability of the sources of information to be used.

The information will be collected independently by the pupils and they are responsible for selecting appropriate methods for presenting, analysing and interpreting these data. The outcomes or conclusions of these enquiries are not always predictable. The processes of learning involved are often as important as the outcomes themselves. It is, therefore, helpful to consider the limitations of the sources of data selected and to review the methods used.

Task 4.1 Alternative styles of teaching and learning in geography

Carefully study the frameworks for looking at teaching styles shown in Table 4.1.

1   Use Margaret Roberts' framework to analyse teaching styles and levels of pupil participation in a geography lesson that you are observing.
2   Record your observations on a copy of Table 4.2 – summarise your observations under each category and then decide whether the approach used by the teacher and the types of task completed by pupils were closed, framed or negotiated.

During your own practical teaching experience, you may wish to ask your tutor or another teacher to observe some of your lessons using this framework. The feedback will help you reflect critically on your own practice. If other student teachers have also engaged in these activities, you will gain a great deal from a group discussion about teaching styles and levels of pupil participation in geography lessons.

The enquiry approach to teaching and learning

In Chapter 2 we discussed planning a geography curriculum using an 'enquiry approach'. In this chapter, we develop the ideas outlined there and consider what 'geographical' enquiry means in pedagogical terms. A central tenant of Margaret Roberts' extensive work on geographical enquiry is that as well as extending pupils' geographical knowledge and understanding, pupils need to also understand something about the provisional nature of knowledge itself. Firth (2012) echoes this, drawing a helpful distinction between 'subjects', which are taught and passive, and 'disciplines', which are practised according to the procedures of subject communities. In the light of this, how can pupils engage with the *practices* of geography in order understand the complexity and provisionality of geographical knowledge? Geographical enquiry is, argues Roberts, an approach to teaching and learning that enables pupils to 'do geography', and thus come to appreciate that the knowledge they unveil through the enquiry process depends very much on the questions that they ask and the processes they engage in; they can begin to appreciate that knowledge is not fixed, but created via disciplinary processes that are part and parcel of the work of disciplinary communities.

As indicated in Chapter 3, the curriculum development projects of the 1970s and 1980s advocated enquiry as an approach to teaching and learning in geography at both GCSE and A-level. The Schools Council 16–19 Geography Project, advocated an 'enquiry-based'

Table 4.2 Using the participation dimension as a framework for analysing 'style' and 'strategy' in a Year 10 lesson about indices of development

Teaching and learning activities	Closed	Framed	Negotiated
Questions: The teacher selects the overall focus: indices of development. The class is presented with a list of indices for which there are data on the ICT database in a file on development. Pairs of pupils are asked to produce their own hypotheses about which indices will show positive correlations, which will show negative correlations and which will not correlate at all. This stage of the scheme of work is negotiated in that the pupils can set up their own hypotheses to explore during the lesson. It is within the broad frame set up by the teacher, however.		✓	✓
Data: The class is given details of what types of information are in the database and what units of measurement are used. The sources of information are not discussed, nor the validity of data questioned. The data are given as authoritative data.	✓		
Interpretation: Pupils are given precise instructions on how to select two variables and draw scattergraphs on the computer. They are expected to follow instructions to use this technique for correlating data. To this extent, the interpretation is closed in that there is no choice of methods for correlation. The pupils have to decide, however, from the scattergraph whether they think there is a correlation, and so at this stage are involved in making their own interpretations of the data.	✓		
Conclusions: There is a class discussion on the findings of pairs of students and lists are made of indices which correlate positively, those which correlate negatively and those where there is no correlation. Pupils are invited to speculate on the reasons for their findings.		✓	

(*Source:* Roberts 1996: 257)

approach to teaching and learning that 'encourages students to enquire actively into questions, issues and problems, rather than merely to accept passively the conclusions, research and opinions of others' (Naish et al. 1987: 45). The project envisaged a continuum of approaches to teaching and learning providing 'scope for an effective balance of both teacher-directed work and more independent enquiry' (Naish et al. 1987: 46). The project's view of 'enquiry-based learning' focused predominantly on 'structured problem-solving' and 'open-ended discovery' (Naish et al. 1987: 45). It is probably fair to say, that for some time geographical enquiry was more associated with fieldwork than classroom teaching, and adopted a very 'scientific' model of investigation: hypothesis testing, data collection and analysis, discussion, and evaluation. There is nothing wrong with this, and still today, good fieldwork is often framed around an enquiry approach that allows pupils to get first-hand experience of collecting and processing and evaluating *their own* data, but geographical enquiry is not just for fieldwork.

The 1995 geography National Curriculum made 'enquiry' a statutory requirement, and it remained such until the 2014 curriculum was published, where enquiry is alluded to, but is not an explicit curriculum requirement. It has, however, remained a feature of both GCSE and A-level geography and therefore, by default has to be a feature of teaching and learning at Key Stage 3.

So, in pedagogical terms, what does geographical enquiry look like? Roberts' research into teachers' perception of geographical enquiry, undertaken in the 1990s, revealed that teachers had different views of what 'enquiry' actually meant and that their views were shaped by several factors including where they went to university and their own experiences of enquiry processes at this level, plus the view of enquiry presented in the examination specifications they used. She also found out that in schools where enquiry teaching was strongly aligned with fieldwork, very little enquiry work was undertaken in classrooms. What emerged from Roberts' research was a distinct lack of agreement about what 'geographical' actually meant. However, important threads that seemed to run through the teachers' understanding was that enquiry involved, to different degrees, pupils working independently or in small groups and using evidence of some sort to learn something for themselves.

But there is more to geographical enquiry than pupils undertaking a 'bit of finding out'. Enquiry is rooted in theories about how children learn and in particular draws on the constructivist ideas of Vygotsky, Piaget and Bruner and the notion that children, through appropriate processes, and *actively* make sense of the world for themselves. The key word here is 'actively'. This does not mean pupils frantically undertaking a vast array of 'activities' such a card-sorting activity, group discussions followed by presentations followed by a plenary activity – which are all activities, but do not necessarily always result in *learning*! We are talking here about cognitive activity stimulated by appropriate learning activities (that may be a discussion or some sort of card-sorting activity), which is necessarily messy involving pupils and teachers feeling their way towards something rather than following a predetermined course with predictable conclusions; it is about possibilities not definites and it is the precursor to creating yet more geographical questions; where one enquiry ends, another one starts!

As a pedagogical approach, enquiry is founded on some important principles. Namely that teachers need to:

> take account of students existing knowledge and ways of understanding allow time for students to explore new information and relate it to what they already know: making sense is not an instant process provide opportunities for students to reshape and reconstruct their existing knowledge in the light of new knowledge make students aware of the way they see things and of different ways of seeing things.
>
> (Roberts 2013: 20)

In terms of 'what' geographical enquiry looks like in geography classrooms, Roberts' framework in Chapter 3 is a helpful tool for thinking about pedagogy as well as for thinking about curriculum planning.

Creating a need to know is vital here and requires some imaginative research and thinking on your part. Norman (2014) talks about her use of 'crazy questions' in stimulating pupils interest in what is to come, and then from 'crazy questions' come other questions for pupils to pursue, or you can encourage pupils to develop their own questions. A bit like a 'curriculum artefact' (see Chapter 3), questions that engender 'fascination and puzzlement' (p. 25) and don't seem to be at all geographical can be a good place to start. Sources for generating crazy questions are many and varied – the news channels, newspapers, magazines, TV programmes – it just depends on what strikes you.

Box 4.1 Crazy questions: an example of a geographical enquiry

How has hair been used to clean the ocean?

1   *Why did the ocean need cleaning?* Pupils watch a video and complete a 'matching statements' activity to discover that the 2010 BP oil spill was the focus of the enquiry.
2   *Where did the oil spill happen?* Pupils use a map to write a detailed description, using key geographical terms, of the location.
3   *What were the effects of the oil spill?* In pairs, pupils speculate on possible effects before being shown an interactive map, detailing the scale of the spill on the BBC News website.
4   *How was the spill stopped and cleaned up?* Pupils find out that hair was collected and stuffed into nylon tights to absorb the thick oil. They consider how such a strategy is effective.

(*Source*: Norman 2014: 25)

In terms of activities to support geographical enquiry, this is a matter of judgement. However, Roberts advocates the use of primary and secondary sources as evidence for pupils to grapple with, the use of dialogic approaches whereby pupils have opportunities to discuss and deliberate their ideas and have opportunities to construct arguments and understand bias and perspective, and that an enquiry lesson is full of rich questions that challenge students' thinking rather than require them to merely recall content (see section on questioning in this chapter). The kinds of activities she describes in her 2013 publication *Geography through Enquiry* include concept maps, mind maps, role-play activities, the use of DARTS (directed activities related to text) and more, and that central to any enquiry is a clear focus on conceptual learning in geography, not just developing generic skills.

Much of what follows in this chapter explores teaching processes that support you in using geographical enquiry as an approach to learning geography. Having said this, these processes can be configured in a number of ways depending on what and how you want pupils to learn – we come back to the notion that the what and how of teaching and learning are, in the main, a matter of professional judgement.

Problem-solving and decision-making strategies

Problem-solving and decision-making are types of geographical enquiry where pupils are expected to become involved in issues, carrying out both factual and values enquiry in relation to them, seeking solutions and considering the possible consequences of these solutions. These are demanding exercises as pupils are required to use their knowledge and understanding of geographical concepts and processes in the interpretation of data which may be complex and wide ranging. They are often based on a wide range of resources including maps, diagrams, photographs, statistics, newspaper or journal articles and statements of views. Sometimes pupils are required to analyse and interpret views presented. On other occasions, they may need to indicate or consider the likely views of individuals and groups involved in the issue. They are also expected to utilise a wide variety of geographical skills and techniques. The task of the teacher therefore is also demanding, helping pupils to develop their understanding of the process of geographical enquiry, their competency in a wide range of skills and their ability to apply in-depth knowledge and understanding of geography.

Strictly speaking, decision-making is not the same as problem-solving. *Decision-making* is the systematic process of identifying an issue, question or problem, investigating the evidence, evaluating the alternatives and choosing a course of action. In geographical enquiry, this involves a meaningful sequence of learning activities designed to provide opportunities for pupils to practise and develop a range of geographical skills and techniques. Decision-making ends with the decision and recommendations for action. However, *problem-solving* involves two further stages: putting the decisions into effect (action); and evaluating the consequences of these actions. Whereas the decision-maker attempts to predict the consequences of decisions, the problem-solver actually follows the progress of these consequences.

Decision-making exercises are designed to involve pupils in the application of skills of geographical enquiry to a particular issue, question or problem arising from the interaction of people with their environments. They are now a well-established part of the assessment process with several GCSE and A-level examinations including decision-making, problem-solving or issues-enquiry components. The independent investigation assesses pupils' abilities in undertaking a structured sequence of enquiry, carrying out both factual and values enquiry about a real situation (Naish et al. 1987). More specifically they are assessed on:

- the ability to follow a logical and well-reasoned sequence of enquiry in the process of reaching a decision;
- the use of appropriate methods and techniques to identify and analyse different resources, data and evidence;
- the appreciation of different values positions in the data provided and the steps involved in clarifying their own values;
- the ability to assess and evaluate alternative solutions and their likely consequences;
- the ability to make logical reasoned decisions and to justify recommendations;
- the quality of reporting.

The craft of exposition

Whilst preparing to teach a group of PGCE students, one of the authors asked her 13-year-old daughter 'So, what makes a good teacher?' Her daughter's reply was perhaps unsurprising but worth thinking about: 'Well, they must have a sense of humour, but actually someone who explain things *really* well.'

The key to helping pupils access your geography lesson is undoubtedly linked to your capacity to express your ideas, intentions and expectation. Exposition is one of the most fundamental and frequently used strategies in teaching. It performs a number of functions and purposes, with pupils learning by listening, thinking and responding to what the teacher has to say. There are three main uses of teacher exposition:

- making clear the structure and purpose of the learning experience
- informing, describing and explaining (or demonstrating)
- using questions and discussion to facilitate and explore pupil learning.

(Kyriacou 1997: 40)

In the early days of learning to teach, being able to 'inform, describe and explain' effectively is, alongside managing discipline, one of the most highly valued skills by student teachers. Good exposition, as indicated above, is also highly regarded by pupils, who feel that enthusiasm for the subject and 'clarity of explanation' make a significant contribution to educational attainment. Joyce and Weil (1980) used Ausubel's ideas to develop a three-phase model of expository learning. In phase 1, the advance organiser is presented to clarify the objectives of the lesson and raise awareness of the learner's prior knowledge and understanding. This is followed by the presentation of the material to be learned or task to be undertaken in a structured and logical way in phase 2. The purpose of phase 3 is to reinforce and strengthen cognitive development by relating this new material to the learner's existing cognitive structures. It is usually a good idea to make the structure of your exposition clear to pupils. The advice frequently given to student teachers goes something like: 'Tell them what you are going to say; then say it; then tell them what you have said.'

Meticulous preparation of expositions in the early stages of teaching will mean that you have thought through what you want to say, how you want to say it, and the sequence in which you want to say it. Sequence is very important. If you introduce new ideas in the wrong order, you will confuse pupils. One author observed a student teacher introducing a group of Year 9 pupils to the concept of sustainable development.

Student teacher:	OK. Who can tell me what sustainable Development means?
	(no response)
Student teacher:	Anyone? What does sustainable development mean?
	(still no response)
Student teacher:	Come on . . . someone give it a try? Just tell me what you think it means.
	(still no response, and getting desperate)
Student teacher:	Ok. Copy down this definition: 'Sustainable development is development that meets the needs of the present without compromising the ability of future generations to meet their own needs.'

Table 4.3 The three main phases of whole-class teaching

The advance organiser	The development phase	The consolidation phase
Whole-class teaching: Teacher exposition to introduce new theme – focus on daily consumption of food and products – lots of questions shared on the board Link with previous learning about industrial change Introduce idea that their lives are connected to the lives of others Explain learning tasks and activities	Pupils work on main task – using atlases and contents of a plastic bag pupils create location maps of where the goods in their bags were made and research the journey of once commodity	Teacher exposition: • using questions to explore understanding of location and production • Summary table of key ideas – understanding of interconnections • end of lesson review emphasising new concept and skills – interconnections, relationships, dependency

This was going nowhere. The student teacher was starting in completely the wrong place. These pupils had never heard the phrase 'sustainable development', let alone knew what it meant. Trying to guess at the meaning was pointless, as was copying down the definition – pupils had no prior knowledge of the concept and were not given any resources from which they could begin to feel their way to a possible answer. A better place to start an exploration of what we mean by sustainable development was not with the big concept, but the students and their lives, possibly tapping into their lives as consumers, where commodities they consume are made, where raw materials come from and *then* when they seem to understand the principles (possible after a couple of lessons) introduce the concept, before then elaborating on the idea by studying, for example, case studies of sustainable development projects and exploring international issues. Sequence was everything in terms of developing pupils' understanding here, because getting the sequence wrong not only prevented pupils from accessing the idea, it actually confused them – the definition was too abstract to be helpful and gradually pupils became disillusioned and distracted.

Waterhouse (1990) describes some of the more common structures used in teacher expositions as:

- The sequential structure – explaining a sequence of events, steps in a process or a chain of causes and effects.
- The deductive structure – explaining and justifying a set of rules or principles followed by a description of examples or consequences derived from these principles.
- The inductive structure – presenting a number of examples or case studies from which the pupils are helped to derive generalisations or rules.
- The problem-solving structure – encouraging pupils to find a solution or make a decision by evaluating evidence and, the strengths and weaknesses of alternative solutions.
- The compare and contrast structure – identifying similarities and differences between various situations or events.
- The subject heading structure – organising the presentation of large amounts of information.

The 'learning about teaching' that results from your early experiences of exposition is usually significant. It takes you forward from thinking just about the geographical content to be covered to a consideration of how to provide a stimulus to elicit audience attention and a framework to support the development of understanding. You are more likely to achieve your objectives if your exposition has a clear structure that the audience can follow.

More recently, we have noticed that with the advent of technology there is a dangerous tendency in beginning teachers to rely very heavily (too heavily!) on PowerPoint presentations to 'do the talking for them'. We wish to emphasise that regular recourse to PowerPoint in this way will ensure that your exposition skills do not develop and that your teaching is dull and lifeless! There is nothing more mind-numbing than a lesson where the PowerPoint replaces the teacher and where lively, interesting explanations of difficult geographical ideas that could be interlaced with interesting/humorous/relevant examples are replaced by screens of dense text to be laboriously read through. With this in mind, we ask you to think carefully about the kinds of resources, including PowerPoint, that you use to support your expositions.

Task 4.2 Explaining geographical ideas

A Planning a piece of explanation

There is no formula for explaining a key idea, no 'right way'. However, more effective explanations tend to include some of the following:

- Planning and rehearsal: organisation, sequence and timing.
- Tell your audience your purpose – provide them with a sense of what this is about.
- Think about your non-verbal communication: smile, make eye contact, stand up straight, try not to fidget or 'wander around on the spot'.
- Include signposts so they can follow your progress and indicate when you are moving on.
- Involve your audience in an activity – use an artefact.
- Be conscious of your audience – their disciplines, experience, needs, levels of engagement – read *their* non-verbal communication.

Do not:

- Describe anything in prolonged detail.
- Read your presentation or parts of it.
- Assume knowledge of specific issues, local features, and so on.

Identify an aspect of geography that you feel you would not be confident teaching. Read around the subject until you feel you have a better understanding of the key concepts associated with your chosen area. Now select one small element of this area and plan a five-minute explanation, using real-world examples to bring your explanation to life. Write down your key ideas, attend to getting the sequence right, and plan what

(continued)

(continued)

artefacts you will use in order to engage you audience. We recommend that you do not 'script' your explanation; this will result in a rather stilted performance. We do recommend that you practise it – possibly in front of a mirror? In the planning process, do not use PowerPoints, other than possibly to include an image such as a photograph or a map.

B Microteaching – preparing and giving a short piece of exposition

Having planned an explanation, the next step is to do it! Microteaching is an obvious but vital activity and is possibly your first experience of teaching. It is an opportunity to begin to understand yourself as a teacher – what you look like, how you sound, and how you communicate your personal passion for geography! Many student teachers report that the prospect of microteaching is far worse than the event itself, and that proper planning and preparation helps to offset any nervousness.

We recommend that you do your microteaching in front of a receptive and supportive audience – your student colleagues should be good for this. We also recommend that you film the microteaching so that you have the opportunity to review yourself and get some sense of how you are as an early career teacher. It is important to remember, however, that it is early days and that you will get better with practice. It is worth repeating the activity once you have had had some teaching experience so that you can continue to refine your practice. Remember that you only have five minutes – be sure to time yourself carefully.

Afterwards discuss the presentation. Invite audience reaction, for example:

a   things they like and why
b   questions about your content and methods
c   their suggestions for improving your presentations.

Kyriacou's (1997) summary of the key features of 'effective explaining' could be used to evaluate your explanation, providing some helpful feedback about the skills that you need to develop for whole-class teaching (see Box 4.2).

Box 4.2 Key features of effective explaining

Clarity	It is clear and pitched at the appropriate level.
Structure	The major ideas are broken down into meaningful segments and linked together in a logical order.
Length	It is fairly brief and may be interspersed with questions and other activities.
Attention	The delivery makes good use of voice and body language to sustain attention and interest.
Language	It avoids use of over-complex language and explains new terms.
Exemplars	It uses examples, particularly ones relating to pupils' experience and interests.

(*Source:* Kyriacou 1997: 42–43)

C Observing lessons

The section below discusses the broader use of exposition at different phases of lessons. When in school, observe an experienced teacher's exposition style. Look carefully at how they make use of :

- advance organisers
- the development phase
- the consolidation phase.

When observing, remember it is the teacher you are focusing on – try not to be distracted by the pupils.

D Filming a lesson

We also recommend that at a later stage in your training you film yourself teaching a whole or part of a lesson. There are clearly issues to attend to, such as getting ethical approval from your school to do this. but most schools are positive about this process as long as you ensure that the film does not leave the school premises and that it is deleted after you have had time to process it. Having filmed a lesson, sit and review the lesson twice. First, view it on your own, making notes on your teaching, including your expositions – explaining, questioning, use for resources to support teaching. On the second occasion, watch the lesson with your mentor/tutor. This second viewing is important because, as we have found in the past, student teachers can be very critical of themselves; you need an experienced eye to help you to apply a more objective analysis of your practice.

(Activity adapted from the PGCE Course at the University of Nottingham)

During these early experiences, whole-class teaching presents two fundamental challenges, both of which require a high level of expertise to be developed. First, your exposition must gain and sustain the interest and attention of pupils. Second, the style and content of the exposition must be 'pitched' at an appropriate level for all the pupils in the class. Gaining and sustaining attention requires stimulating, clear and perhaps even charismatic or inspiring presentation as well as good classroom management skills. We cannot all be charismatic orators, but as geography teachers we can utilise a range of strategies to develop or support our styles of exposition. To illustrate this point, we can draw upon one example used by a student teacher:

In a lesson about tropical rainforests, Richard drew upon his extensive travels as well as his own creative instincts. Bringing in some of the contents of his bathroom cabinet, he tried to establish some links between distant environments that he had visited and the more immediate world of his pupils. Images from his travels showed plants from which medicines have been derived, including alcheloids from which chemotherapy drugs have been developed. A variety of specimens, each with its own story, was circulated around the class. The images and the stories of his travels helped Richard demonstrate the diversity of rainforest environments that exist in the world, indicating their location on the large wall map in the classroom. His exposition drew skilfully on his own unique experiences and provided a source of genuine fascination for the pupils. For them, the textbook descriptions had certainly been brought alive.

Another common use of exposition in geography teaching is the demonstration, often referred to as 'modelling' of some technique or skill such as the drawing of a graph, map or diagram. It is a strategy that is frequently used when teaching mapwork skills. In all these situations, the teacher models the different stages with pupils observing and copying the techniques used. Sometimes pupils are challenged to work out these stages and techniques from the teacher's explanation.

Generally, the modelling of certain skills is usually followed by learning activities and tasks where pupils are required to repeat or apply the techniques in the belief that 'practice makes perfect'. This form of teacher exposition requires careful planning as well as clarity in delivery. Preparation may involve both developing your own resources for doing the demonstration such as a PowerPoint or interactive white board display, *and* producing graph or sketch outlines and other differentiated resources for pupils to use.

Figure 4.2 shows some of the resources used to demonstrate how to draw an annotated sketch map to summarise the impacts of the Volta Dam scheme in Ghana. Pupils could be provided with a blank sketch outline map to use with an atlas map to save time, so that the focus can be on the selection and presentation of information on the map. The teacher could have the same outline projected on to a white board and gradually together, through teacher demonstration, discussion, questions and pupils accessing resources such as the atlas and a newspaper article, pupils 'build' their understanding of the impacts of the dam on the surrounding area. It is too easy, because of the amount of information available on the internet, to simply present pupils with the finished product via a downloaded image. However, the process of gradually, together creating the 'finished product' enables you to:

- model the task for pupils, thus enabling more to be successful;
- question pupils, as they complete the task in stages, and thus check for misunderstandings/misconceptions which can be then be discussed within the lesson rather than being left until end;
- help pupils to see how a geographical skill such as map production can also serve to support their conceptual learning;
- have conversations with groups and individuals to develop their confidence in using and drawing maps.

This example aims to show the impacts of a large dam scheme

Step 1 – Draw a simple outline map showing the main features of the area in the case study.

Figure 4.2a

Step 2 – Mark on important locational information physical geography (rivers, lakes, seas) and human geography (towns, cities, economic activity). Add a title, approximate scale and a north sign.

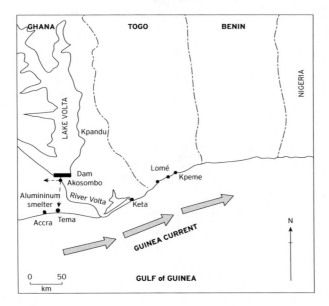

Figure 4.2b

Step 3 – Add important information about the case study using labels and annotations. These should be relevant to the question which the case study is being used to answer.

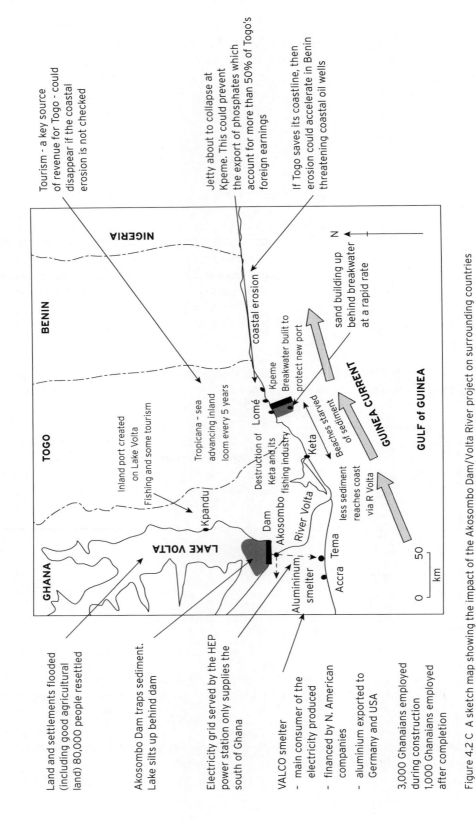

Tourism - a key source of revenue for Togo - could disappear if the coastal erosion is not checked

Jetty about to collapse at Kpeme. This could prevent the export of phosphates which account for more than 50% of Togo's foreign earnings

If Togo saves its coastline, then erosion could accelerate in Benin threatening coastal oil wells

Land and settlements flooded (including good agricultural land) 80,000 people resettled

Akosombo Dam traps sediment. Lake silts up behind dam

Electricity grid served by the HEP power station only supplies the south of Ghana

VALCO smelter
- main consumer of the electricity produced
- financed by N. American companies
- aluminium exported to Germany and USA

3,000 Ghanaians employed during construction
1,000 Ghanaians employed after completion

Figure 4.2 C A sketch map showing the impact of the Akosombo Dam/Volta River project on surrounding countries

Figure 4.2 Demonstrating the technique of drawing an annotated sketch map to show the main features of a case study

By now it should be clear that teacher exposition demands more than just good presentational skills. Being able to explain something effectively requires us to take account of our pupils' existing level of knowledge and understanding, as well as ensuring that the explanation is meaningful by providing an appropriate structure to help them follow and understand its content. As a strategy, exposition can do more than simply relay information to pupils. It can help us to introduce pupils to new or more challenging ideas, explanations and generalisations.

Dialogic pedagogies

As mentioned in the section on geographical enquiry, talking is an important component of your teaching. Teachers and pupils talk a lot in classrooms, some of it is educational, some of it social and occasionally it is distracting. The discussions that follow build specifically on ways of using dialogue to develop pupils' geographical understanding.

Dialogue and talking are not the same. Dialogue requires talking, but the very term 'dialogue' implies more of a mutual exchange of ideas rather than a verbal exchange dominated by one person – usually the teacher. What do we mean by dialogic pedagogies? Alexander (2011) draws an important distinction between 'interactive whole class teaching', a concept which implies teacher-led, whole-class discussions, and dialogic teaching that focuses on the power of talk – whole-class and teacher led, small groups, pairs or whatever – in enabling pupils to learn. The former, an approach to teaching promoted by national initiatives such as the national strategies, was, argues Alexander, less interactive than the term implies and tended to be dominated by teacher talk; it was teacher-led, teacher-controlled, teacher directed – it was all about the teacher and was not about dialogue or learning. Dialogic teaching, however, is about the 'quality, content and dynamics of talk' (p. 23). He goes on to argue that in classrooms talk is essential for learning, because it is the antithesis of the answer-culture evident in so many classrooms. Talk opens-up the content of lessons for scrutiny because it allows pupils to debate, deliberate, question, reflect, and reconsider, new and also taken-for-granted ideas; from talk flows understanding, critical thinking, intellectual engagement.

Alexander suggests five principles for dialogic teaching (see Box 4.3).

Box 4.3 Five principles of dialogic teaching

Dialogic teaching is:

- *Collective*: teachers and children address learning tasks together, whether as a group or as a class, rather than in isolation.
- *Reciprocal*: teachers and children listen to each other, share ideas and consider alternative viewpoints.
- *Supportive*: children articulate their ideas freely, without fear of embarrassment over 'wring answers'; and they help each other to reach common understandings.
- *Cumulative*: teachers and children build their own and each other's ideas and chain then into coherent lines of thinking and enquiry.
- *Puposeful*: teachers plan and facilitate dialogic teaching with particular educational goals in view.

(*Source*: Alexander 2011: 28)

There is something very deliberate about the principles listed above. Dialogic pedagogies depend on talk, but not any old talk – we are not talking here about 'having a natter' or a 'bit of a discussion'. We are talking about deliberate, planned interventions, with clear educational purposes, designed to enhance pupils' understanding.

In the following sections, we consider different approaches to dialogic teaching.

Asking questions in the classroom

Using questioning to develop a class dialogue is an important aspect of whole-class teaching. By asking questions and building on pupils' responses, teachers can skilfully lead or 'shape' pupils' thinking and learning (cognitive development). It is a skill that can be used in a variety of different ways. Simple questions can focus pupils and quickly check on understanding. These lower-order questions require the recall and reporting of information and usually have answers that are clearly right or wrong.

Most questions asked in geography lessons are closed. The teacher's purpose is to structure and control how geographical knowledge and understanding is developed by taking pupils through a particular line of reasoning. The pupils are being asked to tell the teacher what is already known.

Such questioning can actually restrict the learning process as the dialogue between teacher and pupils becomes:

> a guessing game whereby the teacher has the knowledge, and tries through questioning to extract the right answers from the pupil. They in turn reach towards the preferred response, the correct answer. Alternatively they adopt a variety of strategies to keep their heads below the parapet.
>
> (Carter 1991: 1)

Where the intention is to facilitate 'new learning', more open questions can encourage pupils to explore concepts and thinking. More complex and intellectually challenging questions can encourage speculation and deeper thinking. Such 'higher-order' questions require pupils to think about, evaluate or apply information. The answers given by pupils to these questions are often tentative and can be more challenging for teachers to manage as pupils' responses move away from the 'known' and 'expected'. In these situations, the teacher has to be more flexible and responsive, listening to and making sense of pupils' contributions before asking further questions or providing a coherent summary to extend or consolidate learning.

Roberts (1986) offers an analytical framework that can be used to describe the questions teachers ask (see Figure 4.3). This framework considers two dimensions of questioning. One dimension shows how more open questions can encourage pupils to consider a range of answers. The other shows the increasing cognitive demands made upon pupils of questions that promote higher-order thinking. If the majority of questions asked in geography lessons require factual recall or limited comprehension, we may be giving pupils the impression that remembering facts is more important than working things out.

Roberts does remind us, however, that the difference between open and closed questions is not always evident in the words used by a teacher. For example, asking pupils 'What did the programme show you about the impact tourism has had on Thailand?' can be a closed

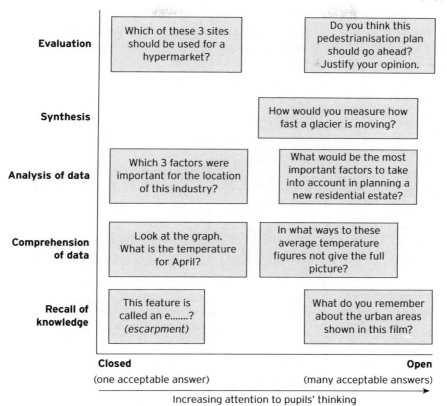

Figure 4.3 Two dimensions of questioning
(*Source*: Roberts 1986: 68-78)

question where the pupils are required to identify the things that the teacher thinks are important. Alternatively, it can be an open question if it is being used to explore pupils' thinking about tourism and its impacts. It depends on whether the teacher is trying to understand or control the pupils' understanding.

One way to tackle the challenge of asking more open and challenging questions is to explore the notion of 'dialogic teaching' (see Alexander 2011, as discussed later in this chapter) and utilise what is known as Socratic questioning. Based on the ideas of the Greek philosopher, Socrates, Socratic questioning is a disciplined approach to questioning that enables a systematic exploration of a concept, issue or dilemma. Socratic questions really probe pupils' thinking. One important aim of Socratic questioning is that, and in time and with practice, pupils use Socratic questioning for themselves, in order to then reason through dilemmas and issues, and understand the thinking of others and the implications of other's ideas. Socratic questioning enables pupils to develop their critical thinking and develop greater independence of thought.

In terms of your practice, Socratic questioning is dependent on dialogue between you and your pupils. Socratic questioning requires thoughtful preparation of the questions you want to ask and careful consideration of how to manage dialogic episodes in lessons. As Alexander (2014) states, 'If we want children to talk to learn – as well as learn to talk – then what they say probably matters more than what the teachers say' (p. 26) – creating a dialogue is also about what happens to pupils' responses.

What are Socratic questions? The table below summarises the main categories of Socratic questions?

Questions that seek clarification, trying to understand what others are saying	Questions about viewpoints and perspectives
What do you mean by . . . ?	Whose points of view are represented?
What is the main point you are making?	What different ways are there of looking at it?
Is your main point . . . ?	Who benefits from this? Who loses?
Could you put it another way?	Why is it better than . . . ?
Could you give me an example?	What are the strengths and weaknesses of . . . ?
How does it relate to what we have been talking about?	Is there another point of view we should consider?
Could you explain that a bit more?	What is the counter argument?
Questions that probe assumptions	**Questions that probe implications and consequences**
You seem to be assuming that . . .	When you say . . . , are you implying . . . ?
Is that always the case?	But if that happens, what else would happen as a result? Why?
Does your reasoning depend on the idea that . . . ?	What effect would that have?
Are you taking for granted . . . ?	Would that necessarily happen or only probably/ possibly happen?
What else could we assume?	What would be the consequence of that?
Why might someone make that assumption?	What are the implications of that?
Questions that probe reasons and evidence	**Questions about the question**
How can we find out if it is true/accurate?	Why is this issue important?
Why do you think that is true?	How can we find out?
What evidence are you basing that on?	Are there other questions we need to ask?
Do you have any evidence for . . . ?	Can we break the question down a bit?
Are these reasons enough?	How far have we got?
Why do you say that?	Are we any nearer to answering the question?
Is there any reason to doubt the evidence?	
Why is that happening?	
Are these reasons a good enough explanation?	
Can you explain your reasoning?	
Could there be another explanation?	

Figure 4.4 Categories of Socratic questions

(*Source*: Roberts 2013: 112)

In order to use Socratic questions to the best effect, there are also some principles to be followed (see Box 4.4).

Box 4.4 Strategies for using Socratic questioning

- Plan significant questions that provide meaning and direction to the dialogue.
- Use wait time: Don't be frightened of silence, students need time to think if they are to feel able to respond.
- Follow up on students' responses with further questions – ask follow up questions rather than just accepting answers.
- Ask probing questions.
- Challenge assumptions.
- Periodically summarise in writing key points that have been discussed so that students can see how ideas are unfolding.
- Involve as many students as possible in the discussion – monitor carefully who is engaged and who isn't, and draw individual pupils into the conversation.
- Let students discover knowledge through the probing questions the teacher poses.
- Think carefully about additional resources that you might use to support a phase of Socratic questioning.

(Adapted from Intel Teach Programme, 2007)

Task 4.3 What kind of questions do geography teachers ask?

1 Observe a geography lesson and note down all of the questions asked by the teacher.
2 Use the framework of Socratic questioning provided in Figure 4.4 to then categorise of the questions that are asked, noting those questions that do not fit into the Socratic categories.
3 What is the balance between Socratic-type questions and other questions such as closed questions?
4 What did you notice about how the teacher manages pupils' responses to questions?

To use questioning effectively, you need to develop a number of skills. Being able to identify appropriate questions and to present them clearly is of fundamental importance and depends on your ability to take account of pupils' existing knowledge and understanding. It is important to use questions to build connections between previous and new learning. It is also helpful to use questions to provide a framework within which pupils can make sense of ideas and new learning.

Sequencing questions helps teachers develop classroom dialogue. 'Staging' questions can be used to increase the level of challenge as the lesson proceeds. This is an important skill when you are trying to develop or explore pupils' understanding. The quality of feedback you provide is vital in terms of both encouraging pupils to participate and challenging their thinking. However, we have observed lessons where, in an attempt to encourage pupils to participate, students teachers have made the mistake of leaving pupils believing that incorrect responses to questions are correct. Every effort needs to be made to create a positive classroom atmosphere in which pupils' contributions are valued and respected. Well-judged praise and encouragement has a profound influence on both the classroom atmosphere and the rapport which develops between pupils and teachers. But at the same time, you have a professional responsibility to monitor pupils' progress and intervene when they clearly do not understand something. In fact, a positive classroom climate includes making it clear that 'being wrong' and making mistakes is fine because this reveals misunderstandings that can then be worked on.

Pupils asking questions

Too often in lessons, pupils only get to ask what 'The Foundation for Critical Thinking' (2013) describe as 'dead questions' – questions such as 'What's the title?', 'What shall I do next?', 'Shall I copy the diagram?'. Yet the discussion above about Socratic questioning identified the importance of helping pupils ask their own geographical questions if you are to develop their capacity to think critically. Pupils are more than capable of asking deep search questions, but it seems self-evident that your lessons need to provide them with opportunities to develop their question-posing skills in order to achieve this. While modelling Socratic questions helps pupils to experience the significance of this way of thinking, at some point you need to hand the responsibility for framing questions over to the pupils.

There are practical strategies you can use to do this, but central to the question-framing process is dialogue. Pupils need to be able to express their ideas and explore their uncertainties, they need to be able to share their thinking – with you and with each other – and they need to have time to reflect and reconsider their own and others perspectives.

Strategies for pupils asking questions

1   Socratic questioning

- Pupils work in pairs or threes and you give them a resource such as a new paper article, a piece of text, an image and so on. Together, they familiarise themselves with the resource.
- You then give them a sheet of 8–10 pre-prepared Socratic type questions (use Figure 4.4 to help you phrase these) to use as prompts to get them started in a debate about a topic.
- One pupil asks the questions and the other pupils draw on any prior knowledge and the resource to answer the questions as best they can. Pupils need know that they cannot give or accept 'yes' or 'no' answers.
- After 3–4 minutes, pupils change roles and another pupil asks the questions.
- Having participated in a short debate, pupils are then asked to work together to devise a new set of questions (a copy of Figure 4.4 might help them here).

2   Snowballing:

- Individually, ask students to write down three questions they would want to ask in response to, for example, a piece of text, an image, a short video clip . . . in order to understand it better! That they should ask three questions, at least, is essential.

- Students then join together in pairs, and you give them three minutes to discuss their questions. They then select what they feel to be the best three questions.
- Pairs of students then join up to form new groups of four and again, between them, they negotiate and agree which are the best three questions.
- Groups then feed back as a whole class, and the best five or six questions are chosen by the class and used to complete work.

3   Hot seating

Organise the classroom with the chairs in a circle.

- Tell pupils that today they are journalists interviewing an expert in the specific topic you are studying (be inventive, e.g. Dr. Mandros Duprey, an eminent French volcanologist, or Lydia Samson, a famous artic explorer).
- You take on the role of the visiting expert (but you have to be convincing – sometimes bringing in some props to show pupils or to talk about can be helpful).
- Pupils work in pairs to support each other in devising a question to ask you. They write their questions down.
- Each pupil has to ask one question – it doesn't matter if it is open or closed, what is important is that they get to *ask* a question.
- The visiting expert answers each pupil's question and pupils , as far as possible, record/ make notes of your responses.
- Pupils work in pairs and then fours to check out the answers to the group's questions and to fill in any gaps they think they might have.
- Pupils then use the interview data to complete a newspaper article.

> (Socratic questioning and 'Snowballing' adapted from Wood (2008),
> *GTIP Think Piece – Questioning*. www.geography.org.uk/
> gtip/thinkpieces/questioning)

While allowing pupils to create their own questions can be a structured activity (see above), be prepared; just when you thought you were safe, someone throws in the unexpectedly challenging question! Wise advice is 'Do not make answers up'. If you really don't know the answer to a pupil's question, then be honest and agree to find out, and/or ask the pupils to do some research. This approach works well if the question really is very tricky. However, you cannot use it as a regular strategy. In order to be confident at handling tricky questions thorough preparation of the subject material – your 'subject knowledge' – is necessary. It is a basic requirement of being a teacher.

Collaborative strategies

Earlier in this chapter, we suggested that some of the terms used to describe different teaching strategies can be value-laden, stereotypical and open to misinterpretation. The use of group work has been the subject of some controversy, partly because it has usually been discussed in the context of the debate over the relative effectiveness of 'traditional' and 'progressive teaching'. It is usually associated with more open-ended investigational tasks carried out by pupils working in small groups.

We prefer to use the term 'collaborative learning' to describe the academic tasks and activities undertaken by groups of pupils that involve some degree of discussion, reflection and collaboration (Kyriacou 1997). There are some educational goals, such as learning to co-operate and learning to work in a team, that can only be attained through group work (Desforges 1995).

Bennett and Dunne (1992) argue that well planned and managed group work can also increase levels of academic attainment and pupils' self-esteem. Learning for understanding is essentially a social process, and collaborative learning can enhance comprehension by creating situations in which intellectual exchanges take place. The broader educational value of collaborative activity is also stressed by Whitaker (1995), who suggests that it:

- creates a climate in which pupils can work with a sense of security and self confidence;
- facilitates the growth of understanding by offering the optimum opportunity for pupils to talk reflectively with each other;
- promotes a spirit of co-operation and mutual respect.

Learning is often seen as an individual process. Although it is certainly true to say that pupils need to internalise learning on an individual basis, it is important to provide opportunities for pupils to work together. Working in groups can promote more effective learning, particularly when it encourages creativity or the clarification of understanding. This notion reflects some of the shifts in conceptions of the learner that have taken place in recent years. These conceptions place far more emphasis on the social nature of learning. Bruner and Haste (1987) argue that '"making sense" is a social process' and stress the importance of the social setting in classroom learning. Bruner was influenced by the work of Vygotsky (1978), who argued that social interaction plays a central role in facilitating learning.

As well as helping pupils to develop their ability to co-operate, collaborative activities encourage pupils to discuss geographical ideas in a purposeful way. The process of selecting, organising and presenting ideas during discussion reinforces and enhances conceptualisation (Stimpson 1994: 154; Freeman and Hare 2006).

To be effective, learning in groups must involve genuine collaboration and purposeful activity. Pupils may sit in groups in many classrooms but most of the time they are working independently and only occasionally are they involved in any collaborative learning activity or required to share answers. This is usually because the tasks that are given to the groups do not require collaboration or co-operation. The main advantages of learning in groups are therefore lost.

The size and composition of pupil groupings is a particularly important issue influencing the success of collaborative learning activities. Teachers often use groups of between four and six pupils. However, it is generally accepted that the ideal group size when working with pupils aged between 11 and 16 is two, three and four pupils. Such groups are large enough for all to participate. Larger groups can inhibit learning if pupils have to wait a long time to give their views or if certain pupils dominate the discussion, leaving others as peripheral non-participants.

Bennett (1995) and others have reviewed evidence from research showing that a number of factors can influence the effectiveness of group work, including:

- group size and composition
- the nature of the tasks assigned
- whether the pupils have been given any training in the use of social and co-operative skills.

Where girls outnumbered boys, or there were equal numbers of boys and girls, both had similar learning experiences. Girls were disadvantaged when outnumbered by boys and tended to speak less and at a lower level of reasoning. Interaction in such groups has been found to be detrimental to girls' achievement (Webb and Kenderski 1985).

Studies comparing (single) ability and mixed-ability co-operative groups have raised substantial doubts about some aspects of ability grouping (Bennett 1995). More able pupils appear to perform well irrespective of the type of group they are placed in. They often talk more, and more of this talk is academic in content. In groups comprising pupils who struggle with learning, substantially less time is devoted to interactions concerning academic content and few relevant explanations are offered. This is usually because the pupils in these groups have a poor understanding of the task or because they do not have the skills or knowledge of the subject matter needed to offer such explanations. These factors lead most advocates of co-operative or collaborative learning to favour mixed-ability grouping. Webb (1989) argues that high-attaining children gain, both academically and socially, from the opportunity to work with and tutor lower-achieving colleagues.

One of the most common ways of organising co-operative and collaborative learning in geography is through the use of various types of card-sorting activities (see section on DARTS in Chapter 5). Such activities are an effective and flexible way of providing a focus and structure for small group work. Nash (1997) identifies a range of benefits from using card-sorting activities as a focus for small-group work (see Box 4.5).

Box 4.5 The benefits of using card sorting activities

- It is a relatively quick and simple method of enabling pupils to work in groups.
- It provides pupils with a clear and focused task – opportunities for them to move off tasks are limited.
- It can be used very flexibly across the full age and ability range.
- It can allow for differentiation even when the same resource is being used in a mixed ability or streamed situation.
- It can be used to impart information to pupils in an interesting and motivating way.
- It allows pupils to develop skills of communication and co-operation.
- It involves pupils actively in their own learning.
- It enables more meaningful teacher-pupil contacts in the classroom.

Card-sorting activities can be used in geography lessons in a variety of ways including:

- labelling features
- matching words and definitions
- classifying features and factors
- ranking and identifying priorities
- looking for relationships and explanations.

(*Source:* Nash 1997: 22)

One of the most common uses of card-sorting activities helps pupils understand how various geographical features, factors or processes might be classified. These activities may require them to decide which groups different cards may fall into. For example, they could be asked to distinguish between benefits and problems resulting from the construction of a large multi-purpose dam, or between the arguments for and against the building of a new road, housing development or out-of-town retail park.

In sorting out statements into two categories, pupils are undertaking a simple form of evaluation. A different form of classification whereby factors that can influence the decisions that farmers make about activities and land use on their farms could be sorted into groups distinguishing between the physical, economic, social/personal and technical influences. Different types of employment or economic activity could be written on cards that pupils then sort into primary, secondary, tertiary and quaternary sectors. In this latter example, pictures cut from magazines could be used in conjunction with vocabulary cards to help pupils with special educational needs such as bilingual learners. Further development of these classification activities would involve pupils looking for and determining their own categories for grouping cards.

Another purposeful discussion task based around the use of a card-sorting activity requires pupils to identify priorities from a variety of alternatives. Diamond-ranking is a technique that is frequently used when asking pupils to distinguish between the 'most important' and the 'least important' ideas, factors, problems or solutions. Working in pairs or small groups, pupils are asked to organise their cards in the shape of a diamond, with the idea they agree most with at the top and the one they least agree with at the bottom (see Figure 4.5).

Using information cards to identify priorities, as in the above example, is an effective strategy for developing pupils' critical thinking and problem-solving skills through more open-ended discussion activities. They can also be used in a purposeful way to provide opportunities for pupils to search for relationships in geographical data, and to suggest explanations and generalisations. Information about particular geographical processes or events can be written on cards that pupils have to organise into some sort of order; for example, into a flow diagram explaining these processes or events.

You also need to develop your ability to observe, listen to and make sense of the learning that is taking place. This 'active assessment' of learning helps you to summarise and

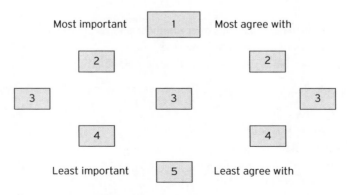

Figure 4.5 Identifying priorities using diamond-ranking

consolidate the learning that has taken place through these activities. It therefore follows that adequate time must be made available to 'debrief' the activities we have described in this section.

Using games and simulations

> The essence of simulation is to provide learning through experience (and through subsequent reflection on experience) rather than by the processing of information through more dialectic means. Pupils involved in a game or role play are likely to come to grapple with ideas based on their own experience and on discussion with their peers, rather than being told about the ideas.
>
> (Walford 1987: 79)

Games and simulations are another way of providing dialogic learning experiences for pupils in geography classrooms. As such, they are an important part of a geography teacher's repertoire of teaching strategies. The games and simulations used in geography lessons can range from simple to quite sophisticated activities. However, what they all have in common is that they 'invite pupils to imaginatively "put themselves in other people's shoes" and exercise thought and reflection in making a decision of some kind' (Walford 1987).

Using games and simulations can certainly improve most pupils' levels of motivation. However, they have a number of other important attributes that make them effective strategies to use when teaching geography. They provide further opportunities for purposeful classroom discussion, negotiation and other collaborative activities.

Another significant attribute of many simulation activities is how they simplify aspects of reality so that pupils can more readily understand the 'dynamics of a rapidly changing world' (Walford 1987: 79). Simulations can also help pupils to 'recognise the "interdisciplinary" nature of real life situations' (Bale 1987: 125). Bale and Walford both comment on the role of classroom simulation in helping pupils to develop empathy, however partial, with people from other places, environment, cultures and occupations. (*Empathy* is used here to refer to the ability to identify with other people's situation or circumstances. It does not suggest that their view(s) should be accepted uncritically.)

Through experience, we have also found that games and simulations can be used effectively with classes where there is a wide range of ability. They often present a variety of problem-solving or decision-making situations that can be interpreted at differing levels of complexity so they can involve the whole class in the same learning activity at the same time.

Grenyer makes a clear distinction between a game and a simulation. He argues that a geographical simulation involves 'a testing of a model against reality in an attempt to predict how a pattern will develop or to analyse the reasons for the development of that pattern' (Grenyer 1985). A geographical game is seen as a form of simulation with 'an element of competition added'. The intention is to simplify reality so that in the process of attempting to win the game, pupils will increase their understanding of that reality.

As your understanding of the principles underpinning the effective use of games and simulations improves, you can begin to develop your own material and adapt existing ones to produce more complex or simpler activities. Spencer (2013) and Clemens, Parr and Wilkinson

(2014) have written articles for the journal *Teaching Geography*, where they report their experiences and successes of devising and using their own games and simulations. While each is very different in content – one is a development of a famous property board game and the other a development of a fair trade game about working in sweat shops – what both examples illustrate is the significance of creating activities that are context specific (designed specifically with their school and their students in mind), that are specific to their curriculum (designed to connect to the concepts they are teaching) and that are enjoyable for teachers to prepare and develop as well as for pupils to use, and if we return to Alexander's notion of pedagogy, they also have specific educational purposes, namely supporting pupils' understanding of global social injustice.

Class management

Your management of games and simulations also needs to be sensitive and responsive. This follows on logically from being confident in your classroom management skills and knowing your classes. Although games and simulations can be very enjoyable and stimulating, different pupils respond in different ways. Some pupils become so 'submerged' in their role or the activity that they react instinctively. Your observation skills can help you monitor the actions of pupils and the learning that is taking place. This is one of the most demanding aspects of managing games and simulations.

You need to monitor a multitude of different exchanges and actions in different parts of the classroom. Decisions have to be made about when and how to intervene. Interventions can be to review events or the learning that has taken place during simulations. Alternatively, the purpose of interventions can be to introduce new factors and situations or to change the direction of particular activities. In making these interventions, you should try to be flexible and not 'pull the reins in' too tightly. Providing too many interpretations along the way can reduce the pace and flow of the activity and inhibit some of the learning opportunities. With some simulations, it is possible to plan the interventions perhaps through the introduction of chance factors. A good example of this can be seen in Spencer's sweatshop game where she has created chance cards such as workers suddenly losing production time because their machine has broken down (vital scissors and glue are removed from a production team for a period of time) or individuals suddenly have to find money to repair a leak in their roof and so have to give up production money.

Debriefing learning

As well as planning when and how to intervene, you should give some consideration to the strategies to be used to debrief and follow-up simulation activities. Pupils need to have opportunities to explore and consolidate the learning that has taken place. Timing and preparation are crucial in this respect. You should plan to allow enough time for discussion and reflection immediately after the end of the game or simulation. Enabling pupils to reflect on their actions, on the way in which the game or simulation operates, and how this mirrors the dynamics of the real world, makes a significant contribution to pupils' learning.

A debriefing session might consist of a number of different elements where the teacher works with the pupils to assess the learning outcomes from a game or simulation. Walford recommends that this should include 'some element of action replay (to recognise key moments and interventions in retrospect)' (Walford 1996: 143). This strategy is often not effectively utilised and consequently an opportunity to help pupils gain a valuable insight into the learning that has taken place is missed. To support the debriefing process, Leat (1998) suggests that teachers carry a notebook keeping a record of interesting interactions between students or significant events that they observe, this can be used to support whole-class discussions. The recording process also serves to keep the teacher focused on the geographical learning and prevents intervention in an activity that is either too early or unproductive.

Too often 'debriefing' is associated with a five-minute plenary at the end of a lesson where pupils do 'thumbs up/thumbs down' actions to indicate levels of understanding. This is not debriefing; in fact we would argue it isn't of any use at all in revealing pupils' levels of geographical understanding. Nichols (2006) reminds us that effective debriefing episodes hinge on:

- use of open (Socratic) questions to tease understanding out of pupils;
- student talk as the dominant voice;
- teachers creating the opportunities for students to explore why they think what they think;
- through reflection students building connections between the processes of the simulation and broader geographical concepts.

Attention should also be given to the affective outcomes of simulations as well as the cognitive ones. As we suggested earlier in this discussion, pupils can become 'submerged' in a role and so their feelings about the learning experience can be used to explore ideas and issues. This is certainly the case in the games described earlier. The main outcomes of the sweatshop game might include an understanding of workers' conditions in other countries and the precarious nature of some people's working lives. Such a game generally arouses feelings of unfairness so it is worth asking groups to comment on how they felt about being financially penalised and the conditions under which they were expected to work. Pupils can be encouraged to recall particular critical incidents in a game and to describe their reactions to what happened.

Skilful debriefing could therefore interweave the affective and cognitive dimensions of pupils' learning experiences. Some may feel that more emotive issues and questions are beyond the scope of geography education in the secondary school. However, we share Rex Walford's view that:

> the essence of many simulations involves feelings as well as minds. Thus some simulations have, as their major objective, the revelation of a particular process in order to have participants re-assess their attitudes towards it.
>
> (Walford 1996: 143)

When reviewing the learning outcomes of many games and simulations, it is therefore worth giving some consideration to the contribution that these learning experiences make to pupils' personal and social education. We can recall many instances where pupils have produced enlightening insights into their feelings and behaviour when describing their reactions to particular experiences during games and simulations. Pupils may also gain some insights into their own strengths and weaknesses in, for example, group work or in a leadership role. The experiential nature of games and simulations provide multiple layers for learning – about geography, about others and about ourselves.

Drama strategies

'Oh no . . . !'
'What's happening?'
'I don't like the look of this!'

The above are just some of the reactions from PGCE geography students prior to a PGCE session on how to use drama strategies in teaching. It is probably important to start this section by being clear that no matter how challenging you may find the idea of using drama strategies in your teaching, many pupils love this approach to learning. We have heard PGCE students say that it not fair to use these approaches as some pupils find them difficult. Our response is that many pupils find writing difficult, but that doesn't mean we don't use it in lessons, and possibly shy/quiet pupils need some of the approaches drama can offer to develop their communications skills and build their confidence. We are not here trying to turn you into thespians, but rather providing another set of alternatives for you to use in your classrooms.

As with any other learning activity drama approaches have to be selected carefully, used judiciously and prepared with a degree of precision. The focus for such lessons is always on geographical learning so you are not looking for a 'polished performance' but evidence that your pupils are learning geography. One anxiety many student teachers have is a fear of losing control of a class if pupils are given the kinds of freedoms that drama-type lessons involve. However ,drama strategies are more than just 'role play' and, if anything, we would argue that the apparent freedoms of drama style lessons are an illusion; to be effective, such lessons need very clear structures coupled with high expectations of behaviour and the appropriate selection of content and teaching strategies' (Biddulph and Clarke 2006).

There are many different drama strategies you can use in geography. Three of these are summarised below:

Box 4.6 Freeze frame as a drama strategy

1   Students create still images, using themselves and available props (tell them they are making a photograph).
2   The teacher explores students' thoughts and feelings about a particular scenario through 'thought tracking' – imaging they have a cartoon-like thought bubble sitting about their head – what would their character think?

Example:

Migration is one possible theme in which to use this convention: pupils could be asked to set up the equivalent of a 'living photo album' where they:

a   develop a freeze frame showing why a group of people have left a place

b   create a second freeze frame showing what the migrants' imagine their destination to be like

c   create a third freeze frame showing the reality of the destination

d   create a soundtrack to go with their series of freeze frames – voice-overs, street sounds, sounds associated with travel such as the sea and boats – they can use their imagination.

Thought tracking the students as migrants can encourage them to think carefully about the hopes and fears of economic or political migrants,

Photographing a freeze frame can support formative assessment processes – pupils can use their photographs, to sit alongside other resources such as maps and text, in order to then complete a piece of extended writing. Capturing the freeze frame in a photograph can jog pupils' memories of their learning, act as a representation of the activities in the lesson, and even become a teaching resource in itself as it can be excellent for developing discussion and in supporting debriefing activities.

Box 4.7 Interviews as a drama strategy

Interviews are a development of hot-seating. Again, the teacher can take on a specific role, or you can invite a 'real expert' in to the lesson. If you decide to do the latter, it needs setting up carefully with students and the visitor; you cannot assume that all visitors know how to relate to teenagers like you do. Get students to prepare questions, and think about how you will organise them (who will sit with whom). Sometimes this activity takes on more significance if done in a space other than the usual classroom. Try to make the event a serious occasion. The difference between interviews and hot-seating is that in interviews pupils are more engaged in asking questions that reveal motives and values. The kinds of questions you want them to ask are those that encourage the 'speaker' (yourself or a visitor) to explain, rationalise, and justify their position on a particular issue. You could add a layer of complexity to this by having two different speakers with different perspectives (perhaps you could involve a colleague to help you). Sometimes pupils themselves, with adequate preparation, can take on the role of the visitor and be interviewed by others. However, you need to ensure that they are well prepared, otherwise the interview process won't add much to pupils' understanding.

Interviews can be a good strategy for teaching about a controversial issue (see section on 'Values education' in Chapter 9).

(continued)

(continued)

Example:

We had been studying about a proposal to build some new houses on some land close to our school. The proposal had caused some debate in the local press because the land, while not particularly beautiful, was the only real piece of green space in the area for some miles. For some pupils, it was something akin to a local park. The pupils socialised there, played there, families took dogs for walks and it was actually well used and cared for by the local community. We visited the space in one lesson and pupils were then asked to draw mental maps of the space as it is; then, in groups, they had to create an annotated map of how they would develop it. We also studied some of the debates about why the land should and should not be developed for housing. By chance, a local counsellor was also on our board of governors and he agreed to be interviewed by the pupils.

In the lesson itself, pupils were very respectful and understood the importance of communicating clearly and giving someone time to respond. They asked questions such as:

- Why do we need more houses in this area? What's the evidence we need more houses?
- Who will benefit from building more houses?
- More houses mean more cars – how will you prevent traffic queues?
- Local people don't want more houses, is there another way the space could be developed?
- Green space is good for people. If you build the houses, what other green space could you provide?

Pupils made notes of the responses and afterwards developed their own letters in response to the information they had gathered and the evidence they had heard. The letters were sent to the council and they did receive a courteous response.

The local debate continues however!

This was a scheme we had taught for a couple of years, and the original plan was not to look at a local issue about land use change. However the local issue emerged and the pupils were interested because any decision would affect them and their families. The 'interview' was an opportunity that presented itself and so we decided to take a risk! Sometimes teaching is about taking calculated risks.

Box 4.8 Role play as a drama strategy

Role play can be an excellent way to really capture pupils' imaginations and involve a wider range of students in different ways, or it can be a disaster! The disaster tends to happen because of:

- Lack of preparation: pupils don't have enough prior knowledge on which to build and participate.
- Poor resources: even very activity-orientated lessons still need good resources to stimulate the imaginations and engender some curiosity – role play is no different.

- Poor planning: the purpose of the lesson is unclear, the structure of the lesson is inappropriate and the content of the lesson muddled.
- Lack of organisation: pupils are not clear about their roles, time frames for completing tasks and where the role play is taking them.
- Low expectations of pupils: just because the activity may be enjoyable, this does not mean that it is not intellectually challenging or that your expectations of their behaviour can slip.

At its best, well-structured, carefully managed role play can stimulate debate, enable students to appreciate the views of others, give otherwise quiet pupils a chance to have their voices heard and give those who either struggle with writing or simply don't enjoy it a change to do something very different. As per any other learning activity, developing geographical understanding is central to the process, and this needs to be clear to pupils.

Role-play activities require pupils to take on the role of another person and take part in a simulated meeting or enquiry of some kind where negotiations take place and decisions have to be made. Examples of the contexts used for such activities might include government or council meetings, public enquiries or even global conventions (e.g. conferences about environmental, economic, trade or development issues). Pupils present or argue viewpoints which may not be ones they hold personally. What you need to consider here is that the contexts listed here are not familiar to students – how will they know what a 'council meeting' is, or a public inquiry – you need to consider how to prepare them for the context as well as the content.

For some role plays, the teacher can issue role cards which describe the role and provide information about people or groups' likely attitudes. Sometimes prompts or questions are used to guide pupils in their preparation of views and arguments to be presented. The cards contain questions which act as prompts to help pupils consider the implications of one possible solution for different groups of people. In such situations, it is interesting to note how some pupils stick closely to the points outlined on their role cards while other more inventive and articulate pupils contribute their own ideas and consider other possibilities.

It is also possible to devise activities where pupils take on similar roles but respond in different ways to the task or problem presented to them.

Example:

In ActionAid's case study of sustainable development on the Altiplano in Bolivia ('Picking up the threads') one activity simulates a year in the life of a Puca Pampa textiles group. Pupils make decisions about how to respond to different situations, design and produce publicity materials for their textiles project and prepare a business plan for their group for the coming year. The activity aims to help pupils gain an understanding of some of the challenges facing people living on the Altiplano and how development projects in the area try to respond to these challenges in a sustainable way.

The presentation phase of a role-play activity is usually very enjoyable, stimulating and, if there has been adequate preparation, contains much worthwhile learning. We can recall numerous occasions where well-motivated pupils have used preparation time between lessons to produce appropriate visual aids to support their presentations and even arrived 'dressed in role'.

The next challenge for the teacher is to ensure that, without diminishing the enjoyment of the occasion, pupils are able to digest, make sense of and internalise some of the worthwhile learning that takes place in this phase of the activity. This could be done using some general questions such as:

- What is the group? Who do they represent?
- What are their views?
- Why do they hold these views?
- What evidence do they use to support these views?
- What was or could be argued to counter these views?

Sometimes the pupils could think of questions that they could ask other groups to challenge or seek clarification of the views presented. Each of these strategies promotes more 'active listening' as pupils are being asked not just to record but to analyse what is being argued.

It is often necessary for the teacher to intervene at different stages during a role-play activity. Sometimes pupils who are relatively unskilled in the 'art' of rational discussion may benefit from guidance to help them to re-focus on appropriate lines of thought and argument when they are losing their way. At some point, you could stop the action and use the break to discuss what has been happening or what particular people or groups are feeling. More information could be introduced, perhaps selectively, in some cases, to benefit particular groups. This information might come in the form of 'chance factors' presenting news of changing conditions or unexpected events. But as Walford reminds us:

> the teacher will need to intervene judiciously here and there – guiding thought or argument away from blind alleys, helping a team understand the deeper implications of an issue that they are discussing, or enlivening a declining discussion with fresh insights or information at an appropriate moment. The teacher mixes administration, management and education for the most part, but the latter may be more effective for not being presented in an obvious expositional mode.
>
> (Walford 1996: 143)

Task 4.4 Using different teaching and learning strategies

It is easy, when you start teaching, to quickly get caught in your own comfort zone. You start to realise 'what works' and so stick with a trusted formula. However, this mind-set can seriously inhibit your professional development in the longer term so we recommend, once on a school placement, that, for a short period of time, you monitor the range of strategies you use with different groups. This is easily done using a monitoring grid where, over a series of weeks, simply tick to indicate the range of approaches you have tried with different groups. The list below is by no means exhaustive and the grid can be adapted, but it can simply start a monitoring process.

Name of group: _____	Subject/Topic _____												
Key area: **Specific detail:**	**Dates used:**												
Approach:	Discussion (class, group, paired)												
	Question/answer												
	Instruction/explanation												
	Comprehension/other written work												
	Creative writing												
	Drama/role play												
	Simulations												
	Mysteries												
	Inductive teaching												
Practical work:	Fieldwork												
	Experiments												
	Work for displays or presentation												
	Project work												
Resources used:	Chalk/dry wipe board												
	OHP												
	Text/workbooks												
	Information/worksheets												
	Video camera												
	Video playback												
	Digital camera												
	Photographs												
	Library												

Differentiating teaching

Effective differentiation is based on an understanding of individual learners, their needs and their strengths as much as their weaknesses. We should select a variety of strategies to provide a range of learning opportunities for all pupils to make progress.

However, achieving differentiation in learning is not just dependent on our ability to design appropriated 'targeted' or open-ended tasks to meet the needs of various groups. Diversity also applies to teaching strategies which have to be used flexibly and implemented success-fully. The quote from the 2011 Ofsted report for geography summarises some of the problems:

When the teaching was no better than satisfactory, an emphasis on covering content did not encourage active learning and, as a result, students' geographical skills were often underdeveloped . . . In far too many classes there was an over-reliance on text books, especially by non-specialist teachers. The result was frequently work that occupied rather than engaged students . . . Higher-attaining students, in particular, were rarely challenged.

Lessons which consistently used a rigid three-part structure did not allow sufficiently for spontaneity and creativity in students' learning. Such lessons also did not always allow them opportunities, the most academically able pupils in particular, to develop the skills of planning and organisation, take responsibility for their own learning or work independently.

(Ofsted 2011: 26)

Breaking this predictable pattern evident in poor lessons requires us to raise our awareness of how we can influence the direction of learning, and how we can provide appropriate challenges for all learners. Differentiation is complex and difficult to do, and, as we stated in Chapter 3 on Planning, is certainly more than just using data, creating different worksheets, and asking targeted questions. It is all of these and more. Figure 4.6 serves as a reminder that effective teaching is a multi-dimensional activity requiring you to hold in balance a significant number of factors all at the same time. When you start teaching, meeting the diverse needs of your pupils seems a lot to ask (and even in groups where pupils allegedly have similar needs, they will, in fact, have diverse needs!). However, and as the diagram suggests, planning, teaching approaches, understanding and knowing your pupils and selecting/developing appropriate resources is the way to think about differentiation in your teaching.

How you intervene in classroom activity has a major influence on the flow of a lesson. Dwelling for too long on particular situations and interruptions, for example when dealing with behaviour or individual needs, affects the momentum of a lesson. Maintaining an appropriate pace is important here as this can influence pupils' interest and motivation levels. Try to avoid slipping into overlong monotone expositions which can create tensions within lessons as pupils' concentration levels fall. However, pace is not about 'speed' and if we want to achieve some of the deep learning advocated in this book then rushing through a lesson will not achieve the desired ends either. Pace is a matter of judgement and is informed by your understanding of learning priorities – in just one lesson you may decide to spend a short amount on time on one idea, for example, where a commodity has come from, in order to then move on and give a substantial amount of time to developing a deeper understanding of a related idea such as the lives behind those who produce that commodity. The pace at each phase of the lesson will be necessarily different.

Skilful teachers appear to attend to a variety of things at one time. This is due to what is sometimes called 'withitness', which describes teachers' awareness of what is going on in all parts of the classroom. Constantly monitoring classroom activity helps you recognise and react to different needs in relation to both learning and discipline. Eye contact and body language can be used effectively to communicate this awareness to pupils and often makes it possible for you to refrain from interrupting the whole class and slowing progress.

To be able to differentiate our teaching, we need to develop these monitoring skills and this is an essential part of what we described earlier as the 'active assessment' of learning. Frequently, teachers use questioning and whole-class discussion to explore and check pupils' learning. A teacher's questioning skills have a significant influence on the quality of

Planning

- clear learning objectives, shared with pupils
- the need to plan small achievable steps
- schemes of work that plan for revisiting
- schemes of work which have a full range of structured and open-ended tasks
- develop the model of core tasks with reinforcement and extension activities
- schemes of work with clear progression

Teaching

- using a wide range of activities and teaching styles
- clear instructions, explanations and expectations
- an awareness that each pupil has unique abilities
- the importance of the pace of a lesson
- the need for a balance of questioning techniques
- the use of open-ended questions and enquiries
- flexibility of approach and response to pupils
- encourage a supportive classroom atmosphere

DIFFERENTIATION STRATEGIES

Resources

- the importance of clearly designed, uncluttered materials matched to pupils' abilities
- using texts of appropriate readability
- using materials that are free of gender/ethnic bias
- the ease of access to learning resources
- classroom display that encourages learning and reflects high expectations

Pupil Needs

- talking with teachers about their learning
- talking to each other about their learning
- sufficient repetition to consolidate learning
- varied activities to match pupils' attention span
- the use of pupil review to set realistic goals
- positive marking which points to improvement

Figure 4.6 Differentiation strategies

(*Source:* Waters 1995: 81-84)

whole-class interactive teaching described earlier in this chapter. Remember that simple, closed questions are only likely to check pupils' ability to recall information, whereas open and more intellectually challenging questions are likely to be more helpful when it comes to exploring thinking and learning.

During a lesson, you will make numerous observations and ask many questions (both individually and collectively) that help you to make judgements about pupils' progress and competence in learning. This process challenges your powers of analysis, as you have your own ideas about what constitutes knowledge and understanding of particular subject matter and what level of competence in the use of different geographical skills is needed by pupils of varying age and ability.

Initially you are very much be guided by your plans and preparation for the lesson. However, avoid becoming a 'slave to the plan'. Your active assessment of the learning taking place will lead you to modify your original objectives, breaking them down into smaller targets for individuals, groups and even the class as a whole. Thus, the process of setting different targets and refining objectives is an effective way in which you can influence the pace and depth of learning during a lesson.

This process of active assessment during lessons is an important part of formative assessment (this is discussed in Chapter 8). Observing pupils working, looking at their work, listening to their conversations about tasks and asking them questions about this work helps you analyse the outcomes of the learning activities that you have devised and the teaching strategies that you are using. You can then make decisions about how and when to intervene and at what level (individual, group or whole class). One of the principles guiding these interventions will be that of 'consequential validity'; in other words, they have a positive impact on pupils' learning. These impacts might include the successful completion of a task, improvements in knowledge and understanding, or the promotion of thinking or critical analysis in response to greater intellectual challenge.

Whether they have these desirable consequences depends on the quality of feedback provided by the teacher. Such feedback should aim to consolidate and extend learning. Once again flexibility is needed in the way that you approach these issues. Sometimes it is necessary to adopt a very 'hands on' approach, taking careful control of each phase of activity to ensure a smooth transition between activities, and thus maintaining the momentum in a lesson. On other occasions, a 'hands off' approach might be preferable as too much intervention will break up any continuity in the learning taking place. Care has to be taken to try to build on pupils' own knowledge and understanding rather than imposing your own version.

As well as mastering these 'techniques', we have to work hard to establish a climate for learning in our geography lessons. If the main goal of education is to promote the social and intellectual development of pupils, then we need to create the conditions in which this can take place. Throughout this chapter, we make frequent reference to the need to create a positive classroom atmosphere in which pupils' contributions are valued and respected. Appropriate praise and encouragement develops pupils' self-confidence and enhances their self-esteem. A phrase used elsewhere is that the 'best resource is a sensitive teacher'. It takes time and effort as well as sensitivity to build a positive rapport with pupils and develop effective working relationships. These are also the conditions needed for developing a teacher's self-confidence, the feeling that you can 'make a difference'!

If we are to 'make this difference' and help all pupils to maximise their achievements in geography, we need to establish a 'culture of success' in our lessons, a 'culture' that is based on high expectations for all pupils and that is closely associated with learning geography. This means establishing an effective classroom presence and a positive working atmosphere. Our own experience of teaching geography and of working with many student teachers is that all these skills help us to differentiate our teaching successfully. They all interact to create something that is difficult to define or describe. Rather, it is something that you feel when you have been part of a successful lesson. This is the real 'stuff' of differentiating teaching and why it is of crucial importance in facilitating intellectual development and the raising of pupil attainment.

There is also that certain something about teaching that is difficult to put your finger on, the atmosphere in those successful geography lessons. You can feel it, but cannot find the words to describe it – you had to be there! The interplay between effective teaching and successful learning has sometimes been referred as 'artistry'. The idea of artistry recognises that teaching is a highly creative and personal activity. We often return to Rubins' words to describe that feeling:

> is a striking quality to fine classrooms. Pupils are caught up in learning; excitement abounds; and playfulness and seriousness blend easily because the purposes are clear, the goals sensible and an unmistakable feeling of well being prevails.
>
> Artist teachers achieve these qualities by knowing both their subject matter and their students; by guiding the learning with deft control that itself is born out of perception, intuition and creative impulse.
>
> (Rubins 1985: v)

Summary and key points

For us, this extensive overview of pedagogy and teaching strategies has provided an opportunity to reflect on just what is involved in teaching geography. We began by drawing you away from simplistic notions of teaching styles and warning about the dangers of being influenced by dogma. What we share with Margaret Roberts (1997) is a belief not that geography teachers should operate within one particular style but that they should use a variety of styles and understand when and how particular styles are appropriate for a particular educational purpose. However, as she also acknowledges, how they teach is 'not simply a matter of efficiency or philosophy' (Roberts 1997: 247). Teachers are influenced by the contexts in which they work, the pupils that they work with and the resources available to them.

This does not mean to imply that there are strategies that cannot be used in particular school contexts. In our work as teacher educators, we rightly ban the use of the phrase 'you can't do that with the pupils in this school'. This is not to deny the influence of particular contexts on how we teach or the autonomy of teachers to decide what happens in their classrooms. Rather it is a recognition that using such a phrase conveys low expectations of what these pupils can achieve and as such is likely to reinforce a climate of underachievement. It should also be clear from this chapter that not using particular teaching strategies results in opportunities being missed for worthwhile learning to achieve certain educational goals.

Further reading

Ferretti, J. (2007) *Meeting the Needs of Your Most Able Students: Geography*, London: Routledge/GA.

The book is an essential resource for secondary geography teachers, it features comprehensive appendices with linked resources available online that feature:

- lesson plans and examples of activities
- departmental procedures and action plans
- identification strategies
- guidance on auditing provision for more able pupils.

Roberts, M. (2013) *Geography through Enquiry: Approaches to Teaching and Learning in the Secondary School*. Sheffield: Geographical Association.

Grounded in ideas from educational theory, this book offers realistic and accessible ideas on how to use geographical enquiry in teaching. It explores both the' why' and 'how' of geographical enquiry, before considering real-world examples to use in geography lessons.

5   Pupils' learning

Some pupils are better at geography than others. Some of this variation is accounted for by interest, motivation and quality of teaching, but much of it must be attributed to intellectual development.

(Leat 1997: 151)

Introduction

This chapter aims to provide you with some guidance about learning in and through geography in the belief that this will help you to do more to promote the intellectual development of your pupils. This requires you to give some attention to processes of learning, the development of learning skills and the fact that pupils learn in different ways. Your planning needs to take into account the range of abilities, aptitudes, interests, personalities, skills, cultural backgrounds and experiences of pupils within your geography classes.

Language plays an important role in the development of children's thought processes. Geography teachers need to explore ways in which work in geography can help to develop pupils' speaking, listening, writing and reading skills. We need to examine how pupils' understanding of geography can be enhanced by developing these skills. Geography has its own technical language which needs to be mastered if pupils are to progress to higher levels of understanding in the subject.

By the end of this chapter, you should be able to:

* describe different ways in which pupils learn in geography
* understand how geography can promote the intellectual development of pupils and how to recognise progress in their learning in geography
* identify ways in which geography can help to develop pupils' speaking, listening, writing and reading skills, and understand how their geographical abilities can be enhanced by developing these skills
* understand your responsibilities in ensuring that all your pupils can access the geography curriculum and feel included in lessons
* develop teaching approaches in geography that support needs and abilities of different kinds of learners.

Pupils learn in different ways

> Learning . . . that effective activity which enables the learner to draw upon previous experience to understand and evaluate the present, so as to shape future action and formulate new knowledge.
>
> (Abbott 1994)

Abbott sees learning as an active process of relating new knowledge and meaning to existing knowledge and meaning. New ideas, thoughts and skills have to be accommodated and assimilated by the learner and connections made between past, present and future learning. This learning process is influenced by the way in which the learning is to be used, and whether this learning can be effectively retrieved and applied in future situations. We also need to acknowledge that some learning may be lost or undone as well as some relearning taking place. This is a person-centred view of learning that has important implications for us as geography teachers. Romey and Elberty (1984) see the task of the 'learner-centred' geography teacher as being to help pupils 'rediscover their "geographic antennae" and to bring the geographic dimensions of all their activities and all events into conscious awareness' (p. 306).

This definition does not, however, take into account the wide variety of factors and conditions that influence this process of learning. For example, how do the characteristics of the teaching (style, skills, strategies, understanding of assessment and learning) influence the learner and the learning process? How do the characteristics of the learners (their expectations, abilities, personalities, preferred ways of learning, motivation, age, gender, social and cultural factors) influence their learning? What influence do the learning contexts (classroom, school and wider society) have on the ways in which the learning process varies for different learners? (See also Capel et al. 2005: 151.)

Teachers use different strategies to achieve different learning outcomes, to facilitate different learning styles or processes, and to respond to the variety of ways in which different pupils learn and thus you need to develop a repertoire of teaching styles and strategies. Several researchers and educationalists have tried to identify different learning styles to describe learners' preferences for particular ways of learning. David Kolb (1976) devised 'learning style inventories' to describe pupils' preferred ways of learning. This work has been adapted and developed by a number of others including Honey and Mumford (1986) and Allinson and Hayes (1996). Fielding's adaption suggested categories such as 'dynamic learners', 'imaginative learners', 'common sense learners' and 'analytic learners' (Fielding 1992). In reality, most people do not conform to just one learning style, but learn in a combination of ways. Pupils will often adopt different approaches to learning depending on the subject, the place or the time. In theory, helping pupils to develop their ability to learn in different ways is more likely to help them to become more 'effective' or better 'all-round' learners with a wide range of learning skills. However, a report by Coffield et al. in 2004 for the Learning and Skills Research Centre entitled *Learning Styles and Pedagogy in Post-16 Learning: A Systematic and Critical Review* identified difficulties associated with using tools such as inventories to make decisions about individual learners and their needs –categorising children into 'types' of learners, could, the report argues, be equally as unhelpful as categories such as 'less able' or 'gifted and talented' (see later in this chapter).

Clearly, you cannot tailor every lesson that you teach to each learning style. However, appreciating that pupils like to engage in different kinds of activities and are motivated to learn when they know that lessons will be interesting and relevant are important principles for teaching.

Did you teach each pupil today, this week, this month or even this term?

Another useful way of looking at how pupils approach learning is to distinguish between notions of surface and deep learning (Marton and Saljo 1976). This suggests that pupils adopt different approaches to learning depending on whether their intention is to remember specific information or to search for meaning. They use a surface-level approach to focus on the most important topics often using rote learning and memorisation so that they can reproduce them accurately. In contrast, pupils who adopt a deep-level approach are motivated by a desire to develop in-depth understanding and to solve problems. A third approach to learning has been identified as the 'achievement' orientation where the motivation for pupils is to achieve high grades with or without understanding. This third style may therefore reflect both surface and deep approaches to learning.

These ways of looking at how pupils approach learning suggests that some can effectively identify the most appropriate strategy for helping them make the most out of the situation or context in which they are learning. Biggs and Moore (1993) argue that this is a 'powerful' concept:

> Teachers need to realise that there is no one way in which students go about their learning; that some ways are more effective than others; and that, most important, there are things they as teachers can do to optimise the chances that students will go about learning in the most desirable ways.
>
> (p. 310)

Task 5.1 Observing pupils' learning

1   Following (or 'shadowing') a pupil or a class of pupils for a school day is a common task during your period of induction in your placement school. If possible, it would be helpful to use this 'shadowing' activity to focus on pupils' learning. In negotiation with your school mentor, identify one student to follow around school for one day, and during the day try to construct a profile of this pupil. It would be helpful if you could also observe the same pupil in a geography lesson. Build up a profile of his/her learning in geography and contrast this with his/her learning in other areas of the school curriculum.

This profile could contain the following:

- age and personal characteristics
- strengths and weaknesses as a learner
- motivation and aptitude to learning
- approaches to learning used in different subjects/lessons
- opportunities to learn in different ways.

(continued)

(continued)

The information for this profile will come from your own observations of the pupil in different lessons and from talking to the pupil about his/her learning. During the lesson observations, you could devise a few simple questions to ask the pupil about his/her perspectives on 'preferred' ways of learning.

2   When completed, you need to find an opportunity to discuss the profiles with your geography mentor or a group of other teachers. Some questions to frame these discussions might be:

- What opportunities do pupils have to learn in different ways in geography compared with other areas of the school curriculum (i.e. learning styles)?
- What opportunities do pupils have to use different approaches to learning (surface, deep, achieving) in different areas of the school curriculum?
- To what extent are pupils aware of the different ways in which they learn? Do they have opportunities to reflect on the ways in which they are learning in different subjects?
- What factors appear to influence pupils' motivation to learn during a school day?

Note of caution: When observing, try not to become too consumed by your pupils' behaviour. We accept that how a student behaves can influence how effectively they learn, and vice versa. However, behaviour is a part of the dynamics of learning, and sometimes when observing in classroom, it is possible for teachers, especially inexperienced teachers, to miss what pupils are achieving in a lesson, because they are drawn, in the first instance by a pupil's behaviour.

3   The concept of 'learning styles' is much debated and not without its critics. The 'note of caution' requires consideration. Read Coffield et al. (2004) (available at: www.voced.edu.au/content/ngv1369). With student colleagues, discuss the implications for your teaching that not all children will 'fit', for example, the learning styles identified by Fielding and others and that, when taken to extremes, the ideas of 'learning styles' can teach children that they cannot learn in certain ways.

Intellectual development through geography

At the start of this chapter, we argued that the 'essence' of being an effective geography teacher involves knowing what to do to promote the intellectual development of pupils through geography. Knowing what is appropriate for pupils of different ages and abilities to learn in geography will help us to match learning tasks to the differing abilities of pupils and to plan for progression in their learning. It should also help us to avoid teaching undemanding lessons consisting of 'busy work' in which pupils do little more than recording or transferring information.

Research into how children's thinking develops is well documented (see, for example Donaldson 1978; Burton in Capel et al. 2005). Although subject to some criticism and revision in recent times, Jean Piaget's studies in child development provide a general framework within which to structure an understanding of children's mental development. This framework, in relation to concept acquisition and logical thinking, suggests that mental development passes through a series of stages: sensori-motor, pre-operational, concrete operations and formal operations (a fully mature form of thinking).

David Leat points out that, in relation to school work, 'formal operational thinkers' have distinct advantages as they can deal with more complex relationships, formulate hypotheses and 'synthesize apparently unconnected information' (1997: 151). Leat suggests that this implies that pupils cannot successfully deal with some tasks because they are beyond their level of intellectual development. Pupils whose thinking is mainly at the concrete level tend to adopt rigid and over simplistic views, and descriptive accounts of issues. In short, they concentrate more on what happens rather than why it happens. Leat comments on how the explanations produced by concrete thinkers often reveal a 'black-and-white' view of the world:

> Having recently studied the work of a Year 7 (11–12 years of age) class on the removal of hedgerows, I was struck by the starkness of their views – this was a black-and-white issue. The common view was that it was bad for farmers to remove hedgerows because it affected wildlife, therefore it was unreasonable for farmers to do this. There was little room for compromise in their plans for the farm that they were studying.
>
> (1996: 253)

Concrete thinkers also find it difficult to hypothesise or to deal with a number of variables. This will limit their ability to develop explanations where they need to demonstrate an understanding of the relationships between several variables. These issues can have important implications for your work with Key Stage 3 pupils as this is the time when many pupils are making the transition between concrete and formal operational thinking.

Recently, one of our student teachers noted in her evaluation of work produced by Year 8 pupils in a unit of work about national parks how most pupils were only able to describe some of the impacts of tourism on the Peak District. During this unit, pupils examined data showing the number of visitors to the national park and the activities that they participated in. Photographic and video resources were used to study evidence of the impacts of tourism and the views of different interest groups were explored through a role-play activity. Finally, a simple decision-making activity was developed to encourage pupils to consider possible solutions to the problems arising from tourism.

The solutions that pupils proposed tended to be simplistic; for example, ban cars and build large landscaped car parks. Some pupils provided explanations of problems arising from some of the impacts and their possible causes, but only at a very basic level. Very few showed any appreciation of inter-relationships between factors such as landscape and environmental quality, access, amenity value, economic value, conservation and land use conflict.

Conversely, more capable pupils might be expected to produce more detailed explanations showing greater understanding of relevant geographical processes. We recall observing a Year 8 group making presentations about possible coastal protection measures for a stretch of coastline that they had been studying. The pupils displayed a number of geographical skills in the visual material that they had produced and they communicated their findings fluently. They also used appropriate vocabulary in a confident way and showed ability to recall knowledge about the places and processes studied. This included describing the way in which different coastal protection measures were designed to work.

It was clear that these pupils' had demonstrated their ability to handle a lot of detailed information and to 'replay' explanations encountered during their study of this stretch of coastline. Their learning had been enhanced by a fieldwork visit to the coastline being studied. This provided a strong visual framework or experience with which to connect future learning. However, most of them were not demonstrating a clear understanding of relationships between various factors and processes. They could describe how coastal protection measures worked but could not evaluate their effectiveness in terms of how they influenced various processes.

Judgements about the ability of these younger pupils in terms of their capacity to recall more specific detail from their knowledge of certain places and processes are clearly valid. The depth and fluency of both written and oral work, and the use of appropriate vocabulary, are frequently used as indicators of pupil's level of attainment. However, developing pupils' capacity to think and their ability to use these powers of reasoning can produce more meaningful learning (Leat 1998: 255). It therefore follows that in order to raise pupils' levels of attainment in geography, we need to consider how to develop their cognitive capacities using strategies that move them from concrete to more formal operational thinking. Strategies for teaching thinking and promoting cognitive development are discussed in Chapter 4 and at greater length in Leat (1998) and in Nicholls (2001), Ireson (in Capel et al. 2005, Unit 4.3) and Burton (in Capel et al. 2005, Unit 5.1).

Understanding pupils' learning in geography

Understanding pupil's learning is one of the key challenges facing us as teachers. Frances Slater argues that more could be done to 'engage the ability of the pupils to think abstractly and logically about their physical, economic, social and political environment' (1970). But what constitutes 'abstract thinking' as part of pupils' intellectual development in school geography?

Learning concepts

In a discussion about 'worthwhile educational objectives' in geography education, Bill Marsden (1995) presents two dimensions of learning as a basis for considering how geography teachers can plan to promote the intellectual development of their pupils. *Abilities* refer to the intellectual skills that are being developed in the learner, while *principles, concepts and exemplars* provide the cognitive frameworks within which statements of learning objectives can be made.

Understanding the nature of concepts and how conceptual learning takes place should have an important influence on curriculum planning (see Chapter 3).

If conceptual understanding is necessary for effective learning and problem-solving, then this suggests that our aim in teaching a subject will be to help children gain an understanding of those concepts which are fundamental to the field of study.

(Naish 1982: 47)

Marsden (1995) uses the common elements identified in the cognitive schemes of Bloom, Gagne and Ausubel to propose a 'four-fold division' of the abilities dimension (see Box 2.2). This classification of objectives provides us with a helpful framework that can be used both to assist with curriculum planning and to evaluate the way in which learning through geography can contribute to pupils' intellectual development. For more about Bloom, Gagne and Ausubel, see Capel et al. 2005.

Principles, concepts and *exemplars* form what Marsden calls the 'raw materials' of the intellectual processes described above under the heading of 'abilities'. He argues that they represent higher levels of generality and thus provide 'the most convenient and cogent structures for curriculum planning' (Marsden 1995: 67). They can help teachers to select content because, as Marsden points out, they are 'derived from the structure of knowledge itself' (Marsden 1995: 67). Principles or *key ideas*, as defined earlier, involve the linking of two or more concepts. They are often used to provide a list of ideas which can be used to plan the objectives that form the basis of a curriculum unit.

Box 5.1 The abilities dimension

Recall   is the process of remembering and is assessed by asking questions requiring recall of memorised material.

Comprehension   is understanding or meaningful learning.

Problem-solving   involves application, analysis and, to some extent, synthesis and evaluation. This ability is commonly associated with enquiry-based learning.

Creativity   is a very broad category emphasising the ability to use a range of principles, concepts and strategies to produce learning outcomes that may be unique and imaginative. The focus is, therefore, as much on the strategies used to facilitate this learning as on the content of the learning. Developing pupils' ability to use problem-solving skills and creativity are crucial if teachers are to help pupils to become autonomous learners.

(*Source:* Marsden 1995: 67)

Developing pupils' thinking through geography resulted in some consideration being given to the idea of concept elaboration. Concept elaboration, based on the work of Charles Reigeluth (1979), proposes that for effective learning to take place pupils' conceptual development moves from understanding simple concepts through to understanding more complex concepts via a process of 'elaboration'. Leat (1997) argues that school geography revolves around a relatively small number of important concepts (see Chapter 3 for more on planning with concepts) and contends that teaching programmes should aim to make these concepts 'visible' and 'potentially transferable', thus elaborating their meaning to pupils over time. Elaboration refers to a process whereby the teacher:

- presents an overview of simplest and most fundamental ideas
- adds complexity to one aspect
- reviews the overview and demonstrates the relationships to the details
- provides additional elaboration of details
- provides additional summary and synthesis.

It is easier to imagine this process as a zoom lens taking a wide-angled view of an idea, zooming in on one piece of detail and exploring it carefully, before zooming out to the big picture again and assimilating the detail into the bigger picture. If we take 'virtual water' as our big idea – you might introduce the idea of water being embedded into food we consume and that this process of water consumption is having global consequences, some good and some bad, before then elaborating on an aspect of virtual water by, for example zooming in on the idea that we consume different foods with distinctive water footprints (see Water Footprint Network for more) and that where these foods are grow and consumed are different. These details can then be assimilated into the big idea – virtual water and global consumption – before exploring further concepts around virtual water and consumption, by for example, considering the threat of 'water wars and the concept of river-basin sharing as the scramble for fresh water intensifies' (see Allen 2011; Swain 2001). The 'zoom' process enables the smaller, more finely grained concepts to continually elaborate on the 'big', more complex concept. It is through this process of 'elaboration' that concepts become powerful and that higher cognitive skills such as explaining, analysing, synthesising and evaluating can be developed. Teachers' subject knowledge has a significant role to play in this process of concept elaboration, for without such knowledge it is difficult to judge what, when and how to 'elaborate' on the concepts being learned.

Slinger (2011) contends that for new conceptual understanding to develop, pupils need opportunities to rework prior understanding. He argues that this can happen in three ways:

1 Differentiation – an existing concept may be differentiated into two or more new concepts. For example, differentiating causes of climate change into natural and anthropogenic causes might quite fundamentally transform the way a student thinks about climate change as they start to balance the relative consequences of each.
2 Coalescence – two existing concepts may be collapsed into one single concept as students understand that some concepts can be 'interdefined'. For example, in the context of studying development, powerlessness and exclusion may be two concepts used to understand groups of people on the margins of a society whereby powerlessness is the effect of exclusion from economic, political, cultural and social processes.
3 Redefinition – concepts can be redefined when considered in terms of relationships as opposed to key properties. For example, a place can be considered as a point in a map, a particular spatial location, or a place can be considered in the context of its relationships – its interconnectedness, its interdependencies, its processes and networks.

(Adapted from Slinger 2011, *Threshold Concepts in Secondary Geography Education*)

Brooks (2013) argues that generally teachers act as a 'conduit' of geographical knowledge, bringing 'outside concepts to the student' (p. 82). Gergen (2001 cited in Brooks 2013) articulates this as an 'exogenic' view of knowledge, namely knowledge that is external to the student. However, there is another highly significant but different view which comes from pupils themselves. Drawing on the work of Hopwood (2004, 2011), Brooks explains the 'endogenic' view of knowledge, as being knowledge developed from within, that is then used by pupils to make sense of the geography presented to them. What this distinction reminds us of is that while we may plan and teach geography in particular ways to bring about particular understandings, failure to take account of pupils' inner conceptual constructions could leave the geography we teach completely out of kilter with what students learn. Slinger (2011) argues that developing more complex conceptual understanding in pupils will stall when students encounter 'troublesome knowledge', namely knowledge that is inert (pupils use it inside the classroom , but not necessarily outside) and/or knowledge that is alien (knowledge that conflicts with students' existing knowledge, such as that brought in from outside school). This links to Thompson's (2002) metaphor of the 'virtual schoolbag', an expression for the knowledge and understanding that students 'bring in' to school from their lives and experiences outside. Thompson and Hall (2008) argue that the personal and community aspects of students' lives, their social and cultural capital is often ignored by teachers in favour of official, or authorised, versions of knowledge. Yet, they contend, it is these more localised knowledges, that offer teachers and pupils the opportunity to bridge the gap between young people and the more official knowledge of the school curriculum (see Chapter 1 for further elaboration of knowledge and school geography).

Ghaye and Robinson (1989) argue that teachers need to develop ways of discovering and understanding pupils' 'structures of thought'. They suggest that concept maps can help us to learn something about the cognitive processes associated with the act of 'constructing meanings'. Leat and Chandler (1996) believe that concept maps have great potential to support pupils' cognitive development by providing 'powerful visual organisers of information' and encouraging them to 'access' their existing knowledge of a subject. In recommending the use of concept mapping in geography teaching, they ask:

> If you were to be offered a teaching strategy that makes learning more meaningful for pupils, improves understanding, helps reveal misconceptions, reduces anxiety in pupils and helps teachers understand their subject matter, ought you to be interested?
>
> (Leat and Chandler 1996: 108)

Leat and Chandler argue that as every concept depends on others for meaning 'the number and quality of connections made between disparate pieces of information' has potential to deepen understanding. They suggest, for example, that the concept of cause and effect, provides a useful way of starting to explore the potential of concept mapping as it is possible to illustrate relationships between a variety of factors. Figure 5.1 shows an example of a concept map produced by a Year 10 pupil to summarise her understanding of problems experienced by national parks.

Concept mapping is a flexible strategy that can be used to serve different purposes. Its potential to provide a good overview means that it can be used at the end of a unit of work to provide a summary or at the beginning to access pupils' existing knowledge and provide

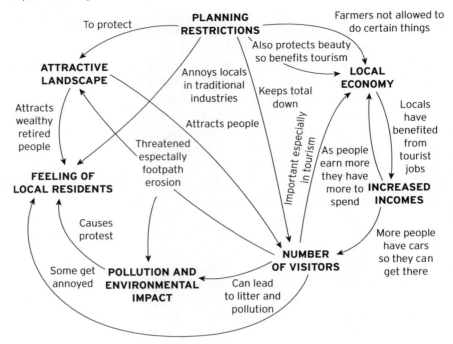

Figure 5.1 A concept map produced by an able Year 10 pupil to show her understanding of problems in national parks in England and Wales

(*Source:* Leat and Chandler 1996: 108)

an advance organiser for the enquiry ahead. This is particularly useful at GCSE and A-level if pupils have encountered some of the concepts and processes at a younger age. It can also be an effective way of preparing pupils for written work, particularly when this work is to be used to reveal the depth of their understanding.

Task 5.2 Conceptual learning in geography

A   Using concept maps in planning:

1   Choose one of the topics listed below and write a list of the concepts you would expect pupils to learn about in this topic:

- The impacts of river flooding
- Urban decline
- Factors affecting coastal processes
- The causes and consequence of a volcanic eruption.

2   Classify your concepts into concrete and abstract concepts and then attempt to arrange them hierarchically.

3   Now try to draw a concept map for your chosen topic and consider how this map could now help you to plan a unit of work.

B   Using concept maps in teaching:

1   Identify a topic that you are teaching where there would be an opportunity to explore pupils 'conceptual learning through the use of concept maps.

2   Prepare a concept mapping activity for pupils studying this topic.

3   Carefully analyse the concept maps produced by the pupils. Is it possible to identify different levels of conceptual learning achieved by pupils? You might try to use these concept maps to classify the degree to which particular concepts appear to have been understood by the pupils.

4   To what extent do these concept maps help you to evaluate the effectiveness of the teaching and learning activities in the unit of work for facilitating conceptual learning?

Understanding issues and approaches in pupils' concept acquisition is crucial if pupils are to make progress in geography. Whilst 'planning for progression' is considered in Chapter 3, it is important to constantly ask yourself: 'What does it look like to get better at geography?', 'What do I need to understand about the relationship between the conceptual structure of the discipline and the conceptual structure of school geography – are they the same or do they overlap or are the completely different?', 'How do I know whether pupils' have understood a concept/group of concepts – what does this 'look' like?'

Spatial thinking and graphicacy

The work of geographers like Peter Jackson's *Maps of Meaning* (1989), Ed Soja's *Post Modern Geographies* (1989), Doreen Massey's *For Space* (2005), and many others, tell us that space is an important idea in academic geography which has long been a topic of popular debate; a highly complex, much contested concept demanding serious attention.

In this section, we consider the ideas of developing pupils' spatial thinking as a fundamental underpinning of pupils' learning in geography. Perhaps too often in schools, the 'spatial' element of geographical understanding gets reduced to a map skills' unit at the beginning of Year 7, and the occasional use of an atlas or an Ordnance Survey (OS) map further up the school. We would argue that it is almost impossible to teach a geography lesson without reference to a map or some sort of or spatial representation somewhere in the learning mix!

There is no doubt that spatial thinking is important in life – it is a form of literacy and so learning how to read and to use maps and understanding maps as representations is a very distinctive part of learning geography. Take, for instance, the iconic example of John Snow's 1855 map of the Soho cholera outbreak. It is perhaps the earliest example of a map being used to plot data and to analyse the patterns – in this case the incidences of cholera in relation to the source of water in the neighbourhood. Although the science of the water-borne disease was not yet understood, the spatial association was strong enough for the water pump's handle to be removed – with dramatic results.

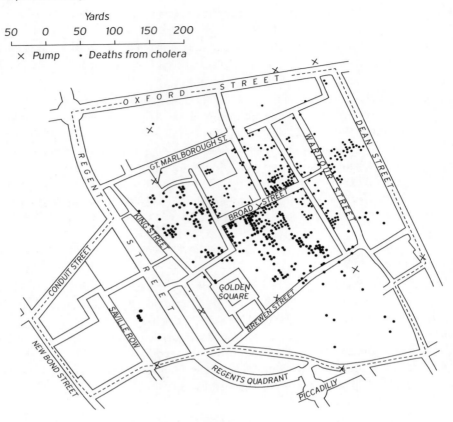

Figure 5.2 John Snow's 1855 map of the Soho cholera outbreak

Thus, to teach geography in secondary schools without including a spatial science element - and, of course, GIS explicitly appears on the National Curriculum and in examination criteria at GCSE and A-level - would be perverse. This is not to say that geography is 'the' spatial science: spatial thinking is taught in mathematics and science too. Nor is it to say that that teaching spatial literacy (with or without GIS) is the be-all-and-end-all of geography: the subject is about other forms of relational understanding too.

What is spatial thinking?

Given how important spatial thinking is, it is perhaps somewhat surprising, if not a little perplexing, how shaky is our grasp of what precisely we mean by the term. To be sure, we can readily point to ideas such as location, distribution, and patterns – the key features of Dr Snow's map. But how and what do we teach in order to enhance and develop spatial thinking abilities in young people? Are there sequences we should follow as teachers? Are some maps more complex or less accessible than others? Is there an identifiable progression (or hierarchy) of spatial thinking skills and concepts that students need to develop gradually? Or do students simply get better at spatial thinking with practice using as big a variety of opportunities and examples as possible?

There has been a growing interest in such questions, especially in the USA where the National Research Council has sponsored a major report on 'Learning to Think Spatially' (Downs and DeSouza 2006) and geography educationists such as Gersmehl and Gersmehl (2006) have sought to identify a 'neurologically defensible' list of spatial thinking skills (see Manning 2014 for a summary). The latter is a blatant attempt to bolster the notion of spatial science with exciting – and somewhat dazzling – medical developments in imaging and understanding of brain function. It is unclear to us what benefits accrue to geography teachers from knowing that different mental functions are performed in different parts of the brain. It is an educational red herring and the consequence of geographers fighting for respectability and curriculum space in time of curriculum competition.

The Association of American Geographers (AAG), in their 'Teachers' Guide to Modern Geography' (www.aag.org/tgmg) identifies eight 'fundamental' spatial thinking skills. Introducing these to a cross curricular audience, the AAG writes:

> Spatial Thinking Skills are an important set of competencies for examining the world around us. These skills enable the geographer to visualize and analyze spatial relationships between objects, such as location, distance, direction, shape and pattern. Any issue or event can be viewed spatially: the spread of Disease, earthquake activity, trade, immigration, and so forth . . .

Eight fundamental spatial thinking skills are listed in Table 5.1.

It is interesting that the AAG overtly present this thinking to an interdisciplinary audience. However, Gersmehl and Gersmehl conclude that it is 'a useful foundation for the kind of

Table 5.1 Spatial thinking skills

Skill	Definition	Example
Comparison	Comparing one place with another	Rainfall, incomes, industry (etc.)
Aura	Describing the influence that a place can have on neighbouring locations	Pollution from a factory, noise from an airport, property values near a park
Region	Drawing a line around places that share similar characteristics or are functionally linked	A biome, an agricultural region, an urban neighbourhood, a city region
Transition	Describing what happens between two places/regions with known (and different) conditions	Do features or conditions change abruptly or gradually as in the case of an 'ecotone'?
Analogy	Finding places on different continents that have similar positions and therefore similar conditions	Mediterranean climates or hot deserts . . . , subduction zones, inner urban zones, deltas, 'rust belt' industrial zones
Hierarchy	Identifying a spatial hierarchy and how 'nested' features relate to each other	River networks, distribution hierarchies and 'central place theory', political relations (e.g. town, county, nation)
Pattern	Describing the distribution of features or conditions	Evenly or unevenly spaced, clusters, strings, core-periphery

Adapted from aag.org/tgmg [accessed 28 May 2014]

discussion that geographers must undertake [to] help spatial thinking become more prominent in the [geography curriculum]' (2006: 25). We tend to agree with this and the ideas in the left-hand column in the table may become useful terms that we encourage students to use fluently to express their geographical thinking, especially when using and interpreting maps and GIS images.

Spatial thinking forms a major part of graphicacy, which also includes the interpretation of photographs and other forms of graphic communication (Boardman 1983). Pupils' spatial abilities are associated with their understanding of 'spatial location, spatial distribution and spatial relations' (Catling 1978). These spatial abilities develop with the cognitive growth of children. For example, in the earlier stages of their development, children move from 'action in space' to 'perceptions of space' to 'conceptions about space' (Marsden 1995: 78). Thus, spatial conceptualisation makes an important contribution to pupils' intellectual development.

Mental maps, in other words maps that people carry around in their minds, are often seen as a useful way of finding out about children's map-drawing abilities and spatial cognition (Boardman 1987, 1989). Research into the ability of children to represent their spatial environment by drawing mental maps has revealed that although they tend to show more information on their maps as they grow older, their learning process does not follow a simple linear progression (Matthews 1984). Children learn about different environments in different ways. Consequently, although pupils' mapping ability and accuracy improve as they get older, they do not acquire these skills in a straightforward way.

In order to learn about the spatial in geography, it is helpful to categorise the skills pupils need to develop. Paul Weeden expresses these skills as:

- using maps – relating features on a map directly to features in the landscape
- making maps – encoding information in map form
- reading maps – decoding successfully the element of map language
- interpreting maps – being able to relate prior geographical knowledge to the features and patterns observed on the map.

(Weeden 1997: 169)

Gerber and Wilson (1984) proposed four essential properties of maps that should form the basis of any programme for developing map-work skills in order to develop spatial cognition:

- plan view (perspective and relief)
- arrangement (location, direction and orientation)
- proportion (scale, distance and selection)
- map language (signs, symbols, words and numbers).

Developing pupils' understanding of each of these properties poses different challenges for geography teachers. Often we need to focus on each one individually before integrating them with other map skills in learning activities that require pupils to apply these skills and their knowledge of geography. For example, until pupils have understood how contours are used to represent relief on a map, they are unlikely to be able to interpret landscape features. Indeed, it is usually the case that they reach higher levels of achievement when the different elements of maps are introduced to them separately (Boardman 1989). Gerber (1981) also observes how pupils seem to be able to handle one element of a map at a time, but often experience difficulty when dealing with several elements together.

Location: Mapping enables places, objects and events to be located in space. Using grid references to locate points on maps is a skill that builds on children's ability to draw and read graphs in mathematics. Techniques used by primary school teachers to help children learn about co-ordinates, can help us understand how to achieve a progressive development of the skills needed to use grid references because only when these principles have been grasped is it possible to move on to using six-figure grid references to locate points more precisely within grid squares.

Direction: Pupils should learn how to describe direction using the points of the compass and encouraged to use the correct terminology throughout their geographical work. It is important to avoid potential confusion by emphasising that wind direction refers to the direction from which winds blow, again with practical examples.

Scale: The concept of *scale* is challenging for some pupils as it requires them to not only measure distances accurately, but also to understand perspective and proportion. Highly structured tasks requiring pupils to use different scales in small steps are needed, particularly when pupils are experiencing difficulties. It is also very important to have maps of the same area at different scales for pupils to compare and to use to make similar measurements. Using scaled plans of the school and maps of the local area can be helpful as pupils are able to see the features that they are measuring.

Route following: Once pupils have learnt the skills needed to use grid references and scale, to describe direction and become familiar with the more common map-work skills, It is possible to devise some imaginative activities that require pupils to use these skills to follow routes or plan journeys such as treasure hunts, mystery tours and fugitive hunts.

Contours: The use of *contours* to show height, slope and relief is another concept that pupils often experience difficulty with. If pupils are to be able to interpret the physical landscape shown on topographical maps, they must be able to identify and understand contour patterns. This is therefore a skill that needs regular revisiting to reinforce and progress pupils' understanding and use of the skill.

When pupils have grasped the basic principles relating the space of contours to the height and slope of land, it is possible to move on to examine common contour patterns and landforms. Pupils should learn how to identify specific landscape components (e.g. hills, valleys, ridges and spurs) before trying to interpret some of the larger-scale features associated with particular types of scenery (e.g. limestone, glaciation).

Cross-section: For younger pupils, it is usually a good idea to start developing this understanding with a simplified contour pattern with a line marked on it along which the cross-section is to be drawn. The horizontal and vertical scales of the cross-section could be marked on graph paper and photocopied so that pupils can concentrate on the steps needed to transform the contours on to the section. You may also find it helpful to produce a resource sheet showing the different stages in the production of a cross-section.

When moving on to draw cross-sections directly from Ordnance Survey maps, it is a good idea to get pupils to first concentrate only on the bolder contours. When drawing their own axes for the cross-section on graph paper, pupils need to be shown how to avoid excessive vertical exaggeration in the scales. Boardman (1996) reminds us that a vertical:horizontal scale ratio of 5:1 is normally accepted as the maximum exaggeration to avoid turning a gently undulating landscape into one mountainous in appearance.

Task 5.3 Map-work skills

A   Arrange to observe a lesson (or lessons) in which pupils are being taught how to use one specific map-work skill (e.g. the use of grid references).

In consultation with the class teacher, identify a small number of pupils (maximum of five) across the range of ability in the class that you will focus on for the purpose of this activity. If pupils are grouped according to ability, it would be helpful to observe different classes learning the same skill.

During the lesson(s), find opportunities to observe each of the pupils working on the tasks set by the teacher. Make a note of which aspects of the tasks each pupil succeeded with, and any with which they experienced difficulties.

- Outline the strategies used by the teacher.
- Summarise the problems and successes experienced by the pupils.
- From your observations during the lesson and by studying the work produced by the pupils, evaluate the effectiveness of the resources and strategies used to teach this particular map-work skill.
- How were the resources and strategies adapted for pupils of different abilities? In what ways could these resources and strategies have been developed further?

B   Evaluate 2–3 schemes of work in your school order to establish the range of maps pupils are using in geography lessons and the different ways they are expected to use them – are they used to establish the location of places, or are pupils using maps in a range of ways – if so how?

C   Talk to pupils about their understanding of maps – prepare 4–5 questions to use to talk to pupils about what they think maps are and what they could be used for, how do they/their family use maps in their daily life? What do they find difficult about maps, what do they enjoy about using maps?

Although it is possible to develop pupils' skills of graphicacy in a progressive way, the learning of these skills is 'seldom linear', and there is 'no one way of setting out the objectives of map learning' (Bailey and Fox 1986: 114). It is important that you are aware of the different aspects of map understanding and use so that you can identify opportunities to introduce and develop them in your teaching. For example, in relation to scale, between the ages of 11 and 14 pupils should learn how to measure distances and convert measurements using scale. They should have opportunities to draw plans to scale, to compare maps at different scales and to describe routes giving distances and directions using information shown on maps.

Between 14 and 16 years of age, pupils might learn how to carry out a range of calculations using scale including gradients, the vertical exaggeration of cross-sections and the approximate areas of landscape features shown on maps. Post-16, scale might be used to carry out more complex calculations such as drainage densities and bifurcation ratios or to delimit areas such as that of a drainage basin.

Alongside developing the skills we associate with *using* maps in geography, David Wright (2000) argues that pupils also need to develop a critical understanding of maps as representations. Achieving this requires teachers to themselves understand different map projections, why they exist and what interests they serve, and to confidently use these different projections, with different centres (Pacific-centred, North Pole-centred and so on) in order to help pupils to understand flat-maps as distortions of the globe.

> The ideal outcome is a school with students who question any world map they see, and who are able to recognise the main qualities and limitations of any world map.
>
> (p. 32)

The significance of understanding maps as representations comes starkly into view when we consider the array of complex cartographical images of places, events and people that now appear in the media. Reporting on local, national and global events in the news is now frequently supported by detailed cartographic images (of, for example, shifting voting patterns in a general election, or reports of international sporting events), and are now coupled with, for example, data on athletic performance, environmental conditions for competitions and maps of venues in relation to local residential populations, resources and infrastructures. In this context, 'maps' – often coupled with satellite images – take on a whole new meaning and therefore require new levels of spatial understanding as spatial relationships are represented in more visual ways. In an article in *Teaching Geography*, Professor Danny Dorling (2012) talks about 'normal maps' that now look strange, and 'no-longer-so-strange-maps' that provide new insights into people and places because of technology-enabled enabled representations. He says:

> When I look at a 'normal' map today I see a strange map. I see a map about places where people almost always don't live. I see almost all human life squeezed into a tiny part of the paper or screen. I see the people living in cities forgotten and imaginations cluttered and confused by images that don't give everyone equal space and equal representation. We are unlikely to see things in much the same ways as our parents did; and the next generation will see things differently to us. On our screens, on our phones, in our textbooks and magazines, our images of the world are changing faster than the world is itself. This is because we are rapidly evolving to think, collectively, differently, to visualize better, and to accept conformity less meekly.
>
> (p. 98)

These' no-longer-so-strange maps' are amazing, beautiful, intriguing and challenging in both what and how they represent geographical information. Described as 're-projections of the world' (Henning 2010) websites such as Worldmapper (available at www.worldmapper. org) provides access to 696 equal area cartograms where pupils and teachers can access, analyse and compare a vast range of 're-projected' maps covering recognisable subjects such as 'Mortality rates', through to 'Radio and TV usage' or even 'Molluscs at risk'. What maps such as these can do is support pupils' engagement with the idea of maps as tools for representing all kinds of data and start to raise questions about spatial patterns, inequalities, relationships and consequences. For example, the 'Television sets in use' map in Worldmapper reveals parts of the world where people have little or no access to television. This raises questions which are less about access to entertainment, and more about peoples' access to news and information. This map can be compared to others such as 'Radio use' or 'Access to electricity' to start to create a more complex picture of resource availability and lead to considerations of the possible consequences for individuals and communities who cannot access or who are denied access to often taken-for-granted resources.

Technology-enabled mapping also comes in conjunction with the world of social media. NeoGeography (Goodchild 2009; Parkinson 2013; Fargher 2013) uses online tools and publically sourced data to create maps of startling precision. For example, 'citizen mappers' (members of a local community using hand-held devices to report what Fargher (2013) calls, 'indigenous data') have contributed to detailed mapping of the Kibera shanty town enabling better-informed decisions to be made regarding resource distribution and infrastructure development. A similar process, of gathering publically generated data from, for example, tweets, enabled both individuals and organisations such as Crisis Mappers UK and Humanitarian Open Street Map to support disaster relief agencies in pinpointing where to target medical and practical support following natural disasters such as the Haiti earthquake in 2010 and Typhoon Haiyan in the Philippines in 2013 (Radio 4 *'Mapping the Planet'*, broadcast Sunday 23 February 2014).

The concept of 'citizen mappers' takes us beyond map reading and into the realms of map making and in ways that are well within the reach of the young people we teach. Using geographic information (GI) in this way is changing the way we conceptualise spaces and throws into new relief how we come to understand key geographical concepts, not just space, but scale, time and interconnections.

Time is an important concept to consider in relation to developing spatial thinking, especially in the context of new technologies. Data can be downloaded and used 'almost' in real time and it would be easy to assume, therefore, that there is a validity to the 'real-time' world of geographic information. However, writing about the use of webcams and the opportunities they offer in enabling pupils to see and appreciate distant places in real time, Mitchell raises some significant questions. He comments on:

> [the] possible simplification of place histories and the development of place, people and culture through the use. It could be that pupils seeing the world with the immediacy of a webcam, jumping from one place to another, seeing those places in real time are learning to think of an instantaneous world, a two dimensional, horizontal world without the depth of a complex history of development over time
>
> (Mitchell 2007, available at file:///C:/Users/user/Downloads/ GA_GeogEdArticle2%20(1).pdf)lping

Developing pupils spatial thinking in ways described in Figure 5.1 should help to guard against the simplification of places and the possible superficiality in learning that would ensue, as suggested by Mitchell and others. However, as we have seen, developing spatial thinking is taking on new layers of complexity as technology enabled mapping is literally changing the shape of maps as we know them, enabling the construction of Dorling's 'no-longer-so-strange' maps, and facilitating the use of 'citizen data' via social media to construct new 'in the moment' maps. Spatial thinking can help pupils make sense of these developments; however, it is probable that pupils will also need to call on other ways of in order to unravel the complexities evident in new ways of presenting data and constructing maps.

Numeracy in geography

An important set of skills that go a long way to enabling pupils to make sense of data and maps are numeracy skills. Numeracy has always been a part of geography, from the work of Aristotle (384–322 BC), who drew on scientific methods to demonstrated that the earth was shaped like a sphere, Eratosthenes (circa 276–194 BC) who calculate the equatorial circumference of the earth to be 40,233 kilometres (just 161 kilometres more than that calculated by satellite technology, which has computed the circumference to be 40,072 kilometres) and Ptolemy's developed of the concepts of geographical latitude and longitude.

The quantitative revolution in academic geography in the 1950s soon found its way into school geography cementing into the fabric of the school discipline a requirement to be both numerate as well as literate in order to 'think like a geographer'. The National Numeracy Strategy (DfES 2000) identified geography as an important subject through which to develop pupils' data-handling skills, map skills such as co-ordinates, as well as the use of and application of calculation skills to real-world situations.

The focus on numeracy has intensified more recently as a result of the UK's performance in 2012 international PISA tests (Programme for International Students Assessment). In these tests, the UK ranked 26th out of the 65 participating countries and economies in mathematics, meaning that there had been little improvement since the 2009 tests (OECD 2012). Despite perceived flaws in the tests, the consequence was a flurry of activity at a policy level, with subsequent curriculum change in England placing increased emphasis on numeracy in all subjects.

There is an important distinction to draw at this point – the priority is not for geography to contribute to the mathematics curriculum, but that being numerically literate enables pupils to get underneath some of geography's big ideas; numeracy contributes to a deeper more critical geographical understanding.

Drawing on the work of Jerome Bruner, Roberts (2013) reminds us of the difficulties many pupils face with numeracy. When working with numbers, essentially, concepts are being represented in symbolic form and symbolic representation is, according to Bruner, the most challenging form of representation. This also means that tables of data and abstract statistics are more difficult for pupils to understand than visual representation of data on maps and graphs. It is also probable that data collected through, for example fieldwork, will have more meaning for pupils because of their involvement in the process, although this data will still need to be processed and some pupils will still lack confidence in their numerical skills.

Numbers can be used to present pupils with all sorts of interesting challenges and develop their critical thinking skills. Numerical data can be used for what Roberts (2013) calls 'intelligent guesswork' where pupils have to apply their existing geographical knowledge to make informed guesses of, for example, a selection of countries average life expectancy at birth. Pupils then have to select the three top and the three bottom countries in terms of greatest and lowest life expectancy and explain and justify their ideas; talking about the factors that they think influence life expectancy in different places requires them to draw different geographical concepts such as health and resource distribution, quality of life and employment patterns, into their justification for the data they have chosen. It is important here to probe their thinking and to encourage students to give full justifications. They then compare their 'guesses' with actual data (the most up-to-date data is important here, for example from the World Health Organisation). The task is then debriefed, encouraging students to consider with which countries their 'intelligent guesses' were most accurate and

Table 5.2 The data-handling cycle and associated questions

Specify the problem and plan	What interests me? What area of geography am I focusing in on?
	How do I phrase an enquiry question?
	How 'doable' is my idea?
	What are my time frames?
	What do I think I need to know that I don't already know in order to carry out my enquiry?
Collect data from a variety of source	Quantitative data and/or qualitative data. How do these different forms of data complement each other?
	How much data to collect? Am I collecting the right data to address my problem?
	How reliable/viable are different sources?
	Are there any health and safety issues if conducting fieldwork?
	How to record data reliably/consistently?
Process and represent the data	How much data do I have?
	Can I use technology to process my data?
	What mathematical/statistical techniques can I use to analyse my data?
	Am I using the right techniques to process my data?
	What kind of cartographical, graphical and statistical representations should I use to present the data I have? Are they the best forms of representation?
Interpret and discuss the data	What does my data mean?
	What patterns and anomalies can I see in my data?
	How does my data relate to my initial problem/question?
	Was my data reliable?
	How does my data relate to bigger concepts, theories and models in geography?

(*Source:* Adapted from Brooks 2006: 139)

why they think this was so? Where were the major inaccuracies and why? Which data sets surprised them and why? A task such as this doesn't require students to manipulate data, but it does challenge them to work with big numbers, to use data and to question data (see Roberts 2013 for a full explanation of this activity).

Linking data processing to geographical enquiry, Brooks (2006) discusses the 'data-handling cycle', a simple representation of the stages of data processing that students will need to engage with if they are to impose a degree of *geographical* understanding on data. Each stage in the cycle raises important questions for geography teachers to consider.

Task 5.4 Developing numeracy skills

When it comes to developing numeracy skills, geography has much to contribute. As you embark on teaching, it is important to get a clear sense of what this means.

A   For a school in which you are placed, carefully review the GCSE and A-level specification being taught. In particular, focus on the numeracy requirements of each of the specifications and keep notes of the range of numeracy skills that pupils will need to be taught. What do you notice about progression in numeracy skills between GCSE and A-level geography? What are the implications of your findings for teaching numeracy in geography at Key Stage 3?
B   Look at a GCSE and A-level examination paper. Which numeracy skills are pupils required to use in order to be successful?
C   Now look at your school's key Stage 3 curriculum. Where and how are numeracy skills developed in geography at this stage? Is there a sufficient foundation for pupils to go on to manage the numeracy requirements of GCSE?

Language, literacy and learning in geography

Being 'literate' has, until relatively recently, been seen in quite technical terms, namely the ability to read and write. However, it is now understood that 'being literate' is laden with values and can in fact be conceived of as ideological in the sense that being literate is framed by a society's culture and power structures, and that language cannot be separated from the society in which it is used and produced (Morgan and Lambert 2005).

Morgan and Lambert (2005) argue that literacy is political because of the value that society places on certain text, forms of writing and ways of speaking, over others. They go on to consider three distinct types of literacy and their contribution to geographical education: functional literacy, cultural literacy and critical literacy. Functional literacy is the ability to read and write, namely the decoding of text into speech and thought, and the encoding of speech and though into written text. Cultural literacy, they argue, involves educating children in particular ways of seeing the world; it requires an acceptance of the status quo and tends to involve pupils in producing 'right answers'. Critical literacy serves a very different purpose as summarised by Moor (2000: 87, cited in Morgan and Lambert 2005: 106).

We might say that whereas functional and cultural literacy seek to help the student to succeed within an unchanged society, critical literacy has in mind a different educational agenda, which is aimed at changing society itself in ways that will help everyone to succeed.

Harrison (2004) argues that developing critical literacy is crucial because of the ways that language practices are increasingly:

determining, reproducing and sustaining the power relations that dominate and control our society, and since many of those language practices operate in ways that are implicit rather than explicit, it becomes a matter of great importance to be able to locate, identify and critique those practices.

(p. 152)

We can see that critical literacy is not functional literacy', but the two support each other and developing pupils' critical language awareness, as suggested above, opens up for scrutiny some of the values and assumptions that underpin society. Understanding something of the relationship between language and learning and the role played by language in the development of children's thought means that teachers can plan and teach in ways that extend pupils' geographical understanding beyond the acquisition of concrete concepts and help them to engage with more abstract ideas (Graves 1975) building their capacity to appreciate the interconnectedness of abstract ideas, see the world in more complex ways and question and challenge the status quo. Teachers need to be ever mindful of the language they select to use, the ways they present ideas to students, both in written and verbal forms, and their expectations of their students: are you using literacy functionally, culturally or critically?

Graham Butt reminds us that the 'action of learning is closely associated with that of comprehending and using different forms of language' (Butt 1997: 154). Frances Slater (1989) describes the two distinct functions of language use in geography lessons as being to communicate what has been learnt and is known as well as being part of the activity of learning. The latter emphasises the importance of 'talking, reading and writing to learn' (Roberts 1986; Hewlett 2006).

Pupils use language in a range of ways in order to learn geography. They:

- use geographical vocabulary appropriately
- describe and compare different phenomena effectively
- structure explanations well, both orally and in writing
- develop their oral skills in order to engage in debate, discussions, presentations and convey their ideas to a range of audiences
- express ideas and hypotheses tentatively orally, and in writing
- synthesise information and ideas and write accurately and appropriately to express understanding and present information and imaginative ideas
- listen attentively in order to empathise with different perspectives and experiences and so sensitively understand the views of other.

(Adapted from Lewis 2005)

Developing pupils' literacy skills helps their learning in geography in a number of ways:

- Pupils need vocabulary, expression and organisational control to cope with the cognitive demands of the subject.
- Reading enables pupils to learn from sources beyond their immediate experience.
- Writing helps to sustain order and thought.
- Language enables pupils to reflect, revise and evaluate the things they do, and the things that others have said, written or done.
- Responding to higher order questions encourages the development of thinking skills and enquiry.
- Improving literacy and learning can have an impact on pupils' self-esteem, motivation and behaviour. It allows them to learn independently. It is empowering.

(DfES 2002: 1)

Geography can provide a wide range of experiences, both in the classroom and through fieldwork, in which pupils can develop their language skills. Giving attention to the use of appropriate skills can also help to enrich pupils' extensive and wide-ranging vocabulary, which needs to be developed if pupils are to gain a sound understanding of the subject. Enabling pupils to write effectively and talk confidently about their work helps them to understand ideas and make connections. Reading and listening are necessary for access to information and ideas from a range of sources, and can thus extend and consolidate their knowledge and understanding.

Talk

Talk has always been one of the essential tools of teaching, and the best teachers use it with precision and flair. But talk is much more than an aid to effective teaching. Children, we know, need to talk, and to experience a rich diet of spoken language, in order to think and learn.

(Alexander 2011: 9)

Providing appropriate opportunities for pupils to talk about geography is important for developing both their language skills and their understanding of the subject. Alexander (2011) reminds us of the substantial body of evidence linking talking and learning and the significance of social interactions in enabling children to construct new meaning. Drawing on the ideas of Lev Vygotsky and the notion of learning as a social process as well as a cognitive one, Alexander presents a complex and convincing set of arguments for the power of talk, or dialogic teaching and learning, in developing pupils' cognitive ability. With talk, he argues, learning becomes less of a 'one-way linear communication, but a reciprocal process in which ideas are bounced back and forth and on that basis children take thinking forward' (p. 24). In talk, you use language to organise your thoughts and give shape to your ideas. Pupils should be given opportunities to talk in a range of contexts and for a variety of purposes in geography including, describing and explaining, negotiating and persuading, exploring and hypothesising, challenging and arguing. Carter describes the ways in which children use talk in learning to:

- engage – relate new information to existing experience and knowledge
- explore – investigate, hypothesise, speculate, question, negotiate
- transform/restructure – argue, reason, justify, consider, compare, evaluate, confirm, reassure, clarify, select, modify, plan
- present – demonstrate and convey understanding, narrate, describe
- reflect – consider and evaluate new understanding.

(Carter 1991: 2)

What we know, however, is that – too often – teacher talk dominates geography classrooms and controls the process by which communication takes place, by deciding what kind of talk is permissible, by whom and for how long (Roberts 1986; Butt 2001). Through their own talk, teachers convey important messages about what they think is important. Roberts reminds us that 'some teacher talk is highly desirable':

> It is a means of conveying excitement in the subject, of motivating pupils and of introducing pupils to the specialist language of geography which is best done in talk where meanings can be fully explored.

(Roberts 1986: 68)

Such teacher talk can be infectious (think about your own enthusiastic teachers and how they communicated this enthusiasm) and serve to capture pupils' imaginations about a topic, motivating them to want to know more. However, by tightly controlling the kind of talk taking place in a lesson, while teachers may feel more secure about how classroom events play out (they make the decisions), and they also run less of a risk of their subject knowledge being tested by discussions that take on all sorts of unpredictable twists and turns, but in restricting pupils' talk to one-word answers to closed questions or to asking technical questions such as 'What's the title', teachers severely limit the potential of talk as a means of learning. Teachers' classroom talk can either be about classroom routines, factual knowledge and their own self-importance, or it can be open discussion, exploratory and inclusive – teachers and students talking together.

It is a good idea to start with simple strategies requiring pupils to talk in pairs and ask them, in the process of talking, to keep a simple record of the ideas they generate through their talk: 'List five points about why you would locate a football stadium in this place', or 'Discuss and write down three ways this area could be improved'. The emphasis is not on the writing, but on the talking, but this way they and you can 'see' the product of their discussion, get a feel for their ideas and then use these as a basis from which to take learning forward. As you get to know students better, and as your own confidence grows, you can think of more open ways to engage students in talking in order to learn (see Chapter 4 for more).

Reading

Enquiry-based approaches to learning geography require pupils to read widely from a variety of texts and other sources of information. They need to select, compare, synthesise and evaluate information from different sources as well as use other skills to distinguish fact and opinion, and to recognise bias and objectivity in sources. Add to this the fact that geography has its own extensive vocabulary which needs to be mastered if pupils are to be able to understand and interpret what they are reading.

Developing pupils' reading ability in order to help them access and understand geographical ideas is not straightforward. In geography, there are many different forms of text that pupils have to be able to 'read':

- maps – Ordnance Survey, atlases, cartograms, mental maps
- diagrams – flow diagrams, concept maps, graphs, tables
- text – short 'chunks', newspaper articles, stories, poems, travelogues
- images – photographs, cartoons, drawings/paintings (published and their own), satellite images, video
- online text such as websites
- text written by other students – for example in peer assessment activities.

Understanding what pupils are capable of reading is important and while there are ways of assessing the 'readability' of written texts such as the SMOG Readability formula devised by Harry McLaughlin in 1969 (see www.readabilityformulas.com/smog-readability-formula.php) such tools cannot replace establishing a good overall understanding of the pupils that you teach. Their attainment levels are one source of information; however, you also need to select and use texts that will interest them, adds variety to their 'reading diet', is sufficiently challenging and is relevant to what you want to achieve. A mismatch between what you want pupils to learn and what you ask them to read will only cause confusion. Other important consideration is presentation of texts – combinations of text and supporting images, page layout, clear labelling and so on all either help or hinder pupils' access to text. Size of print is an issue for some students and for certain kinds of special-needs pupils the colour of paper on which text is printed also needs consideration. Butt (1997) quotes research demonstrating that sixth-form pupils often do not have the 'competence expected of the "implied reader"': frustration was caused by an inability to link together text and the range of illustrative material (maps, diagrams, photographs and statistics) in geography textbooks.

The development of reading skills is often neglected in geography lessons. Evidence shows that most of the reading that takes place in social studies lessons (including geography) is in short bursts of less than 30 seconds, which does not provide adequate opportunity for critical evaluation of or engagement with text (Roberts 1986, 2013). This contrasts with the continuous reading that is frequently required for homework when pupils are less likely to have any support available. Roberts argues that geography teachers can:

> help the development of reading skills firstly by being aware of the difficulties pupils have, secondly by providing a variety of reading materials, and thirdly by devising activities which enable pupils to read intensively and grapple with the meaning of what they read.
>
> (Roberts 1986: 72)

'Reading around the class' is a strategy frequently used that illustrates many of the problems highlighted by Margaret Roberts. Too often used as a control strategy, pupils are usually asked to read a short section of text in turn with the occasional intervention by the teacher, but this rarely was to improve reading skills, evaluate content or to explain meaning.

There is much you can do to help pupils develop their reading skills. Active reading strategies that require students to process text have been around for some time but, as with all learning processes, need to be handled critically. In relation to reading comprehension activities, Harrison (2004) argues that, if text is too easy, it leaves capable readers very frustrated and, if too difficult, it leaves less-confident readers demoralised and disengaged – selecting appropriate text for such tasks is difficult and requires knowledge of your pupils and your subject.

A set of strategies frequently used in many classrooms to support reading development is called DARTS – Directed Activities Related to Text. DARTs came to prominence as a result of the Schools Council Effective Use of Reading project, directed by Eric Lunzer and Keith Gardner in the 1970s and comprising two distinct categories:

- **Reconstruction DARTs** – text is altered in some way so that pupils can reconstruct it perhaps by printing it in sections on card. Sequencing and diagram completion are useful in geographical enquiry (Roberts 2003: 130–132; see also Roberts 2013)
- **Analysis and reconstruction DARTs** – the text is presented as a whole with activities designed to enable pupils to analyse the components of the text (through underlining, highlighting or labelling) and then reconstruct these components into a simpler form (in lists, tables, flow diagrams, and annotated maps and diagrams).

(*Source:* Lunzer and Gardner 1979, The Effective Use of Reading project)

A central underpinning of all DARTS activities is the social interaction that accompanies them. For example, when pupils do an activity such as completing a cloze passage (missing words activities where they insert the correct word in order to complete and make sense of a sentence/paragraph), the process generally does little to *develop* their reading if completed on their own; the task merely confirms what they already know – they can either do it or they can't. However, if such a task is completed with another student, then together they interrogate the text, discuss which word(s) to use and why and come to an understanding of the text as a whole. This more dialogic process gives pupils the opportunity to really scrutinise a piece of text and develop their abilities to become, what Harrison (2004) terms 'thoughtful readers'.

As indicated earlier, *what* we ask pupils to read can be crucial to them being prepared to do any reading at all. Is it short snippets from a textbook, more sustained reading from a newspaper article, reading text from a website or, at worst, reading from PowerPoint slides prepared by the teacher? What other text-based sources can also be used to access geographical ideas?

Novels, travelogues, plays and poems can be great for presenting places in unique ways and, quite literally, engage pupils' geographical imaginations. For example, in Bill Bryson's *African Diary*, Kibera in Nairobi, Kenya, is portrayed as both a place of absolute poverty as well as a place of communities, families and humanity. The writing style is humorous, empathetic, detailed and evocative of a particular place and the people who live there – this kind of rich description is engaging for students, creating a much more powerful 'sense of place' than can generally be achieved when reading a textbook. Opportunities for pupils to read material from a variety of cultures and traditions, including poetry, short stories, fiction and drama, as well as first-hand or eye-witness accounts from different places, can make significant contributions to pupils' geographical learning. Using such material can provide stimulating and challenging ways of studying geographical issues and questions through the eyes of people leading different lives in different places and with different consequences.

Rawling (2010) writes about how poetry can encourage pupils to understand places differently. Writing about a set of ten poems entitled 'Betweenlands I–X' by Philip Gross (2009), she describes how the writer draws on 'geographically accurate observations and poetic definitions of well-known [river] features' to create rich descriptions of places:

> these are no dry descriptions as written in a textbook. Gross's Severn is a real place and we hear the voice of imagination sharpened by experience.

> (p. 94)

Reading to pupils is quite a rarity in secondary geography classrooms, yet *if* done well and *if* the content is sufficiently interesting, pupils tend to enjoy being read to. However, when done badly – lack of enthusiasm, dreary voice, mispronunciation of key terms, too fast and so on – you present pupils with a poor model of how to read. Always practice reading a piece of text out loud, on your own, before you read to pupils. Record your reading and ask yourself how you might improve this aspect if your performance!

Writing

The bulk of the writing that children undertake in school is transactional, involving reorganising, reporting and perhaps translating information. The nature of geography as a subject *demands* that a great deal of writing in the subject is transactional. However, as Butt points out, this 'may not help the pupil learn from the writing experience' (Butt 1997: 160). Roberts (2003: Chapter 7) discusses how pupils' writing can be developed throughout the process of geographical enquiry to promote understanding. She provides a range of examples of practical activities to show how writing can contribute to learning.

There are plenty of opportunities for aesthetic and imaginative writing in geography. Pupils can be offered opportunities to write poems about places they have visited, perhaps as part of a fieldwork activity. David Job (1998) describes how pupils can construct Haiku poems to express their feelings about places. To generate writing for aesthetic purposes in geography requires us to be imaginative when designing motivating learning experiences that will stimulate pupils and encourage them to use all of their senses.

The examples in Figure 5.3 illustrate how pupils can write imaginatively in geography. Simple linguistic devices such as advising pupils to use metaphor and similes when describing a place can provide a helpful structure to their thinking.

Research by Butt (1993) has explored how expressive language can be encouraged in geography by getting pupils to write for different audiences from those which they normally encounter. The aim is to reduce the 'immediacy of the teacher's assessing role' by

The Rainforest
The rainforest: a lush canopy of moist green leaves, An animal paridise, full of tender new shoots, And fruits fell of delicious flavours. A parrot screeches, fluffing up it's vividly coloured feathers, As it sits high up in the trees, almost completely camourflaged, by hanging leaves from the braches above. All kinds of animals scamp along the floor of the jungle, But the most spectacular are the ones which patgrol the airways. Birds are only the beginning of these magnificent airborne creatures. The paradise tree snake slithers up an almost vertical tree, It then drops off in to the air and spreading out it's body, It flattens itself and glides effortlessly to the ground. A gliding squirrel has flaps of extra skin stretching from head to toe, It stretches out it's limbs and drops from a great height, The wind catches this skin like a sail and it swoops to safety, There are all sorts of nasty creepy-crawlies in the Rain Forest, Such as terrantulars and scorpions, But they all serve their purpose as food or to eat others as food. Marmosets swing easily from one tree to another, Collecting tasty tit-bits along the way to feed on. These small furry animals are strong even though they are small. An arrow poison frog is a vey concientious parent, After dispositing each tadpole in a separate pool in a plant it returns every few days to lay unfertilised egg for the young tadpole to eat. There is more to the rain forest than you see at first and it is sad that it is disappearing so fast.

Tropical Rain forests
Tropical rainforests are found in warm, wet parts of the world, such as Brazil, Indonesia and West Africa. Life is abundant here in many forms because of the ideal conditions.

The first thing that would strike you if you entered a tropical rainforest would be the sound. You would hear howling monkeys, screaming and chirping birds and all kinds of other animal noises. You may also see the creatures, but many of them would be camouflaged or hidden in the tops of the trees (the canopy). The tallest tree in a tropical rain forest is the Capoc. Compared with the other layers of the forest not much lives here, only birds of prey like eagles which would kill and eat anything that dares to venture above the canopy. The Capoc grows to a height of 200 ft and the air around it is considerably more breezy than in or below the canopy. The canopy is sometimes known as the pastures of the jungle. Insects, parrots, monkeys and many more animals live here. Nearer the ground there is comparatively little vegetation or animal life, because of the amount of shade provided by the canopy. Only in less dense areas is there a shrub layer which will in turn support it's own variety of creatures.

In the rainforest there are no seasons, it is warm and wet all the year round, like an eternal summer. Consequently plants flower and animals breed at different intervals for each species, anything from every ten months to every ten years. This ensures there is food for everything at all times.

Figure 5. 3 Writing by 14-year-old pupils

(*Source:* Lambert, *Geography Assessment* © Cambridge University Press 1991. Reproduced with permission.)

getting pupils to write for more 'realistic audiences' (Butt 1993: 24). Butt envisaged that using such audiences would encourage more original and creative writing in geography. He found that changing the audience has 'some effect on the learning process' (Butt 1993: 24). Pupils frequently demonstrated 'a deeper understanding of the geography being studied and a greater appreciation of values and attitudes' in their writing. However, to use this strategy effectively some attention should be given to establishing the following necessary pre-conditions:

- that a sense of trust and purpose needs to be established before good audience-centred writing will appear – boys did not reveal this sense of trust as readily as girls
- that removing the idea of teacher as assessor in pupils' minds is important, but also extremely difficult
- that audience-centred writing should be integrated into schemes of work, but not over-used; that audiences should be realistic and plausible
- that if levels of pupil involvement, discussion and enquiry are allowed to increase through audience-centred work, geographical attainment may also rise.

(Butt 1993: 22)

As well as providing opportunities for pupils to write for different purposes in geography, we need to look for strategies that can help them improve the quality of their written work. Too often, assumptions are made about pupils' ability to write in different forms and not enough attention is given to helping pupils develop the skills needed to write effectively in geography. Pupils frequently have the opportunity to draft work in English, yet this is not a strategy in common use in geography lessons.

The use of writing frames to support pupils with writing difficulties was developed by the Extending Literacy Project team at Exeter University (see Box 5.2). The frames are a strategy which help children use their 'generic structures of recount, report, procedure, explanation, exposition (arguing a point of view) and discussion until they become familiar enough with these written structures to have assimilated them into their writing repertoire' (EXEL 1995). A writing frame consists of various key words and phrases in a basic skeleton framework which is used to 'scaffold' pupils' writing. Table 5.3 shows examples of writing frames that could be used in geography.

The intention is that by using different writing frames, pupils will become increasingly familiar with their generic structure:

> The template of starters, connectives and sentence modifiers which constitute a writing frame gives children a structure within which they can concentrate on communicating what they want to say, rather than getting lost in the form.
>
> (EXEL 1995)

Box 5.2 Writing frames

Writing frames can help children by:

- providing experience of a range of generic structures
- offering a structure in which the given connectives maintain the cohesive ties of the text, thus helping pupils maintain the 'sense' of what they are writing
- offering a varied vocabulary of connectives and sentence beginnings, thus extending pupils' experience beyond the familiar 'and then'
- encouraging pupils to give a personal interpretation of the information they have gathered by the careful use of personal pronouns. It is tempting to talk about this process in terms of giving pupils ownership of the information they are working with
- asking the pupils to select, and think about what they have learnt, by encouraging pupils to re-order information and demonstrate their understanding rather than just copying out text
- enabling pupils to achieve some success at writing, a vital ingredient in improving self-esteem and motivation
- preventing pupils from being presented with a blank sheet of paper – a particularly daunting experience for some children especially those for whom sustained writing is difficult
- giving pupils an overview of the writing task.

(*Source:* Wray and Lewis 1997: 122)

The process should always begin with discussion and teacher modelling before moving on to a joint (teacher and pupil/group) learning activity, followed by the pupil undertaking some writing supported by the frame (scaffold activity). It should be made clear that the frame is just a draft which pupils can amend and add to. The aim is to improve the quality of pupils' 'independent' writing at the end of the process, not that the frame should be an end in itself.

Butt (2001) considers the relationship between 'talking' and writing. He argues that providing pupils with opportunities to talk through an issue or set of ideas gives pupils something then to write about – they develop and refine their ideas collectively and then can draw on these ideas in their writing. He also contends that activities such as DARTs are as useful in developing pupils' writing, especially their extended writing, as they are for developing their reading – talking, reading and writing all support each other in developing pupils thinking. George et al. (2002) outline approaches for helping pupils to develop their understanding of the characteristics of 'better descriptions' and 'better explanations' in geography.

Table 5.3 Examples of writing frames in geography

A   Comparing and contrasting places

Although the UK and Italy are different, they are similar in some interesting ways.

For example, they both ....

....

They are also similar in ....

....

They also have the same ....

....

Finally, they both ....

....

B   Sometimes it can be helpful to use a grid to organise information about places and features before pupils use 'comparison and contrast' frames.

Characteristics	UK	Bangladesh
Climate		
Farming		
Population growth		
Health care		
Industry		
Average wealth (GNP per person)		
Education/literacy		

C   Using a writing frame to explain a process in geography

I want to explain how the process of frost-shattering (freeze-thaw action) works ....

It starts by ....

.... and ....

....

This causes ....

....

After that ....

....

and as a result ....

....

Then ....

....

The final result is that ....

....

D   Writing about an issue in geography. Using a writing frame to present arguments and information about different viewpoints.

The issue that we discussed was about whether more new housing should be built in rural areas. Some people think that ....

....

because ....

....

They argue that ....

....

Another group who agree with this point of view are ....

....

They say that ....

....

On the other hand .... disagree with the idea that ....

....

(continued)

Table 5.3 (continued)

They claim that ....

....

They also say that ....

....

My opinion is ....

....

because ....

....

(*Source:* EXEL 1995)

Writing frames should not be used as rigid generic structures. They provide one strategy for extending pupils' experience of writing in a range of genres and contexts. It should also be remembered that not all pupils in a class will need to use a writing frame.

Task 5.5 Language, literacy and learning in geography

These tasks explore 'talking, listening, reading and writing' in geography. They should be carried out during your induction period in school when you are undertaking a broad programme of classroom observation. Discuss your findings with other student teachers and with your geography mentor.

A   Speaking and listening

1   What opportunities are there for pupils to talk about geography? Briefly describe examples from the lessons that you observe where pupils are given opportunities to talk about geography. What evidence is there that the pupils are learning about geography through speaking and listening? What do teachers do and say to 'shape' or to 'guide' this learning?

2   Reflection: What type of learning activities and teaching strategies promote learning through speaking and listening in geography?

3   Summarise the factors that 'encourage' and 'discourage' teachers from giving pupils opportunities to talk about geography.

B   Reading

1   What types of text do pupils use in geography?

2   What kinds of reading take place in geography lessons? What is the purpose of this reading?

3   What difficulties do pupils experience when reading in geography? How can or could some of these difficulties be overcome?

C   Writing

1   What different kinds of written work do pupils undertake in geography? It may
    help to consider three different forms of writing:

- transactional (to inform others and record information)
- poetic (for aesthetic purposes)
- expressive (for thinking and exploring ideas).

2   Collect examples of two or three different pieces of writing in geography. These
    pieces of writing can either illustrate:

- different forms of writing
- writing by pupils of different abilities
- problems that pupils experience when writing in geography.

Be prepared to talk about these pieces of writing.

Make a note of any specific strategies that you observe teachers using to support
pupils' writing in geography.

Inclusion: meeting individual pupils' needs

Teachers should set high expectations for every pupil. They should plan stretching work
for pupils whose attainment is significantly above the expected standard. They have an
even greater obligation to plan lessons for pupils who have low levels of prior attainment or come from disadvantaged backgrounds.

(DfE 2013: 9)

The 2014 National Curriculum in England, and also curriculum reforms in other United
Kingdom jurisdictions are very clear about schools' and teachers' responsibilities when it
comes to ensuring that all students, regardless of their academic ability, ethnicity, gender,
sexuality or social class are 'included' in the curriculum.

Meeting the diverse range of individual learning needs within geography classes is frequently quoted by student teachers as being one of the greatest challenges facing them
during their initial training. For some it can be a frustration. How do I involve pupils for whom
English is their second or even third language? How can I involve Martin when he struggles
to complete any written tasks? Do I have to produce differentiated worksheets for all my lessons in order to support lower-attaining pupils? I've been told I'm not 'stretching' the most
able pupils, what can I do? What do I do if some pupils cannot read any of the material in the
textbooks?

These are familiar stories and ones that are not only experienced by student teachers,
but by very experienced teachers too,

Sometimes the jargon used in education gets in the way of helping us to make sense
of the complex task of teaching, and nowhere is this truer than when applied to the broad
generalisations, frequently used in classrooms, staffrooms and CPD training events when
teachers talk about pupils with different learning needs. In many respects, it is easy to

understand why teachers use terms such as 'less able', 'more able', Gifted and Talented' or 'lower ability' as such categorisations act as conveniences when swift decisions have to be made about support for individuals and when schools are judged on the quality of their provision for different groups of pupils by Ofsted (see the Ofsted *School Inspection Handbook*, 2014) and other accountability measures. However, on a day-by-day basis these generalisations do little to help you understand the needs of different kinds of learners and they run the risk of creating either an 'underclass' of pupils, that is, those stereotyped as having low expectations, low aspirations and low self-esteem, or an 'elite', that is, those stereotyped as having high expectations, high aspirations and enduring intense pressure to succeed. Then there are those pupils who fall between these extremes, those 'in the middle' who fit neither group; what do we do about those pupils? Then there are boys and girls and the debates that abound regarding differences in both attainment and preferred ways of learning exhibited by boys and girls. Layer into this teachers' and schools' responsibilities to also make educational provision for:

- 'looked-after children', i.e. those who are in some way in the social care system
- pupils categorised as 'disadvantaged' and who are judged be at risk of underachieving academically because of their socio-economic circumstances
- pupils who are on the school's register but do not attend school for a range of reasons such as poor health, and/or emotional/psychological/social reasons.

The inclusion debate is long-running and reminds us that inclusion is a complex concept that is difficult to apply in practice. It is complex because rather than labelling pupils or categorising them, it requires you to understand them all as individuals with their own talents, hopes and aspirations.

Teaching geography to pupils with special educational needs (SEN)

It is a requirement of the Teacher's Standards (DfE 2013) that you understand your legal and professional responsibilities regarding teaching pupils with special needs: The current Standards in England state that you are required to:

> have a clear understanding of the needs of all pupils, including those with special educational needs; those of high ability; those with English as an additional language; those with disabilities; and be able to use and evaluate distinctive teaching approaches to engage and support them.
>
> (p. 12)

The Warnock Report, published in 1978, brought about a fundamental shift in our thinking about provision for pupils with special educational needs, establishing the principle, that other than in the most special cases it was the responsibility of all schools to meet the full range of pupils' needs.

Since then, there have been several versions of a 'Code of Practice', a statutory document detailing schools' responsibilities in identifying and providing for the special educational needs of individual pupils. The 1994 Code of Practice required schools to publish an SEN register and every school was (and still is) required to appoint a Special Educational Needs Coordinator (SENCO) to oversee this. Various revisions of the Code, in conjunction with other acts pertaining to the needs of children and young people, including the *2004 Children Act* and the *2012 Health and Social Care Act*, have collectively sought to improve the educational provision for all young people. In accordance with Articles 12 and 13 of the *United Nations Convention on the Rights of the Child*, the 2014 Code in England and Wales gives added weight to the involvement of parents and young people in decision-making processes about any special educational provision. This Code also requires a more integrated approach to special needs support from, not just education providers, but also health and social care providers. This means that, as a geography teacher, you may well be liaising and working with other professionals involved in the care of some of your pupils.

This Code of Practice highlights the role of the class teacher in supporting any individual pupil who has learning or behavioural difficulties. Working with your school's Special Education Needs Coordinator (SENCO), you will be part of what is described as the 'graduated approach' to identifying and supporting pupils who may need special or more targeted support (Draft Code of Practice, 2014: 43). Based on an Asses-Plan-Do-Review cycle, the graduated approach requires increased intensification of support and intervention if, at each 'assess' stage, it is felt that pupils are still not making progress in their learning. This cycle forms the basis of an 'Education, Health and Care Plan', which is an integrated action plan detailing targets, and key personnel involved meeting the specific needs for particular *individual* pupils. Clearly, you have a responsibility to familiarise yourself with the plans for the pupils that you will be teaching and how you might support pupils to achieve their overall targets through their work in geography.

Each school is required to keep a register of pupils' specific needs outlining the strategies that are being used to address these needs. It is important that you know the *specific* nature of the difficulties experienced by particular pupils, and how these difficulties manifest themselves and affect pupil's learning in geography. The geography department should also have its own policy outlining how SEN are being addressed within the subject. Your geography mentor and the school's SENCO as well as classroom assistants are the people to approach for advice and support in this area.

Teaching pupils with specific learning needs and ensuring that they enjoy and are successful in their learning is dependent on careful planning and preparation. Adopting a differentiated approach to lesson planning will help you to address the needs of some pupils with SEN. Battersby (1997) is clear that effective differentiation depends on a sophisticated interpretation of geographical ideas so that you make appropriate decisions about how to make ideas accessible to *all* pupils. Generally is it is a combination of no one strategy, but a combination of different interventions that you use to help pupils make progress. The 2008 Ofsted report criticised lesson planning in geography: 'too often teaching is directed at pupils of average ability so limiting the opportunities for independent inquiry and extended writing' (Ofsted 2008: para 42). Focusing on the 'middle clearly cannot address the needs of pupils with special needs, especially those with SEN'.

Another classroom challenge for you to consider is the impact of teachers' low expectations of SEN pupils, often resulting in pupils with SEN being presented with inappropriate tasks that provide them with inadequate challenges. Some unsatisfactory lessons with 'lower ability' classes often involve pupils in undemanding tasks such as recording or transferring information. Such tasks may not provide any intellectual stimulus or challenge. Pupils with SEN may also find them to be time-consuming and frustrating because their specific learning difficulties limit their ability to complete such routine tasks.

Task 5.6 Understanding the needs of individual pupils

During your initial teacher education course, you will be developing your knowledge of teaching strategies which can be used to support pupils with different special educational needs. In order to do this effectively you need to know your pupils.

It is important before you embark on this task to read the school/department's SEN policy. Having done this, identify – with your mentor – a pupil with SEN. If possible, this should be a pupil with whom you have or will have contact. (Use fictional names to preserve confidentiality.)

Find out the following information about this pupil:

- What are the pupil's strengths and weaknesses?
- What are the specific needs of this pupil?
- What interventions are made in geography lessons to support this pupil in making progress (i.e. what support is provided)?
- Is there any additional contextual information that you need to know, such as how parents and the pupil themselves are involved in and understand school decisions about support?

Work with this pupil during a geography lesson and consider:

- Does the pupil respond well to any particular teaching approaches or activities?
- Does the pupil seek help from other pupils and/or the teacher (and how often)? What is the nature of the support they need?
- What is the relationship between this pupil's geographical understanding when he/she has an opportunity to discuss the work, and how this understanding is represented (or not) in any written or other tasks that have to be completed?
- How does the pupil relate to others in the group – what is the nature of conversations he/she has with others around him/her?
- After the lesson, talk to the pupil about his or her work in geography. Which aspects did he/she enjoy and in what ways he/she they feel successful? Which aspects of the work proved to be more problematic?
- If possible, look at some other work completed by this pupil in geography and try to identify whether there are any common errors or problems. Do not focus just on generic problems such as spelling or presentation, also consider the quality of geographical understanding exhibited in any written work. How much written work is finished by the pupil? What is the nature of the feedback that the pupil receives from teachers?

During this process, keep additional notes on you observations and reflections and also find time to discuss you thinking with your mentor. Consider:

- What do you now understand about this student's specific needs and interests?
- How do you need to plan to meet his/her specific needs in geography lessons

Teaching bilingual pupils in geography

> The desire to answer questions and understand the work about glaciers in geography . . . pushed me to use and extend my vocabulary.
> These classes were the perfect incubators for my language development.
>
> (Giang Vo 2004: 5, cited in Balderstone et al. 2006: 35)

Often, in official documents such as the 'Teaching Standards', reference is made to 'EAL' pupils (English as an Additional Language). However, EAL is perhaps an unhelpful label because of the messages it carries about what pupils cannot do, whereas 'bilingual', by implication carries more positive overtones about pupils abilities in more than one language (Franson 2011). For the sake of this discussion, we will be referring to 'bilingual' pupils.

It is important to remember that bilingual pupils are not a homogeneous group and with language comes an individual pupil's personal and family identity, their sense of belonging – to places ranging from home, to community, to nation state, and attached to this sense of belonging come certain historical and cultural contexts such as religion, music, food and more.

The pupils you teach in geography, for whom English is an additional language, will necessarily be working within bilingual capacities. They may need, at times, to think and speak in their first language in order to access key ideas or, even if they speak relatively fluent English in lessons, they may still be developing their reading and writing skills.

We can see that understanding pupils' contexts is important because it helps us to appreciate what bilingual students bring to geography classrooms. It also helps when making decisions about the kind of support they might need in accessing the geography curriculum. Some pupils may quickly adapt to working in English if their first language is similar in structure, for example, Dutch. For others, the reverse may be true. Some pupils' life experiences may mean that they have a stable life and are in your school for positive reasons, for others they and/or their family may be in the United Kingdom as a result of forced migration and they may have seen and experienced difficult events. Bilingual pupils also have to often cope with the contrasting attitudes of others where either 'bilingualism' is seen as positive and even elitist, or it is seen as a deficit and in need of remediation.

Many of the approaches discussed earlier in this chapter to develop all pupils literacy skills will help you also support bilingual pupils – the additional factors to consider are language and culture.

Talking

Bilingual pupils need to practise their use of English orally as exploratory talk helps them to develop understanding through the metacognitive process of 'thinking out loud' (DfES 2002). In your geography lessons create opportunities for pupils to:

- 'think out loud'
- rehearse their ideas orally before committing themselves to writing
- use their first language where appropriate

- operate within clear ground rules for talking in the classroom
- enjoy some silence so that they can process information
- converse with you, taking care with your diction and your use of colloquial vocabulary, which may just confuse pupils.

Listening

If you have ever watched a foreign language film without subtitles and struggled for a couple of hours to make sense of the plot, then imagine what it is like, all day, every day, to sit in classrooms trying to listen to and make sense of the language you hear – it is probably exhausting! Use your non-verbal communication to help pupils to begin to make some sense of what you are saying in terms of instructions and explanations. Pointing at relevant resources such as an image or title on a slide, hand gestures, facial expressions, voice tone and pace, all help to give subtle cues about the nature of what you are saying.

Reading

Bilingual pupils can experience a variety of challenges when using written texts in English, depending on their previous experiences of reading (DfES 2002: 16). Confusion can arise as a result of cultural differences, for example when reference is made to aspects of life in the United Kingdom with which they may be unfamiliar. The use of metaphors, imagery and the passive voice in geography textbooks can also be source of confusion.

Writing

In your geography lessons, you can support bilingual pupils' writing by:

- providing opportunities for discussion, in pairs and small groups before writing begins
- providing opportunities for pupils to establish their understanding of key vocabulary
- supporting writing skills via writing frames
- modelling different forms of geographical writing with and for students
- allowing students to use ICT where appropriate as this can build confidence and enable a certain degree of self-checking of written work
- providing clear diagnostic feedback and manageable targets.

While much of the above may seem like fairly generic advice, we must also be clear that the very subject matter of geography lends itself to creating an inclusive classroom. If your pupils have travelled, lived in different places and have life experiences that could contribute to all pupils' geographical understanding, then encouraging them to bring these experiences in to lessons is good for everyone. Such an open disposition on your part will encourage openness in your pupils.

Social class and school geography

In recent years, the idea of providing an inclusive education for all has been founded on some important new debates, not least of which is the way social class either inhibits or enables educational success. While academics such as Stephen Ball (2012, 2013) and Danny Dorling (2011) argue that inherent injustices in the education system mean that children from disadvantaged backgrounds are more likely to underachieve academically and so are less likely to access opportunities such as a university education, Ofsted (2013), in a report entitled *Unseen Children: Access and Achievement 20 Years On*, is emphatic that social deprivation should not and need not be a barrier to educational success. Much of the Ofsted argument in the 'Unseen children' report centres on lack of challenge, low expectations by teachers, lack of or inadequate intervention strategies and inadequate teaching of fundamental skills such as oral and written communication. The group the report identifies as begin at significant risk of under achievement in school is white British children from low-income backgrounds (Ofsted 2013: 17).

For school geography, there are some particular issues to consider here. We know that the numbers of students studying GCSE geography declined overall between 1997 and 2010. We also know that in that period the majority of students studying geography at GCSE tended to be in either independent or grammar schools, or in high-performing suburban comprehensive schools (see Weeden and Lambert 2010). Research undertaken by Paul Weeden, at the University of Birmingham, clearly revealed that pupils attending inner-city comprehensive schools and living in areas of social and economic deprivation were significantly less likely to study geography post-Key Stage 3. This pattern was reinforced in the 2011 Ofsted report for geography, which expressed concerns that there was a trend of some schools failing to enter any students at all for GCSE geography.

The bigger picture here suggests that for students in certain kinds of schools in certain geographical areas, opportunities to study geography were severely restricted or even denied.

However, geography and/or history, is now one the 'entitlement' areas which schools are required, by law, to teach. GCSE entries for geography have increased in England as schools have had to rethink their GCSE provision (Geographical Association, *GCSE Entries and Results 2013, Final Report*). This means that a wider range of pupils, from different socio-economic backgrounds are now expected to study geography up to the age of 16.

Being mindful of pupils' socio-economic context is important for several reasons. In 2011, the UK government introduced a system of additional funding called 'the pupil premium' for all pupils who have been in receipt free-school meals in the last six years, or are 'looked after' in the care system or have parents in the armed forces. It may be that you teach pupils who receive additional support as a result of the pupil premium funding and so you need to know what form this takes. More importantly, understanding pupils' socio-economic context should inform decisions you make about what and how to teach. This brings us back to the debate about knowledge, discussed in Chapter 1 and the purpose of education:

> [to]enable students to acquire specialised/disciplinary knowledge that is not accessible . . . in their everyday lives, and enables those who acquire it to move beyond their experience and gain understanding of the social and natural worlds of which they are a part
>
> (Young 2008: 164)

Creating an inclusive school geography and ensuring that all pupils are able to access geographical knowledge in its widest sense (i.e not just content knowledge) requires you to utilise many of the ideas already discussed in their book. You will need to attend to developing generic skills of numeracy and literacy in geography lessons, consider how to develop students spatial thinking and other cognitive capacities and draw on the wide range of teaching approaches and learning resources that are part and parcel of learning the school subject.

However, you can do all of this and still be unsuccessful. What you will also have to consider are the ways that material poverty and social immobility leave some pupils out of kilter with the mainstream curriculum, so specifically you will need to attend to how to mediate pupils' life experiences and how these can be utilised as a bridge between pupils' existing cultural capital (and all will have this) and the new geography that you want them to learn.

Teaching very able pupils in school geography

'Bright' or 'gifted' pupils show a high level of general intellectual ability or specific academic aptitude which may be accompanied by creative thinking.

(Grenyer 1986: 171)

We know that pupils we might label as 'gifted' or 'talented' or 'very able' or ' high achieving' or 'high attaining' are not a homogenous group. We can also see that identifying pupils who we would regard as exceptionally able is less than clear cut. Identifying which pupils are and which pupils are not the 'most able' in our schools has a long and contentious history, starting with the establishment of a tripartite educations system of grammar schools, technical high schools and secondary modern schools in 1944, through to the establishment of a comprehensive education system in 1965, and on through significant shifts in government policy ever since!

Grenyer's definition of 'gifted' pupils may not be accepted by all and some prefer not to talk about 'gifted' pupils at all because they associate the term with elitist ideas. David George argues that 'definitions abound and create much confusion' (George 1992: 1) and he urges us to get away from 'pseudo-scientific labelling' of pupils, suggesting that the term 'intellectually underserved' may have some value when describing pupils with exceptional ability.

The 'Excellence in Cities' programme set up in 1999 under New Labour introduced a new definition into the education lexicon. Many schools in England used and still use 'G and T' (gifted and talented) to denote their most academically able pupils, selecting the top 5-10 per cent, *per school*, from national test data and other data sources in order to satisfy the then-requirement for all schools to identify and track the progress of their most able pupils.

Gagné (2003) argues that *potential* is the key signifier of 'giftedness', where students display above average potential in one or more of the following areas: intellectual ability, creative capacity, social abilities and physical abilities. He contends that while pupils can possess natural capacities in these areas, unless these are in some way systematically developed through learning and practising, then these 'gifts' cannot become 'talents'. More recently, the Sutton Trust report 'Educating the Highly Able' (Smither and Robinson 2012) suggested that the term 'Gifted and Talented' was confusing and should be abandoned in favour of 'highly able' to denote pupils who are excellent in certain school subjects. The report also recommends that schools, rather than national initiatives such as the National Academy for Gifted and Talented Youth, are best placed to make provision for their academically capable pupils.

While at a policy level terminology changes and meanings and interpretation shift position, ultimately you have to think carefully about how you plan and teach in order to ensure that *your* most able pupils make the progress they are capable of.

Table 5.4 identifies a set of characteristics of pupils with high levels of ability or potential in geography.

Table 5.4 Possible characteristics of high levels of ability or potential in geography

Possible aspects	Possible student responses
Curiosity	Students will seek information and understanding beyond that which is immediately presented to them. They raise questions and are motivated to find the answers.
Scope of general knowledge	Students will want to discuss topical issues relating them to the work being covered in class. They will have a wide range of interests and an excellent memory for detail.
Conceptual understanding and application	Students quickly and easily grasp new ideas and theories and are able to apply them to real situations. It will sometimes feel as though full explanations from the teacher are unnecessary.
Perceptiveness	Students appreciate the complexity of the world around them. They can identify and justify other people's viewpoints. They have acute observation skills.
Well-developed thinking skills	Students demonstrate originality and divergent thinking when they approach problems. They can see many different routes for getting to the same end point. They are capable of metacognition (thinking about thinking) and can help to raise the roof off the classroom.
High levels of geographical literacy	They are accomplished at matching style of communication (whether oral or written) to the task and audience. They are also likely to have an advanced vocabulary. They will be excited by and sensitive to the fact that geography has its own language for learning and will enjoy technical terms and precise definitions.
High levels of geographical numeracy	Students very quickly pick up on sequences and patterns. They are confident in applying mathematical principles such as area and shape. They enjoy looking for spatial patterns in map-work tasks and will be excited by learning situations involving statistical testing or geographical information systems.
Attitude towards less formal learning experiences	Some students will come into their own in situations where they are asked to take part in a role play or simulation. They will display innate confidence and adopt a leadership role. They will tend to be very enthusiastic about fieldwork and relish the challenge of setting and testing hypotheses.
Interaction with peers	Gifted students have no consistent manner of interaction with their peers. Some may display a preference to work alone or with older students. Others will relate very well with their peers and be keen to help those who are not as quick to grasp new ideas. Some will look to hide their ability from the rest of their classmates.
Teacher perceptions	This list does not profess to be exhaustive but students may be considered to be one or more of the following: aloof, arrogant, eccentric, impatient, insensitive, intolerant, intuitive, lazy, nonconformist, obstinate, opinionated, perfectionist, persistent, precocious, preoccupied, rude, sensitive, underachieving, withdrawn.

(*Source:* Enright, Flook and Habgood 2006: 370)

Self-motivation and working independently are often qualities used to characterise pupils viewed as being academically more able.

Ofsted, in 2011, reported that more able pupils were underachieving in geography because classroom activities were not challenging enough and pupils were not afforded sufficient opportunities to develop their capacity to think and work independently. However, pupils with exceptional ability do not necessarily have the skills needed for effective independent learning. These pupils may need to be taught these if they are to become successful independent learners. For instance, a very able pupil may spend an excessive amount of time searching out information but not necessarily have the capacity to analyse it and apply it to particular problems. Such a pupil needs teaching information-handling skills in order to be able to both select and *also* deselect information.

When considering how to develop more able pupils, it is worth thinking in terms of *challenging* their ability and *enriching* or *enhancing* their learning. The approach you adopt should not encourage these pupils to be passive receivers of information. Learning activities should challenge them to analyse, interpret and evaluate information, to search for meaning and derive theories and generalisations. Pupils should be encouraged to ask, rather than just answer geographical questions and they need to have opportunities to make, understand and question the big ideas in the discipline. For example, presenting land use data can be a fairly undemanding task unless pupils are required to make decisions about appropriate forms of presentation before looking for patterns and suggesting reasons for these patterns.

Above all, you must be flexible in the way you respond to the needs of these pupils. There are a wide range of approaches you can use to do this such as: games and simulations, fieldwork, strategies used to promote values education, developing critical insights into the media, and using multimedia technology to harness pupils' technical and creative capabilities in order to present their work to different audiences (all of these are discussed in detail other chapters).

What all of the above suggest is that meeting the needs of very able pupils need s thinking about and planning – 'bolt-on' activities that are simply 'more of the same' will not provide the challenge these pupils need. One of the best resources very able pupils need access to is you, their geography teacher. It is you who can ask the more searching questions that give them pause for thought; it is you who can direct them to read and review different and more challenging sources of information; it is you who can provide opportunities for open dialogue with other students and with you; and it is you who can judge the quality of their geographical understanding, identify misconceptions and guide then forward in their geographical learning. It is tempting to assume that building autonomy in able pupils means leaving them to their own devises, but these pupils need your time and attention too.

Task 5.7 Working with pupils with exceptional ability in geography

Educating the most able children in appropriate ways is a challenge that society must take seriously. We cannot afford to foster under-achievement, disaffection and alienation amongst these children.

(George 1997: 111)

A   As suggested earlier in this section learning about pupils as individuals is an important key to unlocking how to teach them. Look back at Task 5. 1 and now, with your mentor, identify a pupil who is very able in geography. As suggested in Task 5.1, find out as much contextual information as you can and then work with the pupil in a geography lesson in order to find out how they respond in the lesson, to both the geographical content and the tasks they are required to complete. Consider:

- To what extent is this pupil cognitively challenged by the work they have to complete? What kind of progress does he/she make in their geographical understanding?
- How does this pupil go about the required tasks – alone, in discussion with other pupils, with support from the teacher?
- What kinds of task is this pupil asked to complete – is there scope for him/her to work independently in the lesson? Are tasks open-ended enough?

Talk to the pupil after the lesson and try to get some sense of his/her perception of his/her learning in geography.

Gender and learning geogrpahy

One issue that permeates all of the discussions above is that of the difference in achievement between boys and girls in geography. In 2013, there was a rise in the total number of pupils studying geography with slightly more boys studying geography at both GCSE and A-level. However, in both qualifications girls consistently outperformed boys at the higher grades (Geographical Association, *GCSE entries and results 2013, Final Report,* and Weeden 2013, *Geography A-level and AS results 2013*). Both the 2008 and 2011 Ofsted reports for geography also highlight that there is a gender issue in geography:

> Survey evidence suggests that the gender gap is, in part, attributable to boys' poorer attitudes to learning, but there are also problems associated with boys' writing and literacy skills, especially the extended writing required for some assessments. In discussion, boys are frequently able to outline and recall the work covered and speak about the main issues far better than they can record them in writing. In particular, with some notable exceptions, boys' coursework is of a poorer quality than girls. They are especially poorer than girls at articulating explanations and developing reasoned argument in writing. Frequently, boys will spend more time on describing processes and graphing and mapping data but they appear less interested in interpreting and analysing this in depth. This often inhibits them from attaining the higher levels.
>
> (Ofsted 2008: 19)

It seems to be a significant challenge – how to support boys in developing the necessary skills, dispositions and understandings needed to be 'good geographers': how to develop their argumentation skills and get to grips with some of geography's big ideas, how to develop their critical evaluation skills and question these ideas, and how to support them in expressing their ideas and understandings in written as well as oral form.

Butt, Bradley-Smith and Wood (2006) observed that boys appear to be more oral than girls, they dislike writing and they tend to dominate practical activities. Wood (2002, cited in Butt et al. 2006) in his research found that boys preferred to work on computers and liked discussing geography more than they liked writing about it; the pattern of boys preferred ways of learning points to the value of building discussion work into your geography lessons, whereas developing writing skills will need structure in the form of scaffolds such as DARTS activities and writing frames.

While there are practical steps you can take to support boys more in lessons, you also can consider the geographical content of lessons – what kinds of geographies are more likely to interest/enthuse/engage them? This is not to say that you pander to the interests of boys at the expense of girls, but that at different points in a teaching year, tapping into their natural enthusiasms may help with their levels of engagement and enable them to develop ways of thinking geographically that they can then apply elsewhere in the geography curriculum.

One group we hear relatively little about in research in geography education is the group Bradley-Smith (2002) calls the 'the invisible girls'.

> always quiet and compliant; they demand little and contribute little. They draw so little attention to themselves that it is often difficult to recall whether or not they were actually present in a particular lesson
> (Bradley-Smith 2002: 143, cited in Butt, Bradley-Smith and Wood 2006: 388)

What Bradley-Smith found is that despite their 'invisibility' these girls had developed strategies to ensure that their learning was not necessarily inhibited. They used peer-interaction as a means of addressing any difficulties they were having, what Bradley-Smith calls 'horizontal interaction'. The research also reveals that the girls enjoyed group work, and that they were more than happy to remain invisible to the teacher.

It is probable that 'invisible' girls are not just an issue for geography lessons, but that they repeat this behaviour in other areas of school. Bradley-Smith's work makes several practical recommendations such as being aware of these girls' existence and learning their names quickly, use direct questioning to draw them into lesson discussions (this can also offset the impact of 'noisy boys'), plan group work ensuring that group membership changes from time to time and anticipate neat but not always geographically complex work and so be careful not to judge ability on presentation skills. You need to make the invisible girls visible!

Creating an inclusive geography classroom means planning for the specific needs of individual pupils and to do this, you will need to identify the pupils who may have additional needs and then consider approaches to meet these needs. It is in this context, however, that we also wish to offer an important note of caution. There is an excellent TED talk given by the Nigerian author Chimamanda Ngozi Adichie in which she reminds the audience of the 'danger of the single story'. What she means by this is that if we repeatedly only ever see people through one particular lens, then eventually this is what they become – they become the stereotype we create. This is particularly true of pupils with distinctive needs. While it would be professionally irresponsible to ignore the particular needs of groups and individuals, at the same time there is a danger that labels end up defining individuals – pupils become their labels. What we urge is that you are open to the possibilities of what pupils can do, can achieve and can bring to geography lessons – let them surprise you!

We accept that this section has merely scratched the surface of the complex topic of learning and inclusion, but we hope that at least your appetite is whetted sufficiently to persuade you into a long-term commitment to learn more about how your pupils learn.

Summary and key points

This chapter has been about learning – specifically, about learning in geography and the approaches and issues you will need to consider when learning to teach. We have explored a range of areas such as literacy, numeracy and spatial thinking in geography, and have considered the contribution each make to developing geographical understanding.

Ultimately, on a day-to-day basis, a key factor helping your pupils to learn is embedded in the attitude that you adopt towards *all* your pupils and how you understand the specific needs, interests and aptitudes that that they have. The 'sensitive teacher' seeks to develop pupils' self-esteem, values pupils for who they are and creates a classroom climate in which all pupils can succeed. This is about developing inclusive classroom practice so that all pupils feel part of learning geography

Further reading

Roberts, M. (2013) *Geography Through Enquiry: Approaches to Teaching and Learning in the Secondary School*, Sheffield: The Geographical Association
While there are many practical ideas in this book, all are underpinned by careful consideration of how young people learn in school geography.

Manning, A. (2014) 'Gersmehl and Gersmehl's Wanted: a concise list of . . . spatial thinking skills', *Geography* 99, 20: 108-110.
This article raises questions the notion of a 'taxonomy' for spatial thinking and the implications of this for teachers planning and teaching.

6   Resources

A major part of school geography is about what can be seen in the world, and geography teachers rely heavily on visual material to bring some reality into their classrooms.

(Robinson 1987: 103)

Introduction

If we recognise some of the notions of what geography is about (as discussed in Chapter 1), the nature and quality of the resources that we use are of fundamental importance. Echoing Roger Robinson's quote above, we rely, as geography teachers, on the quality of the materials that we use as well as the quality of our teaching to bring the subject alive in the classroom.

There should be a very close relationship between the planning processes described in Chapter 3 and the preparation of resources. When identifying and selecting resources or designing and preparing new resource materials, you should have a clear idea of their purpose. In other words, the resources needed are determined by the nature of the teaching strategies and learning activities that have been planned. However, the discovery of a particular resource or activity may in itself provide the source of inspiration for a lesson or sequence of lessons (see Chapter 3 for discussion on curriculum artefacts). The quality, variety and use of resources will have a significant influence on pupils' interest and motivation to learn, and the resources that pupils use can significantly influence the images they develop about people, places, events and issues.

As well as the resources teachers bring to geography lessons, learners themselves bring a wealth of experience, insight and perspectives into the classroom. By virtue of the lives that they lead, they themselves can be invaluable 'resources':

> Young people participate in their own 'lived geographies': on a day to day basis they interact simultaneously with other people and are part of different social groups. They interact with others at both a local level (friends, family, school/college, unknown others) and at greater distances, including the global (often via the internet). They navigate very complex networks of participation from informal social groups (friends, school groups, shared social activities) to more organised social activities (such as leisure activities, sport and music concerts) and formalised group activities especially in school. Their access to spaces, places and environments and other people are enabled and/or

hindered by a range of factors and influences including parents, financial considerations, age group, gender, ethnicity, feelings of safety, personal interest and so on.

(Firth and Biddulph 2009: 14)

You might also like to consider how you use your own experiences in your teaching. If you have travelled, not necessarily extensively, then gathering images, visual resources and experiences of people and places in the process can be used to bring some 'reality' into the classroom in a stimulating way. We are not advising here that your lessons to slip into non-stop anecdotal episodes of your travels, but that the stories you have to tell (and they need to be well told) of where you have been and what you have seen are more likely than not to capture pupils' imaginations.

With these considerations in mind, we need to critically evaluate the geographical resources we encounter, both for their potential to engage pupils' interest and motivation, *and* to facilitate successful teaching and learning in geography, so in this chapter we will discuss some of the issues that you need to consider when using different kinds of resources in teaching. While there are practical issues to consider, more importantly there are philosophical issues to keep in mind. This is because the resources you select, create and use convey important messages about you, as a teacher, and what you believe to be important in school geography.

> By the end of this chapter, you should be able to:
>
> * identify and critically evaluate resources available to support and facilitate teaching and learning in geography
> * create and produce your own resources for teaching and learning in geography
> * appreciate the nature of the relationship between resource quality and teaching quality in geography.

Developing your own resources

The preparation of resources is an important part of your lesson planning. Producing resources to a high quality is a time-consuming and demanding task. However, it gives you an opportunity to be creative and imaginative in your attempts to provide interesting and stimulating learning in the classroom. Figure 6.1 is a useful framework to help you to think about the process of developing your own resources for teaching. It shows the process of planning and preparation of resources as a series of stages. Many of the questions relate to practical issues, and the role of evaluation in developing your understanding of factors influencing the production and use of resources.

Selecting and using geography textbooks

One of the most interesting – and enduring – characteristics about teaching geography in the UK is the existence of what the eminent educationist and historian of geography education Bill Marsden called an 'anti-textbook culture' (Marsden 2001). On the face of it, many creative and imaginative geography teachers find the idea of basing their teaching on textbooks abhorrent: how *restricting* they would say; how *limiting*; how *unimaginative* and *uncreative*.

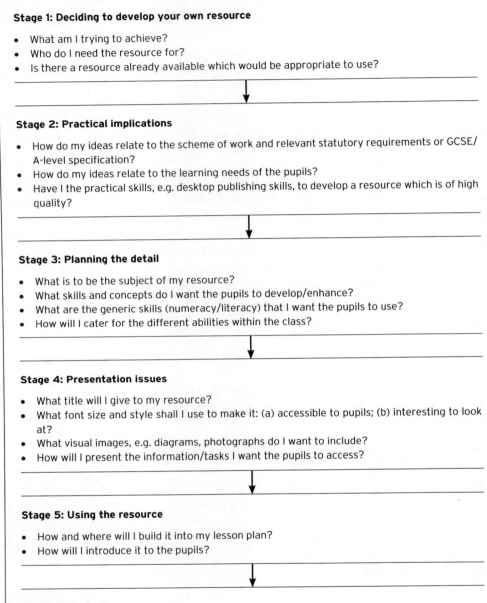

Stage 1: Deciding to develop your own resource

- What am I trying to achieve?
- Who do I need the resource for?
- Is there a resource already available which would be appropriate to use?

Stage 2: Practical implications

- How do my ideas relate to the scheme of work and relevant statutory requirements or GCSE/ A-level specification?
- How do my ideas relate to the learning needs of the pupils?
- Have I the practical skills, e.g. desktop publishing skills, to develop a resource which is of high quality?

Stage 3: Planning the detail

- What is to be the subject of my resource?
- What skills and concepts do I want the pupils to develop/enhance?
- What are the generic skills (numeracy/literacy) that I want the pupils to use?
- How will I cater for the different abilities within the class?

Stage 4: Presentation issues

- What title will I give to my resource?
- What font size and style shall I use to make it: (a) accessible to pupils; (b) interesting to look at?
- What visual images, e.g. diagrams, photographs do I want to include?
- How will I present the information/tasks I want the pupils to access?

Stage 5: Using the resource

- How and where will I build it into my lesson plan?
- How will I introduce it to the pupils?

Stage 6: Evaluation

- Did the resource help me to achieve my objectives?
- Were pupils of different abilities able to use it?
- Do I think the pupils enjoyed using it?
- Was the outcome relevant to the demands of the scheme of work?
- If I were to change it, what changes would I make?
- What have I learnt about the planning and use of resources?

Figure 6.1 Stages in planning, preparation and use of resources

In this light, textbooks are easily seen as dusty relics of times gone by. Marsden and others point out that such a response has led many teachers to proclaim almost as a badge of honour that they 'don't use textbooks'.

It is therefore easy to find geography departments where the head of department asserts that courses are 'not textbook-led' implying that the teaching is (therefore) lively, topical and in tune with the students' interests. This unfortunately leads to a very significant professional tension, and an almost unspoken but widespread *pretence* – for textbook sales are in fact still measured in millions of units. *Someone* must be using them! Yet, the pretence remains that departments buy sets of textbooks mainly for 'cover teachers' who need materials to teach with at the drop of a hat. Some will say that a set of textbooks is a good 'fall back' resource for non-specialists. The message is clear: textbooks are not to be used except in emergencies, or if you are somehow deficient as a teacher.

Textbook denial, the result of an anti-textbook culture that is almost unique to the UK, is a phenomenon that heaps responsibilities on to the teacher. It is based on the conceit that all teachers are excellent, autonomous curriculum *development* experts as well as the *makers* of the curriculum as experienced by students.

'But textbooks are always out of date' some geography teachers may go on to argue. Geography, they reasonably say, is about the contemporary world and textbooks are by definition unable to compete with the World Wide Web! However, good textbooks have a 'pedagogy' – a methodology by which they accomplish this – but they do not in themselves 'teach'.

Using a good textbook well can be the cornerstone of excellent teaching and this section shows you why this is the case. Note the cautious choice of words: there are no guarantees of excellent teaching. However, we would be prepared to argue that excellent teaching is more likely to follow the careful use of a good textbook than a dogmatic decision not to use a textbook at all in pursuit of 'creativity'. After all, what often replaces the textbook as the corner stone or central spine of geographical learning is a sequence of highly detailed PowerPoint slides or, even worse, a steady accretion and accumulation of 'handouts'.

In this section so far, we have made a strong case for the serious consideration of the place of good textbooks in geography classrooms. We should also note the dangers of geography teachers relying too heavily on textbooks. This of course a serious problem if the textbook itself is poor, and in this context we are reminded of Rex Walford's (1995a) research into the changes he observed in the balance between text, illustration and activities in geography textbooks. In discussing the 'strange case of the disappearing text', Walford provides further evidence of the changing role of textbooks in geography over the last 20 years. The dominance of the 'double-page spread', the variable quality of often repetitive activities and the lack of genuine problem-solving or decision-making tasks can limit the breadth and depth of geographical enquiry. As a consequence, there may be insufficient challenge for more capable pupils, thereby placing a ceiling on their achievements. A reductionist view about the amount of text that pupils are capable of dealing with can also restrict the potential of geography for developing pupils' literacy and use of language. Although most textbooks contain a good range of different types of resource material, a shortage of text limits opportunities for pupils to undertake extended reading in order to develop their geographical understanding. Likewise overuse of graphical devices such as talking heads and cartoon sketches, rather than photographs, can lead to over simplification and stereotyping (SCAA 1997).

Textbooks have to meet a huge range of often conflicting needs from different potential users (including non-specialist teachers), but the characteristics of good textbooks, are
fairly constant. In addition to publishers attending to the way textbooks are structured, an
important area of development has been in their giving more consideration to issues relating
to equal opportunities in the production of textbook resources and to the reduction of bias
in the use of language and illustrations.

Several authors have warned about the dangers of ethnocentric bias in geography textbooks. Christine Winter has provided a significant contribution to the debate about these
issues in her account of an attempt to 'raise pupils' awareness of the subjectivity involved
in representing knowledge about people and places in geography' (Winter 1997: 180). She
uses principles taken from McDowell's (1994) cultural geographical perspective as a basis for
analysing a case study of the Maasai way of life in the *Key Geography: Connections* textbook
(Waugh and Bushell 1992: 78–79) which in its day was by far the best selling KS3 geography
textbook. This analysis aims to deconstruct the authors' interpretation of the geography
National Curriculum in relation to the Maasai people of Kenya. The following extract from
this analysis illustrates how ethnocentric bias can manifest itself in a geography textbook:

> In spite of the frequent reference to the idea of change in the National Curriculum policy
> document, the authors make no reference in the textbook pages to the Maasai places
> and people as undergoing change; instead, a picture of a static way of life is presented.
> There is no mention of the reduction in Maasai grazing ground as a result of the appro-
> priation of land by the European settlers; soil erosion caused by the overgrazing of pas-
> ture on reduced amounts of land; the employment of Maasai people as cattle-herders
> by European ranch-owners and employment in the tourist trade. Neither are the devel-
> opment of fixed villages with wooden homes, more sedentary lifestyles, tanked water
> supplies, schools and community healthcare projects mentioned.
>
> The representation shows no evidence of a range of voices involved in the place
> being studied. The text is dominated by a white, male, western voice, with no views of
> the Maasai people about their places, history, stories and lives. If Maasai authors had
> written the two pages, what would they have looked like? How would they have repre-
> sented themselves and their land? What do the Maasai women say about their places?
> And what about the other voices to be heard in a study of this place; the voices of the
> Kenyan government, the tourists, the cattle ranchers and the safari travel firms?
>
> (Winter 1997: 183)

Winter's deconstruction of this case study shows how one textbook's interpretation of the
then National Curriculum can present an ethnocentric view through a 'one-dimensional,
static, unproblematical representation' of Kenyan people and place (Winter 1997: 184). She
then uses the same principles to reconstruct the case study providing alternative suggestions about how more appropriate teaching materials and activities could be developed. In
doing so, Winter demonstrates the crucial role of geography teachers in developing in pupils
the ability to think for themselves, to ask questions, to make decisions and judgements on
the basis of their own rational reflections, supported by materials and teaching which uphold
a notion of social justice' (Winter 1997: 187).

As specialist geography teachers, we need to be aware of the messages that geography textbooks give about people and places. As with all resources used for teaching and learning, we should critically review their contents and approaches to learning in geography as well as consider the potential learning outcomes (knowledge, understanding, skills, attitudes and values) that ensue from using them. As geography teachers, we need to question ways in which certain textbooks develop or reinforce negative stereotypes of people and places, and we need to look out for misconceptions about issues and big geographical questions that can also be found in some textbooks.

Task 6.1 Evaluating published resources

These two activities are designed to help you look carefully at the published resources you use in your teaching.

A   Evaluating textbooks

For this activity, you need a range of textbooks and it would be helpful to work with a small group of other student teachers to discuss your findings. Consider the evaluation questions below:

1   How are the contents organised and expressed?
2   How is text presented and organised?
3   How clearly are key concepts, themes or ideas signposted?
4   How successfully are photos and artwork integrated and used?
5   How useful is the 'text' in the textbook?
6   What forms of activities have been designed?
7   What appears to be the 'ethos' of the book?
8   Is the presentation appropriate for the age group?

(Adapted from Boardman 1996)

Points for group discussion:

- What are the fundamental differences between the textbooks you have evaluated?
- Are there any significant similarities between books that you have evaluated?
- Which textbooks would you prefer to use and why?

B   Identifying bias in published resources

Select a number of case studies about people and places from a small range of textbooks. Carefully study the text, illustrations and activities in these examples.

1   Examine the way in which these case studies portray people and places.
2   Describe any examples of gender or ethnocentric (or any other form of bias) that you have identified.
3   Suggest alternative ways in which people and places could have been portrayed. Could the resources in the textbook be used with pupils in different ways so as to avoid the development of biased views?
4   Develop an activity to be used with pupils to find out how aware they are of bias in the textbook resources that they use in geography.

The introduction of the revised National Curriculum for Geography in 2014, with its emphasis on the subject's important concepts and 'core contents', should bring a fresh approach to the production of textbook resources. Widdowson and Lambert (2006) raise questions about the role of textbooks in an 'information age' and the balance between the teacher, students and the learning resources in generating the 'learning energy' of a classroom. They conclude that textbooks do still have a role in geography classrooms, but that it is unlikely to be the same role they had in the past (Widdowson and Lambert 2006: 157).

Clearly your thinking about textbook resources will develop further when you have gained more practical experience of planning lessons and using textbooks in your teaching. However, it is helpful to raise your awareness of the design and presentation of resources and activities for teaching and learning that are to be found in geography textbooks.

Using maps and atlases

Dorling and Fairbairn (1997) argue that a map is:

> a fundamental form of representing space and location and it occupies a central place in the experience and development of the majority of people who have lived in large groups.
>
> (p. 3)

Maps are one of the geographer's most important tools, providing useful ways of storing and communicating information about people and places. If geography involves the study of the relationships between people and places, then maps help geographers to present, describe and explain the spatial information, patterns and processes that they observe in the world around them. Dorling and Fairbairn (1997) discuss in detail not just the institutional creation and use of maps, by governments and large organisations, but the increasing tendency for individuals to create their own maps for a wide range of personal and social purposes. They argue that technology-enabled map production has led to what they describe as 'a new renaissance in mapping' (p. 156), which for teachers, opens up a vast array of opportunities for all sorts of creative mapping with pupils (see Chapter 5).

How to read and understand maps is a central to learning geography. However, drawing and creating maps, *in order* to understand maps, needs to be a feature of pupils' geographical education. Maps can, unfortunately, be reduced to stereotypical notions of 'colouring and labelling'; however, we would argue that, in the right context, there is a place for pupils' to take the time and develop the patience to hand-draw their own maps and to develop the skills and understanding necessary to create maps using the facilities now afforded by technology.

Maps have several main functions:

- location, enabling the user to find a place (e.g. in an atlas, on a street map);
- route-displaying, allowing the user to get from A to B (e.g. a road atlas, underground map or street map);
- storing and displaying information, allowing the user to isolate and sort information from a wide range of different items (e.g. Ordnance Survey maps), or to consider patterns and relationships of selected information (e.g. distribution maps);

- problem-solving, helping the user to solve problems by interpreting or inferring from the information provided (e.g. why a road does not take the most direct route or where to locate a factory). Skilled map-users have learnt to 'see' the landscape from the information on the map;
- developing pupils' technical competence using mapping techniques and conventions;
- making meaning from patterns observed on maps.

(Adapted from Weeden 1997: 173)

Ordnance Survey maps

During their secondary school education in geography, pupils are required to use and interpret Ordnance Survey maps and plans at a variety of scales. The OS did for several years offer all Y7 pupils a free 1 : 50000 map, delivered via the school. Most schools took advantage of this offer. By 2008, over five million maps had been distributed in this way. Most schools have a good range of Ordnance Survey maps including ones of the local area as well as a collection of map extracts of other areas from previous examinations.

In addition to paper maps, you can also access a range of digitised Ordnance Survey maps via the Digimap website. Specially designed for schools, this site provides a range of resource opportunities for teacher. Via the site, you can:

- view and print anywhere in Great Britain (but not Northern Ireland)
- search for locations by place name, postcode or national grid reference
- print maps out at A4 or A3, landscape or portrait size, depending on availability of suitable printers
- measure distances and areas on the map
- add your own points, lines, areas and text on any map. These annotations can be saved or printed
- print maps with your own title and name on them
- use the maps with interactive whiteboards and digital projectors
- access annually updated maps.

(*Source*: Digimap for Schools)

Through the Digimap site, you can access a range of different types of maps including Explorer and Landranger maps and you can also access scanned historic maps from 1890 onwards.

The versatility of the facility means that Ordnance Survey maps can be used for: whole-class teaching where maps can be electronically displayed; for groups where, in a geographical enquiry, pupils can use maps and photographs and other sources of data; and in individual work when developing pupils map skills such as measuring distances or developing pupils understanding of compass directions. The historical maps on the site enable you to explore how an area has changed over time, with the slider function enabling you to fade between the current and the historic map, making the tool really useful for exploring land use change overtime, for example industrial expansion or decline, or you can examine changes in physical landscapes such as the impacts of coastal erosion. The line tool enables you to mark on specific events such as flood events or proposed landscape change such as new route ways (roads or railways) or building proposals, thus enabling you to consider how lives and land-scapes will change in the future.

The Ordnance Survey is a strategic partner of the Geographical Association, and there is much collaboration between the two organisations to help teachers. The GA and OS produced materials to help teachers plan for progression in using maps: www.geography.org.uk/resources/ordnancesurveymappingresource/achieveyouraims/planningforprogressionusingmaps%E2%80%93secondary/#top

Weather maps

Weather maps or synoptic charts provide a summary of the weather conditions being experienced in particular places at a particular point in time. A synoptic chart gives an indication of air pressure, temperature, wind strength and direction, and the amount of rainfall received. From this, judgements or forecasts can be made about probable future weather conditions.

As with other types of map, pupils need to understand the essential elements and features of synoptic charts before they are able to interpret weather patterns. These skills can be developed systematically and progressively so that able pupils can be challenged by interpreting more complex patterns and relationships. It should also be remembered that pupils can encounter synoptic charts alongside other resources in tasks (such as those in examination questions) that require them to describe and explain ways in which weather and climate can affect people's lives and activities. Pupils should, therefore, have opportunities to apply their understanding and skills. For example, an A-level student might be asked to use the synoptic chart in Figure 6.2 to explain why the Meteorological Office might have issued a severe weather warning for midnight for the London area. Sometimes, synoptic charts are used with satellite photographs: for example, to examine a weather system such as a depression or a tropical cyclone. This can help pupils visualise features like weather fronts and the cloud patterns associated with different weather systems.

You can access a wide range of meteorological data and maps online. Both the Met Office and the Royal Meteorological Society provide online educational materials to support your teaching about weather and climate.

Atlases

The power of the atlas came into sharp focus when one of the authors was observing a Year 8 geography lesson. Two girls, at the back of the classroom, were pouring over a map of the world when the following interaction took place:

Pupil 1:   *Look! Look! Madagascar . . . it's a real place!*
Pupil 2:   *What? No . . .*
Pupil 1:   *It is . . . look, it's a real place, see here . . . (pointing to Madagascar on the world map)*
Pupil 2:   *Well, I didn't know that . . .*

The popular animated film had been on television the night before, yet clearly, these pupils had no idea that Madagascar was a real place. In a similar vein, a group of Year 9 pupils

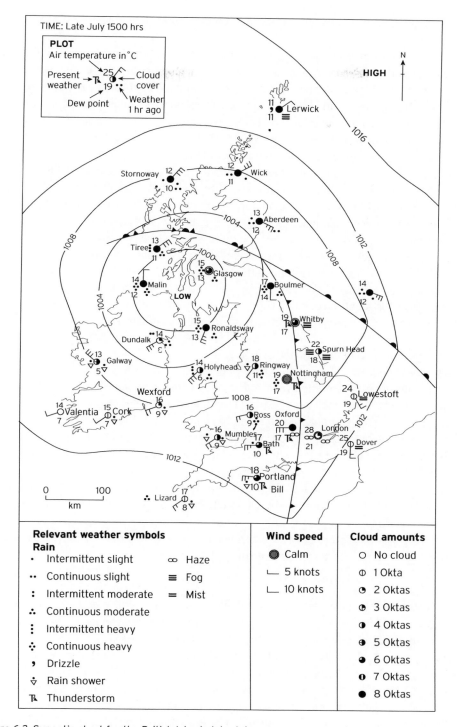

Figure 6.2 Synoptic chart for the British Isles in late July

learning about China's 'One Child' policy, had no idea where China was – no one had ever shown them on a map.

Pupils' lack of locational knowledge has long been bemoaned in the press, and the 2011 Ofsted report indicates that in geography lessons opportunities are being missed to develop pupils wider locational knowledge. We now have electronic resources at our finger tips in the form of electronic maps and atlases, and many classrooms still have hard copies of maps and atlases, and even the occasional globe! We would argue that these resources should be a feature of every geography lesson; we would go as far to say that it is impossible to teach a geography lessons without a map of some sort being used at some point!

There is now a great range of atlases (including electronic atlases) available to support and enhance pupils' learning in geography. Notwithstanding the changing nature of the world around us, the atlas still has an important role to play in helping pupils to both locate places within their regional, national and global contexts and study a wide range of geographical phenomena. Many atlases produced for schools are often textbooks in their own right, containing a variety of different kinds of maps, as well as a wide range of data and other information to support teaching and learning.

While geographers marvel at the range of maps now at our disposal, for pupils accessing the information on an atlas requires a certain level of 'abstract thinking'. A number of interpretation problems can be associated with the use of these maps including:

- complex patterns of colours and symbols
- a wide variety of typefaces and type styles
- a high density of information which can make the maps difficult to read
- the inter-cutting of map labels and labels with lines and colour
- certain place names that can be difficult to spell and to pronounce
- the use of colours with ambiguous meanings (e.g. green areas on topographic maps can be read as 'grassy' or 'fertile' when the colour is being used to indicate the height of the land)
- choropleth and isopleth maps that can mislead pupils into believing that sudden changes occur at the zone boundaries when in reality there is likely to be a transition from one zone to another
- standard world map projections, when used in isolation from alternatives, or a globe, can distort pupils' understanding of spatial relationships.

(Wiegand 1996: 125–126)

These problems are not always readily evident to a teacher and they can often be overlooked. We should be aware of the fact that, like any other reference book, an atlas presents only a 'partial and selective view of the world' (Wiegand 1996: 126).

Another issue that is often neglected is the importance of the type of projection that is used for different maps. Pupils need to be familiar with a variety of different projections and to understand that the selection of a projection is determined by the purpose for which the map is used. It is not possible to have a map that accurately shows both the relative shape and the area of land masses; being aware of potential problems that could hinder pupils' learning means spending some time examining the differences between projections in order to remove a possible cause of misinterpretation when pupils are using atlas maps in the future.

In order to make effective use of atlases, pupils need to develop a range of interrelated skills:

- locational skills – using the index and system of co-ordinates; understanding latitude and longitude
- symbol skills – learning about the different uses of colour and point symbols; using the key to interpret symbols
- sense of scale – using scale to compare areas and to estimate distances
- interpretation of data – describing, retrieving, using and comparing information about places shown on thematic maps.

A 'progressive teaching sequence' for developing pupils' understanding of longitude (meridians) and latitude (parallels) could be:

- The earth has two poles.
- There are two sets of imaginary lines circling the earth (lines that go round the earth at its maximum extent).
- Parallels do not join and only one of them (the equator) is a 'great circle'.
- Meridians and parallels are numbered in degrees.
- Some parallels have special names – the equator, the tropics and the polar circles.
- Meridians are numbered east and west from the prime meridian.
- The prime meridian is not 'natural'. It is only fixed by international agreement.
- Parallels are numbered north and south from the equator.
- The equator divides the world into north and south hemispheres.

(Wiegand 1996: 130)

Electronic atlases offer a vast amount of information in a range of formats including maps, text, statistics and both photographic and video material. When electronic atlases are used flexibly and interactively by pupils, there is a great deal of potential to enhance their learning. An example is the World Health Organisation's *Global Health Atlas*, which allows you to select specific areas and create maps showing the location of infrastructure such as healthcare facilities, schools, roads and geographic features, and map the spread of diseases.

Other kinds of maps and atlases

What is starting to unfold here is that fact that there are numerous different types of maps we can use in school geography, and that we *expect* to see maps such as Ordnance Survey maps, meteorological maps and other recognisable maps being used in geography teaching. In Chapter 3, we discussed pupils drawing their own mental maps and how these can support geographical learning. However, there are other kinds of maps and atlases that we can also use in geography teaching that represent the power of the imagination in creating alternative views of reality. Atlases such as Antonis et al.'s *The World According to Illustrators and Storytellers* (2013), Obrist and McCarthy's *Mapping It Out: An Alternative Atlas of Contemporary Cartographies* (2014) or van Swaaig, Klare, and Winner's *Atlas of Experience* (2000) all use maps in highly creative ways to represent people, places and personal experiences.*The World According to Illustrators and Storytellers* is a form of 'visual story telling' using maps and illustration techniques to tell stories of experiences, people and places. *The Atlas of Experience*, produced by Dutch cartographers, is a set of beautifully presented conceptual maps onto which the reader can impose their own particular narrative (Guignard, 2001). Maps such as the 'Map of Creativity' , The Map of Secrets' or the 'Map of Health', are all imaginative maps, created using cartographic techniques, and comprising recognisable map characteristics such as topography, trade and travel routes, ecosystems and weather. Such maps can be important for helping pupils to understand ways in which maps can be used to represent almost anything we want them to represent, without necessarily compromising the conceptual idea of what maps are. The maps in the *Atlas of Experience* can serve as models for pupils developing their own 'maps of experience' and can be particularly useful for debriefing learning, allowing pupils to express their learning experiences in cartographical form rather than more benign, less imaginative and less thought-provoking 'sticky notes'. We would argue that alternative types of maps have their place in teaching geographical ideas and understanding.

Task 6.2 Teaching and learning with maps

1   Review an existing scheme of work looking in particular for the ways that maps are embedded in the scheme. If maps are conspicuous by their absence, think about how maps could be embedded in the scheme in order to maximise pupils' geographical learning.

2   Observe a series of geography lessons, noting in particular the ways that maps are (or are not) embedded into lessons. How is pupils' location knowledge developed in the lessons you observe? What other resources do teachers use to support this process (photographs such as aerial photographs, text, numerical data, or other kinds of images such as art work)?

3   After some initial teaching experience, review your lessons for your own particular use of maps: what types of maps have you used in your teaching, how did you use them, what additional resources did you use and what do you think pupils gained from the opportunities you provided?

Using images

Aerial photographs

Aerial photographs are often used in conjunction with Ordnance Survey maps and with electronic maps to help pupils visualise landscapes shown on the maps. Pupils should be helped to understand the important elements of aerial photographs if they are going to be able to use these resources effectively. The effect of perspective will influence the shape and spatial arrangement of features viewed in a photograph. The effect of scale means that as the scale of a photograph becomes smaller it becomes more difficult to identify the detail of features. Whereas the scale of a map is consistent over the whole of the map, the scale of a photograph varies with distance from the camera. Pupils often overestimate the size of areas shown on a photograph when they are comparing it with a map, so it is useful to get them to measure the distances across the various components of the area shown on the photograph using the scale on the map.

For pupils who are unfamiliar with aerial photographs, a useful strategy to illustrate the effect of perspective is to start with ordinary ground-level photographs before moving on to investigate the different perspectives shown in oblique and vertical aerial photographs. Ground-level photographs show features in the foreground more prominently than those in the background and the variations in scale mean that distances cannot be measured. The transition between this view and that shown by a vertical aerial photograph is provided by an oblique aerial photograph. As such, it forms an intermediate stage in the mental processes involved in transforming the three-dimensional landscape of the real world to the vertical representation on the map (Boardman 1987: 133).

Figure 6.3 summarises a possible approach to the progressive development of these skills. As with all geographical skills, the aim is to move from an awareness of the important

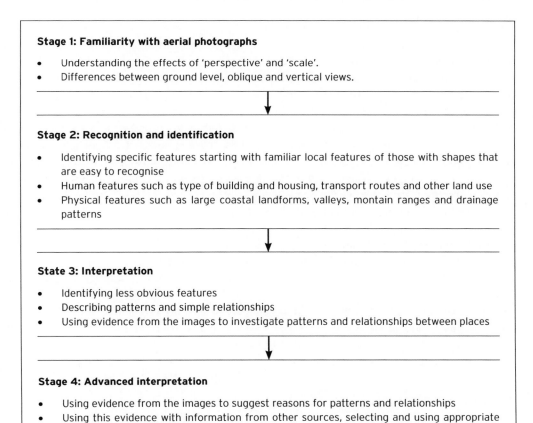

Stage 1: Familiarity with aerial photographs

- Understanding the effects of 'perspective' and 'scale'.
- Differences between ground level, oblique and vertical views.

Stage 2: Recognition and identification

- Identifying specific features starting with familiar local features of those with shapes that are easy to recognise
- Human features such as type of building and housing, transport routes and other land use
- Physical features such as large coastal landforms, valleys, montain ranges and drainage patterns

State 3: Interpretation

- Identifying less obvious features
- Describing patterns and simple relationships
- Using evidence from the images to investigate patterns and relationships between places

Stage 4: Advanced interpretation

- Using evidence from the images to suggest reasons for patterns and relationships
- Using this evidence with information from other sources, selecting and using appropriate skills in geographical enquiries

Figure 6.3 Progression in the development of skills used to interpret aerial photographs

characteristics of a resource, through an understanding of how to identify features and interpret evidence, towards the ability to select and use appropriate skills in the study of particular geographical themes and places.

Satellite (remote-sensing) images

'Remote-sensing' is a term used for a method of obtaining information about a place or an area from a distance. This information is collected by cameras and scanners that are carried by aeroplanes and satellites, and is presented in the form of photographs and images. As described earlier, aerial photographs usually show this information in much the same form as the human eye would see it (Barnett et al. 1995). However, information collected by the scanners carried by satellites goes beyond what the human eye can see so the images are often presented in 'false-colour' (unnatural colour) schemes that highlight interesting features.

There are two main types of satellites providing images which can be used in teaching:

- weather satellites such as METEOSAT
- land observation satellites such as the American LANDSAT and the French SPOT.

Remote-sensing images often motivate pupils as they can show more detail and depth of information than can usually be found on a map. They can also bring genuinely inaccessible areas of the world into the classroom, allowing pupils opportunities to see for themselves changes in rates of deforestation, examine evidence for resource exploitation or monitor glacial retreat. Understanding these images can be challenging so you need to consider how to teach pupils how to 'read' and interpret satellite images, or even how to use image-processing software to investigate a sequence of weather images; for example, to study the passage of a depression. As with aerial photographs, there is no strict progression in the way that pupils' skills for interpreting satellite images should be developed. However, as a general rule, the sequence suggested for aerial photographs in Figure 6.3 may be helpful to follow. To stimulate pupils' interest, it is helpful not to provide a key for the image at the outset and encourage them to think about the following:

- What do the different colours mean?
- What patterns or simple relationships can now be described?
- What factors have influenced the development of these patterns or relationships?

As is the case with many teaching resources, satellite images are not an end in themselves, and to support the enquiry work where pupils generate a series of enquiry questions that could be used as a basis for investigating the image, you need to carefully select other resources to support the process; local area maps, historical data or maps, and photos can all be part of a package of resources, which in combination with satellite can support pupils geographical learning.

Other types of images

Make every lesson a geographical experience; a journey of the geographical imagination.

(Durbin 2006: 232)

Photographs

Photographs, films, YouTube videos and so on are important sources of visual material that help geography teachers bring reality into their classrooms. The key role that visual images play in helping pupils to acquire knowledge about and perceptions of people and places means that, as teachers, we need to give careful attention to the strategies we employ when using different types of images with pupils.

Opportunities for pupils to share ideas and to explore values and attitudes in relation to issues can be exploited through the appropriate use of visual images. Robinson and Serf (1997: 58) identify learning skills that can be developed using photographic material:

- Making careful visual observations and verbal comments
- Acquiring information from a visual source
- Analysing and evaluating information
- Relating one's own views to the image
- Recognising the value of different interpretations
- Producing a written or oral interpretation of an image
- Empathising with the people or situations portrayed
- Forming links between photographs.

The use of photographic material can help pupils to develop a variety of learning skills. Skills of photographic interpretation should be developed gradually and it is important to focus on some basic skills before challenging pupils to make more detailed analyses. For example, pupils should be encouraged to look carefully at and assimilate the content of a photograph before attempting any interpretation. They should also be given the opportunity to relate what they see to their own experiences.

Below is a list of questions you could use with pupils to engage them in a critical analysis of an image:

- Who took this photograph?
- Why did they take it? Who was it taken for?
- How is the image organised: Foreground? Background? Representation of people? Camera angles?
- How is colour/shading used?
- What is the title of the photograph? Does the title convey a particular meaning? What could an alternative title be?
- Are there other photos of this place/event that convey different meanings?
- Do you think the photo is trying to convey a particular message? If so, what?
- What might be missing from this photograph?
- What might be happening around this image that you cannot see?
- How might the same picture look different in ten years' time?
- How might this place/these people be connected to other places?

(Adapted from Robinson and Serf 1997)

These kinds of questions are designed to encourage pupils to examine photographs with a more critical eye and to help them to understand that photographs are not neutral representations of people, places and events, but that they are perspectives and therefore in some way biased and so open to interpretation.

Hawley (2014) suggests several ways for using photographs to help pupils move beyond landscape description in developing their understanding of physical landscapes. The activities he suggest are engaging, but are specifically designed to ensure that pupils are challenged to examine photographs analytically and think carefully about the geographical content they can see. Pupils are expected to develop and use their geographical vocabulary, and apply their geographical knowledge and understanding to different contexts.

Landscape Bingo encourages students to develop their geographical vocabulary via geographical terms on 'bingo' cards and apply their understanding via a set of images. Pupils are given 'bingo' cards comprising a range of words relating to landscape features and landscape processes they have been studying. As a whole class, they carefully examine different photographs (presented on a white board) which you have selected from a range of locations, showing relevant landscapes. Pupils have to either identify relevant landscape features or make judgements about processes the landscape is likely to be subject to, and if they have the correct term on their bingo card then they can cross it off, but only after they have explained their thinking.

Six-degrees of Separation requires students to apply their geographical understanding when examining 'before' and 'after' photographs of an event such as the 2004 Boxing Day tsunami, or a volcanic eruption. Working in pairs (A and B), and siting 'back-to-back' and with a six-box story board between them, pupil A describes in detail the 'before' image to B, who has to draw it in the first box of the story board. As a whole class, you then show the students the 'after' image and they draw this in box five together. They then have to complete the interim four boxes, applying their geographical knowledge of processes in order to represent the stages of landscape change. The sixth box is there for students to consider what a future landscape might look like. The aim of the activity is 'to go beyond the "end point" of physical features often shown in diagrams and to think independently and inferentially to suggest possible and probable future landscapes' (Hawley 2014: 27). In addition, frameworks like the Development Compass Rose (shown on page 289 of this book) can also be useful in supporting photographic analysis as pupils are invited to interrogate the social, environmental and natural elements in evidence in any one particular image.

What the above tells us is that photographic analysis cannot be left to chance and should not merely be an opportunity for pupils to 'have a quick look' at a geographical feature or phenomenon. If pupils are to really learn to make sense of photographic evidence, they need scaffolds and processes that help them to do this. Activities drawn from media education, like scripting a documentary using a selection of photographs, provide creative and motivating strategies for promoting discovery learning (see Durbin 2006: 234–235).

Pupils also learn by taking and using their own photographs to record their observations in fieldwork activities. This can be particularly useful when analysing attitudes and values involved in issues. For example, when investigating the impacts of recreation in an area within a national park, pupils could be asked to take photographs to show evidence of particular recreational activities and their impacts. Alternatively, pupils could investigate the regeneration of an urban area and take photographs to support a particular viewpoint. For example, one group would take appropriate photographs to construct a display to show that the regeneration had been successful while another group would attempt to show evidence of failure, concentrating on the negative impacts.

In both examples, follow-up activities, such as a poster display or a discussion/presentation/role play, could be developed so that pupils could represent different viewpoints and demonstrate their geographical understanding.

An interesting fieldwork investigation could be set up by providing groups of pupils with different sets of photographs of geographical features and locations in an area to be visited. During the visit, the pupils would have to match the photographs to particular locations, which would then be identified on an Ordnance Survey map of the area.

There are other types of images we can use in conjunction with photographs in geography. These include simplified or idealised maps, which are effective when used to show the main features of geographical patterns or the typical spatial impacts of processes involved in a geographical model. Flow diagrams are also frequently used to show the impacts and consequences of different geographical processes and graphical representations of models are used to show changes in geographical phenomena over time. As geographers, we are familiar with such diagrams as a method of communicating geographical ideas and we are experienced at interpreting them. But do our pupils see things in the same way? How do they interpret diagrammatic representations of reality?

Moving images

> Because so much of our geographical source material is derived from television, it is vital that in a secondary school geography curriculum we take account of the distortions that can result from this particular source of images and ideas. Many television genres are constructions of reality and can bias our views, albeit unintentionally.
>
> (Durbin 2006: 229)

Moving images make a significant contribution to teaching and learning in geography. However, if films and so on are to fulfil their educational potential, we need to adopt active strategies that encourage pupils to 'use and analyse' the material provided rather than just 'watch and see'. Writing about her experiences of working with a group of PGCE students, Margaret Roberts described the rather disappointing outcome having allowed her students to 'just watch' the film:

> A group of student teachers were shown a television programme and asked to take notes on what they learned from it. The programme was stopped after five minutes and the transcript of the commentary was read out. The students were asked to delete from their notes anything which they had written down during the programme that was in the transcript. Not a single student had anything left! They had made no record of what they had just seen. This revealed that the students were not interpreting the pictures; they had behaved as if it was a simple dictation exercise. Visual information was not recorded.
>
> (Roberts 1987: 116)

Using clips from television programmes can serve a number of purposes. They can be very effective in 'capturing' pupils' interest or providing an 'inspiring lead into' an activity. As well as being used to 'capture interest', video clips can be interspersed with key questions and activities as part of a geographical enquiry. Feretti (2009) discusses the use of film and television to support pupils 'intelligent guesswork' (p. 110) as they are shown a clip and then asked to predict what they think will happen next. Alternatively, brief video sequences can be recorded from news programmes and accompanied by enquiry questions to bring in topical items with geographical relevance.

Chris Durbin (1995) suggests that television and other film resources are helpful because they:

- bring distant places to the classroom
- enable people's views to be heard, although they are often short sound bites
- can explain a difficult concept or process using a combination of images, graphics and commentary
- can relate the location of a place to a wider region or even the world, through a series of 'nested' maps
- can give a visual impression of change over time in relation to various geographical phenomena.

However, Durbin reminds us that it is difficult for television and film to:

- convey detail on maps and also specific locational knowledge
- convey complex geographical data
- give subtle and complex viewpoints about an issue
- allow enough time to dwell on images to enable the viewer to absorb complex information.

Media literacy is a vital part of geographical education and, as geography teachers, we must ensure that pupils are aware of how their views of the world are shaped by the images and messages they receive from the media:

> As geography teachers we have a particular responsibility because our subject is full of partial truths, is in many ways an uncertain science, and involves issues in which there are vested interests and about which there are varying opinions.
>
> (Durbin 2006: 236)

Table 6.1 suggests a range of ways that moving images can be used in geography classroom. What is important in this list is the relationship between activities and outcomes. The activities have been deliberately designed to promote critical medial literacy.

Although it is time-consuming, you should always preview and evaluate televisual materials that you intend to use in the classroom and ensure that they meet the needs of the geographical learning you want to take place. You should also analyse the content of televisual resources for gender and ethno-centric bias (Butt 1991). Geography teachers can draw upon a variety of strategies to address bias in visual material by involving pupils in an evaluation activity. Table 6.2 is one approach you could use.

The work of Urban earth (http://urbanearth.ning.com/video) brings geographical film-making into a new perspective. Geography educators such as teachers have created a range

Table 6.1 Using media literacy techniques creatively in geography

Basic technique	Possible teaching activities	Learning objectives
Freeze frame	While watching a film clip which has strong landscape scenery (e.g. *Lord of the Rings* trilogy to illustrate the landscapes of New Zealand) the pupils write down adjectives which will support written description, classifying them into colours, shapes, patterns and textures.	Pupils should learn that: • Film-makers choose camera position, framing, angle and movement to create a particular impression of landscape, weather and human activity. • Films can be shot in different ways to portray a place.
Sound and image	• While watching a film sequence, without sound, set in a specific location, pupils hypothesise the sounds suggested by the visuals. • With another piece of video and three or four pieces of music or sound effects, pupils work in pairs to evaluate the effects of music on the image of the place.	• Sound is as influential as pictures in creating an image of place. • The image of the place conveyed in a film is influenced by the nature of the sound tracks. • The atmosphere of the place is conveyed by the choice of music.
Top and tail	• Pupils are given a printout of some of the credits from a diverse range of films about the rainforest or another issue of human impact on the environment (e.g. natural history documentary, adventure fiction, charity appeal, etc.). They are shown the tops of the programmes including the first few minutes of the film and they have to match them with the credits, justifying their choices.	• The values and attitudes of film-makers, sponsors and production companies can differ and these differences can often be evident in their programmes or films. • Moving image texts targeted at different audiences can have different perspectives on their subject.
Cross-media comparisons	Pupils evaluate the portrayal of an earthquake or volcanic eruption, comparing a fictional film interpretation such as *Dante's Peak* (Roger Donaldson 1997) with a television documentary.	Fact and fiction provide different kinds of evidence about natural phenomena: fiction may provide emotional involvement but be unreliable as evidence; documentary may fail to communicate the immediacy of the experience.

Source: British Film Institute 2000: 25, 'Moving Images in the Classroom'

of films designed to 're-present' some of the world's largest urban areas. Film-makers have walked across cities, such as London, Mexico City and Mumbai, and every eight steps they have stopped to take a picture, regardless of what they can see. These pictures have then been cut together to give the viewer a unique perspective on how these places change from the outer limits, through the centre and then out to the other side. These films are unique in their design and are deliberately free from background music and commentary. The intention

Table 6.2 Evaluating televisual resources with pupils

Characteristic	Criteria	
Purpose	Why was the film/clip/ programme created? To entertain, inform?	
Who owns it?	Commercial company, aid agency, government organisation personal, other?	
Age	How old is the film/clip? Why might this be significant?	
Geographical content	What are the key geographical themes you can see in the film/clip:	1 2 3 4 5
Coverage	Does the film/clip leave out anything that you think might be important?	
Bias	Does the film/clip represent a very particular point of view and how do you know this? How are different groups of people represented? How are different places represented?	
Presentation	Is the film/clip easy to see? Is the sound clear and easy to hear? Are any captions relevant and useful?	
Audience	Who is the film/clip's intended audience? What impact might this have on its content?	

(*Source*: Adapted from Lederer 2013)

is that the viewer watches, without interruption, and sees and thinks for themselves about how these cities are, as places to be.

Small hand-held devices and mobile phone technology means that the kind of production undertaken by Urban earth is well within the reach of even young pupils, and pupils and teachers can use this technology creatively in their geographical enquiries (Raven-Ellison 2005). Filming can be used to great effect, by teachers developing 'virtual fieldwork' resources, possibly for preparatory work before pupils actually visit a place. Pupils can also be asked to capture their fieldwork experiences in film. Perhaps using the approach of Urban earth, or teachers can set pupils a particular task whereby pupils have to gather evidence (newspaper articles, tourist information leaflets and so on) and then write and edit together their own 'documentary' representing a place from a particular perspective. The process of constructing a film such as this encourages pupils to carefully consider what they are representing about a place and therefore how they are re-presenting it.

Film-making can be used in other ways. Jones and Ryecraft (2007) describe how PGCE geography student teachers, using modelling clay, hand-held cameras and stop-frame animation software, produced their own films of different landscape formations. While this may sound like a lot of fun, do not under-estimate the degree of geographical reasoning that has to go into such a process. As they explain:

At the different stages in the process, PGCE students actively discussed the geographi-cal principles that they were basing their decisions on as they planned and carried out their animations. Such discussion involved the PGCE students actively questioning, rea-soning, challenging, justifying, compromising and confirming the processes and the ver-sion of geography they would be presenting to an audience.

(Jones and Ryecraft 2007: 95)

Doing this kind of activity requires a degree of preparation and Jones and Ryecraft recom-mend that you first of all complete a similar task yourself, before asking pupils to do it. In setting up the film-making, they also recommend that pupils prepare a 'script' for their anima-tion, via a storyboard, before they begin preparing their models to make sure that they make effective use of the time available. They also recommend that pupils have an audience for their film in order to add a sense of purpose to the process. Involving pupils in making films this way can really concentrate their thinking on the fine detail of landscape formation and can provide evidence for formative assessment purposes about pupils' geographical understanding. Figure 6.4 shows the role of careful planning and preparation to support the use of digital video.

Alongside films produced specifically for educational purposes, there are great many fea-ture films that can also support geographical learning. Feature films can convey the magnifi-cence of landscapes (for example *The Lord of the Rings* trilogy filmed in New Zealand), the impact of globalisation (*Blood Diamonds*) or the cyclical nature of poverty (*City of God*, set in one of Brazil's poorest barrios). While there are an almost infinite range of geographical themes you can elicit from feature films, di Palma reminds us that:

The use of visual teaching material alone is not sufficient enough to enhance visual thought. . . . Simply presenting photographs, drawings, models or practical exhibitions as aids for study is no guarantee that the subject will be understood deeply.

(Arnheim 1969: 361, cited in di Palma 2009: 48)

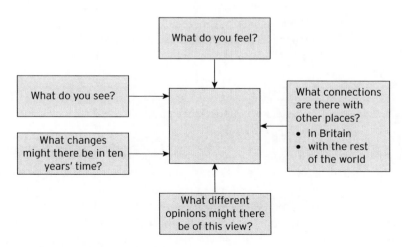

Figure 6.4 Stages in the animation process

(*Source*: Jones and Ryecraft 2007: 93–96)

Feature films have to be mediated and used in conjunction with other resources if they are to realise their educational potential in geography. In the context of using feature films, di Palma (2009) identifies four specific tensions that require some thought:

1   Viewing vs knowledge – in turning viewing a film into geographical knowledge, pupils have to become what she described as 'attentive observers' (p. 49).
2   Fiction vs reality – pupils need to appreciate how the message of a film is conveyed via camera angles, use of light and colour.
3   Stereotypes vs. complexity – films are a form of cultural matrix so pupils need to access multiple sources in order to be able to question the content as represented in a film.
4   Passive vs active learning – pupils will need to be actively engaged in viewing, analysing and critiquing films if their geographical knowledge and understanding is to be developed.

As a response to these four tensions, Morgan (2003) and Balderstone (2006) suggest that school geography can provide pupils with opportunities to question cultural representations and that this can perhaps best be done by using advertisements, television programmes, films, music and travel guides to help students explore how particular views of how the world are constructed (Morgan 2003). As an example, Morgan describes how the film *The Full Monty* can provide significant opportunities for teaching geography in ways that reflect developments in the subject discipline, particularly drawing upon cultural geography. Geography teachers have used this film successfully, exploring themes about the gendered nature of work, the separation of private and public spheres and the gendered use of space, to enrich geographical enquiries about economic change.

In exploring the everyday landscapes of national identities, Winchester, Kong and Dunn (2003) describe films as form of text or cultural product in the social construction of such identities. They observe how Australians increasingly identified with the 'red centre' (Uluru) and areas of wilderness such as Kakadu in films like *Priscilla: Queen of the Desert* and *Crocodile Dundee*. Such films were also seen as an attempt to counter Australia's perceived vulnerability to the cultural dominance of the United States and they observed how urban landscapes were often portrayed as a 'site of problems and injustice', whereas rural and wilderness areas are portrayed as 'harsh, but communal and level playing fields' (Winchester et al. 2003: 47).

Task 6.3 Developing your use of images in geography

1   With a group of other PGCE students, identify possible feature films (or more realistically, clips from films) that could be used in geography lessons. Discuss what films you would use, how you would use them and why you think they would be the best medium for you to use to convey a particular concept or issue.
2   Plan a geography lesson where you use a range of different photographs to develop pupils' understanding of a specific process or issue. What other resources, in addition to the photographs, will you need to support pupils' developing their geographical understanding?

3   Using Jones and Rycraft's suggestion for developing animations of physical processes, set aside some time to develop your own 'stop-frame' animation of a physical geography process such as waterfall retreat or features of coastal erosion.

4   With a group of pupils, use digital cameras (either mobile phone technology or hand-held cameras will do) to create your own 'geographical film'. These could be almost anything you decide but examples could include:

- pupils filming their own pre-prepared weather forecast
- pupils filming a news programme or documentary about an enquiry into, for example, land use change in the local area
- pupils filming their own fieldwork
- working with pupils to create a 'walk through' of your local town or city, similar to those on the UrbanEarth website.

Think carefully about how you would need to prepare pupils for any filming and also be mindful of any school regulations regarding the filming of pupils and how this is subsequently used.

Using newspaper resources

Newspapers provide us with opportunities to bring up-to-date information and events into the classroom. They can help us develop case studies about people and places, as well as about global trends and issues that are of current relevance and concern. They often provide us with information about the opinions and views of different people or interest groups involved in or affected by geographical issues.

The style in which most newspaper articles are written makes them a lively and informative geographical resource. Articles are sometimes accompanied by maps showing the location of places referred to in the article or displaying relevant spatial information. These are particularly useful when they show spatial patterns or distributions revealed in recently published statistics; for example, in social, economic, health or crime statistics. They can also update some atlas maps showing the impact of recent political developments such as regional and national boundary changes. However, we should be aware of the fact that these maps are not always accurate and there are numerous examples of distorted patterns or incorrect locations being shown on newspaper maps. However, generally, using such material also helps to support our claim that geography is a dynamic subject relevant to young people growing up in the world today.

The Royal Geographical Society's 'Geography in the News' website (www.geography-inthenews.rgs.org) is a useful resource for busy geography teachers looking for information about topical geographical issues and events.

While acknowledging the benefits, we also need to be aware of the limitations of newspaper material. Articles are usually, by their nature, concise (one of their advantages) and can therefore oversimplify information and explanations. The bias of the writer (and sometimes of the newspaper itself) also needs to be recognised because of the way this influences the selection, interpretation and presentation of viewpoints.

Even with these limitations, newspaper articles can have a valuable role to play in helping to develop pupils' critical thinking. Pupils should be encouraged to identify which information is critical and relevant as well as consider any conflicting evidence or viewpoints not included in the article but in other sources.

The following framework could help pupils to not only learn about geographically relevant events and their impacts, but also to examine them critically:

- Why did they happen?
- Why did they happen here?
- What are the possible consequences going to be in both the short term and long term?
- What do the pupils themselves wish to understand about the issue?
- What are the social, political, economic and environmental causes of the event?
- What can geography contribute to the analysis of this event?
- What are the opportunities for bridging to other examples or case studies?
- What predictions can we make about the long- and short-term effects of this event?

(Brooks 2003: 70)

Task 6.4 Geography in the news!

Find two or three examples of newspaper articles about one particular geographical issue or themes.

1   Identify the key ideas, facts and geographical words in each article.
2   Consider how the article is organised in terms of headlines and subheadings, use of images and other visual sources such as maps, diagrams or data.
3   Is there any other information or evidence that could or should have been included to ensure balance?
4   Identify any opinions or viewpoints expressed about the issue or theme. Are there any other views, or other interest groups with views, about this issue not in the article?
5   Think carefully about how you might use one of the articles with a class. Consider:

   - language level – how will you help pupils access the text?
   - how you will use any images/data/maps
   - other supporting resources you might need to find to support pupils' geographical understanding.

Pupils can be very keen to contribute to discussions about current events so asking them to, if possible, look at home or online for news reports of a major event can be a good way of encouraging them to engage with news sources. Once pupils have developed the skills needed to use news articles effectively, newspapers and other news sources can become useful in terms of setting meaningful homework activities. On a regular basis, pupils could select a relevant article about a geographical issue, note the key facts and summarise the key ideas covered in the article.

Using cartoons

Cartoons have become an increasingly used resource in geography teaching. They are to be found in published resources such as textbooks and have featured in GCSE and A-level examination questions. As teachers, we are also likely to come across cartoons about a wide variety of geographical issues in newspapers and magazines, usually when these issues are topical.

Clearly the apparent simplicity of cartoons and their potential to generate humour makes them appealing resources to use with pupils. As well as being motivating to use for many pupils, cartoons are flexible resources which, like other visual material, can be used in a wide variety of ways. They can be particularly useful for helping pupils to recognise and evaluate different viewpoints about an issue. However, as with all resources, we must be aware of their limitations when selecting cartoons for use in the classroom. We should also be careful to devise appropriate strategies for using cartoons that challenge rather than reinforce bias and stereotypes.

Marsden has raised concerns that cartoons could become the 'new stereotyping' in geography. He urges us to balance the advantages and disadvantages of the various types of cartoon material. He is particularly concerned about the use of comic-type caricatures, which he regards as 'the most dangerous manifestation of the "new stereotyping"'. Marsden reminds us that the process of 'caricaturing' is the 'art of pictorial ridicule which, through grotesque exaggerations of human features into debased likenesses, implicitly dehumanised' (Marsden 1992: 128). In doing so, he argues that such material can be 'educationally and socially damaging in that while complex reality has to be made more clear-cut than it really is, the crass over simplification sometimes presented can reduce important issues to triviality' (Marsden 1992: 129).

A general perusal of the geography textbooks being used in schools today is likely to reveal a number of what might be described as 'narrative *talking-head* depictions' of people presenting different viewpoints. These are often used to simplify the attitudes and values of different individuals or groups involved in an issue. However, they can sometimes reveal more about the humour or creativity of the graphic designer than the real-life people that they are supposed to represent. The absence of real places in most cartoons can also be an issue of concern. Fortunately, as we mentioned earlier, most publishers are becoming more aware of these dangers.

The perceived advantages of using cartoon material in geography texts include:

- motivational – providing 'entertainment value'
- pedagogical – a way of simplifying the complexities of reality
- presentational – adding to the variety of stimulus materials
- logistical – a convenient way of providing generalised impressions of life in other places (in the absence of 'real photographs')
- cognitive – using cartoons as teaching material requires the 'application of often high level interpretational skills'.

(Marsden 1992: 128)

Marsden's final point about the potential 'cognitive value' of using cartoons highlights the importance of the teaching and learning strategies employed. The apparent simplicity of the cartoon and its captions may conceal more complex messages. The interpretation of these hidden messages and agendas could provide the focus for many worthwhile learning activities.

The 'arts' as imaginative resources for geography

> We hope that the National Curriculum in geography will stimulate the use of painting, photography, music, prose, poetry, dance and drama as well as radio, film and video. They are of value in the evocation of a sense of place and can stimulate hearts and minds. They also add immensely to the enjoyment of geography.
>
> (DES 1990: para 7.20)

Literature and poetry

Literature and poetry can be exploited in imaginative ways by geography teachers. Rawling (2010) turns to new interpretations of cultural geography in helping us make sense of places, explaining how 'literature, painting, walking, photography, playing sport and exploration are all seen as activities with the potential to show how our "being in the world" takes shape'. (Rawling 2010: 93). These 'ways of being' provide many interesting opportunities for developing a 'humanistic' approach to the study of places and provide some weight to the significance of drawing on the senses, emotions and feelings in understanding our engagement with places (Rawling 2010). She considers the significance of a new relationship between the arts, particularly poetry, and school geography in helping young people to 'reflect on the way their own lives are intertwined with the places and landscapes they inhabit, or to introduce them to more personal responses to places' (p. 93).

Fieldwork provides many opportunities for different sensory learning experiences that can inspire poetry, such as 'Haiku' poetry. Haiku is a Japanese term describing a simple three-line poem consisting of 17 syllables. Using Haiku writing as a way of raising pupils' awareness of their surroundings would require them to find a suitable place to sit and to relax. They should be encouraged to clear their minds so that they can then become aware of stimuli (visual, sounds, smells) from their surroundings. A blindfold could even be used to help them concentrate on sounds and smells for a few minutes.

After about ten minutes, they should write down some words to describe the sights, sounds, smells and feelings. These words can then be arranged in a Haiku structure. This can be done individually or collectively. By having five syllables in the first and last line, and seven in the middle line, the Haiku has a balanced form. The examples shown below are not quite as they should be!

Haiku poems about the environment:
Swirling green water
Flows endlessly on to the
Limitless ocean

Your time here is short
Thinks the round golden pebble
In rhythmical waves

Fumes from a taxi
Swirl round the face of the child
As she sleeps unaware

(Acknowledgement: These examples were provided by David
Job in a workshop for geography teachers at the Institute
of Education, University of London)

There are many novels which provide what Rex Walford has called a 'regional comprehension'. Appropriate extracts from novels by authors like Thomas Hardy could be read and analysed as a way of exploring the sense of place they seek to invoke. There are also novels that focus on geographical themes and issues. For example, Steinbeck's *Grapes of Wrath* explores the impact of the motor car on transport in the USA, while *Paradise News* by David Lodge describes the impacts of tourism.

Despite the 2014 debate about what kinds of books pupils should read as part of the English Literature curriculum, it is useful to become familiar with books that pupils read in their English lessons. Such texts are often valuable to use in geography in terms of both creating some curriculum coherence for pupils, but also novels often contain examples of 'rich description' of places rarely found in geography textbooks and so can provide alternative sources of inspiration for teaching and learning about places.

The following are some novels that pupils may have read:

Holes by Louis Sachar
North of Beautiful by Justina Chen Hadley
Of Mice and Men by John Steinbeck
Kiss the Dust by Elizabeth Laird
Kakadu Calling by Jane Garlil Christophersen
Journey to the River Sea by Eva Ibbotson
Miraculous Journey of Edward Tulane by Kate DiCamillo
Walkabout by James Vance Marshall
Al Capone Does My Shirts by Gennifer Choldenko (no journeys but the place is very significant).

Also, Sidall (2009) *Landscape and Literature* introduces you to the process of exploring different ways in which landscape has been represented in literature.

Art

While poetry and literature can help teachers and pupils develop their affective understanding of places, so too can art, both 'traditional' paintings and also less conventional representations. It is now possible to obtain posters and postcards of many famous landscape paintings. These lend themselves to a number of interesting tasks, not least to consider the impression of a landscape that an artist is trying to convey. In what ways do the artists use the weather to evoke a mood? What images do Lowry's paintings present of industrial north-west England? There are, therefore, several opportunities for meaningful co-operation with art teachers, including the development of pupils' field sketching skills.

Less conventional ideas might include Slinkachu's (2008) *Little People in the City* where tiny figurines, 1/87 in scale to the 'real' world, are situated and photographed in urban settings, surrounded by seemingly disproportionate urban paraphernalia; the images provoke questions about urban scales and structures and provide an interesting lens through which to view the urban environment. In a similar vein, urban street art provokes us to see the urban landscape differently and to question different artistic representations of and engagement with places and spaces.

While the art of others can be used to promote geographical conversations, pupils own artwork can really engage pupils in seeing and interpreting the world in different ways for themselves. One of the authors, working with a creative practitioner (an installation artist), a group of Year 9 students and their geography teacher set about developing pupils' understanding of global water inequalities. Their teacher created a set of profiles of different countries fresh water availability. In groups, the pupils completed research of their country and then, with the help of the creative practitioner and using a range of collectable objects, including the inimitable 'squeezy bottle', set about creating an installation that in some way represented their nation's water supply. For example, one group created an elaborate network of wool, string, straws and bottle tops to represent their nation's need to gather fresh water via desalination processes. Another group, a nation with abundant fresh water, creating a sophisticated systems or straws and toilet rolls to represent water transfer around the country. Applying their understanding of fresh water availability to some form of creative representation seemed to focus the pupil minds on thinking about water supply, storage and transfer. Asking them to then trade water with each other enabled them to begin to appreciate the politics of global fresh water supply.

Music

There are several different ways in which music can be used in geography lessons. Short sections of instrumental music can help to focus pupils on a task such as watching sequences of images. Playing music can also help to evoke images and develop a 'sense of place'. For example, slides showing views of coastal landforms could be accompanied by Debussy's *La Mer* while Wagner's *Flying Dutchman Overture* provides more dramatic sound to use with images of Australia, showing stormy seas around the 'Seven Apostles' on the coast of Victoria.

The role of music in creating moods and evoking a sense of place suggests possibilities for more direct use of music in learning activities. Music is often used to emphasise the impact of visual images in documentaries and other television programmes. Pupils could be shown the visual sequences without the sound and asked to write down words to describe their feelings about what they are looking at. They could also describe the type of music that they might use as background for these sequences and why. The sequence could then be replayed with the sound and the role of the music in influencing the impact of these images discussed.

Music is a powerful source of images and symbolism. It is possible to identify references to geographical terms, places and issues in the lyrics of contemporary music. Through these lyrics, songwriters impart images of popular culture. How these images are perceived and interpreted depends on the listener. However, the use of geographic symbolism in contempo-rary music is extensive and, as most cultural geographers would argue, the dynamic nature of culture puts it at the heart of human geography. (See the section on curriculum artefacts in Chapter 3 for an example of how an Irish folk song can be used in geography lessons.)

Music, of course, has its own geographies and themes such as the geography of music festivals (which contain significant environmental issues to explore – transport, waste, green policies and so on), the impact of music movements on the socials and cultural geographies of cities (the Beatles in Liverpool, Punk Rock in New York and London, Northern Soul in Northern England and the Midlands and the impact of Tamla Motown on Detroit), and the cultural geographies of young people all mean that music is not just a resource; it also influ-ences and is influenced by place and space.

Models

Despite limited time available for teaching geography in many secondary schools, it is pos-sible to create opportunities to use models in geography lessons. Taking time to use them can be justified in terms of both the impact they have on pupils' motivation and how models support pupils' understanding of concepts and processes. As Yoxall argued in relation to the use of hardware models in earth science instruction: 'Often an hour of relatively simple experimentation can teach more than pages of book reading or hours of classroom talking' (Yoxall 1989: 169)

Yoxall is referring to the use of larger-scale hardware models that only tend to be found in the earth science laboratories of some universities; however, his justifications can be applied to the use of a range of different kinds of models. Scaled models, whether they are relief models or models of coastal landforms in a wave tank, help pupils to gain a more 'holistic perspective' of landscape systems because, especially if they are dynamic, they 'compress time' and thus can help pupils to conceptualise links between form and process more eas-ily (Job and Buck 1994: 106). However, these models are actually closed systems, but they are representing open systems in the natural environment; this is an important discussion point to have with pupils. Inman (2006) suggests a range of other creative approaches to what he calls 'classroom fieldwork' to bring alive the study of environmental processes in the geography classroom. These include the use of analogies, or 'models of the mind' to aid 'visualisation' and learning about processes and landforms (Inman 2006: 273–274).

Helping pupils to understand the role of contours in depicting the relief of an area on a flat topographical map can present a challenge. Until pupils have grasped this concept, they find it difficult to interpret relief on a map and to transform contours into a cross-section of a landscape. Relief models of an area can be built using thick corrugated card or polystyrene tiles which pupils cut and layer in order to reconstruct a 3-D model of a landscape. They then paint and label accordingly.

Parkinson's 'miniture landscapes' (2009) are what he describes as: 'a creatively subver-sive way of approaching the study of physical geography' (p. 120). Using take-away packag-ing from a fast-food outlet, Parkinson describes how pupils were instructed to construct a mini-landscape to fit inside the box. This then remained a secret until they revealed all in their lesson. Parkinson asked his pupils not to construct an imagined landscape, but to search out maps and images of real places in order to construct a miniature version of a real place. They also had to be prepared to explain their landscape to the rest of the class.

Parkinson recommends that to ensure that the activity supports geographical understanding, then some search questions need to be asked as shown in Box 6.1.

Box 6.1 Questions to encourage students to think about the contents of the box as an actual place

1   Describe the landscape that is in your box, using as many appropriate adjectives as possible.
2   Imagine standing in the landscape in your box. What would you see, smell, feel, hear?
3   What changes are likely to take place in your landscape over time – either short term or long term?
4   Now look at your neighbour's landscape and imagine spending time there – what would you do in that landscape?
5   What similarities and differences are there between your two landscapes?

(*Source*: Parkinson 2009)

The activity is also not particularly age-specific; one of the authors asks her PGCE students to make a 'mini-landscape' of the university campus at the very start of the course; in this context, the activity proves to be is good for team building and area familiarisation, and it marks the PGCE students' first foray into peer assessment! There are also variations on this 'mini' theme including using recyclable material instead of the polystyrene products of fast-food outlets, and the idea does not have to be restricted to landscapes – one of our PGCE students asked her pupils to make 'biomes in-a-box'.

Balderstone and Payne (1992) describe their squatter settlement model-making. The stimulus for the activity was provided by using photographic images and video clips of different squatter settlements; this helped to develop a 'sense of place'. Profiles of families from the video clips, who are having to build their homes in squatter settlements were detailed on study cards to help pupils get to know them as individuals and thus develop some empathy with those involved.

Over a few weeks, a large collection of simple materials had been assembled to provide the resources for this activity. These included scraps of paper and card, matchsticks, match boxes, lolly sticks, paper clips, twigs, sticky tack, clay, string and plastic. These materials formed a city dump on a separate table. The pupils were organised into small groups (2–4 pupils) and were allocated a short period of time to collection of materials and plan their family shelter. Each group was given a piece of card on which to build their house. Once the context for the activity had been established, the pupils were given the remaining 30 minutes of the lesson to construct a basic shelter. In the subsequent lesson, settlement building continued, but, with the teacher representing the city authorities, various issues were introduced to simulate to difficulties families can face. The impacts of these on those trying to live in the squatter settlement were periodically evaluated. New materials were provided to help some pupils improve the construction of their houses (stronger card, glue and scissors for some), yet some were given difficult sloping sites on which to build their homes. You can use a watering can (if the settlement is built outside!) to simulate the impact of heavy rainfall on squatter settlements.

Pupils are certainly motivated by learning experiences like this. However, the teacher's skill in debriefing the pupils, helping them to make sense of what has been happening and how it relates to reality is *crucial* if the intended conceptual understanding is to be achieved. Inman (2006: 272) warns that the 'realism' and strong visual quality of the model itself can sometimes inhibit pupils' ability to transfer their understanding from the simulation to reality. This is why careful debriefing is vital to develop conceptual understanding. Linking the above activity with appropriate visual images and information about real case studies helps to maximise the potential of this learning experience. It can also be integrated effectively with role play or decision-making exercises about ways of addressing housing problems in a large city in a less economically developed country.

Technology

Technology enables the bringing together a range of resources in order facilitate more active learning. Many of these resources (e.g. photographic images, maps and video) have been available for some time, but it is the ability to integrate their use in more efficient and, hopefully, more effective ways that ICT has improved so significantly. Recent years have seen the growing use of 'virtual learning environments' (VLEs) in which pupils and teachers interact online. These learning platforms and their 'virtual learning environments' provide pupils with access to learning resources and activities from anywhere in a school, at home or elsewhere so that they are able to work collaboratively online as well as in a classroom. Many geography departments now have their own websites with a wide range of resources and activities to support teaching and learning including images, webcams, animations and links to other useful websites (Mitchell 2007).

You cannot avoid using technology in your teaching; not least because pupils are required to develop their skills and geographical understanding through the use of technological systems such as Geographic Information Systems (GIS) at all key stages in geography, but also because technology is now an embedded aspect of classroom practice meaning that geography teachers have opportunities to 'bring the world into the classroom' in ever more stimulating ways. One such opportunity is Gapminder (www.gapminder.org/) a website that provides you access to statistics and other information about social, economic and environmental development at a range of scales. The power of Gapminder is in the high quality of the available data (and there is plenty of it) as well as the tools the site uses to illustrate how different statistics give us very different messages about a country's state of development. One very powerful attribute of the site is its potential to challenge many misconceptions that teachers and pupils have about development data and what it actually means. Visually, the site is impressive and helpful videos demonstrate how to use the vast range of resources available.

Keeping up to date with 'what's out there' in technological developments for geography teaching seems almost impossible. The Geographical Association (GA) and the Royal Geographical Society (RGS) both have websites where you can at least get some sense of latest developments. In particular the GA's publication *GA Magazine*, published three times per year, contains a regular feature called 'Webwatch' where new sites, resources, blogs and Twitter accounts are reviewed and reported on in terms of what they have to offer geography teachers . In the Summer 2014 edition alone, we were introduced to I-Use (www.i-use.eu), to support the teaching of statistics, London Mapper (www.londonmapper.org.uk) which describes itself as a 'social atlas of London' covering topics such as poverty and wealth and inequalities in London, and a new online ArcGIS.

Not unsurprisingly, all online resources require careful evaluation before they are used. Not all sources are reliable and pupils need to understand the importance of checking information such as data age and origin before they make assumptions about the validity of different sources. Developing pupils' critical literacy when it comes to internet and other electronic sources is an important responsibility of all teachers. There is an additional health warning that comes with the rapid increase in technological developments. This is that, despite the educational potential of many different forms of technology and regardless of the temptations to get embroiled in shiny new toys and their applications, technology is only as good as its user; careless and inappropriate use is as much a waste of time as is the careless and inappropriate use of any other resource. Parkinson (2013) asks the question 'is technology always the best tool to use?' (p. 202). Clearly the answer is 'No': the way to avoid the technology trap is for the geography you want pupils to learn to remain at the forefront of your lesson planning and curriculum development.

Geographical information systems

> geographical information systems (GIS) were revolutionising and extending their [pupils] experiences. Visual images from around the world provided via internet links gave immediacy to their learning, and satellite technology brought landscapes to life. Higher-attaining pupils were challenged by being able to overlay data and explore interactive maps to interpret patterns and solve problems.
>
> (Ofsted 2011: 28)

Although geographical information systems (GIS) have been around for some years, only now are they beginning to be used more widely in geography classrooms and fieldwork, but as indicated in the OFSTED inspection report of 2011, access to high-quality GIS remains limited. This limited use is in the main attributed to teachers' perceptions of what it means to use GIS effectively in classrooms. Fargher (2013) highlights the increase in level of pedagogical understanding that teachers need to develop if they are to better embed technology in their teaching – they not only need to understand their subject, how to teach and how students learn, but in addition they need to understand how technology works and how it contributes to pupils' cognitive development in both geography *and* technology subject understanding.

Having said this, GIS is one of the fastest growing applications of ICT in the world and is already part of our everyday lives in satellite navigation systems used in cars, providing government information online, supporting emergency services and enabling market research via supermarket loyalty card schemes. Thus, GIS is an obvious way of illustrating the value of geography in the current and future world of work, enabling pupils to apply what they learn in geography to real-world situations (Balderstone 2006: 24–25). However, recent times have seen the emergence of a more critical perspective on GIS, one that emphasises the potential of GIS to engage less with the scientific and more with the social, political and environmental aspects of people's lives. This, argues Fargher (2013), means using more complex, not less complex data. We are talking here about a form of 'public geographies' (see Fuller and Askins 2010) where data sources emerge from localised issues, thus raising questions about data reliability.

If teachers choose to adopt conventional GI in geography, what are the implications of constructing geographical knowledge through predominantly quantitative technology? Which elements of geography can/cannot be measured? If teachers opt to use VGI [volunteered geographic information] in their lessons where has that information come from? How trustworthy or reliable is geographical information uploaded from the web?

(Fargher 2013: 210)

A geographical information system has three components: a digital map, digital data to be displayed on the map and a piece of computer software (GIS) that links the two together. More sophisticated commercial GIS also incorporate spatial modelling, spatial query and analysis functions. GIS can enhance pupils' learning in geography by enabling them to produce more professional maps and helping them to visualise landscapes through 3-D imagery, aerial overlays on maps and 'fly-throughs' (Martin 2006; Freeman 2005). It also enables them to experiment with cartographic techniques and significantly, leaves more time for higher level thinking and decision-making by replacing time-consuming and tedious mapping with interactive manipulation of digital mapping (Freeman 2005). Table 6.3 summarises some of the geographical skills developed using GIS.

Using free internet GIS resources and activities is the best way to get started using GIS (Mitchell 2007). The Geographical Association's 'Spatially speaking' project web pages (www. geography.org.uk/projects/spatiallyspeaking/) provide guidance and exemplars to help you get started, while the Ordnance Survey's GIS zone in its Mapzone for schools (http://mapzone. ordnancesurvey.co.uk/mapzone/giszone.html) has resources and activities to support decision-making and problem-solving exercises using GIS. Flood risk can be investigated using a GIS-based flood-risk map on the Environment Agency website (www.environment-agency.gov. uk/subjects/flood/). This can be used with maps and images from mapping sites (www.multi-map.com and www.ordnancesurvey.co.uk/oswebsite/getamap/) and Google earth to assess areas at risk of flooding. There are also further resources to support enquiries into flooding on the Geographical Association website (www.geography.org.uk/resources/flooding/).

While the potential of this kind of technology to develop pupils spatial literacy seems immense, there still remain important questions to consider, not least young people's use of geographical information outside the classroom; their personal and social use – to find shop locations, to arrange social gatherings, to locate recreational facilities and so on, all enabled via

Table 6.3 Geographical skills developed using GIS

Geographical skills may be extended into the use of digital mapping and GIS. The list illustrates how skills gained using more traditional methods may be transferred to digital mapping and GIS.
Use an extended geographical vocabulary • New vocabulary includes ICT keywords (such as raster and vector) and specific GIS terms.
Select and use appropriate fieldwork techniques and instruments • Small hand-held computers (PDAs or palmtops) may be used to enter data directly in the field for transfer to GIS. • Hand-held GPS systems are now accurate enough to collect location information for transfer to GIS. • Weather monitors and environmental data loggers may collect information for transfer to GIS.
Use maps and plans at a range of scales, including Ordnance Survey 1:25,000 and 1:50,000 maps • Ordnance Survey digital map data provides the basis for vector and raster mapping.
Select and use secondary sources of evidence: aerial photographs, satellite images, ICT sources • Aerial photographs and satellite images may be used in digital mapping and GIS. • Ground level digital photographs may be linked to 'hotspots' on a map.
Draw maps and plans at a variety of scales, using symbols, keys and scales . . . **GIS explores raster and vector maps:** • Draw and edit maps and plans in a GIS editor • Import a variety of digital maps and plans in different formats • Add information to maps and plans from a set of data • Select separate vector map layers • Zoom in and out at different scales and pan around an enlarged map • Measure distances (in a straight line or along a feature), areas or perimeters accurately; understand geo-referencing • Select and use appropriate graphical techniques to present evidence on maps and diagrams including the use of ICT.
Present data at points, lines and areas (closed polygons) on maps using the functions of a GI. • Areas: Choropleth and thematic maps. • Lines: Flow lines of traffic or journeys by people. • Points: Diagrams (bar charts, pie charts, divided pie charts, proportional circles and pie charts) at places on the maps. • Add pictures and notes at locations on the maps.

(*Source*: Freeman 2005)

their often proficient and prolific use of mobile technology such as smart phones, tablets and other mobile technologies. Young people can now access an enormous quantity of geospatial data. However:

> there may be a need for educators (particularly those in geography classrooms) to enable young people to learn which geospatial data is useful and which is not; and with so much data in 'techno-savvy' students' hands (via smartphones, tablets and other mobile technologies), offer guidance and training in how to use it effectively
>
> (Manning 2014: 108)

Google earth is an earth viewer which enables pupils to explore anywhere on the earth, with the high resolution enabling them to zoom in and out to view buildings and even individual cars. It is a good way to introduce pupils to GIS, not least because you can download a simple viewer for free (www.earth.google.com). Google earth makes it relatively simple for teachers to introduce the location of new places, and also reinforce more familiar locational knowledge. However, Google earth is more than just a high-tech facility for showing pupils where places are. Facilities such as tagging, line-drawing tools and additional layers such as weather layers mean that Google earth is a powerful visual tool for helping pupils develop their spatial literacy. They can interrogate spatial data, identify and critique spatial patterns and begin to appreciate spatial relationships. Weather layers can be used to teach about depressions, and the line-drawing tool can be used to delineate spheres of influence, and additional facilities such as Google Ocean can be used to teach about ocean terrain such as deep sea vents, or ocean acidification, or dive and surf spots if you are studying tourism. Pupils can use a variety of digital map overlays to analyse spatial data and its relative simplicity of use enables you to create stimulating decision-making and problem-solving activities to develop pupils' geographical understanding and skills.

Once pupils have been introduced to the basic principles and tools, they can practise using these tools to 'fly around' and view places from different angles. They can also develop a range of geographical skills using compass directions and latitude and longitude as well as planning and measuring routes. An attractive feature of Google earth is the way pupils can use screen grabs to copy what they are viewing into another document so that they can annotate, describe and explain features. Aerial images from Google earth can also be combined with maps (e.g. from www.multimap.com, www.google.com and www.ordnancesurvey.co.uk) to investigate land use patterns and transects.

Google earth also makes it possible to create 'virtual fieldwork' using digital media (maps, photographic images and video) from real fieldwork or expeditions that you and others may have undertaken. Although virtual fieldwork is no substitute for the 'real thing', it can help pupils to develop a 'sense of place' and experience places it is not possible to visit in a typical school field trip. Virtual fieldwork can also be used to enhance and reinforce learning from fieldwork pupils have experienced. Images, video and digital data can be combined with fieldwork data the pupils have collected to support their analysis of geographical phenomena, patterns and issues

Via a technique known as 'mashups', pupils and teachers can combine information from different data sources to create 'new maps'. For example, data from the Unites States Geological Survey (USGS) and Google earth can be used together to study tectonic activity and also to track earthquake activity in real time (see Google earth for educators website http://sitescontent.google.com/google-earth-for-educators/).

The scope is enormous. However, all this potential also comes with a 'health warning', which is that a resource such as Google earth loses its potential when reduced to 'game playing' at the end of lessons. This type of facility has to be embedded into schemes of work and into individual lessons if it to realise its potential in geographical learning. As with other ICT applications, it is important to think about how progression will be developed in pupils' understanding and use of GIS. You will need to consider how much pupils need to know about

Table 6.4 Progression in the use of GIS skills

Data processing and analysis skills level	Knowledge of GIS theory required	Knowledge of GIS software required	Teaching examples
Basic	Qualitative and quantative map classification techniques Map symbolisation and the use of size, shape, colour hue, colour intensity and texture Bivariate data display techniques Map layout and design issues Measurements of lengths, perimeters and areas	Students need to develop an understanding of the range of classification, symbolisation and mapping design techniques available within the software and how to access them Students need to gain experience of how to output data using the software in the form of maps, images, graphs, tables and reports	Year 9: Mapping the historical and future growth of Bishop's Stortford Year 12: Mapping and symbolising global tectonic activity
Intermediate	Data selection and queries Principles of basic logic (Boolean operations) Data aggregation techniques Statistical techniques 3-D mapping and display	Students need to become familiar with the statistical and data processing capabilities of the software, the options available and their limitations and applications with various data types	Year 10: Identifying areas of high and low levels of economic development on a global scale Year 13: Hazard mapping, assessing the vulnerability of the USA to earthquake activity
Advanced	Data reclassification Buffering and neighbourhood functions Map overlay Spatial interpolation and density mapping Analysis of surfaces		Year 13: Advanced GIS techniques most usually applied with experienced GIS users as part of A-level projects and fieldwork

(*Source*: O'Connor 2008: 149)

the theory of GIS to be able to use the technology effectively and how much time they need to become proficient in the use of GIS applications (O'Connor 2007). Table 6.4 suggests three conceptual levels for developing progression in the use of GIS moving from the presentation of spatial data to the processing and analysing of spatial data. More advanced use of GIS involves the input and editing of spatial data (O'Connor 2008: 148–149).

Task 6.5 Using technology in your geography teaching

1   Establish where and how technology is used to support teaching in your school. Review schemes of work, and also any fieldwork provision, to get a sense of whether technology is embedded in the geography curriculum, or whether it is 'bolted on' to certain schemes.

2   Devise a series of lessons (two or three) where you use an online source to support your teaching – Gapminder or WorldMapper might be places to start your thinking:

  •   Devise an appropriate enquiry question for the pupils to explore.
  •   Think about how to ensure that pupils can access the ideas as well as the content of your selected site.
  •   Plan any additional resources that will be needed to scaffold pupils use of the site.
  •   Consider what additional resources you will need to develop to support the enquiry process – photographs of places? Text descriptions of places?

3   Review an online GIS site that you could plan to use in your teaching and consider:

  •   Is the site easy to access in terms of navigability?
  •   What are the data sources on the site?
  •   Are maps and other tools clearly presented and easy to use?
  •   What kind of geographical knowledge will be developed if you use the site with pupils?

4   Use the site with a class of pupils:

  •   Explore pupils' response to using GIS (it can be useful to just have a conversation with a group after the lessons have finished).
  •   Evaluate the quality of the geographical learning, evidenced in work developed by the pupils.
  •   Evaluate the quality of pupils technological understanding after they have used the GIS.
  •   Reflect on your own professional development as a result of using GIS in your teaching.

Summary and key points

This chapter has introduced you to some of the many resources that are available to geography teachers. Most of your pupils have not had any direct experiences of many of the places and issues that they study in geography, so the range and quality of the visual materials that you use has a significant influence on their geographical education. Hopefully, you are now aware of some of the important considerations that

(continued)

(continued)

should influence your decisions about which resources to use and how to use them. In particular, you should be concerned to identify and, where possible, to avoid using resources that show evidence of gender or ethnocentric bias. Where this is not possible, you may be able to devise strategies for using those resources that seek to address issues of bias.

We hope that you look for opportunities to be creative in the way that you develop and use resources to support teaching and learning in geography. Make use of your own interests and experiences as well as those of your pupils. Put the pupils at the centre of your decisions about which resources are used in your lessons. Will these resources stimulate your pupils' interest and motivate them to learn? How will these resources be used by pupils? Which skills will they develop through using these resources? What knowledge, understanding, attitudes and values will pupils develop? Will all pupils be able to learn successfully using these resources?

Remember that the care and effort that you put into the preparation and selection of resources has a positive impact on pupils' interest in and motivation to learn geography!

Further reading

Fargher, M. (2013) 'Geographic information – how could it be used?' In D. Lambert and M. Jones (eds) *Debates in Geography Education*, London: Routledge.
This chapter raises some important questions about the development and use of GIS in school geography. In particular, it questions the kinds of geographical knowledge developed through GIS and it also encourages us to consider the complex relationship between subject and technical pedagogies.

O'Connor, P. (2008) *GIS for A-Level Geography*, Sheffield: Geographical Association.
While not a book to 'get you started', this text is full of practical advice for using GIS with A-level students. It will support your own knowledge development about GIS as well as provide you with real and realistic ways of using GIS to enhance A-level geographers knowledge and understanding.

7 Fieldwork and outdoor learning

So, do you remember that fieldtrip we went on when we were measuring that water with the tape measure and I slipped on that rock and my wellies got full of water?

(A chance conversation with an ex-GCSE student some 15 years after the event!)

Introduction

Fieldwork is one of the distinctive attributes of geography and, in Britain, has a long tradition as an established component of geography education. There is substantial evidence indicating that when planned rigorously, well-taught and effectively followed up, fieldwork provides learners with opportunities to develop their knowledge, understanding and skills in ways that add value to their everyday classroom experiences (FSC 2004). Indeed, we hope that most readers of this book will have fond memories of fieldwork, both in relation to contribution that fieldwork made to your love of geography, but also the social and emotional benefits that accrue from well-planned and well-taught fieldwork experiences. The 2011 Ofsted report for geography, *Learning to Make a World of Difference* (Ofsted 2011) is clear about how fieldwork enhances pupils' geographical understanding. The report also states that good fieldwork also has the added advantage of encouraging pupils to continue to study geography beyond Key Stage 3. It would seem then that there are clear reasons to consider what constitutes 'high-quality fieldwork' – love of the subject, contribution to learning and sustaining the subject in schools.

Fieldwork tends to be highly valued by pupils: it transports them out of the classroom; it allows them to work collaboratively, often on tasks that last for several hours or even a whole day (in contrast to the bitty school day of possibly as many as eight single lessons); it is often very much 'hands on' kind of work; it is generally very 'learner-centred' in the sense that pupils are involved in formulating questions to investigate, engaged in seeking answers to their questions, and are involved in communicating the outcomes of their work in geographically appropriate ways. Residential fieldwork in particular often provides intense group feelings of achievement and togetherness. Fieldwork can also open up access to, and engagement with, the spiritual aspects of learning, stimulating interest in the environment and passion for outdoor education (May and Richardson 2005: 6). For many young people, the impacts of fieldwork and outdoor learning are lifelong and life-changing experiences.

By the end of this chapter, you should be able to:

- identify the different purposes of and approaches to fieldwork in geography
- understand how to use a range of fieldwork strategies
- plan and prepare geographical fieldwork that is of a high quality, safe, successful and sustainable
- understand how to ensure that pupils can make progress in both developing their skills and in extending their conceptual learning through geographical fieldwork.

What is fieldwork and why should we do it?

Fieldwork, which can be defined as any curriculum component that involves leaving the classroom and engaging in teaching and learning activities through first-hand experience of phenomena out-of-doors, has a long tradition in geography and in certain of the sciences, notably biology and environmental science/studies.

In geography, learning in the 'real world' is thought to be absolutely essential, contributing particular qualities that run through geography's identity as a subject discipline from primary education to undergraduate study. It expresses a commitment to exploration and enquiry, and geography's concern to discover and to be curious about the world.

(Lambert and Reiss 2014: 5)

In some respects the quote above answers the question posed at the top of this section. It gives us a definition of what geographers think fieldwork is, and offers some sort of rational for the purpose of 'doing' fieldwork. However, in recent years doing fieldwork has come under some pressure as senior managers in some (but not all) schools seem increasingly reluctant to allow pupils to work away from the school site. There are many reasons for this, including concerns for the safety of staff and pupils, the financial cost of running fieldwork trips but, less convincingly, concerns that time away from the classroom will in some way jeopardise pupils' performance in lessons they may miss. It is because of concerns such as these that, as geography teachers, we need sound and well-articulated justifications regarding the value of fieldwork, and we need to be confident in expressing these justifications in whatever arena we find ourselves.

The purpose of fieldwork?

Thinking geographically

Earlier in this book we explore the notion of 'thinking geographically' using both the language and the grammar of geography (concepts and content) to develop young people's geographical capabilities. Fieldwork is a 'real-world' opportunity for pupils to develop and extend their geographical thinking as it affords unique opportunities for pupils to experiment with their geographical imaginations, to explore their geographical understanding and to demonstrate and expand their geographical knowledge, in ways that are simply impossible to do in the classroom alone. If we consider the aims of education as well as the aims and purpose of the geography curriculum, it is almost impossible to imagine how we could claim to meet these aims, with any quality, if we do not allow our pupils to experience high-quality fieldwork.

Geographical research skills

To reach a satisfactory position on fieldwork, we need to focus on it as embodying a range of *skills*. By focusing on skills, we do not mean to be exclusive of knowledge and understanding – indeed the aim of fieldwork will often be to gain knowledge and deepen understanding. However, we do wish to show that the strength of fieldwork is that it requires pupils to project a range of practical, organisational and intellectual skills onto a 'real-world' question or issue. What characterises the real world is that it is complex and messy rather than simplified and neat (or archetypal). Because geography is concerned with making sense of physical and human environments and their interactions, it follows that pupils must have the chance to 'have a go' at the interpretation of the world at first hand, or else their instruction in geography (and how geographers make sense of the world) will be deficient.

The approach you adopt for fieldwork very much depends on what you are trying to achieve educationally. The traditional teacher-led 'field excursion' fulfils a particular role, possibly in introducing pupils to an area or setting a location in a broader geographical context, before more hands-on work begins. Field research (or hypothesis testing) uses a scientific approach to test models or expected trends, providing pupils with a clear structure and purpose as they work through a series of stages to find the answers. Pupils develop a range of skills in collecting, presenting and analysing data, enabling them to dig deep into a specific, often very localised issue (such as the causes of footpath erosion in a specific location, or the consequences of erosion and deposition processes on the profile of a specific river). Enquiry fieldwork involves pupils in exploring a range of geographical factors to investigate an issue or question. They are thus required to draw upon different aspects of the discipline and work at different spatial scales, with subsequent benefits for their conceptual learning. Through values analysis, pupils are likely to develop their decision-making skills and ability to identify geographical questions.

In terms of 'research methodologies', fieldwork gives pupils the scope to use a range of methods of 'finding out' beyond those embedded in just the scientific model. Well-planned fieldwork gives pupils first-hand experience of using both quantitative and more qualitative approaches to 'data' gathering. Evaluating the different ways a town is represented through tourist brochures, newspaper reports, advertising campaigns, or even how it is represented in art and photographs and so on requires a very different view of and use of 'data'. Using social science research methodologies, or even more creative methodologies such those in the arts and humanities, in conjunction with the more fine-grained picture that generally is the consequence of hypothesis testing, can provide opportunities for pupils to see the local and 'bigger picture' through different geographic lenses.

Affective learning

While geography fieldwork makes significant contributions to pupils' intellectual development in a number of ways, when planned appropriately, good fieldwork also contributes to pupils' affective learning. Affective learning was one of the three 'domains' (areas) of learning identified by Benjamin Bloom in 1956. While the categories in his cognitive domain (knowledge, comprehension, analysis, analysis, evaluation) are much used in schools for a range of purposes, the affective domain (receiving, responding, valuing, organising, internalising) is less visible. However, we would argue, that alongside developing pupils' cognitive capacities, fieldwork can make a substantial contribution to pupils affective learning because of the unique opportunity that fieldwork experiences provide. Fieldwork can:

- enable pupils' to develop/express *feelings*, about places, experiences, landscapes
- enable pupils to question their own *values* and those of others
- provide opportunities for pupils to *appreciate* landscapes, environments, alternative approaches
- engender *enthusiasm* for and commitment to particular geographical issues, dilemmas, events
- develop pupils' *motivation* to, for example, participate and collaborate, on a joint venture
- provide opportunities for pupils to engage with the *attitudes* and values of others and in doing so reflect on their own.

(Adapted from *Bloom's Theory of Learning Domains*)

Set within the context of environmental education, Job (1966) makes the point that fieldwork often stops short of asking critical questions concerning alternatives; for example, while a common field activity might be to examine the arguments surrounding the siting of a new reservoir, less common is the consideration of whether rising demand of a finite resource such as water should simply always be met, or whether demand could be managed more effectively by introducing conservation measures. This type of thinking requires that pupils utilise their more affective understanding in order to appreciate that there are alternatives, what these might be, the relative strengths of these alternatives, and also what the pupils themselves think and why. This is not about emotional thinking at the expense of evidence, but it is about appreciating that any evidence can be used in particular ways, often driven by peoples' values and attitude.

Interpersonal skills

While a key aim of geography fieldwork is to develop pupils' geographical knowledge and understanding, and to enable them to see and experience geography 'first hand', there is little doubt that an important by-product of fieldwork is the benefits it brings in terms of developing pupils' social relationships, with each other and with their teachers:

Certain social gains derived through fieldwork form highly valuable soft outcomes of the study of geography or science at school: we focus here on the social construction of meaning through collaborative enquiries. Done well, fieldwork engages students in the iterative processes of drafting and redrafting data collection instruments (including the identification of good questions to investigate) as well as analysis and drawing conclusions; that is, situations where students learn with and from each other as well as with and from their teachers.

(Lambert and Reiss 2014: 8)

Claiming that fieldwork builds a greater sense of self, develops intellectual *and* personal confidence and extends/develops pupils' social skills is hard to quantify, but the experience of working together in a unique environment on a shared project is the context in which such growth is likely to take place.

We have considered above possible ways that fieldwork can be rationalised. What we now need to unravel is the relationship between your approach to fieldwork and the different learning gains that can be made.

Fieldwork strategy

As stated above, the educational purpose of geographical fieldwork has an important influence on the fieldwork strategy you choose to use and therefore how you structure the fieldwork experience for pupils.

Table 7.1 summarises the main categories for fieldwork strategies and their purposes (Job et al. 1999). These broad approaches to fieldwork have different purposes and can be associated with different learning styles and strategies that pupils may be required to use. Fieldwork in geography may be dominated by a particular approach in some schools. This may be due to the experience and educational philosophy of individual geography teachers or to the influence of particular examination specifications. However, you are more likely to find a range of approaches in evidence so that there is variety in pupils' experience of fieldwork and in the learning outcomes derived from these experiences.

Field teaching and field research can bring about a range of desirable educational outcomes. The practical nature of many tasks observing, collecting and recording data helps pupils to acquire new skills and develop 'technical competency' in a range of fieldwork, laboratory and data-handling skills. Focused investigations and carefully structured approaches to geographical enquiry help pupils to transfer these skills and frameworks to their own independent investigations. There may be some gains in conceptual understanding and the development of technical and specialised vocabulary is usually strengthened.

In addition to approaching fieldwork from a scientific perspective, Job (1996) suggests a variety of less structured fieldwork activities that can be used to encourage deeper thinking about landscapes and environmental issues. These more qualitative activities, some derived from the work of Steve Van Matre (1979) and others involved in earth education, which aims to promote love and respect for nature, can be used as starting points for fieldwork investigations raising pupils' awareness of an environment based on their own personal experiences and perceptions. Job emphasises the importance of this 'engagement with places at an emotional or sensory level' in developing pupils' 'sense of care and concern about places and landscapes' (Job 1997: 156), which is a key element of any deeper environmental perspective.

What we are saying here is that rather than the 'single fieldwork 'exercise, we believe that it is important to consider, at the planning stage, how you can build in opportunities for pupils to experience a range of fieldwork approaches in order to enhance their understanding of the varied work of geographers. You may, for example, want your pupils to learn about how the characteristic features of a river change as you move downstream. A number of fieldwork tasks could be devised to observe, measure and record features such as the channel characteristics (width, depth, cross-sectional area, wetted perimeter, hydraulic radius), the velocity of the river and the nature of the load that it is carrying. As you have particular learning outcomes in mind, you might adopt a hypothesis testing approach to the design of this fieldwork. You present hypotheses about how these characteristic features might change between different sites along a river, select the sites for study and the techniques to be used to measure these characteristics. The pupils follow your instructions in collecting these data and in using various graphical and statistical techniques to present and analyse the data. The findings are more or less what is expected with possible reasons suggested for any that do not fit the predicted patterns.

However, you might also 'layer in' to this more scientific fieldwork, opportunities for pupils to practise their OS maps skills, tasks designed to develop pupils' understanding of how this place is connected to other places (possibly if the stream is located near footpaths and there are walkers/other visitors using the area), time to look for evidence in the landscape for how this place has changed over time (think of this place as a palimpsest), or even simply time to enjoy sitting together by the stream, appreciating the differences between places (for example the difference between school and this new place), to question why this place is like it is and what they (pupils) like/don't like about it – these informal conversations, which are difficult to create in school, can be excellent opportunities for exploring geographical ideas.

This idea of 'layering' fieldwork in this way, rectifies some of the concerns that Job (1996) expresses about the 'hypothesis' testing model, which he argues is reductionist and narrow and fails to 'deliver a holistic and integrated landscape view in which interactions between subsystems [are] vital to an understanding of the functioning of the whole' (Job 1996: 37). You have to consider to what extent you agree or disagree with this, and if you agree, how you would address the concern in the plans that you draw up and the activities you ask pupils to undertake in the field.

Geographical enquiry, discussed elsewhere in this book in relation to curriculum planning and teaching, provides a more open approach to fieldwork (see Chapters 3 and 4). By adopting a more 'framed' style of working, a teacher could create a decision-making exercise as the structure for a fieldwork investigation into the impacts recreation has on the countryside, and the ways in which these impacts can be reduced or alleviated. This issue provides a good example of people-environment interactions, the investigation of which requires pupils to use a range of data collection techniques. Also, by presenting the pupils with a problem to solve there are opportunities for them to establish priorities, interpret data in different ways, consider viewpoints about the issue and show their ability to apply their understanding of geographical ideas relating to this issue.

Table 7.1 Fieldwork strategies and purposes

Strategy	Purposes	Characteristic activites
The traditional field excursion	• Developing skills in geographical recording and intervention • Showing relationships between physical and human landscape features • Developing an appreciation of landscape and nurturing a sense of place	Pupils guided through a landscape by a teacher with local knowledge, often following a route on a large-scale map. Sites grid-referenced and sketch maps to explore the underlying geology, topographical features, the mantle of soil and vegetation and the landscape history in terms of human activity.
Field research based on hypothesis testing	• Applying geographical theory or generalised models to real-world situations • Generating and applying hypotheses based on theory to be tested through collections of appropriate field data	The conventional deductive approach involves initial consideration of geographical theory, leading to the formulation of hypotheses which are then tested against field situations through the collection of qualitative data and testing against expected patterns and relationships.
Geographical enquiry	• Encouraging pupils to identify, construct and ask geographical questions • Enabling pupils to identify and gather relevant information to answer geographical questions and offer explanations and interpretations of their findings • Enabling pupils to apply their findings to the wider world and personal decisions	A geographical question, issue or problem is identified, ideally from pupil's own experiences in the field. Pupils are then supported in the gathering of appropriate data (quantitative or qualitative) to answer their key question. Findings are evaluated and the implications applied to the wider world and personal decisions where appropriate.
Discovery fieldwork	• Allowing pupils to develop their own focus of study and methods of investigation • Encouraging self-confidence and self-motivation by putting pupils in control of their learning	Teacher assumes the role of animateur, allowing the group to follow its own route through the landscape. When pupils ask questions, these are countered with further questions to encourage deeper thinking. A discussion and recording session then identifies themes for further investigation in small groups.
Sensory fieldwork	• Encouraging new sensitivities to environments through using all the senses • Acknowledging that sensory experience is as valid as intellectual activity in understanding our surroundings	Structured activities designed to stimulate the senses in order to promote awareness of environments. Sensory walks, the use of blindfolds, sound maps, poetry and artwork are characteristic activities. Can be used to develop a sense of place, aesthetic appreciation or critical appraisal of environmental change.

(*Source:* Job et al. 1999, *New Directions in Geographical Fieldwork*, Cambridge: Cambridge University Press/Queen Mary Westfield College)

Box 7.1 The 'framed approach' to fieldwork: an example of a geographical enquiry

1   Create a need to know

Sites are identified around a popular attraction in a nearby national park. The pupils consider the different types of recreational activity in the area and how the impacts of these activities might manifest themselves around this honeypot site. The teacher suggests a variety of relevant enquiry questions that guides the fieldwork and encourages the pupils to suggest some other questions that might be worth investigating.

2   Plan and prepare

The pupils then decide what information can be collected to investigate these enquiry questions and what fieldwork methods could be used for this data collection. The teacher guides this preparation by drawing pupils' attention to sampling issues and by helping them plan techniques for assessing visual quality, footpath erosion, vegetation trampling and other environmental impacts. The pupils have been organised in groups for these tasks and for the fieldwork itself as the teacher believes that this collaborative effort will help the pupils understand the relevance of the enquiry questions as well as the principles guiding the planning of methods of fieldwork data collection.

3   'Do' the fieldwork

Each group is provided with equipment needed to measure footpath erosion (tape measures, quadrants and so on) and large-scale plans of the sites visited to record information about some of the impacts of recreation observed. In addition, each group is provided with a film to take photographs of these impacts and any management strategies observed.

4   Making sense of data

The pupils' findings are presented in poster reports illustrating the evidence collected about the impacts of recreation and suggesting possible strategies for reducing these impacts. The pupils are encouraged to use a range of different techniques to present their findings graphically and cartographically. Appropriate photographs are selected and annotated to illustrate the impacts observed and to justify the group's management plan for the area.

5   Reflect on the learning

In the final follow-up lesson, each group makes a short presentation describing the problems observed, the methods of data collection used and explaining their choice of management strategies. The teacher explores with the pupils the rationale for the different management strategies selected. In this way, the outcomes of the fieldwork can be considered critically and also are related to the key ideas and generalisations in the examination specification.

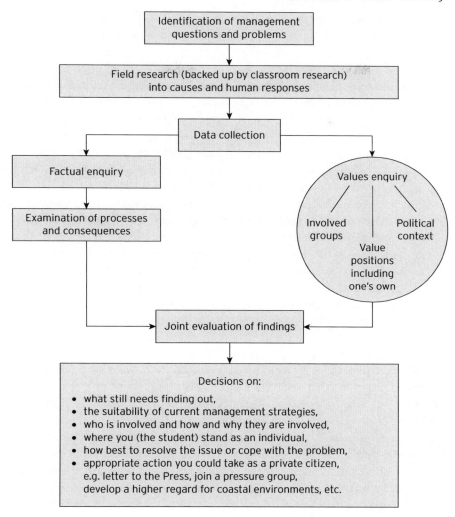

Figure 7.1 Enquiry fieldwork

(*Source*: Naish, Rawling and Hart *1987*. *Geography 16-19: The Contribution of a Curriculum Project to 16-19 Education*, p. 135 (Figure 67), Harlow: Longman)

The benefits of this framed style of working are not only the development of pupils' knowledge and understanding of geographical ideas and issues, or their skills of data collection and analysis, but by controlling the development of the 'frame' the teacher is able to 'induct the pupils into the techniques and principles of geography' (Roberts 1996: 245). The teacher is able to help pupils understand these principles and to appreciate the need to make choices between different ways of collecting, representing and analysing data. In this way, pupils can become aware of the strengths and limitations of these different methods.

What the pupils learn may be less predictable than that suggested in the scientific approach where the data collected and skills developed are still largely controlled by the teacher. In an enquiry, the data are presented as 'evidence' to be interpreted and there are opportunities for conflicting information or opinions to be explored. It is also possible for pupils to reach different conclusions which can be debated and challenged. A framed style of working in fieldwork can thus create opportunities to use a wide range of teaching and learning strategies leading to 'deeper' understanding as well as enhancing pupils' problem-solving skills.

At A-level, independent fieldwork provides opportunities for 'negotiated' styles of field-work enquiry. The requirements of an examination specification and its approach to the study of geography may influence the choice of topic, issue or question to be investigated. However, the 'essence of the start of the negotiated sequence is that the questions which form the basis of subsequent enquiry come from the learners' (Roberts 1996: 245). It is the learner who makes the choices about which sources of primary and secondary data are appropriate to answer the questions to be investigated in the enquiry. The learner also chooses the methods to be used to analyse the data collected and is responsible for the interpretation of these data. The role of the teacher in this 'negotiated' style is as a 'consult-ant' advising and supporting the pupil. This advisory role is particularly important when the pupils are selecting appropriate enquiry questions and methods, and when they are evaluat-ing the outcomes.

Individual studies, while no longer required for assessment purposes as part of GCSE examinations (see Chapter 8 on Assessment), look likely to be reintroduced at A-level, having been removed in 2010 amid fears of inappropriate levels of teacher and paren-tal support for supposedly independent coursework. However, such a study, when con-ducted with clear principles in mind, in many ways represents the 'pinnacle' of pupils' achievement in relation to geographical enquiry: it provides an opportunity to demon-strate knowledge and understanding of geographical ideas and skills as well as an ability to apply these successfully when investigating an issue or question in the messy and unpredictable real world.

What should be clear from this consideration of different approaches to fieldwork is that in order to carry out an *individual* enquiry successfully, pupils need to have supported expe-riences in using a range of fieldwork styles and strategies. You will need to develop an under-standing of how different strategies can be employed to help pupils develop appropriate enquiry skills and then how they can learn how to apply them independently.

Task 7.1 Thinking about fieldwork

A   Analysing provision in geography fieldwork

This activity can either be carried out independently with you examining the nature of fieldwork provision in your placement school, or collaboratively with a group of pupil teachers examining a range of examples from different schools.

1   Collect examples of different fieldwork activities from one or more schools. These should be from a variety of age groups. You can include:

  - the resource sheets to explain the fieldwork activities
  - any data recording sheets
  - examples of work produced by pupils as a result of fieldwork.

  If you have participated in any of these fieldwork activities, describe the role of the teacher and the strategies used by the teacher.

2   Try to classify these examples of geography fieldwork using the approaches identified in Table 7.1.

3   Discuss the role of the teacher in the fieldwork – are they leading an 'excursion', setting up an enquiry or supporting more discovery learning?

4   List the positive learning outcomes from the fieldwork activities.

5   Consider the limitations of each approach to fieldwork in relation to the learning outcomes.

B   Alternative fieldwork approaches

Consider the examples you have now analysed and discuss what additional or alternative approaches to the fieldwork could have been used/layered in to the experience, possibly to create a more holistic understanding of the area where the fieldwork took place. How was technology used to enhance the fieldwork – was it effective in this?

Planning fieldwork

Fieldwork is an entitlement for all pupils. The aims of the geography National Curriculum state that pupils should be 'competent in the geographical skills needed to: collect, analyse and communicate with a range of data gathered through experiences of fieldwork that deepen their understanding of geographical processes' (DfE 2014). Fieldwork is also a requirement of GCSE and A-level specifications. However, as with any other educational encounter, fieldwork requires careful and thoughtful planning:

  - of the geographical learning
  - of the management and organisation
  - of the health and safety/legal requirements.

Figure 7.2 provides a useful timeline indicating the key decisions that have to be made, in what order and by whom in order to assure parents, pupils and school leaders of the need, viability and the safety of the fieldwork you have planned.

Health and safety/legal requirements

More recent government policy has sought to ease the administrative/legal burden (often seen as prohibitive) on schools and teachers conducting off-set work with students

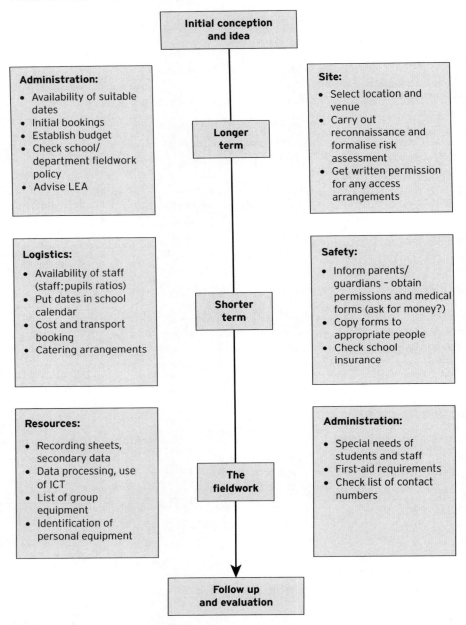

Figure 7.2 Planning fieldwork – some important considerations

(Source: Holmes and Walker 2006, in Balderstone, D. (ed.): 211)

(see *Health and Safety: Advice on Legal Duties and Powers for Local Authorities, School Leaders, School Staff and Governing Bodies*, February 2014). It's important to remember is that whenever you are doing fieldwork with students you are in fact *in loco parentis*, meaning that when working with pupils you are in effect in a role equal to that of a responsible parent and should make decisions for their well-being in the light of this responsibility.

The Geographical Association has published guidelines for geographical work outside the classroom and every school has a policy for the organisation and planning of visits and activities outside the school. This policy must be consulted and its requirements followed rigorously; to be safe as well as successful, nothing must be left to chance in the organisation of fieldwork.

Achieving safe, yet challenging fieldwork experiences means acting responsibly towards yourselves and others as well as recognising and following good practice in preparing for the fieldwork. Helpful checklists to guide the organisation, preparation and conduct of fieldwork can be found in May and Richardson (2005). There is no substitute for first-hand knowledge of the area where you will be undertaking the fieldwork, so site-visits are an essential part of preparation, particularly when completing the obligatory 'risk assessments'.

The aim of risk assessment is to anticipate, minimise and manage possible risks for all those involved in the fieldwork activity (Holmes and Walker 2006; May and Richardson 2005). Site assessments and appraisals are carried out in advance to evaluate the potential risks to those taking part and to plan how to remove or control those risks. A 'hazard' is anything that could reasonably be expected to cause harm, while the 'risk' is the chance, however great or small, that someone participating in the fieldwork activity might be harmed by that hazard (DfEE 1998). Risk assessments need to take account of:

- hazards specific to the location (i.e. rural or urban)
- weather conditions likely to be experienced
- the age and experience of the group and its leaders
- students with special needs (e.g. mobility or visual impairment, medical conditions).

(Bland et al. 1996)

When assessing risk, you should consider how likely a risk is to occur and then the likely severity of the outcome. On this basis, decide whether the risk is acceptable or if the work can be modified to reduce the risk level to one that is acceptable. Examples of risk assessments can be found in Holmes and Walker (2006: 214), in May and Richardson (2005) and in school policy guidelines. Fieldwork providers such as the Field Studies Council (FSC) also provide risk assessments for their fieldwork activities and these provide a good example of best practice to follow. You might also wish to consider taking a specialist course in safety management or first aid leading to a recognised qualification.

Management and organisation

Your legal responsibilities and obligations as a teacher, particularly in relation to health and safety, demand that your management and organisation of fieldwork are of the highest standards possible. There are important time-scales to consider and so planning and organising fieldwork cannot be left to the last minute The management and organisation issues that need to be addressed include:

- Timing of the fieldwork – in relation to the whole-school calendar of commitments (clashing with GCSE or A-level exams may not be a good idea), and also in the context of where you are in terms of subject teaching – conducting fieldwork in the midst of a unit of work on volcanoes may be confusing for pupils.

- Undertaking/updating risk assessments in line with school policy/expectations.
- Ensuring that all other necessary 'paper work' is completed on time and forms such as parental consent forms returned in good time.
- Ensuring that additional transport is booked.
- Planning, preparing, developing resources for the geographical learning.
- Staffing – which members of the geography team will attend? Will you need additional staff? If so, who and how will they be briefed on the work to be completed?
- How will pupil groups be organised? How will pupils' special needs be catered for/ managed/supported?

Although it is unlikely that you will take full responsibility for much of the above in the early phase of your career, what you cannot be sure of is when you might find yourself in a situation where you have to take responsibility for fieldwork or make swift decisions for pupils' and colleagues' well-being and safety. This means that growing your knowledge and understanding of the necessities of fieldwork is crucial, whether you are 'in-charge' or not!

Geographical learning

Given the limited resources (financial and time) available for fieldwork, careful and imaginative planning should include thorough preparation of all stages of the experience from the initial development of ideas through the fieldwork itself to the post-fieldwork follow-up activities that will embed the learning gains made by the pupils in their longer-term conceptual learning and development of skills. To ensure that pupils learn the geography you want them to learn while in the field, you need to (a bit like lesson planning) attend to some key dimensions of fieldwork planning and preparation:

- the learning framework
- the fieldwork style and strategy (see Table 7.1)
- resource preparation
- organisation (including health and safety).

Hart and Thomas recognise the importance of pre-fieldwork preparation and post-fieldwork follow-up in achieving the desired learning outcomes. You should identify what the pupils need to do to prepare for the fieldwork activity. This preparation should focus on what they need to know, understand and are able to do if they are to derive the maximum benefit from the fieldwork. This may in part be driven by the assessment objectives of an examination syllabus or relevant aspects of the geography National Curriculum. But it may also be influenced by wider curricular and cross-curricular objectives.

Identifying relevant geographical ideas, processes and, where appropriate, people – environment interactions helps you decide what data need to be collected before planning the techniques to be used in the field enquiry. These considerations will in turn influence decisions about learning objectives and enquiry processes. Although fieldwork provides pupils with experiences that are intrinsically valuable, you should plan follow-up that uses the findings and experiences to consolidate and extend learning. This involves more than just writing up and presenting data collected. Try to be imaginative and creative with this follow-up phase.

There is a wide range of fieldwork styles and strategies that can be used. It is common to classify these into three broad categories or approaches to fieldwork (see Figure 7.1). In reality, geography teachers draw upon a range of styles and strategies, particularly when devising fieldwork courses lasting a few days. It should also be remembered that interesting fieldwork investigations can be carried out around the sites of a school or its local area in a single lesson or part of a day (e.g. the microclimate of a school, land use in the local area).

Once the structure of a fieldwork enquiry has been planned and the objectives and strategies identified, attention can be given to the preparation of appropriate resources and equipment. Fieldwork usually involves collecting information for a specific purpose. Resources may need to be prepared to provide instructions for pupils to follow or frameworks within which to record the data collected. This preparation needs to take into account the skills that you are intending the pupils to use and develop, as well as the degree of autonomy that you would like to see in the use of these skills. Highly structured resources are often produced to support the collection, presentation and analysis of fieldwork data. There are numerous examples of such frameworks in the wide variety of fieldwork textbooks and resource packs. However, you may want your pupils to use *their* initiative and creativity to develop greater independence in their use of enquiry skills in fieldwork.

You will inevitably need to consider how to differentiate the fieldwork in terms of how groups are organised, how any additional support is deployed and how resources are presented. For pupils with mobility issues, you will need to consider site accessibility and what kinds of support you and the pupil will need to ensure that all can participate. Such issues must not prohibit individuals from participating in the fieldwork; discussions with parents are very important in such circumstances, but ultimately it all just needs careful thinking through. Some centres offer additional support for pupils with a range of learning needs. They tend to operate on the basis that fieldwork is for everyone so can offer very particular support and advice to ensure that your fieldwork is safe and inclusive.

Teaching in the field

With all the detailed planning required to make fieldwork safe and successful, it would be easy to neglect the role of the teacher. Field teaching is not easy. You do not have recourse to the same structures (behaviour management, technology and so on) available in school, and so you are dependent on carefully created and communicated systems that ensure the work can get done and pupils and teachers can enjoy the experience. Your communications skills, your natural enthusiasm for geography, your knowledge and understanding of what you are doing and your relationship with the pupils, all serve to ensure that fieldwork, especially off-site fieldwork, goes well. Planning needs to be detailed and if you are unfamiliar with the area where you are going to be doing fieldwork, then a pre-course visit for your own knowledge development is, as far as is reasonably possible, essential.

One thing to be mindful of is that for teachers, once off-site on fieldwork, there is no such thing as 'down-time' – you are with the pupils ALL day, or even all week, so alongside the teaching you do there is also a lot of 'pastoral' care to be done too:

- managing relationships between pupils and between teachers and pupils;
- maintaining motivation levels in sometimes challenging situations (eating a packed lunch in the pouring rain can challenge even the most motivated pupils!);
- ensuring that pupils are appropriately dressed for the work and weather (most schools send out a 'kit-list' in advance and some residential centres have systems that allow pupils to borrow wet-weather clothes);
- ensuring that pupils work co-operatively together;
- striking a balance between allowing pupils space and time to enjoy the experience, but offering support and encouragement when needed to ensure that the opportunity of being 'in the field' is maximised.

The pastoral role becomes even more significant when you are away on residential fieldwork. Ensuring that domestic routines are attended to, having appropriate rules and regulations in place and understood (but at the same time that don't want to stifle pupils' enjoyment of being out together and away from school), being clear about the needs of pupils with special dietary requirements, understanding specific medical needs, and for some pupils, being away from home for the first time, all need sorting, organising and acting on.

In terms of actually teaching in the field, the same rules apply as to classroom teaching, except that the degree of planning required is much greater. We have already mentioned earlier in the chapter the need to 'layer in' learning opportunities during field days. Plans need to have a clear purpose, a range of activities, and in any one location pupils need to be 'doing' the fieldwork. Get the pupils involved! Encourage them to use their imaginations ('close your eyes and imagine we are . . . ') and give them some opportunities to 'explore' the areas being investigated, within acceptable safety constraints. Get them to use their senses to describe how it smells, feels and looks. Use appropriate questioning to elicit what they know to reinforce and extend their understanding. Formative assessment (see Chapter 8 and Caton 2006) is also important during fieldwork activity. Don't leave it until the end of the activity to find out what they haven't understood; check what they have learned and summarise regularly.

Manage the physical position and movement of the groups carefully. Use open body language, relax and smile! Use stories and anecdotes, particularly from your own experiences to hold their attention. Point to what you want them to look at and use drama techniques to bring in some fun and make the learning active (see Chapter 4, Caton 2006 and Biddulph and Clarke 2006).

Above all, be creative and imaginative when designing fieldwork enquiries. Think 'outside the box' and try out new ideas that will stimulate and engage pupils. Fieldwork does not always have to be driven by the need to achieve particular outcomes such as examination coursework or case studies, and even then it is possible to be imaginative and original to create more meaningful, motivating and open-ended fieldwork enquiries.

What kinds of fieldwork?

Ultimately the fieldwork you plan needs to ensure that pupils' learning experiences are worthwhile and that they make progress in their geographical understanding. The activities they engage in should reflect the purposes and frameworks you have identified for the field-work and should enable pupils to experience unique learning opportunities they would not otherwise be able to experience in a classroom.

We think it is important that you do not to draw distinctions in your mind between 'traditional' fieldwork and more 'creative' fieldwork – this is an unhelpful dichotomy that undermines the value and purpose of fieldwork; like any learning approach, fieldwork has to be fit for purpose and as we indicated earlier it is more likely that you will combine approaches depending on what you want to achieve. There is plenty of advice and ideas available to you through publications such as the Geographical Association's journal *Teaching Geography*, or online via organisations such as the Field Studies Council, exam boards and other professional outlets. But of course, any advice or ideas you hunt down, while helpful, they have to be tempered by your pupils' needs. Ideas need adapting to ensure that they are relevant to both your professional context and the location where you are conducting the fieldwork.

We have already mentioned some 'old fieldwork favourites' such as the river study outlined on page 222. Holmes and Walker (2006) suggest a range of different approaches to fieldwork in Box 7.2.

Box 7.2 Creative approaches to geographical fieldwork

Ideas that are worth trying include:

1   Geographers as artisans: Design a fieldwork activity which appeals to pupils who have strong artistic and visual tendencies. Take a physical geography theme and incorporate creative responses to the environmental processes. This might involve ideas using poetry, drama, sculpture, song or dance.

2   Making connections – linking local to global: A fieldwork experience which explores interconnections between people and places at a range of scales. For instance, collect a series of images to illustrate how the area studied links with other parts of the world. What are the implications of such linkages and how do they influence other people's quality of life?

3   Web-designers: Use a web storyboard as a mechanism for learning about a place. Encourage pupils to carry out internet research to construct a virtual field course that could be used prior to the real excursion. How would they design navigation around their site? What would people like to know? This activity will engage and connect the pupils to the location while forming an important part of the pre-course preparation.

4   Tricky trails: Ask the pupils to design two short trails around a local town. The first is a route which shows the best elements, high quality of life, best sights, etc. The other trail is an 'eyesore' route, which takes in the worst parts. Explore how the use of photographs and captions could illustrate these contrasts in such a small geographical area. This activity could be extended to introduce the more complex idea of bias and selectivity – how do these affect our views about both people and landscapes?

(*Source*: Holmes and Walker 2006: 218)

House et al. (2012) discuss the notion of 'risky' fieldwork. They argue that it is easy to become complacent with fieldwork and to get into a 'fieldwork rut' where processes, procedures and outcomes are so familiar we almost don't notice what learning is actually happening in the field – as long as the pupils get the answers we want, then all is well. Risky fieldwork means everyone, including teachers, stepping outside their comfort zone, often undertaking work in locations that are relatively new to everyone. They observe that too often the hard thinking that fieldwork requires is done, not in the field, but 'back at base' (in a classroom or a field centre), thus undermining the challenge of thinking geographically *in* the real world. Strategies need to be in place that require pupils to think in the field as well as when they are back at base. They suggest strategies such as of 'geo-squishing' where pupils take photos of landforms and explain them to each other, creating opportunities for peer assessment in the field and providing insights into pupils' understanding for teacher to use too.

Charlton et al. (2012) suggests similar approaches for coastal fieldwork where more familiar activities such as beach profiles and measuring longshore drift can be supplemented with activities that encourage pupils to take a broader view of the local area. 'Mapping viewpoints' requires pupils to follow a map and then at different pre-ordained points pupils can either:

- ask questions
- make a statement
- express an opinion
- query their own knowledge.

They have ten seconds to film their idea/question/musings, with the landscape feature in the background, before moving on. They can then, at the end the day or once back in school, edit their fieldwork presentations to create a short news programme explaining the landscape or rising questions about how it was formed and what might happen to it in the future. This could form the basis for interesting peer assessment as well as provide some important 'advertising' material for school open days!

Witt (2013) introduces the notion of 'playful' fieldwork. This approach to fieldwork is rooted in the French Situationist tradition of wandering through spaces and seeing and experiencing places and the environment in new ways. The idea of a 'dérive' is for the individual, rather than follow a prescribed route and look at particular thing, they 'encounter' the landscape, they observe, they look up and notice.

This is an unstructured approach in the spirit of discovery (Kinder 2013) and 'risky fieldwork' (House et al. 2012). It involves journeys which are not predetermined by a set of learning objectives or a fixed purpose, but are serendipitous and unpredictable. The students' route is randomly determined by a set of cards which are selected at appropriate intervals. These cards may be directional instructions, for example turn left, turn right, travel straight ahead. The cards could also suggest activities along the way, for example follow a bag, sit quietly for two minutes and observe what happens, find something red and so on (Witt 2013: 114).

Witt goes on to suggest how the activity can be adapted, allowing pupils to be more involved in the planning, possibly writing their direction cards. During the dérive they can also be encouraged to record their experiences using sound or images and then 're-create' or represent their experiences using 'messy maps' (see Barlow et al. 2010) and artefacts collected along the way.

The value of this approach to fieldwork is to encourage pupils to look differently at places, and it can be especially useful when undertaken in places that pupils think they know well. When one of the authors completed this task with PGCE geography students, working in collaboration with English PGCE students, the outcomes were fascinating. They went out with their 'dérive kit' (direction cards, city tourist map, recording devices and their imaginations) and a certain degree scepticism, but came back quite enthralled, claiming to have spoken to people they would never normally have spoken to, and to have visited parts of the city they had never been to, and did not even know existed. They brought back their own soundscapes and urban detritus in order to create a piece of 'urban land-art' (rather like land-art which can be the creative part of more environmental fieldwork) in order to represent their experiences and imaginings of the day.

The approaches above remind us that fieldwork is not one thing or the other (traditional vs creative), but it is a subtle blend of carefully planned and organised experiences that then allow pupils to develop their understandings of how geographers work in order to create new understandings.

Cross-curricular fieldwork can provide an added dimension to fieldwork. Collaborating with history colleagues can help pupils to understand how places change and develop a more informed insight into some of the events that have brought about change. Collaboration with English colleagues can help pupils look at a place as it is represented in the media or in literature and thus develop their critical capacities. Even working with less obvious subject areas provides unique opportunities. Collaboration with the modern foreign language (MFL) department provided support for a group of PGCE geography students (working in small teams, with MFL PGCE students) to conduct geography fieldwork *in French* during a visit to Lille. As mentioned elsewhere in this book, a great deal of work has taken place on the potential of pupils learning geography through the medium of a modern foreign language (see Coyle 2007; Coyle et al. 2010) and fieldwork, if abroad, provides an excellent opportunity for pupils to build geographical understanding as well as application of language knowledge.

Fieldwork and new technologies

Technology can make a valuable contribution to geographical fieldwork especially in supporting the collection and processing of accurate and reliable data. Digital and electronic monitoring equipment can be used to collect environmental data, for example to measure light, heat and humidity levels when investigating the microclimate of an area. There are also sensors for measuring noise levels and soil pH levels. Spreadsheets can be used to process data and facilitate effective presentation and analysis of this data. Another benefit of using spreadsheets is that they can facilitate multiple access for entering and sharing data (Holmes and Walker 2006: 223). Digital cameras (photographic and video) are increasingly being used as part of data collection (see above) with images edited digitally, presented to whole classes using digital projectors and shared with others via the internet. The internet can also be used to research additional secondary data sources to support enquiries. The use of technology can also promote creativity and give pupils more autonomy in designing and developing geographical fieldwork enquiries.

As new technology develops, there are even more creative ways in which technology can be used to enhance fieldwork. Mobile technologies have an increasing range of applications that can be utilised in fieldwork. Most mobile phones have cameras for taking digital images and video that can be downloaded for use in data analysis and presentation. Schools increasingly offer pupils opportunities to use devices such as tablets which can support data collection, process digital images and provide access to other data. Global positioning systems (GPS) can be used to enhance fieldwork providing pupils with insights into 'real world' applications of technology (Martin 2006: 141-142). Fieldwork data can be recorded along a transect or at sample points with the GPS used to record the position where this data was collected. Data can then be presented and analysed spatially using Google earth or another mapping program.

For pupils with special needs, mobile technology can reduce the need for writing in the field, but can speed up data processing as well as help pupils to organise and present their work in ways they can be proud of, without detracting from developing their geographical understanding. Again, the Geographical Association's publication *GA News* has a section entitled *Webwatch*, dedicated to updating geography teachers on technology developments, including developments for fieldwork.

Progression in fieldwork

As in other areas of the geography curriculum, we should expect pupils to experience progression in their learning through geographical fieldwork between phases and age groups. They should make progress in relation to the skills and techniques used, the range of places and themes experienced, the degree of complexity and difficulty in conceptual learning and enquiry, and in the degree of independence required in undertaking fieldwork enquiry (see Table 7.2). Older pupils should be expected to use more sophisticated fieldwork techniques and where appropriate devise their own. They should appreciate the significance of sampling issues and demonstrate a greater range of skills in presenting, analysing and interpreting their findings. Careful planning is needed by a geography department to ensure that pupils continue to make progress in developing their skills and in extending their conceptual learning through geographical fieldwork.

Table 7.2 Progression in geographical fieldwork

Key Stage	1	2	3	4	5
Enquiry related skill	• Other responses to questions. • Some simple analysis of results.	Simple line of enquiry followed, teacher led/guided. Some will undertake additional independent investigations. Ask questions to help design enquiry, begin to hypothesise. Devise some fieldwork techniques. Decide how to record and present the data. Review fieldwork and the impact on their understanding.	Ask geographical questions. Suggest an appropriate sequence of investigation and plan an enquiry. Collect record and display information. Analyse and reflect critically on their evidence and methodology, when presenting and justifying conclusions. Solve problems and make decisions, developing analytical skills and creative thinking.	Use of initiative in independently developing the enquiry process. Identify and collect a range of appropriate evidence and justify choices. Evaluate the whole enquiry process, including the limitations of their evidence and conclusions. Understand and apply the geographical principles and theory that underpin the enquiry.	Individual ownership of investigations. Understanding of piloting. Development of original data collection techniques. Systematic and robust enquiry process. Evaluate thoroughly and self-critically including constructive proposals for further development. Wider geographical context fully explained and integrated throughout the enquiry.
Data-orientated skills	• Local walk making observations. Simple surveys and questionnaires (such as a traffic survey). Simple graphs. Simple maps and plans. Use of maps to record information.	Sketches including field sketches. Use of photographs. Measurements recorded using field equipment. Land-use survey using tally chart and colour coded key. Simple charts and graphs. Data used to answer question and interpret results.	Annotated field sketches. Maps interpreted (range of scales). Design surveys and interviews. Environmental assessments. Detailed, extended land-use mapping of multiple types of data. Range of data collected from a variety of sources including the internet, digital media and GIS. Sufficient data interpreted to substantiate conclusions. Data represented using a range of methods including ICT and GIS.	Precise data collection. Application of sampling. Data presentation using a wide variety of appropriate cartographical, graphic and numerical techniques including: choropleth and isoline maps, proportional symbols, annotated sketch maps. Quantative analysis. Detailed analysis cross referencing a range of data, establishing links, extrapolating and making inferences.	Rigorous data collection, high level of accuracy and detail. Full explanation of sampling strategy. Quantitative and qualitative data. Annotated data presentation; kite and vector diagrams, triangular graphs and other complex graphical, diagrammatic and cartographic techniques. Statistical analysis of data. Explanation of anomalies. Analysis effective, coherent and independent. Conclusions fully justified and synoptic.

(continued)

Table 7.2 (continued)

Key Stage	1	2	3	4	5
Example of fieldwork: 1 day River Study data collection	• Possible use of stream in school grounds, or river in a village being visited, to make observations.	Short section of river visited, simple data collection at 3 sites. Predictions made. Method devised using field equipment provided. Field sketch completed.	More detailed data collection at 3 sites, including use of hydroprops. Limitations discussed. Detailed annotated fieldsketches. Landscape features interpreted to support results analysis. Maps interpreted (range of scales).	Wider range of data collection – type and amount, completed with high level of accuracy. Discussion of sampling techniques. Methodology justified. Photographic evidence used to support observation.	Extensive data collection at 5/10 sites, detailed, thorough and precise. Hypothesis specific and individual. Additional sketches/ notes to inform results and explain anomalies. Methodology and sampling techniques critically analysed and justified. Wider drainage basin features analysed, comparison with textbook river.
Examples of appropriate fieldwork equipment		Rulers, tape measures, stop watches, clinometer, thermometer, soil auger, digital cameras, video.	Hydroprop/flow meter, ranging poles, anemometer, light meters, digital media, GIS, GPS, environmental sensors	Digital meters – decibels, pH, PDAs with spreadsheets.	

Source: Turney, A. and Jakeways, E., Field Studies Council, Brockhole

---

Task 7.2 Progression in geographical fieldwork

1   Working with a small group of other geography teachers, collect examples of field-work activities developed for pupils working in the following phases of education:

  • Key stage 3 (11–14-year-olds)
  • GCSE (14–16-year-olds)
  • GCE AS and A2 Level (post-16).

2   For each age range, identify:

  • the skills and techniques developed
  • the range of places experienced
  • the range of geographical themes covered
  • the level of complexity and difficulty in the conceptual learning
  • the degree of independence required
  • the range of fieldwork approaches and purposes.

3   Compare your findings with the framework outlined in Table 7.3.
4   Where are the 'gaps' in pupils' experiences of geographical fieldwork?
5   Discuss possible reasons for these 'gaps' and suggest how they might be addressed.

Summary and key points

Geographical fieldwork should not be seen as a 'one-off' and isolated learning experience. It needs to fit coherently within the wider curriculum experience through geography. This further emphasises the importance of careful and thorough planning and preparation. Pupils must be prepared in advance so that the learning gains from the fieldwork experience are maximised. Careful attention also needs to be given to how these learning gains will be built upon after the fieldwork in what Holmes and Walker (2006: 224) describe as 'closing the loop'. Evaluating all aspects of the fieldwork also makes an important contribution to your own professional development and to ensuring the success of future fieldwork.

   This chapter has explored many of the important issues involved in planning high quality, safe, successful and sustainable fieldwork. To conclude this discussion, we have chosen to draw your attention to David Job's challenge when thinking about the significant role geographical fieldwork can play in a young person's education:

> Engagement in real fieldwork, particularly of the deeper kind, addresses almost the full range of intelligences and learning styles. To promote and justify real field-work, it needs to be demonstrated that the experiences offered include not only the development of cognitive skills but also the nurturing of aesthetic sensibility, creativity, critique, co-operative endeavour, caring and healing. These attributes, rather than technical and rationalist aptitudes alone, form some of the foundations for the growth of ecologically and emotionally literate citizens.
>
> (Job 2002: 144)

Further reading

www.teachernet.gov.uk/teachingandlearning/resourcematerials/outsideclassroom/
The DfES launched the 'Learning Outside the Classroom Manifesto' in November 2006 to promote the value of learning beyond the classroom, including fieldwork. This document shows how direct experience outside the classroom provides a powerful approach to learning that can raise achievement.

St. John, P. and Richardson, D. (1997) *Methods of Presenting Fieldwork Data*, Sheffield: Geographical Association.

St. John, P. and Richardson, D. (1996) *Methods of Analysing Fieldwork Data*, Sheffield: Geographical Association.

Both of these publications are excellent if your statistical understanding is either rusty or in serious need of support. With the renewed emphasis on developing pupils' numerical capabilities through geography, then each of these texts will support you with accessible worked-through examples of how to plan and develop the statistical element of fieldwork.

8 Assessment

> Assessment is not an exact science and we must stop presenting it as such.
>
> (Gipps 1994: 167)

Introduction

For those outside the teaching profession, assessment is often caricatured by red ticks and crosses littered over pupils' work, teachers' mark books comprising illegible codes and squiggles meaning nothing to anyone other than the owner, and silent examination halls full of weary pupils struggling to get to the end of an exam. Of course, assessment maybe some of this, but high-quality assessment practice is more complex than this caricature represents. In this chapter we will consider two, now-common notions of assessment – formative assessment and summative assessment, the relationship between assessment and progression and some of the more practical practices associated with assessment such as managing day-to-day assessment and recording and reporting pupils' progress in geography.

In formal terms, we can define assessment in education as 'the process of gathering, interpreting, recording and using information about pupils' responses to an educational task' (Harlen et al. 1992: 217). This is an excellent definition and in this chapter we explore what it means in practice, particularly in terms of your developing the professional attitudes and skills needed to get to know your pupils and, through their geography, to help them improve. What all this requires, literally, is learning how to value pupils' work.

By the end of this chapter, you should be able to:

- identify the broad principles of educational assessment
- identify the principles of 'assessment for learning'
- understand some of the threats to high-quality formative assessment
- understand the purposes of and practice of marking pupils' work in assessing pupils' progress
- use appropriate recording and reporting systems
- appreciate the changing landscape of summative assessment and the implications for pupils' geographical learning.

Assessment: some contextual insights

The Teachers' Standards In England (DfE 2011, updated 2013) place considerable emphasis on teachers' understanding of assessment practice and their use of assessment outcomes for different purposes. For teachers in England, the Standards state that teacher must be able to:

- make accurate and productive use of assessment
- know and understand how to assess the relevant subject and curriculum areas, including statutory assessment requirements
- make use of formative and summative assessment to secure pupils' progress
- use relevant data to monitor progress, set targets and plan subsequent lessons
- give pupils regular feedback, both orally and through accurate marking, and encourage pupils to respond to the feedback.

(p. 12)

Understanding assessment is a statutory prerequisite of being awarded Qualified Teacher Status in England. However, we would argue that high-quality assessment practice, which is an embedded characteristic of high-quality teaching, is a professional responsibility. High-quality assessment practice is, of course, a somewhat vague term. What do we mean by 'high quality'? Does it mean the same thing to everyone including head teachers, teachers, pupils and parents? What does it look like in practice?

The recent history of assessment presents something of a confused and confusing picture. In 2000, the educationist Mary James wrote an influential paper outlining the changes in assessment practice in England. Entitled *Measured Lives: The rise of assessment as the engine of change in English schools*, the paper summarises her own child's experiences of the new testing regime introduced in the wake of the first National Curriculum. In that time (between 1989 and 2000), the curriculum and its formal assessment requirements have changed many times, and further changes since 2000 have left English youngsters with the reputation for now being the most assessed young people in the world (Elwood and Lundy 2010). Much of the assessment rhetoric has focused on the more managerialist aspects of assessment such as: assessment systems and organisation, schools' use of assessment data, teacher accountability through assessment, the relationship between assessment and 'raising standards' (a popular euphemism for 'yet more testing', as if testing and raising standards go hand-in-hand!), rather than more educational aspects of assessment such as curriculum coherence, progression in learning, and meaningful assessment. James reaches some difficult conclusions about assessment policy and practice in England, views which are supported by others (see Reay and William 2006; Elwood and Lundy 2010) and which in summary include:

- the negative impact of relentless assessment on the emotional well-being of young people and their teachers;
- the risks involved in emphasising performance over learning;
- the risk of jeopardising 'life-long' learning as an educational goal by focusing too much on out-of-date assessment practices which are inappropriate for the twenty-first century;
- the consequence of such a 'meritocratic vision' on social ambitions to promote increasing degrees of social justice.

(p. 361)

International comparisons show the education system in England and Wales to be somewhat overloaded with external, state-controlled examinations of one sort or another, designed to sift and grade young people into fairly fixed categories of 'ability' or 'potential' at the beginning of their adult lives. However, in recent years, there has been a growing realisation of the destructive impact of the assumptions that underpin such an assessment regime. If you assume that intelligence is general, inherited and pretty well fixed, then you will continue to 'prepare' pupils for their tests, knowing deep down that the results are more or less determined. You will make sure they cover the syllabus, practise answering questions, learn to avoid classic errors (for example, by using 'along the corridor and up the stairs' as a prompt for reading grid references) and boost confidence whenever you can.

If, however, you believe intelligence to be multifaceted, and that intelligences can be learnt (see Perkins 1996), you will do all the above but with important and potentially liberating differences; for example, you will not so readily adopt teachers' short-hand terms such as 'the less able' with their deterministic and, in fact, damning connotations about the general characteristics of groups of pupils. You might think of your class not as passive 'pupils', the sometimes reluctant recipients of what you have to give, but as active 'learners'. Part of your job in the latter regime is to 'tune in' to these learners as individuals, getting to know their work and its strengths and weaknesses; you may then use this knowledge to find ways of helping them meet new work more intelligently (and experience more success).

Figure 8.1 shows how the different purposes and functions of teaching, learning and assessment are inter-related. It highlights the important questions for both teachers and pupils during the assessment process. It also emphasises that the learner is at the centre of this assessment process with the information obtained being used to support learning through 'feedback' and 'feedforward' (Weeden and Hopkin 2006).

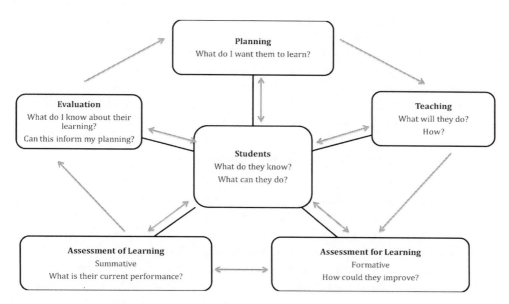

Figure 8.1 Teaching, learning and assessment

(*Source*: Weeden and Hopkin 2006: 415)

Assessment practice is influenced by four important assessment principles, outlined below.

Assessment must be planned

> All lessons should be planned with assessment in mind. Indeed, as we travel through the various 'scales' of planning – from individual lessons, to units of work, schemes of work, specifications, syllabuses and curricula – all these educational 'episodes' need to give a clear indication of the role of assessment within them. Therefore at the 'sharp end' – where the teacher is working day-to-day with pupils in classrooms – there should be a keen awareness on the teacher's part of the ways in which pupil achievement can be measured.
>
> (Weeden and Butt 2009)

Self-evidently, assessment is not something to be left to the end of a teaching episode, and nor is it something that can be applied without considerable forethought. In other words, assessment is a process which needs planning well before the children walk through the classroom door. As we have seen in Chapter 3, planning occurs at three levels. In assessment terms, we can summarise these as:

- *Level 1 The general level:* The assessment requirements and arrangements of the external agents such as examinations providers. These are published and updated annually and usually supplemented with materials designed to assist teachers. For example, make sure that you read the Chief Examiner's annual report for the GCSE or A-level syllabus you teach.
- *Level 2 The school level:* Your department plans the geography for the pupils at your school by devising a scheme of work. In addition to detailing what and, possibly, how to teach, this should also show the overall scheme of assessment: when more summative assessments take place, but also the identification of variety and range in assessment opportunities. Analysing the scheme of work for assessment opportunities is a good discipline: what different kinds of writing do the pupils have the chance to try? What other forms of expression does the geography department value? Do we ever ask pupils to produce extended writing, perhaps based on extended reading?
- *Level 3 The classroom level:* The day-to-day marking or on-going assessment of pupils. The evidence of your planning at this level is in your lesson plan, and it concerns what you do, to (or with) whom and why.

Assessment must have 'consequential validity'

This chapter explores how geography teachers can place value on, and respond to, children's work. It is driven by the concept of 'consequential validity' (Gipps 1994). This concept identifies a basic touchstone of educational assessment: that its validity depends upon it having consequences for improving learning. This is a good test of worthwhileness; for example, how will marking this pile of books have consequences? Will not marking them have consequences? How do I mark these books to have the maximum positive impact on future learning?

The idea of consequential validity takes us to the heart of what Gipps means when she reminds us that assessment is 'not an exact science' (Gipps 1994: 167): that highly 'scientific' assessment (i.e. standardised testing under controlled conditions), with its emphasis on exactitude, does not serve well the educational purposes of teachers. Good assessment is altogether more messy – more 'art' than 'science' – and rests on teachers making dependable and fair judgements of value on pupils' work. By good assessment, we mean assessment that is formative – literally, assessment for learning: this is different from summative assessment because the latter cannot feed back to pupils (it is undertaken at the end of the course) and therefore has very limited potential in feeding forward to inform future learning. This distinction is an important one (see Box 8.1 for a summary of others) and signals the persistent need for teachers using assessment to clarify purpose.

Assessment must be 'fit for purpose'

That assessment has to be 'fit for purpose' is another touchstone to be guided by. Much assessment in education serves purposes other than educational ones and teachers need to be clear about this. Generally speaking, four broad purposes of assessment in education can be identified:

- Formative: recognising the positive achievement of the pupil, feeding back in terms that the pupil can understand and feeding forward in terms of next steps or targets.
- Summative: recording the overall achievement of the pupil, usually in the form of a useful summary that can be compared (i.e. ranked) with others, such as a grade.
- Diagnostic: designed to identify and measure particular learning difficulties which may be classified and scrutinised so that remedial action can be planned and implemented effectively.
- Evaluative: fulfilling the needs of the state or administration which legitimately needs some way of assessing the effectiveness (value for money) of the education service at various levels – individual teacher, school, national and so on.

If the main purpose identified for assessment is evaluative, the occasional testing of a sample of pupils would suffice. In practice, the summative assessments of all pupils by examination are taken to be the appropriate data set: hence the introduction of league tables of examination results in the early 1990s. Examination results therefore have a high stake, not only for the individual pupils concerned, but also for the teachers: there is pressure to improve results year on year. This is fine so long as the distorting tendencies of high stakes assessment are understood and kept in check: primarily, the risk arises from pressure to 'teach to the test' and only to value achievement which 'scores' in examination terms. The way such pressure can (but need not) distort the geography curriculum is by reducing:

- time for fieldwork
- time in class devoted to open-ended, speculative or creative discussions or enquiry
- class time devoted to topical issues or particular interests/experiences of pupils or the teacher.

At the same time, there may be an increased:

- reliance on classic case studies or examples, which can become stereotypical
- tendency to teach (and learn) simple answers to complex questions, uncritically copying.

If the main purpose of assessment is formative, the priorities are quite different. Formative assessment may be combined with assessments designed for diagnostic purposes, but it is very difficult to see how, in practice, assessments may serve both formative and summative/evaluative purposes at the same time. Whereas, for example, high-stakes summative assessment rewards people who can avoid mistakes, play safe and commit to memory the information and rules, low-stakes formative assessment often centres on analysing mistakes and encourages risk taking. It exploits a range of assessment opportunities from the more formal, to the informal, from the written to the oral, from work done at home to work done at school, from work done individually to work done as a member of a group or team. And all the while, the purpose is not to compare and rank the pupil with others, but to get the pupil – and the teacher – to understand each other better and what it is they have to do next.

Another crucial distinction between summative and formative assessment is that the former, being designed mainly with the need to grade pupils in relation to each other (that is, essentially, to rank them for selection purposes), is likely to be norm-referenced (see Box 8.1). The latter, however, ought to be criterion-referenced, as we shall see below.

It is interesting to make the historical note here that the influential TGAT Report upon which the initial National Curriculum assessment framework was orginally based (see Lambert 1996; Marsden 1995), while recognising different assessment needs, tried to create a single, criteria-referenced system to meet all assessment purposes. It failed.

Educational assessment must be criterion-referenced

The principle here is simple and expanded upon later in this chapter. If we intend to engage pupils-as-learners in conversations about their progress, next steps or targets, we need a transparent common language. There are undoubtedly many readers of this book who have experienced for themselves the opaqueness of traditional assessments for which the criteria on which the mark or grade were based were not identified.

The usefulness of assessment criteria reinforces the point made repeatedly in this book that effective planning for learning requires teachers to become fluent and adept at identifying 'lesson objectives'. It is difficult to see how, without a clear sense of the teacher's objectives, it would be possible to articulate very clearly the success criteria in learning.

So, we clearly need criteria on which to base assessment. What may not be quite so clear is the subtle interplay of norms with criteria. We do not want you to think that norm-referencing is 'bad' and criteria-referencing is 'good'; they are not polar opposites. It has long been realised that 'behind every criterion lurks a norm'. To illustrate with an example: it is impossible to provide the exact, objective criterion for assessing success in explaining the location of the biotechnology industry in the Cambridge area, or outlining the arguments for and against eco-tourism in Costa Rica. It is not even possible to say exactly how to award marks for reading pie charts or Ordnance Survey maps. Any general guidance that criteria can provide has to be brought alive by the process of establishing norms – of skimming the work and setting expectations or standards. Without criteria at all, however, this process is without basis: teachers, even in the same department, will have different – and to pupils confusing – standards.

These principles, despite their apparent lack of precision, are nonetheless important in underpinning our understanding of how to assess pupils' learning and communicate our thinking, as a teacher, in clear and transparent ways.

Assessment for learning: using formative assessment in geography classrooms

Have established some principles for good practice, we now consider one particular and important aspect of assessment practice in schools – formative assessment. As the discussion above suggests, there is history of using formal, summative assessment in the English (and other) education systems, in other words *assessment OF learning*. As a student, you will have had experience of this type of assessment via the tests that you took at school, including KS2 and KS3 SATs (Standard Assessment Tasks), GCSE examinations, and also A-level examinations. We can add to this the exams and other assessments you sat for your degree, as well as public assessments such as your driving test!

In schools, in an effort to redress the balance and raise the status of internal assessment, two researchers (Black and Wiliam 1998a), both of them heavily involved in the initial design and the implementation of National Curriculum assessment, undertook an exhaustive review of research into formative assessment over the last decade of the twentieth century. What they were investigating was the potential benefits to pupils' learning if assessment is focused, not on end of unit testing or examinations, but on classroom practice, or what is now commonly referred to as *Assessment FOR Learning (AfL)*. Their quest was to answer the question: is there evidence that improving formative assessment raises standards? Their conclusion was that 'innovations including strengthening the practice of formative assessment produce significant, and often substantial, learning gains' (Black and Wiliam 1998b: 2). Furthermore, the evidence they found showed that formative assessment helps the (so-called) low attainers more than the rest.

Thus, according to evidence from the several hundred research reports studied from around the world, the effect of good formative assessment, they stated, is that attainment is raised overall and the spread of attainment is reduced. This suggests that any 'tail' of low achievement in a school (or whole-education system) is a portent of wasted talent, and produces young people who come to believe that they are 'no good' and unable to learn. These are bold claims. A lot hinges on exactly what the research counts as formative assessment.

Box 8.1 Characteristics of formative assessment

In essence, formative assessment is characterised by:

- clarifying and understanding learning intentions and criteria for success
- engineering effective classroom discussions, questions and tasks that elicit evidence of learning
- providing feedback that moves learners forward
- activating students as instructional resources for each other, and
- activating students as owners of their own learning.

The 'big idea that ties these together is that we use evidence of student learning to adapt teaching and learning, or instruction, to meet student needs.

(*Source*: Wiliam 2006: 8)

Box 8.2 Improving formative assessment practice

Black and Wiliam's (1998b) research review also offers signposts for the improvement of formative assessment practice. Teachers, the research suggests, should adopt the following goals:

1   Use feedback that identifies particular qualities about the pupils' geographical work and which offers precise advice for improvement. Comments on presentation and so on are to be avoided because they are superficial and do not support pupils' capacity to understand their geographical learning needs.

2   Encourage a 'culture of success' in which pupils take risks and are not afraid of making mistakes. This requires that the comfortable but unchallenging 'contract of contentment' which often exists between pupils and teachers (lots of 'busy work' like colouring in the sea) needs renegotiating.

3   Begin to train pupils in self-assessment and peer-assessment so that they come to understand for themselves the criteria for judging success in geography and gain a sense of longer term learning goals.

4   Work to break down the common pattern of passive learning and make the learning goals explicit (especially the 'big picture' – how each lesson relates to the longer term goals).

Formative assessment in practice

Questioning and dialogue

Questioning and dialogue in geography classrooms provides many opportunities for you to promote successful assessment for learning. We spend a considerable part of lesson time engaged in class discussions or question-and-answer sessions. However, this questioning and dialogue needs to create new knowledge rather than just rehearsing existing knowledge. Weeden and Lambert (2006) outline the essential features of learning activities that can provide rich evidence to enable geography teachers to make judgements about what the next steps in learning might be and how they can be made:

- challenging activities that promote thinking and discussion
- rich questions
- strategies to support all learners in revealing their ideas
- opportunities for peer discussion
- group or while class discussion which encourage open dialogue.

(Weeden and Lambert 2006: 8)

Black (2004: 1) argues that formative interaction in classrooms involves far more than having good questions. He warns of the dangers of 'recitation' styles of questioning:

What matters is both the question and the way in which the teacher handles the responses which it elicits. If a question is asked, but students given little time to think, with the inevitable one-word responses rewarded if correct or brushed aside if wrong, then there is no formative dialogue as the teacher continues along his/her predetermined path. A lack of dialogue means that it is difficult for teachers to get inside their pupils' thinking and it is therefore difficult to make informed judgements about what pupils actually understand.

The reinforces the problem identified by Bennett (discussed in Chapter 2) where what we can *infer* about pupils' geographical understanding is severely limited if they don't get a chance to say or do very much. We discussed different types of questions and the notion of dialogic teaching in Chapter 4 on Pedagogy.

Clarifying and sharing learning intentions and criteria

Low achievement often results from pupils failing to understand what is required of them (Black and Wiliam 1998b). The principle here is simple. If we intend to engage pupils-as-learners in conversations about their progress, next steps or targets, we need a transparent common language. There are undoubtedly many readers of this book who have experienced for themselves the opaqueness of traditional assessments for which the criteria on which the mark or grade were based were not identified.

This is not about posting the learning objective on the board at the start of a lesson. It means clarifying and sharing learning intentions that focus on what pupils will learn rather than what they will do in a lesson. These learning intentions should be achievable and realistic. The criteria for success should always be transparent to pupils and in language they can understand. Sharing examples of work completed by previous year's pupils can prompt discussion about quality; what's good about the good ones and what's lacking and needing improvement in the weaker ones?

A range of strategies can then be used to discover what pupils have actually learned. There has been a focus in recent years on the role of a 'plenary' in creating time and space at the end of a lesson to do this. Quite a lot of emphasis has been on using fun activities to support the process of making judgements about learning. This is all well and good; however, we would argue that leaving judgements about learning until the end actually flies in the face of good formative assessment practice and in reality makes no sense; moving on to teach a new concept or skill before pupils have grasped the current one seems pointless, and only finding this out at the end of a lesson will have serious consequences for pupils' ability to make progress. Creating opportunities within lessons to really find out what pupils are understanding and using these insights to adjust your lesson *as* you teach is much more realistic in terms of supporting pupils' learning. By all means, work together with pupils at the end of your lesson to establish what has been achieved in relation to your initial intentions, to give and receive feedback and to give pupils some sense of 'where next' – but your objectives or enquiry questions need to be embedded elements in the lesson and therefore present in the work pupils produce and in the conversations that you have with them.

Giving feedback

An important part of the dialogue we have with our pupils is the feedback dialogue – how we intervene in pupils' work and learning to help them see what they understand and where they need to go next in their learning in order to make progress – this is feedback. Feedback takes on two forms – verbal feedback and written feedback. Pupils report that the kind of feedback that they feel is most useful to them is verbal feedback. This 'on the spot' feedback, evidenced in the kinds of conversations teachers have with pupils *in* lessons, helps pupils to make progress because they can respond to it in the moment, they can ask for clarification if they don't understand and they can see their work develop in the lesson. Do not underestimate the impact of this kind of dialogue, both on your understanding of your pupils' work and on pupils' ability to make progress. This kind of dialogue provides you with invaluable, but generally subliminal 'data' about who understands what, who needs more support or advice and who needs more challenge. Being more conscious of the kinds of conversations you are having enables you to make subtle but significant adjustments in your teaching to help pupils access the key ideas in the lesson.

Table 8.1 is a list of the kinds of evidence pupils will produce in geography lessons and as homework that can then be used by teachers to make judgements about pupils' geographical understanding. From this evidence, teachers can then give advice on what pupils can do next to improve. The list is a useful indication of the kinds if evidence you can use to support formative assessment, but what it also reinforces is the notion that pupils do have to 'produce' something for you to assess. Tim Oates (2014), Chair of the Review Panel for the National Curriculum, is very clear that in high-performing contexts, pupils 'produce a lot' of work, oral or written, or visual, that provide insights into pupils thinking that teachers can then use to support learning.

Table 8.1 Learning activities which present opportunities to assess pupils' work

Oral evidence	Written evidence	Graphic evidence	Products
questioning	questionnaires	diagrams	models
listening	diaries	sketches	artefacts
discussing	reports	drawings	games
presentations	essays	graphs	photographs
interviews	notes	printouts	
debates	stories	overlays	
audio recording	newspaper articles		
video recording	scripts		
role play	short answers to questions		
simulation	lists		
	poems		
	descriptions		

The other form of feedback that is part and parcel of teachers' work is 'marking': looking at the work that pupils produce, reading it/listening to it/looking at it (depending on the type work), checking it carefully for understanding and having a written dialogue with your pupils in order to help them make progress.

It seems that a plethora of practices have emerged in the name of 'marking', often in the rush to provide attainment evidence for senior managers and Ofsted inspectors rather than necessarily to support progress. What we mean by this is over-elaborate form-filling, box-ticking, sticker-giving and record-keeping, at the expense of a genuine written dialogue with pupils. At its best, however, written feedback can help pupils to understand their achievements and at the same time know what they need to do to improve.

When marking, we need to make some choices – and realise that we do not have to:

- assess every piece of work a pupil does
- assess everything possible in the piece of work we are marking (What are the priorities? What is the focus this time?)
- assess every pupil in the class every time work is handed in.

In other words, less frequent, but higher quality, pupil–teacher interactions may have beneficial effects on learning, and the pupils' understanding of their progress.

Marking and written comments are the most common way in which we have a written dialogue with pupils and provide them with feedback. However, comments are often unhelpful or not used by pupils. A challenge for you is therefore to develop strategies that make comments more effective in developing pupils' learning and then find ways of engaging them in dialogue about their learning (Weeden 2005). Feedback on tasks that are more challenging, requiring reasoning rather than simple recall, provide more evidence about learning. Such tasks often involve more extended writing.

Paul Weeden (2005) provides a helpful range of suggestions about ways of providing effective feedback comments. These include examples of prompts that can support students in making immediate improvements:

- Reminder prompts – 'Say more about . . . '
- Scaffold prompts – 'Can you explain why . . . . ?' (questions)
- 'Describe why . . . ' (directive)
- Example prompt – 'Choose one of these statements or create your own.'

Evidence suggests that a teacher will typically spend more time marking a student's work than the student will spend following it up – which runs the risk of undermining the feedback process (Wiliam and Black 2002). In response to this, schools are increasingly introducing whole-school policies requiring teachers to provide explicit feedback that pupils then have to respond to. The expectation is that pupils are given time, either in lessons or at home, to do this, the rationale being that feedback and targets are senseless if pupils just read and ignore them; they need opportunities to participate in the dialogue and actually respond in some way. The main problem seems to be that the 'paraphenalia' gets in the way of the process (Lambert 2011), as schools/departments introduce a multitude of coloured forms for ticking and sticking, and teachers and pupils are required to use different-coloured pens to, respectively, set and respond to targets. The question is, who is this all for? Does it improve the quality of feedback to pupils? Does it make their engagement with their targets more purposeful, or is it merely for surveillance purposes and ease of accountability?

So the security for teachers is in their planning. It can be decided at the beginning of the year how frequently pupils will receive in-depth feedback which may involve face-to-face contact for some minutes (three or four pupils a week?). The focus for the rolling programme of ongoing assessments is also decided and identified on the scheme of work. Lessons plans can then identify 'in-the-moment' assessment. It is unlikely that such planning translates into action without a hitch; in fact, the actual process is likely to be messy and, as you get to know your pupils better, it will become obvious that some require more attention than others. The best-laid plans are adaptable.

Using peer- and self-assessment

One of us once observed a student teacher using peer-assessment at the end of a sequence of lesson about 'The Weather'. In groups, the pupils had prepared weather forecasts which they were to present these to the rest of the class. The rest of the class (individuals) were then to each evaluate the forecast using quite a complex grid and scoring system (see below).

Criteria	Grade 1	Grade 2	Grade 3	Grade 4
Quality of poster display				
Clarity of presentation				
Use of weather words				
Group organisation				

As the lesson progressed, several problems emerged. First, the class did not know what the grades meant: some thought Grade 4 was very good, and others thought Grade 1 was very good – the system had not been explained. Second, the pupils were not allowed to discuss with each other their ideas about the quality of each presentation – the task had to be completed in silence. Third, the assessment criteria were mainly about generic issues rather than geographical understanding so the focus of any feedback was not going to help pupils 'get better' at understanding the weather. Finally, by the end of the lesson the student teacher found herself with numerous completed copies of the grid, yet had no idea how to share the outcomes of the peer-assessment process with the pupils.

Peer assessment is difficult and takes time for teachers and pupils to use with any effect. We also accept that this was a student teacher trying something new and feeling her way into a very different way of thinking about assessment. However, this example illustrates the sorts of problems that arise when the system, that is, the mechanism of completing the grid, dominates in lessons, at the expense of finding out what pupils know, can do and understand.

Helping pupils to develop peer- and self-assessment skills is one of the most challenging aspects of assessment for learning. Pupils often lack the understanding and skills necessary to assess work and progress in learning against criteria for success and learning intentions. Giving and receiving feedback are important skills in peer-assessment, but It also takes time to develop their skills in communicating their judgements to each other. Peer work where pupils learn by trying to teach others and by being assessed by their peers will help them to develop these skills. Some advantages of peer assessment include:

- pupils receive rapid feedback
- pupils learn, through doing, the meaning of attainment according to the assessment criteria
- the teacher is 'released' during the period when pupils are marking to focus on other classroom priorities
- assessment is focused
- assessment is being used to improve performance.

A fear for some teachers is that one pupil's misunderstanding could be transferred to another, but choosing groups carefully and monitoring discussions can help to alleviate this problem. Weeden and Lambert (2006: 18–19) suggest starting in a small way and then evolving pupils' practice gradually perhaps by getting them to exchange books once a week and check for specific items such as key words. This can be progressed to getting them to write a comment about at least one good point made and if possible, one thing to consider to improve in the future.

Pupils may at first demand that the teacher 'ratifies' (or corrects) the peer marking. If so, there exists a splendid opportunity to get them to engage constructively and individually with their work, and to redraft it in the light of their feedback. You can then mark the redraft – their 'best shot'.

Task 8.1 Getting to grips with classroom-based assessment

The following activities are designed to encourage you to think critically and analytically about how you assess pupils' learning and how you help them to make progress in their geographical understanding through assessment.

A   Marking policies

Schools now have clear marking policies that they communicate to pupils and parents. When first in a school, it is important to understand the marking policy and consider how it translates into practice. Read your school's marking policy; how does this relates to the geography department's marking policy – what procedures does the department follow regarding marking and assessment and how this is recorded in mark books/on databases.

(continued)

(continued)

B   Formative assessment practice

1   Observe 2–3 lessons looking specifically for:

- How learning attentions are shared and used in the lesson.
- How the teacher uses questions to probe pupils thinking and support their learning. What does the teacher 'do' with pupils responses to questions?

2   Observe 2–3 lessons and discuss with the class teacher the kinds of targets they set pupils; if possible, look at a sample of 3–5 books/folders and look at the different kinds of target set for different pupils, and consider:

- How do teachers use oral feedback in lessons? How is pupils' progress monitored?
- How do pupils respond to written feedback on their work? What are they expected to 'do' with the feedback they receive?
- How the class teacher records pupils' progress.

C   Marking your first work

Before you set your first homework or classwork to be marked by you, you should have spent some time preparing in the following way:

1   Examine with the teacher a range of work from the class. You analyse it in terms of:

- accuracy of the content (the geography)
- the style of work (how it has been structured – by the teacher or by the pupils?), presentation
- spelling, punctuation and grammar
- how it has been marked – use some of the issues emerging in the present discussion to guide you:
  - o   How is it graded?
  - o   What are the grades for?
  - o   Does the teacher comment?
  - o   How? With what tone? Is the pupil expected to respond?

2   With the teacher's help and advice, identify an individual, pair or threesome of pupils with whom you can have a discussion about their work. Your aim is to find out:

- what sense they make of the work
- what they think it is for
- why it is marked
- what sense they make of the marks.

(Use this as an opportunity to practise the art of engaging young people in a serious but unthreatening manner and finding out about their views, without interrogating them.)

3   Nothing, however, can prepare you fully for that first pile of exercise books or file paper. It is useful to articulate on paper how you approach the task in detail. It is likely that you will take steps to skim the work in order for you to establish your expectations, norms or 'standards'; you may revise your judgement of earlier work in the light of later work. What were your feelings, your uncertainties or anxieties about the whole process? Discuss these with your mentor.

The purpose of records is to enable a fair and reasonable picture of the pupil to be communicated to others. This is the purpose of your mark book.

Recording and reporting assessment

Commenting on her marking, a teacher wrote that little of her dissatisfaction with marking

could have been deduced from my 'mark book', a large buff coloured commercially printed creation, containing hundreds of pink lines dividing large pages into thousands of little boxes, into which I carefully inserted the codes, grades and symbols derived from the rather cursory assessment process. At a glance everything appeared in order: there was something in every box, but what did it all mean? Not much actually.

(Sutton 1995: 65)

The problem for her was that the records seem to have taken a life of their own – rather like the columns of figures which occupied the red-faced, fat man (an accountant) in Saint-Exupéry's *The Little Prince* (1943), who was always too busy with adding up neat columns of figures (his 'important matters of consequence') to talk to the little boy. Sutton's records were not part of a wider process with a distinct role to play. So, when she asks, 'What impact did this relentless effort have on my teaching or the pupils' learning?' she answers, honestly: 'Too hard to judge, and it never occurred to me to try' (Sutton 1995).

Our response to the familiar conundrum of how to handle recording both effectively and efficiently (i.e. in a manageable way) is a familiar one: the system we adopt should be determined by its purpose (i.e. by the information it needs to record) and not the other way around. What information do we need, for whom and for what purpose? You do, of course have to have in mind school and departmental policies and practices, but even then it is important to be professionally thoughtful about purpose – records have to be fit for purpose too.

Records should not be seen as a collection of discrete or finite assessments but as a profile of interim judgements that provide a basis for making composite, multifaceted or 'synoptic' assessments. The distinction being made here is similar to the distinction made between formative and summative assessment: the interim judgements are part of the formative process involving lots of interaction between the teacher and pupils, while the teacher's growing knowledge of pupils can, at intervals, be summated to provide a rounded, overall judgement (or synopsis) of each one.

Such assessments are required for a variety of purposes including writing reports, parents' evenings and case conferences, so to have a rich knowledge of pupils based upon different types of evidence enables teachers to use their information flexibly, tailoring it for the particular purpose. However, assessments are also contingent – not only in the light of further information which may force a change of view, but also in terms of the audience: other teachers, the head teacher, parents and the pupil each require different kinds of assessment information which your records, ideally, should enable you to supply. Note that your records (of what we have called interim judgements) should be serving your purposes.

Issues in formative assessment

Having opened up for consideration the benefits to pupils' learning of using of using formative assessment processes, the following discussion tackles some of the issues you need to consider when using formative assessment. Some of these are very practical and can be remedied; others, while seeming quite theoretical, nonetheless have significant implications for practice.

Since the research and development work on formative assessment entered the public domain (Black and Wiliam 1998b; Black et al. 2002), the ideas and practices advocated have been promoted widely and used in national strategies at both primary and secondary level. However, Paul Black and Dylan Wiliam have raised concerns in recent years that practical implementation has often been based on limited understanding and superficial adoption of these ideas and strategies. They argue that 'doing assessment for learning' may fail to implement the crucial features of formative assessment if teachers are not supported by sustained commitment over several years (Black 2004; Marshall and Drummond 2006, cited in Weeden 2013). Black and Wiliam's research has shown that it takes at least two years before changes become embedded in teachers' classroom practices enabling pupils to become more confident and effective learners. So the message is clear: it will take longer than your initial training to feel confident in the application of these practices, but in the longer term the benefits for pupils' learning will be significant.

Box 8.3 Impediments to effective formative assessment practice

Research also shows the hazards lying in wait to neutralise attempts to introduce innovative formative assessment, such as:

- too much generous – but unfocused – praise is unhelpful to pupils
- too many tests often encourage surface learning as opposed to deep learning (e.g. the 'facts' and not the processes)
- classrooms are still too often like 'black boxes' – we do not share practice with colleagues, nor challenge each other about 'best practice'
- quantity and presentation tend to be over-emphasised in marking
- comparison of marks and grades tends to be over-emphasised, diverting focus away from self-improvement
- feedback tends to be 'social and managerial' rather than about specific learning functions of pupils
- although teachers can predict external examination results accurately, this shows only that they have a good understanding of the examination – not necessarily the individual learning needs of the pupils
- the bureaucratic imperative (to collect a complete set of marks) can outweigh the educational (to analyse pupils' learning needs).

Box 8.3 is a long – but very useful – list. It forms the basis for identifying evaluation criteria for you to use in order to analyse your own practice and the practice you observe in your department.

In addition to the 'impediments to formative assessment' identified in Box 8.3 and also some of the concerns raised by Black and Wiliam themselves, Bennett (2011) has written about more theoretical issues, which warrant serious consideration as they relate to practise. Bennett has identified six inter-related 'issues', which, he argues, if not given serious consideration in the formative assessment debate, will continue to undermine the true potential of formative assessment.

Box 8.4 Issues in formative assessment

Definitional issue: The term 'formative evaluation' was initially applied to the evaluation and development of teaching programs, not to judgements about pupils' learning and progress. In the USA, 'formative' refers to interim tests that can be used diagnostically – the focus is on the test, whereas in the UK 'formative assessment', often referred to as 'assessment for learning' refers to the process, used on a daily basis, with pupils in classrooms to support their progression learning. An additional complication is that while terms are not used interchangeably, summative assessment outcomes can be used formatively with pupils. This raises questions about whether one assessment can serve different purposes? (Weeden 2013)

The effectiveness issue: Bennett argues that, while Black and Wiliam provide a useful 'qualitative synthesis' of international research, they do not provide (and they are clear about this) any quantitative evidence that formative assessment can achieve the rate of improvement so often (mis) quoted in the academic literature. Describing it as 'the educational equivalent of urban legend' (p. 12), Bennett is clear that, while formative assessment probably does support improvement in pupils' performance, the evidence for the rate of improvement via formative assessment does not exist.

The domain (subject) dependency issue: Much of the discussion about formative assessment practice is generic in nature. This, argues Bennett, is likely to mean that any developments in practice, if they remain at the generic level, are likely to be weak and therefore purposeless. Good quality formative assessment is dependent on the quality of teachers' subject knowledge in order to make judgements about what questions to ask and to whom, what to look for in terms of quality outcomes, and how to decide when and when not to intervene in a pupil's work.

The measurement issue: Bennett argues that we can only infer, from observations of pupils' work, what pupils understand, and therefore the idea of 'measuring' pupils' performance is misleading (see the discussion 'Life without levels' below). At any one time, a pupil's response to a question or task could be inadequate merely because of an error or a slip (not paying attention or simple carelessness), it could represent a misconception (some conceptual confusion) or it could reflect a worrying lack of understanding. Each type of response requires a very different response from the teacher in order to address the problem – pupils may need a simple reminder about the task in hand or pointing to a resource to trigger their thinking, or they may require

(continued)

(continued)

a more significant intervention, such as a different example of a phenomenon or some additional resources to clarify their understanding, or they may need you to start again and re-explain a concept or skill, but in a much more 'step-by-step' way. An additional layer of complexity to the measurement issue is the impact of hidden assumptions on judgements we may make based on race, gender, ethnicity or disability.

The professional development issue: Bennett calls for more professional development opportunities for teachers in order to develop their knowledge and understanding of formative assessment that is subject-specific as it relates to both the context of classroom teaching, but, and at the same time, is understood within the context of the subject their subject – that is, geography.

The system issue: Finally, Bennett argues that 'the effectiveness of formative assessment will be limited by the nature of the larger system in which it is embedded and particularly by the content format and design of the accountability test' (p. 19); that is, the wider assessment system gets in the way of effective formative assessment.

The issues identified by Bennett provide us with a useful set of ideas with which to think critically about formative assessment. This is not to undermine teachers' use of formative assessment; we would still argue that good teaching will inevitably be characterised by formative assessment processes, but the issues can help to understand practice more critically and thus avoid the kind of 'paraphernalia' mistake the student teacher above made.

In the next section, we develop the formative assessment discussion, by introducing the changing educational discourse around assessment practice, with particular focus on the changing landscape of National Curriculum assessment.

Progression and assessment

As we have seen (in Chapter 2), progression is an important – and challenging – issue. One of the questions that arises from considering progression in learning is how (or even whether) to measure it. In recent years, the notion of assessing pupils' 'levels of attainment' has become familiar to teachers. In this section, we consider this idea in some detail.

The origin of 'levels'

The idea of assessing students into criterion-referenced 'levels' came into being as part of the National Curriculum which was introduced to England (and Wales) following the Education Reform Act of 1988. During the initial National Curriculum deliberations, the proposal was to define levels of attainment in geography according to five distinct 'attainment targets'. This was logical, recognising different aspects of geographical knowledge and skill. However, in asking teachers to assess every student against five attainment targets was quite complicated! By the time the curriculum became law in 1991, geography as a whole had become a single attainment target. However, attainment was defined by no fewer than 184 'statements of attainment'. These were distributed across ten 'levels' of attainment. These levels were intended to describe 'progress' in geography from age 5 through to 16 years of age.

Precise statements of attainment, which in effect attempted to define the national, statutory standards of geography, were difficult to write. Teachers expecting these statements to be usable as assessment criteria were quickly disappointed. On the one hand, they were too general, too rough-hewn and distant from what was actually being taught. On the other hand, they proliferated. To many teachers, they resembled simply a list of what had to be covered.

Statements of attainment didn't last long. By 1995, the curriculum had been reviewed and statements of attainment abolished in favour of 'level descriptions'. The ten-level (5-16 years) model remained, but this time described not by atomistic statements but by holistic paragraphs that tried to grasp, in the round, what distinguished the levels of attainment. Teachers were meant to use a 'best fit' methodology to assign periodic level judgements to their students' attainment in geography.

Were levels a good thing?

Ten 'level descriptions' seemed to offer more promise than 183 'statements of attainment'. They were written more 'generically', which reduced the need for a 'mad dash' to get through the content that statements of attainment encouraged. They also seemed to avoid the 'Holy Grail'-like search for precise, objective and easily agreed assessment criteria and instead restored broad teacher judgement of student achievement.

However, under pressure from school leaders and managers, who were themselves under intense pressure from Ofsted and the government to produce quantitative measures of school performance, teachers were instructed and encouraged to misuse levels. Read, for example, the following extract from an open letter to the new Secretary of State for Education in 2014:

> Two years ago I worked in a school that had experienced an unprecedented level of staff turnover. 'You should probably know that we're all leaving,' one teacher told me, kindly, in the staff room. This was during a phase in which Ofsted had told the school – and many others – that pupils must be constantly evaluated using something called National Curriculum levels – numerical ratings that measure how advanced pupils' skills are in particular areas of the curriculum. This should happen throughout the school day, the inspectors said, every twenty minutes.
>
> (*Source*: https://www.opendemocracy.net/ourkingdom/teacher/
> open-letter-to-nicky-morgan)

We can find no evidence that Ofsted really did demand this. But the writer of this blog was not alone in believing that this is what was being demanded by 'the system'.

Remember, the main intention was to use level descriptions periodically as a basis for summative teacher assessments. They were broad brush. Think about it: 10 levels across 11 years of school. It would not be surprising if individual children failed to progress a single level in a whole year! This simply would not supply adequate performance data. Thus, levels were sub-divided, often into three 'sub-levels'. But think about this: can we really imagine describing progress in geography across what became 24 'levels' (3 times 8)? This takes us back to the Holy Grail! It is an impossible task, accomplished only by falsification: we make it up and we fit the evidence to suit our needs – to show progress.

The machine needs data on 'progress'? We can supply data. It is, though, on the whole, pretty meaningless data. In its most absurd manifestation, students were expected in some cases to show 'progress' in a single lesson.

So unsatisfactory was this situation that Tim Oates, Chair of the National Curriculum review, strongly recommended that the levels be abolished. This was done. Attention was turned to 'assessment without levels', together with a mild panic as to whether this was even possible, such was the attachment of the machine to data that showed 'progress'.

Assessment without levels

Earlier in this chapter we distinguished formative from summative assessment. As we have stated, reduced to its essence, formative assessment is an integral aspect of effective teaching: it is the usually dialogic process through which the teacher gets to know students – their experiences and capacities, what they find difficult, enjoyable, motivating, supportive. In turn, the students gets to know what the teacher is driving at: the teacher's expectations, what quality means in geography, what they are being asked to do and why.

Put this way, it is perhaps perfectly clear that in formative assessment we simply do not need 'levels'. Research is overwhelmingly supportive of this. As soon as grades, percentages, and especially levels are introduced to assessment, these are all the students see. This is partly the result of the very natural desire to know how one is doing in relation to others (where you are on the pecking order), whereas what we really want is the student to focus on how well they have grasped the material being taught and to understand that in relation to themselves and their previous work (the latter is what we call 'ipsative' assessment).

Formative assessment, therefore, is based on rich and varied classroom interactions – and lots of student 'productions' – oral presentations and varied forms of writing and drawing resulting from decision-making exercises, investigations and so on. The professional judgement of the teacher is guided by criteria that relate directly to the material being taught – and dialogic assessment processes aim to make sure that the students grasp these, using techniques such as peer assessment of work, the provision of precise subject-focused feedback.

It is almost inevitable that when marking students' work teachers will, at some point, use a system that includes grades; indeed, as a teacher you may be required to do so by your senior leadership team. So be it, but keep any system simple and focused on the work. The question requiring your professional judgement, and the one raised earlier in this book, is: Has this student grasped what I was intending to teach?

Perhaps the most straightforward marking system, therefore, is something like a three-grade system: where B = yes; A = very well; and C = not yet. Even if you use the traditional 'marks out of ten', you will almost certainly be using the same system: where 6-7 = yes; 8-9 = very well; and 4-5 = not yet. Using such a system is criteria-related (but the teacher needs to identify the criteria in relation to the particular content being taught); easy to understand by pupils, parents and other teachers and, crucially, does not involve shoe-horning children into levels which are essentially generic (i.e they do not relate to the particular content). In assessment, there has been a tendency for it to become over-bureaucratised: the approach we want to encourage is one that centres on the relationship between the teacher and the pupils, and so keep things simple.

Summative assessment is periodic. It is an overall judgement based on meaningful evidence (which ultimately is the students' work) of what the student has learned by the end of a course of study – say a year or even the whole key stage. It is in this context that an end of key stage 'bench mark' statement may be very useful. There is enormous expertise in the system as to how to conduct effective summative assessments through examinations (GCSE; AS/A-levels and so on) and teachers can draw from this to devise 'in-house' assessment opportunities, possibly tests, but other forms of summative assessment too such as presentations, reports, creative writing and so on. In addition, it is perfectly reasonable to use the accumulated evidence of attainment built up through formative assessment processes – sometimes referred to as 'teacher assessment' to distinguish this evidence base from formal tests or examinations.

Assessing without levels – potential opportunities

The following activity is designed to help you to begin considering how to make judgements about pupils' progress and attainment in geography, particularly by the end of Key Stage 3. Tim Oates, Chair of the National Curriculum Review Panel, explains that in order for teachers to do this effectively, then pupils need to produce 'stuff' – through talking, writing, drawing or whatever – this 'stuff', he argues, is what gives teachers an insight into the 'mental life of the child', teachers can then use this 'stuff' to support pupils' learning because from it they can make subject-specific judgements about pupils' understanding.

The intention is to encourage you to really look at pupils work, to share this with other beginning teachers and consider what kind of geographical knowledge, understanding and skill they demonstrate in the different type of work that thy produce.

Task 8.2 Assembling and moderating a portfolio (groups)

A   You are going to construct a portfolio of work for one student you teach. The student should be in Year 9. This portfolio is to show a range of evidence for this pupil's geographical understanding. To complete this activity, you will also need to draw on how you now understand making progress geography developed from Task 8.1 (c) Marking your first work.

Preparation phase

1   Identify one pupil in a group that you teach; the class teacher may help you with this – you are not looking for 'the best', just a student whose work you can talk about (but remember, in the spirit of ethical behaviour, pupil anonymity is important). Select 4–5 different pieces of work that you feel exemplify different knowledge, skills and understanding in geography. These may be presentations completed by the pupil, a piece of extended writing completed for homework, an investigation undertaken using GIS . . .

(continued)

(continued)

You need to consider:

- Do you select real work or photocopies of work for inclusion in the portfolio?
- How much work needs to be selected, will 4–5 pieces be enough? How voluminous is a portfolio?
- Over what time span was the total work completed (2–3 months? 1 year?)
- What kinds of work can a portfolio not show and how do you take account of this when making judgements about a pupil's geographical understanding?

2 For each piece of work, complete a 'context sheet' (see Figure 8.2). The aim of the context sheet is to make explicit the purpose of the work, what the pupil was trying to achieve and the extent to which he/she was successful.

Carefully consider any success criteria for individual pieces of work and then annotate each piece indicating what evidence you have that demonstrates:

- the quality of geographical understanding
- the appropriate use of geographical skills
- evidence of subject knowledge
- appropriate use of geographical vocabulary.

You may like to also consider more generic issues such as quality of communication, but this should not dominate your thinking or conclusions.

Analysis phase

3 Before you start this activity, it is important to remember that the analysis focuses on the work, *not* the 'ability' of the pupils.

In groups of about four, take it in turns to share one piece of work, including the context sheet, at a time. Tell your colleagues your thoughts about the overall quality of the work and what you feel it reveals about one pupil's geographical understanding and why – what is your evidence for your conclusions about the work? Be prepared to discuss, argue and defend the standards you have applied and the way you have interpreted and annotated the work. When each person has had the opportunity to present their first piece of work, take time as a group to discuss the evidence you have, how you have used it and be prepared to rethink your ideas and amend the context sheet accordingly.

Repeat this process for other pieces of work.

Conclusion phase

4 When you have each had a chance to explain and justify the work you selected, as a group discuss what you feel to be the advantages and disadvantages of an evidence portfolio of this kind.

How did you take account of more ephemeral evidence (pupil's response in lessons, quality understanding demonstrated in discussions and so on) when drawing conclusions about this pupil's knowledge and understanding in geography?

What did this overall process tell you about how we judge the quality of a pupil's work and what do you now think are some of the challenges we face in geography when making judgements on progress in learning?

B   With the onset of the new National Curriculum in 2014, and the abolition of level descriptions, the Geographical Association has adopted a new approach to how to judge progress, which includes the use of 'benchmarking statements' for each of the key stages. Benchmarking statements, while not prescribing content, serve as reference points for planning and are statements of the academic standards a pupil would be expected to reach at the end of a course of study.

   1   Using the portfolio of work you have now discussed and moderated, consider the pupils' achievement in relation to the expectations set out in the bench-mark statement for Key Stage 3 (see Box 8.5). What might each one need to do to improve? What other curriculum opportunities' might your school's cur-riculum need to provide to support this improvement, for example fieldwork opportunities?
   2   How will the benchmark statements such as that in Box 8.5 below help you to make a summative judgement of an individual's achievement at the end Key Stage 3?

Box 8.5 Benchmark statement for Key Stage 3 geography

By the age of 14, pupils are able to draw on an extensive world knowledge of places and significant geographical features. In this locational framework, and in the par-ticular context of Asia, Africa and the Middle East, they can demonstrate that they understand the distribution of a range of human and physical geographical phenom-ena and the significance of inter-relationships between physical and human systems. Pupils are able to explain change in physical environments, including the role of ice in shaping landscapes, within an accurate conceptualisation of geological time. They can also account for change in human environments and in particular the results of urbanisation. On a range of scales including the global, pupils are able to describe the nature of unequal economic development and some of its consequences. They demon-strate a grasp of how different perceptions and competing interests between groups and nations can result in conflicts, for example concerning boundaries and resources. Pupils can demonstrate the ability to analyse and interpret a wide range of geographi-cal evidence, including primary data from fieldwork. In evaluating evidence, they show sensitivity to different viewpoints and are able to make careful judgements and draw effective conclusions about environmental questions, issues and problems.

> (*Source*: This is an exemplar 'benchmark statement' based upon extensive and continuing work from the GA. Go to the GA's website to discover further versions of this, and advice on how to use such statements of 'expectations' in the planning and assessment of your teaching. www.geography.org.uk/ news/2014nationalcurriculum/assessment/ benchmarkexpectations/#16858)

Subject: Date:

Topic/unit:

Context Description: Describe what the work was intending to show, success criteria, how it relates to the scheme as a whole.

What does this piece of work show in terms of this pupil's geographical understanding, skills, knowledge, values/attitudes?

What does this piece of work not show, that it should, in terms of this pupil's geographical understanding, skills, knowledge, values/attitudes?

What advice would you give this pupil to improve his/her geographical understanding?

Figure 8.2 Context sheet for Task 8.2

(*Source*: Adapted from Sutton 1995: 94)

Box 8.6 Compiling an evidence portfolio: a checklist of key points

- A 'piece of work' is a completed task of some description; it may be a single home-work or a more lengthy task representing several lessons' work.
- It is the work, not the pupils, that the portfolio exhibits.
- Each portfolio must not become too voluminous, so the copying should not be prohibitive. To get pupils to complete a 'best draft' is also a possibility.
- The portfolio is meant to be indicative, not a document of 'proof'. It needs to be digestible and its contents easily accessed. It must not become too large therefore, and experience indicates that about six to eight 'pieces of work' are appropriate.
- When selected, each piece of work needs detailed (but not copious) annotation in clear handwriting (green or red pen – whichever colour you choose, use it con-sistently) focused on *what the work shows* and *what it fails to show* in terms of elements of learning.
- Each piece of work needs a completed context sheet. This helps other teachers 'read' the work and understand your assessment of it; increasing such transfer-ability ultimately contributes to increasing dependability of assessments.
- Thought needs giving to who will see the portfolio – parents? Head teachers? Ofsted inspectors?

(The 'Evidence Portfolio' is an activity adapted from a previous
activity entitled 'Compiling a Standards Portfolio'
by D. Lambert and D. Balderstone 2010: 400)

While evidence portfolios as discussed above can be regarded in many senses as sources of data that allow teachers and pupils (and others such as parents, head teachers and even Ofsted inspectors) to carefully consider evidence for progress, it is true today that the accu-mulation of other sources and types of data, especially statistical data, regarding pupils and their performance in school, are part-and-parcel of teachers' working lives.

Using data to support teaching and learning in geography

> If the profession is to take greater ownership of accountability, data remain key. It is data that will challenge thinking and stimulate discussion leading to improved practice. It is data that enable progress to be monitored. The role of quantitative data as a tool for school improvement is well rehearsed and widely accepted but data can emerge from a range of activities, principally observation, but also others, such as analysis of problems and case studies, or from interviews or focus groups. This sort of data supports profes-sional accountability within and across schools.
>
> (Gilbert 2012: 13)

There is now a wealth of national and internal information available to schools, and to teachers in individual subject areas, which provide data about students' attainment and progress. This data is generated from statutory end-of-key stage assessments, external examinations and a range of school-based assessments. It is used to analyse student achievement and to evaluate the performance of schools, subject departments and individual teachers. The teaching standards require teachers to use relevant data to monitor students' progress, set targets and plan subsequent lessons. This includes being able to assess students' attainment against national benchmarks. It is important that geography teachers are fully aware of the data available to support target setting and how this data can be put to good use.

A major difference between the core and foundation subjects is the amount of subject-specific data on students' performance available in Year 7. In English, mathematics and science, the amount of data available on entry, or from assessments carried out early in the school, can be considerable. This data can provide baselines against which future progress can be measured. Without specific data from national tests, foundation subjects like geography have to build an accurate picture quickly through their own testing and other forms of assessment when students join the school.

There are two broad types of data:

- Raw data: this refers to published National Curriculum scores and examination results.
- Value added: this refers to examination results that have been adjusted to take account of (a) prior attainment and (b) the social context of student cohorts including gender, free school meals, socio-economic indicators, level of special educational need, English as an additional language and mobility.

Schools are expected to make progress with respect to both raw results and value-added scores. The range of data that is used in schools to inform target setting and support teachers' monitoring of students' progress includes the following.

End of Key Stage 2 test results in English, mathematics and science

These are used to generate school and subject targets for individual students. The level of input that geography departments will have on establishing subject targets for students in geography at Key Stages 3 and 4 will vary between schools so it will be worth asking your geography mentor or head of department how this is done in your placement school.

Fischer Family Trust (FFT) data

This is a package which uses a database of historical performance to analyse the progress made by students in different subjects (value added) between Key Stages 3 and 4. One of the most useful features of this package is the data it provides about the 'chances' (in percentages) of students achieving particular grades in different subjects at GCSE and at A-level. This is often used by schools to identify the most likely and aspirational target grades for students in each subject.

Cognitive ability test (CAT) scores

Some schools use cognitive ability tests (CATs) when students join the school in Year 7 and/ or at other points (for example later in Key Stage 3) to provide an assessment of their reasoning ability. These assessments are sometimes regarded as providing more reliable indicators of subsequent performance in GCSE examinations than end of key stage assessments because they can provide a standardised measure of a child's ability largely independent of which school the child went to, and what learning experiences he or she had there.

RAISEonline

This interactive online package is published annually for every school and includes contextual information, raw attainment data and simple (non-contextualised) value-added data. This is used to evaluate schools' performance including the progress made by different groups of students and value added in different subjects.

Other commercial packages include Yellis and MidYiS produced by the University of Durham which are used by some schools to provide baseline assessments and then predict and evaluate the performance of their students in GCSE examinations (Yellis) and in Key Stage 3 assessments (MidYiS). Schools also use packages such as ALIS and ALPS to predict and evaluate the performance of students at A-level in different subjects against national benchmarks for these subjects. It will be important to find out which data is used in each key stage in your placement school and how it is used to establish the targets for students and then evaluate their performance.

Another useful source of data can be found in the online data analysis tools provided by the examination awarding bodies to help teachers and subject leaders to analyse the performance of their students in different aspects of subject examinations at GCSE and A-level. These include tools for question-level analysis which can help you to identify students' strengths and weaknesses in different types of questions as well as comparing the performance of the students with that of those in similar types of school.

Data plays an important role in the process of monitoring and evaluating the progress that students generally and those within specific target groups make in relation to their expected progress. The emphasis is on how much progress students make in relation to their starting points, especially the progress made (value added) between Key Stages 2 and 4. Schools are also judged on how effectively they are narrowing the gap between the performance of different groups of students both within the school and when compared with national expectations. As well as focusing on gender, ethnicity and different ability groupings, there is a particular emphasis on the progress made by students in disadvantaged groups including disabled students, those with special educational needs and those eligible for the pupil premium. Schools in the UK receive significant additional funding to support their provision for these pupil premium students. Students eligible for this funding include:

- all children eligible for free school meals (FSM) at any point during the previous six years
- looked after children (LAC)
- children with one or both parents in the armed forces (service premium).

The government holds schools to account for the attainment and progress made by these students through performance tables and school inspection. The aim of the provision supported by this funding is to reduce the gaps in attainment and progress between disadvantaged students and their non-disadvantaged peers.

When preparing to take on the teaching of classes, you should obtain the data available about the targets and expected progress for the students in these different groupings within your classes. You should identify students belonging to any of the target groups listed above together with any specific information about their learning needs and the support they receive either within lessons or as part of their wider educational provision (learning mentors, literacy and/or numeracy support, attendance support and access to extra-curricular activities). You should seek to address any particular learning needs as part of your normal planning for differentiation but also pay particular attention to the progress they are making in school assessments. You should also ensure that staff supporting them (e.g. learning mentors) are made aware of specific learning needs and tasks within geography and your lessons (e.g. homework) so that they can provide appropriate support for these students. Some schools expect you to indicate who these students, their targets and current progress in seating plans and other essential information provided for lesson observations.

The culture of a school always has an important influence on how data is used – whether it is 'data-driven' or 'data-informed'. Your own 'data-literacy' will develop as you become more experienced in interpreting and using the data available to you. But effective target-setting cannot rely just on number crunching and strategies have to be developed by teachers based on their professional judgement of how to close the gap between students' current performance and their 'desired goal'. Gilbert (2010) reminds us that 'data are only numbers on a page, or a spreadsheet on a screen. They only measure what has been tested. And people often only test what they feel they can measure.'

The challenge is to understand the data and use it alongside a range of sources of evidence to identify areas of students' learning that can be improved. These areas for improvement become curricular targets that need to be understood by the students themselves if they are to make progress in their learning in geography. Royce Sadler (2003) summarises this challenge:

> When anyone is trying to learn, feedback about the effort has three elements: recognition of the desired goal, evidence about present position, and some understanding of a way to close the gap between the two. All three must be understood to some degree by anyone before he or she can take action to improve learning.
>
> (Sadler, cited in Black et al. 2003)

Examinations in perspective

Though few people would deny that external examinations are necessary, and play an essential role in education, the current system is considered by many to be flawed. As a result, the field of external examinations is an uncertain one with significant changes currently taking place. It is not the purpose of a book such as this to second guess what those changes may be in any detail or attempt to describe in detail the external examinations available in geography. Such a list would quickly become dated. Instead, we provide a short description of how the system is changing and has evolved in recent years and this is followed with an outline of some principles that have helped shape the design of public examinations in geography (see Lambert and Lines 2000 for a general overview). Our overall purpose is to help student teachers see how they may support pupils preparing for this major hurdle in their lives. We are mindful that preparing for public examinations is also a major hurdle for teachers as, rightly or wrongly, raw data on pupil attainment are used increasingly as an indicator of teacher effectiveness as well as pupil attainment.

It is worth saying at this point that the announcement made in 2010 by the then Secretary of State for Education, Michael Gove, in the government's White Paper *The Importance of Teaching*, that he would be introducing a new accountability measure for schools called the English Baccalaureate (EBacc) was something of a boost for school geography at GCSE level. In their data, schools would now have to account for pupils' performance across a range of subjects including geography or history. The consequence of this was that almost immediately many schools had a rethink about their GCSE option systems and an increasing number of pupils were both encouraged and able to study geography at GCSE level. Since 2010, the number of pupils studying geography at GCSE has risen steadily and the numbers studying A-level geography have remained relatively consistent (see the Geographical Association website for detailed annual analysis of GCSE and A-level results). In 2012, the same Secretary of State announced new qualifications called the English Baccalaureate Certificates (EBCs); again, geography was included in the announcement but the new qualification was abandoned less than one year later in favour of revised GCSE qualifications with a new grading system (1–9 to replace A*–G), new (and more challenging) content and new assessment systems. New GCSEs are first taught in 2016.

The next section maps out the relatively recent history of examination reform which goes some way to highlighting the some of the thinking that needs to underpin any principled changes I how we summative assess young people.

How examinations have changed

Traditional public examinations were strongly criticised over many years for being dominated by the academic interests of subject specialists. 'If the "candidate" can't perform in the exam, too bad' . . . the examination seemed to say . . . 'we just want to sort out the best'.

Indeed, this was the purpose of the GCE O-level, and to some large extent it remains the purpose of the A-level examination. Essentially, such norm-referenced examinations (i.e where pupils' work is judged in comparison with the performance of other pupils) serve the interests of selection well. However, because they guarantee failure for a substantial proportion of the candidature, they are not appropriate if the candidature consists of most of the year group: they stand little chance of motivating pupils who know they are likely to fail. Traditional examinations were also narrow in the range of skills and attributes they demanded of candidates and suited certain kinds of abilities (e.g. memory) far more than others (e.g. analysis). They tended to be opaque to many pupils, who found it difficult to 'crack the code' and therefore please the examiner. 'I can't do exams' was an often heard admission of pupils, who were resigned to their incompetence or at least lack of certain ill-defined capacities. But surely pupils should not have had to shoulder all the blame!

The introduction of the GCSE in 1986 signalled an enormous effort to reform not only the structure of the system, but also the internal dynamics and design of the examinations themselves in the light of those well-understood limitations outlined in the previous paragraph. In essence, the GCSE is built upon the ideal of finding out what candidates know, understand and can do – not what they do not know and cannot do. This became expressed by the phrase 'positive achievement' and the early rhetoric emphasised the role of criteria referencing (pupils' work is judged solely in relation to explicit criteria), in devising an examination which could recognise positive achievement. It was recognised that the criteria would need to encompass a wider notion of achievement than perhaps most examiners and teachers were accustomed to, and thus issues concerning the validity of the examination assumed equal status to that more traditional (and still important) concern of examinations' reliability (reference to how well standardised the questions, procedures and marking are). From this basis emerged new examination paraphernalia, elements of what we might call an 'examinations technology' in which geography teachers require management and organisational skills as well as technical expertise. The main elements are:

- assessment objectives and specification grids
- grade descriptions and criteria mark schemes.

You will get to know the particular details of these in relation to the examination specification your department has chosen to follow. The following brief comments are designed to help you place the particular detail into a general framework.

Assessment objectives and specification grids

All GCSE syllabuses have to conform to the National Criteria for Geography, which sets out the broad aims of studying geography at this level and the content requirements (the A-level Core performs a similar function). In addition, the syllabuses set out what 'abilities' are to be tested by the examination. This is achieved through assessment objectives. GCSE examinations test knowledge, understanding, application and skills, including geographical enquiry, each assessed at several levels (see National Criteria for Geography, 2014).

The Criteria lay down weightings for the each objective in the 'scheme of assessment, giving broadly equal balance to knowledge, understanding and skills'. Precisely how many marks are awarded for each can vary within the limits shown, but are stated in the syllabus specification grid.

One of the great achievements of the GCSE was the realisation that for the examination to be valid such skills could not be tested via short answer questions under timed conditions. Thus, all GCSE geography examinations had a coursework element which included 'a geographical investigation supported by fieldwork'. The wording of this was significant. It did not lay down that each GCSE pupil must undertake individually a piece of field research entirely independently; so long as some kind of fieldwork investigation (undertaken in groups, for example) could be shown to support the pupil's individual coursework submission, then all was well. This considerably eased the management problem of supervising possibly hundreds of GCSE candidates annually, though the organisation and management challenge was still considerable; it was fieldwork enquiry that was required, not merely 'experience' in the field. As we shall see below, the 'coursework' component of GCSE geography has been removed.

Grade descriptions and criteria mark schemes

The current GCSE is criterion referenced, that is a statement is made of what the pupil needs to do in order to attain a given grade, that is, the level of achievement in a given skill. It proved difficult for Awarding Bodies to reference every grade and only Grade A, C and E are criterion-referenced. These statements are the basis for the marking scheme, presented as a marking grid.

The structure, procedures and design of GCSE examinations are sophisticated. In addition to the technical aspects discussed above, examiners have devised techniques to ensure fairness and maximum access to the questions. Take some past papers and examine for yourself how the rubric is designed to help the candidate, how the layout of the paper has been carefully considered and how the wording of questions is controlled and clear. Also note how the questions themselves usually have an internal structure designed to invite 'positive achievement', that is, they have a built-in incline (or a number of clear steps) of difficulty. Even the best-designed examination paper cannot, on its own, successfully examine the entire cohort of 16-year-olds.

Examinations at post-16

When the majority of the population left school in their mid-teens, it made sense to have a system of terminal examinations at 16. The main purpose of the exam was to inform the selection processes of employers and institutions of further education such as sixth forms and colleges. GCSE was introduced in 1986 to combine under one roof a two-track terminal examination system (of O-levels for the 'brightest' 20 per cent and CSEs for the next brightest 40 per cent) that had begun to emerge in the 1960s. It is still a terminal examination in the sense that it comes at the end of compulsory schooling and is now inclusive of nearly the entire age-cohort of pupils (i.e. very few 16-year-olds in any one year do not acquire any GCSEs). But its role in selection is not as profound as in former years since the majority of 16-year-olds now expect to continue in full-time education. Indeed, it is now a legal requirement for all pupils to continue in education or training until the age of 17 (this is likely to be 18 in the near future).

In 2013, the government announced major reforms to GCSE qualifications. The reformed GCSEs will remain universal qualifications accessible to the same proportion of pupils that currently sits GCSE exams at the end of Key Stage 4. The level of what is widely considered to be a pass will be made more demanding, and at the upper end they will aim to provide better preparation for A-level. This will be achieved through a balance of more challenging subject content and more rigorous assessment structures with a focus on final rather than modular exams. The aim of these changes is to raise standards, restore rigour, end perceived grade inflation, and to better prepare students for future studies and employability. The government also intends these qualification reforms to help pupils in the UK to match the achievements of those in the highest-performing education systems around the world.

The Department for Education introduced new criteria for geography GCSE qualifications in April 2014 for first teaching in September 2016. The revised criteria include a number of significant changes, including a rebalancing between physical and human geography content, a requirement that all pupils study the geography of the UK in greater depth and use a wide range of investigative skills and approaches, including mathematics and statistics. There is also a requirement for at least two examples of fieldwork to be undertaken outside school. There have also been significant changes made to the assessment arrangements with the removal of controlled assessment and tiered exams. The assessment of fieldwork by external examination rather than by controlled assessment or coursework is another change and one that has divided opinion in the profession with many geography teachers and the subject association arguing that this will not give pupils opportunities to show evidence of the applied knowledge, skills and understanding they have developed through their first-hand experiences.

A major overhaul of post-16 examinations is also taking place. From 2016, the government proposes that the AS-level will be separated from A-level to become a standalone qualification. A-level students will sit examinations at the end of their two-year course, although AS- and A-level will, theoretically at least, be 'co-teachable'. This change will in itself have significant implications for teaching and assessment but also for universities who have traditionally used pupils' results in their AS-level examinations to inform the offers they make for higher education courses.

Core content will be introduced to each geography specification, requiring pupils to study a balance of human and physical geography. This will include four core themes that will be common to all A-level specifications (Physical – Water and carbon cycles; Landscape systems; Human – Global systems and governance; Changing places). A balance between physical and human geography is also required in the non-core content which addresses people–environment questions and issues, and which will be chosen by each Awarding Body. One of the key aims of the proposed changes is to ensure that the core content provides an appropriate level of challenge to prepare pupils who progress to study geography and geography-related subjects at university as well as being relevant for those who end their studies of geography at A-level. Pupils will also need to be given opportunities to apply geographical knowledge, concepts and skills, and to engage critically with real-world issues and real-world locations.

Fieldwork will be assessed in a teacher-assessed independent investigative report contributing 20 per cent of the A-level qualification but by examination at AS-level. This will have important implications for planning, teaching and resourcing fieldwork at AS- and A-level. Pupils will require sufficient time in the field to develop the required depth of understanding and to develop the ability to apply their geographical knowledge and appropriate data collection techniques in real-world contexts.

At both GCSE and A-level, there is an increase in emphasis on the role of geography in developing pupils cartographic, graphic, numeric and statistical skills, and overall there is an attempt to ensure greater continuity between Key Stage 3, 4, and 5 geography, with national criteria containing specific 'progression' statements to this effect.

Other qualifications in geography

In addition to GCSE and A-level geography, geography also contributes to other qualifications such as the International Baccalaureate (IB), IGCSEs (International GCSEs) and there are elements of what we might call 'geography' in Travel and Tourism (a vocational qualification).

Over the course of the two-year IB Diploma Programme, students study six subjects chosen from the six subject groups, complete an extended essay (4,000 words), follow a theory of knowledge course (TOK – assessed via presentation and essay) and participate in creativity, action, service (CAS). Geography is situated in 'Theme 3 – Individuals and Society' (see www.ibo.org/diploma/curriculum/core/).

Pupils can study at two levels – the Standard Level (SL) and the Higher Level (HL). In geography, there is a common core to both levels consisting four compulsory topics:

1   Population in Transition
2   Disparities in Wealth and Development
3   Patterns in Environmental Quality and Sustainability
4   Patterns in Resource Consumption.

There are also optional themes at both levels. HL students study three options. SL students study two options from:

A   Freshwater – Issues and Conflicts
B   Oceans and their Coastal Margins
C   Extreme Environments
D   Hazards and Disasters – Risk Assessment and Response
E   Leisure, Sport and Tourism
F   The Geography of Food and Health
G   Urban Environment.

At the higher level, pupils also study additional compulsory topics under the heading 'Global Interaction' and are expected to exhibit a greater capacity to synthesise ideas and also apply a greater level of criticality to the work that they do. There is a fieldwork report of 2,500 words.

A further international qualification you may encounter is the International GCSE. Originally developed by *Cambridge International Examinations*, a provider of international examinations, the specifications and examination process is generally regarded as being 'more traditional' than the English GCSE. IGCSEs, to date, have generally been a qualification studied in international and independent schools rather than with the English state school system. Their popularity increased in the state sector as Ofqual (Office for Qualification and Examination Regulation) started to accredit an increasing number of courses. However, in

2014, under the UK government's review of national qualifications it was announced that IGCSEs would be 'axed' from schools' league table data, possibly because they do not conform to the same design and structure as the new GCSEs (*BBC News*, 1 July 2014). This decision, coming late in the day in terms of the remit for new GCSEs, probably means that state schools will forego the choice of teaching international GCSEs because of the consequences for their data.

In geography, the Cambridge IGCSE requires the teaching of recognisable themes such as population and settlement, the natural environment, and economic development and the use of resources (Cambridge International Examinations 2013: 11). However, some other boards also currently offer their own IGCSE in geography.

The third 'alternative' qualification that you may encounter being taught in a geography department or by geography colleagues is a vocational qualification in 'Travel and Tourism'. Vocational courses comprise a very different assessment system including practical work, portfolio evidence and independent research. The geography element of a BTec in Travel and Tourism is relatively light on content other than the expectation that pupils can locate places (national and international) on maps and also understand how disaster scenarios (including the weather) can effect holidays (e.g Edexel BTEC, Level 2).

Developing examination skills

To help prepare your pupils for public examinations, you should become familiar with the specifications of your examination syllabus. This document, together with past examination papers will be available online on the Awarding Bodies' websites. Make sure that you understand the marking scheme. Another important resource is the Chief Examiner's Annual Report, particularly the section dealing with candidate performance (see their Figure 9.3). You should teach your pupils how to develop study skills, how to revise and examination techniques to use in the examination (Balderstone and King 2004; Chapman and Digby 2006; Warn 2006). Given the improved emphasis on study skills and greater focus on preparing pupils for examinations, it is not surprising that standards have risen in recent years.

One concern that has increasingly emerged in recent years is that creativity and other crucial intellectual aspects of learning have been sacrificed in the drive for higher standards of achievement through improvements in examination results. Pupils are increasingly taught how to meet examination criteria and to accumulate knowledge rather than develop conceptual understanding and higher-level cognitive skills (Bell 2006: 13). The changes taking place in the geography qualifications at GCSE and AS-/A-level will have important implications for teaching and learning in geography as much as they will for the way you prepare your pupils for examinations. There is an increased emphasis on pupils being able to think geographically, to apply geographical knowledge, theory and concepts creatively to real world issues and locations. The revised subject criteria for geography at both GCSE and AS-/A-level emphasise the need for pupils to be able to develop well-evidenced geographical argument drawing upon their knowledge and understanding. 'Rigorous understanding of processes' shaping physical and human geography appears frequently alongside the need to understand and use concepts at a range of scales and in a range of locational contexts. This can only be achieved by developing this knowledge and understanding, and these argumentation skills progressively over time. Such changes can, in our opinion, only increase the value of geography teachers developing and strengthening the professional knowledge and skills outlined in earlier chapters.

Task 8.3 Exploring a school's use of data

When in school, discuss with your mentor the kind of data collected:

- at a school level
- at a subject level.

Try to establish the different ways this data is used in relation to:

- supporting pupils' progress in geography and in identifying pupils' learning needs
- how data is used when communicating with parents
- how the school uses data to develop school action plans.

What appear to be some of the problems with the different ways schools/departments gather and use data?

Task 8.4 Examinations

Look at the nationally prescribed *Subject Content* for GCSE and A-level geography. Can you identify threads of progression between the different key stages in terms of subject aims and purposes?

Carefully read the GCSE and A-level specifications studied in your school. Look for how each specification presents the geography students are to learn. In particular look for:

- which geographical themes and issues permeate the specification
- how does the specification articulate both breadth and depth of content to be taught (and knowledge of place context)
- how are geographical skills assessed
- how is fieldwork assessed
- how are decision-making skills assessed

What appears to be the underlying philosophy of the subject as represented in the specification.

Discuss with your mentor in school why they have chosen to use particular specifications at GCSE and A-level – what is distinctive about the specifications that means they are the best option for pupils in the school? How do they use the specification to plan schemes of work and why have they decided to teach the geography in a particular sequence? How is progression planned for? What is the role for fieldwork in the specification and how does this translate into action in the school?

Summary and key points

This chapter has concentrated mainly on assessment that takes place within the geography classroom. This is not to undervalue external assessment such as GCSE and AS/A2 examinations: indeed you need to get to know the syllabuses, or 'subject specifications', well and you need to learn how best to prepare pupils for the examinations. The best way that practising teachers have of learning the expectations of the examination is to become an assistant examiner themselves – a goal for the future maybe?

This chapter has also explored the purposes of assessment, the principles and practice of both external and educational assessment. The overall message is that using information about pupils, acquired through the assessment of their work, can and should influence the teacher's planning of lessons and response to individual pupils. Can you show how your understanding of educational assessment has influenced your practice in these ways?

It is almost certainly the case that your level of effectiveness can be traced right back to your marking practice. If, within the necessary bounds of what can be achieved in the time you have at your disposal, your marking is analytical, focused and accompanied with precise, individualised feedback to inform the pupil of their next steps, it follows that your assessment practice is also effective and fully integrated into your curriculum planning and lesson design.

Further reading

Oates, T. (2010) *Could Do Better: Using International Comparisons to Refine the National Curriculum in England*, Cambridge: Cambridge Assessment.
A very useful wide-ranging view of the National Curriculum, including notions of international comparisons and the issues associated with 'levels' in the English system. Although quite lengthy, and also generic, the report provides a fascinating insight in to the principles driving educational change, and in particular the dilemma posed by international comparison tables in shaping English education.

Weeden, P. (2013) 'How do we link assessment to making progress in geography', in D. Lambert and M. Jones (eds) *Debates in Geography Education*, London: Routledge.
This chapter highlights some of the debates and dilemmas geography teachers have to navigate in terms of how to understand pupils' progress in the subject.

9 Values in school geography

geographical context is significant to moral practice, and [...] ethical delibera-
tion is incomplete without recognition of the geographical dimension in human
existence

(Smith 2000: viii)

Introduction

In this chapter we discuss the debates, dilemmas and controversies around the contribution
that geography can make to pupils' understanding of complex and often highly controversial
issues. As a starting point we must accept that some of what follows will in itself be controversial, for as Roberts (2013) states: 'Almost anything anyone writes about the teaching
of controversial issues in geography is in itself controversial' (p. 114). Therefore, in reading
this chapter you are likely to encounter ideas and perspective that you find you may well
disagree with. However, much of what we express in this chapter is ultimately about why it
is important to develop pupils' capacity for critical thinking and the need to build a culture of
argument in geography classrooms, we also hope that the discussions that follow build such
a culture with geography teachers too.

Accepting this, and if we think about the quote from Smith above, it is impossible to
imagine how we could teach geography without recourse to values, morals and controversial
issues – a geography curriculum that disregards values and controversy would not only be
very dull (and also very thin in terms of content), but more importantly would fail to educate.
The question is how to teach controversial ideas and issues in geography in principled ways
and in doing so maintain the integrity of the discipline in schools; how do we ensure that we
educate young people to think intelligently and critically about some of the significant issues
of our time rather than *indoctrinate* them into particular ways of seeing and being?

We start this chapter with an overview of values education and teaching controversial
issues in school geography which then serves as a backdrop for subsequent discussions
about key educational themes: environmental geographies and education for sustainable
development, teaching geography through a futures dimension, and concluding with some
consideration of geography and citizenship.

By the end of this chapter, you should be able to:

- understand the contribution that school geography makes to pupils' understanding of controversial issues
- identify ways of engaging young people in thinking about their future adult life and the potential for exploring these aspects with children in geography lessons
- make a judgement about the value of critical thinking in geography teaching and learning
- identify the value and the potential pitfalls of offering a futures perspective in your teaching.

Teaching for a 'good cause'?

Before we get into the 'nitty-gritty' of contemporary debates about teaching controversial issues, we want to start with a word of warning, and one that we hope will inform your reading of the remainder of this chapter. Bill Marsden (1995) has reminded us that moral dimensions to geography teaching have existed for a long time and have, not unexpectedly, stirred up argument. From the early part of the twentieth century, teachers have objected to the amount of 'imperialist' and, later, racist or Eurocentric geography in school textbooks. Here, Marsden quotes two Sudanese teachers writing 70 years ago:

> Teachers who have vivid imaginations, but little knowledge of the facts, find it easy to interest classes by telling exaggerated stories of the strange customs of savages ... They emphasise the strange things in other people's lives and ignore what is similar to our own.
>
> (Griffiths and Rahman ali Taha 1939, cited in Marsden 1995: 125)

Though extreme imperialist and racist views, are for the most part avoided in textbooks (most publishers have clear policies and guidelines for authors), Hicks (1981), Wright (1985) and Winter (1997) have shown that stereotyping people and places is a persistent problem. Marsden's analysis of such trends gives pause for thought, for he shows how the relationship between society and education is one which uses:

> the curriculum and informal channels of education to serve the ends of significant power groups, whether church, the state, or some other body, even the 'educational establishment', so that explicitly or implicitly employed techniques of inculcation, indoctrination, and loaded selection of material, dictate the content, values, attitudes and beliefs to be transmitted.
>
> (Marsden 1989, cited in Slater 1996: 224)

Frances Slater picks up this point when she asks: if Mackinder (see Box 9.1 below) reveals the values of his time in describing the imperialist 'good cause' for teaching geography, then 'who is making equally loaded statements today and what effect are they having?' (Slater 1996: 224).

Box 9.1 Geography 'in a good cause'

In 1911, Halford Mackinder wrote:

> Let our teaching be from the British standpoint, so that finally we see the world as a theatre for British activity. This, no doubt, is to deviate from the cold and impartial ways of science. When we teach the millions, however, we are not training scientific investigators, but the practical striving citizens of an empire which has to hold its place through the universal law of survival through efficiency and effort.

(*Source*: Mackinder 1911: 79–80, in Slater 1996: 225)

The quote in Box 9.1 is fascinating, partly because it would not be too fanciful to imagine parts of this being written today: think of what our politicians say about globalisation, for instance, and the need for efficiency in the face of global economic threats. Equally interesting, and a different kind of response to Slater's question, is to imagine substituting 'environmental' for 'British': there are those who would say that geography's current 'good cause' should be environmental concern – to the extent that certain values should be inculcated. The damage this could do, ironically to environmental education, could be as great as that which Mackinder's good cause did for international understanding.

Following Marsden, Alex Standish (2009) has taken up the arguments concerning the dangers of 'good causes' assuming too prominent a role in geography lessons. His main argument is that 'global education' in fact has little to do with education. His view, argued even more forcefully in his 2012 book, *The False Promise of Global Learning: Why Education Needs Boundaries*, is that global education is a policy-driven agenda and anti-intellectual in the sense that, ironically, it undermines pupils' curiosity about the world and how it works. Instead, he argues that 'geography has embraced the themes of global education/citizenship . . . in place of teaching children about the geography of the world' (p. 59). In other words, according to Standish, the ill-defined assertions from global *education* are closer to indoctrinating pupils in a particular way of making sense of the world, rather than *educating* them with disciplined geographical knowledge that enables them to think independently – this is a key challenge that geography teachers have to confront and this is where an exploration of values education can help.

Values education

Values and attitudes

It is perhaps important to start by distinguishing values from attitudes. Slater uses Rokeach's (1973) definition of a value being 'an enduring belief that a specific mode of conduct or end state of existence is personally or socially preferable to an opposite mode of conduct or end state of existence' (Slater 1982: 90). Some of these values are central to what we consider to be important in life, whereas others may be more peripheral and therefore receive less personal commitment.

Attitudes can be defined as 'packages of beliefs which influence us in decisions' (Slater 1982: 91); in other words, when we focus on a particular situation, they 'predispose' us to act in a particular way. Slater summarises the distinction by suggesting that 'attitudes are value expressive', whereas 'values are strongly held attitudes'. Michael McPartland (2006: 172–173) classifies the values which underpin the study of geography into:

- *Social values* (e.g. the need to respect human rights)
- *Economic values* (e.g. the need for wealth creation)
- *Environmental values* (e.g. the need to maintain biodiversity)
- *Aesthetic values* (e.g. the need to conserve forested landscapes)
- *Political values* (e.g. the need to participate in the life of the local community)
- *Moral values* (e.g. the need to act in accordance with a moral code).

He suggests that all values, in whatever arena they are located, may take on an ethical dimension and become, therefore, moral values. Thus, if you regard an issue as a moral issue, then social, economic, environmental, aesthetic and political values related to the study of this issue can become subsumed within the category of moral values (McPartland 2006: 173).

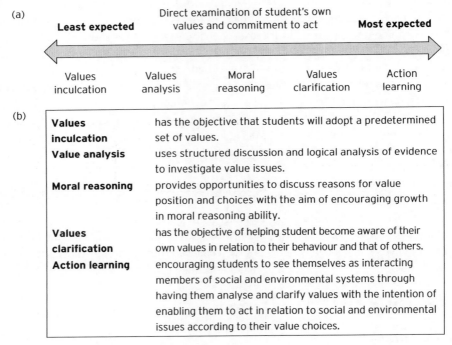

Figure 9.1 Approaches to values education
(a) The degree of student involvement in examining own values and actions
(b) A brief description of approaches to values education

(*Source:* Fien and Slater 1981)

Each of the different teaching approaches identified in Figure 9.1 have been designed with different 'valuing objectives' in mind. To be effective, the approaches selected by geography teachers should therefore reflect the objectives of their teaching programmes (Fien and Slater 1981; Huckle 1981). The teaching strategies that can be used in values education range from individual reflection and writing to group discussion, role playing and structured analysis of situations where there is conflict (Rawling 1986).

Values analysis emphasises that judgements are based on facts and values. Marsden describes the objective of values analysis as being to equip pupils with the 'capacity and inclination to make rational and defensible value judgements' (Marsden 1995: 6). Fien and Slater (1981) outline a sequence of procedures for achieving this which involves:

- identifying the decisions to be made to resolve the value issue
- assembling the purported facts on the issue
- establishing the veracity of the purported facts so that decisions will be based on objective evidence
- establishing the relevance of the facts and removing distracting information
- arriving at tentative decisions
- testing the value principles involved in the decision.

The role of the teacher is to help pupils understand the decision-making process while leaving pupils free to make their own independent judgements. The intention is that by studying relevant factual evidence, and clarifying appropriate policies pupils will engage, at their own level, in the type of decision-making carried out by, for example, planners and others (Huckle 1981). Thus pupils use a process of rational analysis to conceptualise and interrogate their own values.

As a strategy for values education, values analysis does have its limitations. Huckle points to its 'readiness to cling to what some consider a debased form of rationality' (Huckle 1981: 156) and the continued promotion of ideas and cognitive skills at the expense of values and feelings. He suggests that the desire for balance and consensus can dominate approaches to rational decision-making in the classroom which 'merely reinforce the status quo' and create a 'false confidence in democratic society which is likely to be frustrated later in life' (Huckle 1981: 158).

Moral reasoning has similar objectives to values analysis but pursues them in a less structured way using small-group discussion and debate (McPartland 2006; Marsden 1995). Case studies are presented to pupils as moral dilemmas to be resolved. The moral reasoning strategy is based on Kohlberg's (1976) theory, which suggests that an individual's ability in moral reasoning passes through a series of stages (now questioned) before attaining moral autonomy. Kohlberg developed the use of the 'moral dilemma', a story in which there is no clear cut answer.

Box 9.2 is an example of a moral dilemma based on an imaginary character. McPartland (2001, 2006) provides helpful guidance for geography teachers about how to create and use moral dilemmas successfully.

Box 9.2 An example of a moral dilemma

Nestor is a graduate student living in England, studying for an MSc in Chemistry. He is from Benin. He came to the university on a scholarship financed by the Benin government. His father, Desire, is a cotton farmer in the Borgou province in the north of Benin trying to earn a living from his three hectares of land. The cotton he produces is exported to Italy to make jeans. The lack of urban centres, the undeveloped infrastructure and high transport costs all make it difficult to grow crops so cotton is the main cash crop. But the soil is degraded. Cotton cultivation robs the soil of nutrients. Crop rotation and use of fallow periods are not used, and so artificial chemical pesticides and fertilisers are used to maintain yields. There is some concern that the use of pesticides is having a negative impact on river quality, biodiversity and the health of workers in the ginning mills. Last year, one of Nestor's cousins was poisoned eating corn which was growing near his father's cotton field.

Nestor is in the final stages of his MSc. He is an excellent student, hard-working and committed to his research. Last week, a well-known international French chemical company offered him a well-paid job based in Paris. Nestor is fluent in French, the official language of Benin. His job will be to develop a new range of pesticides.

He has to make a decision by next week.

What are the moral reasons and, therefore, moral requirements underpinning his decision: to take or not to take the job. How finely balanced are they?

(*Source:* McPartland 2006: 175)

Approaches such as moral reasoning contribute to pupils' moral development supporting their understanding the concept of 'morality' – that sometimes tense and conflicted combination of personal beliefs and values, the beliefs and values of social, cultural and religious groups to which a person belongs and the customs and laws of wider society of which they are members.

Lambert and Balderstone (2000) and Lambert and Jones (2013) argue that geography teachers occupy a moral space and that it is morally careless not to provide opportunities where pupils can consider, for example, what is right and wrong. The phrase 'there is no right or wrong answer' is frequently heard in geography classrooms, and Mitchell (2013) argues that this implies a degree of moral ambivalence, especially when 'there are occasions, when something is clearly (in moral terms) either right or wrong' (p. 239). It is perhaps more helpful for pupils and teachers to consider how different perspectives on a particular issue are likely to intersect, overlap and conflict with each other; this way pupils can understand the messiness of moral positions and come to appreciate that in some circumstances 'there are no clear cut answers' is a more viable framework to think with (Lambert and Balderstone 2000).

Values clarification helps pupils to use both rational thinking and emotional awareness to examine their personal feelings, values and behaviour patterns (Huckle 1981). According to Frances Slater, this process of 'articulating and understanding the basic values which underlie and inform one's attitudes towards people, places, object or issues' is important for two reasons. First, it is important because it helps pupils to recognise the 'processes underlying preferences and judgements'. Second, pupils can use a variety of issues to provide the context through which the 'implications and consequences' of holding particular values can be explored (Slater 1981: 85).

Marsden reminds us that 'values clarification' does have its limitations as a strategy for values education as it 'suggests that values are subjective and all a matter for individual choice: that everybody's opinion is as good as everybody else's' (Marsden 1995: 6). He warns that it could 'tend to foster the primacy of self-interest'.

Action Learning is a combination of values analysis and values clarification that enable pupils to act upon their value choices. Action might involve pupils participating in projects that could improve the environment of the school site or that could change practice within the school community, such as developing recycling schemes managed by the pupils themselves.

Action could involve pupils in community-wide projects such as small-scale local conservation projects, fundraising activities, school-linking projects (with schools, often in economically developing countries). These, argues Fran Martin, require careful consideration if schools and teachers are to avoid reinforcing the kinds of stereotypes of 'others' they are actually seeking to challenge. Drawing on post-colonial theory, Martin (2011) draws attention to the possibility of international school partnerships contributing to a new form of colonialism where the discourse about countries in the southern hemisphere is dominated by concepts such as poverty, dependency and environmental degradation. This risk, Martin argues, is that whilst school partnerships may engender in UK pupils a commitment to help others, the reality is that all too often schools merely use the experiences of people in economically poorer countries as resources for the school curriculum.

Controversial issues

Many of the issues explored through values education are by their nature controversial. Almost any issue can become controversial if individuals or groups hold differing views or offer differing explanations about events, what should happen and how issues should be resolved (Oxfam 2006). They can also be controversial if these views and explanations are presented in a way that raises an emotional response from those who might disagree. Controversial issues can be personal, local or global and they are often complex with no easy answers with people holding strong views based on their different experiences, interests and values:

> Issues that are likely to be sensitive or controversial are those that have a political, social or personal impact and arouse feeling and/or deal with questions of value or belief
>
> (QCA 2001)

However, there are concerns about the dangers of geography teachers being 'morally careless' if they fail to adopt appropriate values education strategies when investigating issues which are often controversial in geography lessons. Bill Marsden argues that there is a difference between what we would all agree to be 'laudable educational aims' and the possibility that what we teach becomes so dominated by *the issues* that the 'self-evident good causes embraced appear to justify indoctrination'. Further dangers can be seen in some of the issues-dominated texts and teaching materials at Key Stage 3 in which superficial enquiry approaches lack any cognitive rigour and adequate engagement with geographical data. Over-simplistic presentation of issues can lead to 'little more than an incitement to offer an opinion' (Marsden 1995: 143).

So to respond to these concerns it is important that not only should the issue selected for study carefully taught, but it should also have a strong and geographically distinctive conceptual structure. Consideration should be given to how pupils are able to recognise the distinctive contribution that geography can make to an understanding of this and similar issues. Appropriate geographical concepts should be identified and attention given to how they are developed through enquiry.

Sue Warn (2012), writing about the geography of war and conflict, suggests that the four strategies outlined in Table 9.1 provide useful frameworks to help teachers avoid accusations of bias and indoctrination. By taking account of the relative strengths and weaknesses of each approach, teachers can make conscious choices about the approach they adopt and the likely consequences it will have. She also suggests that untended bias, often a feature of teaching under pressure, can be avoided by:

- not reporting opinions as if they were established facts
- not giving your own accounts of the views of others, i.e., allowing the students to see the
- raw material, and letting the facts speak for themselves
- not setting yourself up as the sole authority on a subject
- not challenging a one-sided consensus if it emerges too quickly in a classroom
- trying not to allow your own opinions to be implicit in the way you describe a particular issue, or in your choice of sources to analyse
- not orchestrating the discussion so that competent, articulate speakers dominate and those with more tentative minority views are ignored.

(Warn 2012: 58)

However, the strategies outlined in Table 9.1 are unlikely to be successful without careful attention to classroom atmosphere. The generation of an atmosphere of mutual trust and respect in the classroom is important. Such an atmosphere is not only a reflection of positive teacher–pupil relationships but also of pupils' respect for each other. However, there will be times when controversy unexpectedly emerges out of something you are teaching. It is important to respond positively to such a challenge and manage pupils' evolving interest in an issue positively, respond constructively to any strength of feeling that emerges as a result, and also foreground the geographical dimension as a means of supporting pupils' understanding of the issue.

The 'unexpected' reveals that geography teachers are rarely far from having to face the challenge of teaching controversial issues. David Mitchell (2013) equates this with geography's 'relevance', pointing out that this is in itself quite a tricky idea. Good teaching does not always have to be relevant in the sense that it is 'of today', or that it relates directly to pupils' everyday lives. However, good geography teaching does need to recognise that a changing world is (more often than not) a contested world: there are different perceptions and opinions about the change itself, the causes of change and its consequences. As Mitchell points out: 'School geography is therefore "shot through" with values (Slater 1996) and where values arise, controversy follows' (ibid.: 232).

Table 9.1 Four teaching approaches for dealing with controversial issues in the classroom

	Potential strengths	Potential weaknesses
Procedural Neutrality In which the teacher adopts the role of an impartial chairperson of a discussion group.	Minimises undue influence of teacher's own bias. Gives everyone a chance to take part in free discussion. Scope for open-ended discussion, i.e., the class may move on to consider issues and questions which the teacher hasn't thought of. Presents a good opportunity for pupils to exercise communication skills. Works well if you have a lot of background material.	Pupils find it artificial. Can damage the rapport between teacher and class if it doesn't work. Depends on pupils being familiar with the method elsewhere in the school or it will take a long time to acclimatise them. May only reinforce pupils' existing attitudes and prejudices. Very difficult with the less able. Neutral chair doesn't suit my personality.
Stated Commitment In which the teacher always makes known his or her views during discussion.	Pupils will try to guess what the teacher thinks anyway. Stating your own position makes everything above board. If pupils know where the teacher stands on the issue they can discount his or her prejudices and biases. It's better to state your preferences after discussion rather than before. It should only be used if pupils' dissenting opinions are treated with respect. It can be an excellent way of maintaining credibility with pupils since they do not expect us to be neutral.	It can stifle classroom discussion, inhibiting pupils from arguing a line against that of the teacher's. It may encourage some pupils to argue strongly for something they don't believe in simply because it's different from the teacher. Pupils often find it difficult to distinguish facts from values. It's even more difficult if the purveyor of facts and values is the same person, i.e., the teacher.
A Balanced Approach In which the teacher presents pupils with a wide range of alternative views.	Essential: I think one of the main functions of a humanities or social studies teacher is to show that issues are hardly ever black and white. Necessary when the class is polarised on an issue. Most useful when dealing with issues about which there is a great deal of conflicting information.	Is there such a thing as a balanced range of opinions? As a strategy it has limited use. It avoids the main point by conveying the impression that 'truth' is a grey area that exists between two alternative sets of opinions. Balance means very different things to different people. The media's view of balance is not mine. Teaching is rarely value-free. This approach can lead to very teacher-directed lessons. Like media interviews, you are always interrupting to maintain the so-called balance.
The Devil's Advocate Strategy In which the teacher consciously takes up the opposite position to the one expressed by pupils or in teaching materials.	Frequently used by me. Great fun, and can be very effective in stimulating the pupils to contribute to discussion. Essential when faced by a group who all seem to share the same opinion. Most classes which I have taught seem to have a majority line. Then I use this strategy and parody, exaggeration, and role reversal. I often use this as a device to liven things up when the discussion is beginning to dry up.	I have run into all sorts of problems with this approach. Children identifying me with the views I was putting forward as devil's advocate; parents worried about my alleged views, etc. It may reinforce pupils' prejudices. Only to be used when discussion dries up and there are still 25 minutes left.

(Source: Slater 1993: 114 (after Stradling et al. 1984))

Task 9.1 Teaching controversial issues

1   Think about your own geographical education (at all levels). What kinds of issues did you learn about and what strategies can you recall your teachers using to support your learning?

2   Use Table 9.1 to help you to plan a lesson where you will be teaching a potentially controversial issue. What are your geographical questions for framing the lessons? What 'position' will you adopt in the lesson and why? What resources will you use to support your teaching and in what ways will you engage your students in a 'culture of argument' in order to help them understand the complex nature of the issue they are studying.

3   Review a scheme of work in your school. Consider:

- What are the main geographical concepts and themes in the scheme and how they are developed?
- What skills, values and attitudes are developed?
- What range of participatory approaches are used?
- How is pupils' progress in understanding judged?
- Does the scheme suffer from promoting 'a good cause'? How could the scheme be developed to ensure that pupils develop their critical thinking?

Sustainable development

Environmental geography has been in the school geography curriculum for some time, and from the 1950s onwards was a particular response to the significant changes taking place in both urban and rural landscapes – the growth of towns and cities, industrial expansion to support growing demand for consumer goods at home and abroad, and the industrialisation of agricultural production resulted in teachers trying to help children make sense of these rapidly changing landscapes at a local level (Morgan 2011). The 1980s marked a shift in focus as education turned its attention to more global issues and by the 1990s, in response to global debates about planetary management, education for sustainable development came onto the education policy radar.

As Chapter 2 makes clear, all curriculum change is located in broader social, cultural and ideological contexts, we can see this clearly in the way the curriculum responded to Education for Sustainable Development (ESD) where from the mid-1990s to the present (2014), we saw what Eckersley (2004) describes as the emergence of the 'green state' based on a new form of environmental politics (see Eckersley 2004, cited in Morgan 2011: 132). It was within this political and ideological context that ESD was introduced into the National Curriculum in 2000 by the last Labour government and in the wake of this came a series of related initiatives including the sustainable schools initiative (the intention of which was to ensure that all schools in England were sustainable schools by 2020) and the inclusion of 'The Global Dimension and Sustainability' as one of the six over-arching cross-curricular dimensions in the 2007 National Curriculum Review in England. In 2010, the coalition government halted the Sustainable Schools Strategy and 'ESD' disappeared from the education policy agenda: ESD, sustainable development, sustainability – none of these concepts are mentioned at all in the 2014 National Curriculum (including geography) and only receive limited mention in GCSE and Draft A-level subject content criteria for geography.

It seems somewhat ironic that the 'green' policy initiatives of the early twenty-first century seem to have disappeared while at the same time we acknowledge the Anthropocene as the new geological 'epoch'. We would argue that, despite a lack of obvious presence at a policy level, sustainable development should be taught in school geography. This in itself is controversial, not least because the concept is much contested leaving decisions about how to teach highly problematic.

According to the the Brundtland Report, sustainable development, is:

> Development that meets the needs of the present without compromising the ability of future generations to meet their own needs.

(Brundtland 1987)

This famous, but somewhat brief definition needs unpacking in more detail. 'Sustainable development', as Figure 9.2 shows, refers to the intersection of processes leading to environmental quality, social equity and economic security. Some would include additional aspects, including governance and cultural processes, but the three main pillars, the environmental, social and economic, are fundamental. Thus, the implications for the school curriculum are very interesting. Although aspects of sustainable development may be addressed through traditional subjects – arguably geography in particular as it promotes a holistic 'synthesis' of physical and human knowledge – education for sustainable development implies the

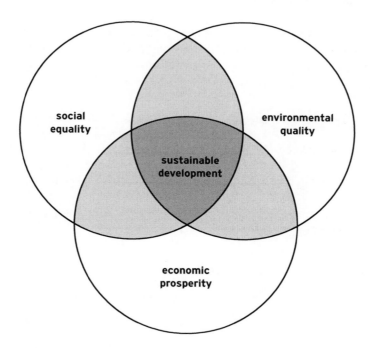

Figure 9.2 Sustainable development

development of multidisciplinary understandings. There is a good case for geographers, scientists and historians, and indeed other subject specialist communities, to work in partnership when it comes to education for sustainable development.

Sustainable development: a contested concept

The meaning of sustainable development takes on different forms with different political ideologies, and within different forms of knowledge, values, and philosophies, within different cultures. For instance, a technocentrist viewpoint, such as might be held by liberal and social democrat reformers, would support weak sustainability, whereas at the other end of the spectrum, ecocentrists such as green socialists and those holding post-modern holistic views would support strong sustainability (Smith 2013: 258).

The quote above highlights the extent to which sustainable development is a contested concept. Morgan (2011) identifies two levels of controversy around sustainable development. The first is controversy rooted in the social impacts, the solutions to which are often rooted in different ideologies, but where there is a degree of agreement over the science and geography of sustainable development. The second is what he calls a 'double level of controversy', which is rooted in disagreement about the science/geography *and* the social impacts/solutions. It is these layers of controversy, embedded in sustainable development issues that give rise to very distinct tensions, namely, education–advocacy–indoctrination – a sort of continuum along which ESD can slide depending on how it is taught.

We would argue that it is inappropriate to teach sustainability as if it were simply a matter of identifying the 'right answer' to problems and then implementing the policies which subsequently flow, and in our view geography classrooms oriented only to inculcating certain 'sustainable' ways to live are deeply suspect. This could be viewed as indoctrination. Far more useful, and legitimate educationally, are geography lessons that enable young people to think creatively and critically using ideas such as interdependence, differential impact and so on. Morgan (2011) considers two approaches to ESD:

ESD1: learning for sustainable development

- Promoting positive behaviours where it is fairly obvious (or is apparently so) what these need to be.
- It is an approach that suggests that those in authority know what good SD practice looks like.
- Practice at the school level includes activities such as energy efficiency; fair trade tuck shops; charity fundraising for a partner school; recycling.

ESD2: learning as sustainable development

- Building learners' capacity to think critically about the issues and what experts (including teachers) say.

- Exploring the contradictions inherent in those very practices considered to be 'good SD practice'.

ESD1, argues Morgan, on its own is not enough; it needs ESD2 in order for the 'education' element of ESD to be foregrounded. School geography can contribute a great deal to ESD2 as approaches such as geographical enquiry invite pupils to engage critically with what they see, hear, read and experience and encourage them to take nothing for granted. Lambert and Morgan (2010) agree, stating that sustainable development should be taught in ways that:

> introduce them [pupils] to instances of how the world is made through economic, social and cultural argument. Such an approach may reveal the values basis of decision making, including people's attitudes to 'nature' itself.

> (p. 139)

Planning tools such as the Development Compass Rose can help with developing the ESD2 approach advocated by Morgan. The intersection between social, political and environmental elements is essential to the understanding of people and places and the environment.

Task 9.2 invites you into a serious debate which inevitably considers the form that education for sustainability should take.

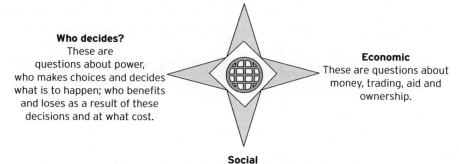

Natural
These are questions about the environment – energy, air, water, soil, living things, and their relationships to each other. These questions are about the 'built' as well as the 'natural' environment.

Who decides?
These are questions about power, who makes choices and decides what is to happen; who benefits and loses as a result of these decisions and at what cost.

Economic
These are questions about money, trading, aid and ownership.

Social
These are questions about people: their relationships, traditions and culture, and the way they live. They include questions about how, for example, gender, race, disability, class and age affect social relationships.

Figure 9.3 The Development Compass Rose

(*Source*: Robinson and Serf 1997: 12)

Task 9.2 A question of values (individuals or groups)

1   Read the following passage, which deserves critical analysis:

> For the survival of the world and its people teachers must do far more than just teach about global issues. We must find ways to change hearts and minds. This can be a response to reasoned argument and evidence or to experience where empathy leads to commitment to action.
>
> Teachers hold the responsibility for educating their participants to work for future change that will help create a better world for all. Together we must work towards a more ecologically sustainable and socially just society locally, nationally and globally.
>
> (Calder and Smith 1993: 2.1, cited in Tilbury 1997: 105)

2   As an aid to analysis, copy out each sentence of the passage onto a separate card or piece of paper. Re-read each sentence. Write down your reaction to it on the card:

- Do you agree with it?
- If necessary, write down what it says to you in your own words.
- What does the sentence leave unsaid?
- What does it seem to assume?
- Identify a 'key word'.

3   Fien and Slater (1981) identify different approaches to values education including values clarification, where pupils understand their own behaviour in relation to others, values analysis which involves pupils in analysing where different 'players' are coming from (i.e. their value position) and values inculcation where the teacher attempts to proselytise a particular value position (see p. 134).

   In your analysis of the passage:

- Which of the values approaches do the authors appear to be advocating?
- Discuss the pros and cons of each in relation to education for sustainability.

4   Discuss the key words you identified in question 1. For example:

- Is there significance in the use of the term 'participants' rather than 'students'?
- What is meant by 'empathy'?
- What is the implication of the use of the word 'action'?

Discussion: Present-day ways of living are probably unsustainable – ecologically, socially, economically and politically. If you believe this, then teaching geography for a sustainable world sounds like a sensible idea. Nobody could entertain the idea of doing the reverse (teaching for an unsustainable world). But the activity shows that identifying, let alone achieving, our teaching goals in this field is by no means a straightforward matter.

In this sense, geography teachers do have a great responsibility, to keep up to date and work in appropriate ways with young people. But to inflate this responsibility in the way that some readings of the quote at the start of Task 9.2 may imply is not all that helpful. Teachers have enough to do without taking on the responsibility of changing society or saving the human race. Their achievable aim is to change the individuals they teach, principally by enabling them to respond to issues, and each other, more intelligently. If success at this individual level also leads to more informed personal choices and behaviours, it could also contribute to the creation of a better world. But the main interest of the teacher is with the person.

Holistic geographies

Because of geography's breadth and its well-known openness to change and development as a discipline, it is well-placed to help young people to find ways of analysing the super-complex world in which they now live; where nothing is certain and change is inevitable (see Lambert 1997, 1999; Barnett 2000). Keeping problems whole, rather than fragmented and isolated, enables pupils see the relationships between issues and thus come to understand how they are connected: pupils can see certain issues in relation to others, though none of this necessarily presents 'solutions' to the world's problems. Read, with these thoughts in mind, how Fritjof Capra introduces one of his books:

> The more we study the major problems of our time, the more we come to realise that they cannot be understood in isolation. They are systemic problems, which means that they are interconnected and interdependent [in time and space]. For example, stabilising world population will only be possible when poverty is reduced worldwide. The extinction of animal and plant species on a massive scale will continue as long as the Southern Hemisphere is burdened by massive debts. Scarcities of resources and environmental degradation combine with rapidly expanding populations to lead to the breakdown of local communities, and to the ethnic and tribal violence that has become the main characteristic of the post-Cold War era.
>
> Ultimately, these problems must be seen as just different facets of one single crisis, which is largely a crisis of perception. It derives from the fact that most of us, and especially our large social institutions, subscribe to the concepts of an outdated worldview, a perception of reality inadequate for dealing with our overpopulated, globally interconnected world.
>
> (Capra 1996: 3–4)

Rawding (2014) is a strong advocate for developing an approach to geographical education that requires pupils to come to understand the world more holistically. He contends that there are two types of holistic geographies that connect to each other:

1   Elements of the earth that are fundamental to our understanding of a wide range of topics, for example: continentality, oceans, atmosphere.
2   Single-issue geographies that have a global dimension, such as climate change, capitalism, environment.

Rawding argues that studying the earth as a 'whole' enables pupils to better understand that the world is in fact 'joined-up' and that events in one place have significant consequences for what happens elsewhere. He cites numerous examples such as the eruption of the Eyjafjallajökull volcano in Iceland April 2010 and the consequences this had for global air travel, or the impact of globalisation on our local-level lives – the food we eat, the goods we buy and the places where we live and work, which are now inextricably linked to places elsewhere. Holistic geographies, argues Rawding, help pupils to better understand these connections:

> A student needs to be aware of how the local fits into the global and how the global influences the local at all sorts of levels. At the most basic level, it is the role of the geographer to be able to explain where and why people sunbathe in summer, skate in winter and play conkers in the autumn. Equally, it is essential for the geographer to be able to explain that such practices do not apply worldwide.
>
> (Rawding 2014: 13)

Achieving this kind of understanding is no small task and it requires that geography teachers themselves understand these holistic geographies and then draw on this knowledge and understanding to create appropriate learning opportunities for pupils. As indicated elsewhere in this chapter when discussing values education and ESD, it is essential that pupils have opportunities to both develop their geographical knowledge and understanding – they need to know something about the processes and cost of, for example, food production or commodity production elsewhere in the world, and how such goods are transported and by whom, before they can begin to consider ethical issues relating to global consumption and the ways that their lives and choices are connected to the lives and choices of people living elsewhere in the world.

Box 9.3 Commodity geographies

Commodity geographies provide an interesting context for holistic geographies because by their very nature they are concerned with connected lives. Pupils can select a commodity and then undertake some 'geographical detective work' (generally online, but not always) as they trace their chosen commodity back from the point of consumption, through marketing, distribution and processing, along the transport network, to the site of production and back to where workers live (Cook, cited in Firth and Biddulph 2009: 24). What they gradually unfold, as they follow lines of enquiry and critically interrogate sources, is that the link between production and consumption is far from linear – the commodities they consume are the products of a web of complex global connections. As a teaching approach, this detective work is very unpredictable; you do not know what lines of enquiry your students will take or where it will lead them.

The 'Follow-the-things' website is deliberately designed to look like a shopping site with shopping departments and different commodities to 'buy'. This is a good starting point from which to begin investigating the holistic geographies of 'stuff' (available at: www.followthethings.com/).

While the point about commodities being made by people you don't see is hardly a shock revelation, the detective work aims to vividly bring that to life and take students on a journey through a quirky, clicking little universe of its own in which every piece of the puzzle fits and everybody has a part to play.

(Cook et al. 2007, cited in Firth and Biddulph 2009: 24)

Task 9.3 Geographical detective work

Figure 9.4 is an example of a spider diagram showing how a pair of socks bought in a shop the UK is connected to India, China, the Middle East and Europe.

1   Become your own geographical detective and try to trace the networks of connections for a commodity of your choice. Use the Follow-the-things website to get started.
2   Create your own spider diagram demonstrating how people and places are connected – what do you notice about the nature of the different connections.
3   What would be some of the issues you would need to anticipate if you undertook such an activity with pupils in school?
4   How would you capture pupils' learning – what would you ask them to produce to demonstrate geographical understanding?

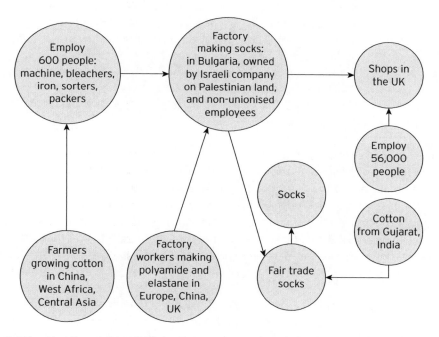

Figure 9.4 A spider diagram showing how pupils can make connections between themselves and the lives of others

(Adapted from Cook, in Biddulph and Firth 2009: 26)

A futures-oriented geography curriculum

If you think about it, most of the curriculum experience of pupils is derived from the past – the past discoveries, achievements and products of human beings. This is not surprising. The curriculum is a selection of the society's science, art and culture that it chooses systematically to 'pass on' to the next generation.

And yet, as John Morgan (2011) has shown, 'it is clear that human beings are now living in an environment that is increasingly a matter of their own making' (p. 145). Morgan's point is to show that there is an increasing consensus among expert opinion that we are living in a geological epoch known as the Anthropocene (see also Castree 2015) – that is, replacing the Holocene epoch, the interglacial period of stable climate that has allowed for the development of agriculture and urban growth for the last 10,000 years. Morgan (2011) concludes: 'there are significant challenges in developing a geographical education that is appropriate to the Anthropocene' (p. 146). But what does this mean?

Thus it is arguably the case that all education is *for* the future, and that a curriculum that does not overtly prepare young people for thinking about alternative futures is inappropriate to 'life in a changing world'. This thought encourages us to rethink the purposes of school subjects: rather than bodies of knowledge to be passed on to young people, they are better seen as resources which introduce students to productive and significant ways of thinking about the world. This argument takes us back to Chapter 1 and the purpose of geographical education being to develop pupils' capacity to 'think geographically'. This, we argue, provides them with an intellectual framework, which in addition to helping them make sense of the world they see and experience *now*, can also support them in the process of thinking about possible futures: 'to see that the world is not reducible to what we experience or what happens, there is much that could happen and understanding this is necessary if we are to think the unthinkable and the not-yet-thought' (Wheelahan 2009: 2)

Rex Walford, addressing the Geographical Association as President, expressed the need for a futures orientation to geography teaching:

> The sustained study of a number of possible geographies of the short-term and middle-term future will encourage the student to consider those aspects of the future which are desirable and those which are not. Hopefully such geography teaching can vitalise school students into an interest in their own futures . . . In urging that we teach a geography of the future, I do not mean to say that we should give up teaching the geography of the past: but we should make the past the servant of the future. If the future is unavoidable, let us at least not walk backwards into it.
>
> (Walford 1984: 207)

Of course, to suggest that young people do not think about the future would be absurd. They do, as Figure 9.5 shows. They have concerns and anxieties about the future and the majority of pupils surveyed think that school should teach more about the environment, for example. For the geography teacher, the task is to identify approaches and resources which enable us to structure ways for pupils to investigate and imagine alternative futures. This needs to be done within a theoretical framework, so that bolt-on 'discussions' about the future, which can be repetitive, frustrating and confusing, can be avoided.

If we agree that a futures dimension is a legitimate, indeed essential, component of geographic enquiry (which has an established sequence of questions such as: What is this place like? Why is it like this? How did it come to be like this? How ought it to be? The final question in this enquiry sequence is futures-oriented and political), we must be prepared to endorse its consequences. Asking questions of the future, about the future and for the future takes

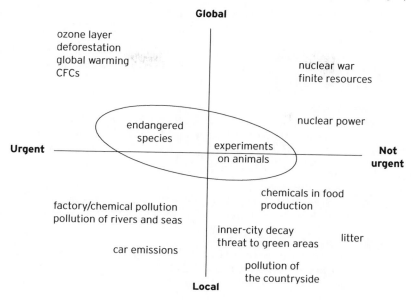

Figure 9.5 Children's environmental concerns

(*Source:* Young Eyes, Henley Centre for Forecasting 1991, in Hicks 1994: 2)

us into the realms of choice, priorities and, therefore, politics. A futures-oriented curriculum could make a useful contribution to pupils' political education. For example, understanding local, national and international political structures can help pupils appreciate the role of politics in decision-making *for* the future. Understanding these structures can contribute significantly to pupils' citizenship education as they engage critically with questions about democracy and political and ideological alternatives.

We believe that geography teachers, because of the nature of their subject, involving analysis and synthesis across a wide spectrum of contents from the physical and human worlds, are particularly well suited to the kinds of pedagogic demands of a futures-oriented curriculum. What is underrepresented in Table 9.2 is the more 'hard-nosed' knowledge and understanding educational outcomes. We would certainly agree that an educational rationale for a futures dimension in the curriculum is arguably incomplete without reference to knowledge and understanding – it *matters* that processes such as the greenhouse effect are understood, and that they do not just become slogans or icons designed to elicit only certain kinds of emotional response.

A broad framework for a futures orientation

Writing more recently about a futures-orientated geography curriculum, David Hicks has considered 'optimism and hope' to now be educational imperatives (Hicks 2007, 2014a, 2014b). Presenting pupils with 'wicked problems', that is, those to which there is no easy solution, or even 'super wicked problems', that is, those where time is running out yet there is a lack of authority to respond to them (see Roberts 2013: 116 for more) runs the risk of seriously demoralising them and leaving them with a sense of helplessness and hopelessness

Table 9.2 Educational rationale for a futures dimension in the curriculum

---

1   Pupil motivation
Pupil expectation about the future can affect behaviour in the present, e.g. that something is, or is not, worth working for. Clear images of desired personal goals can help stimulate motivation and achievement.

2   Anticipating change
Anticipatory skills and flexibility of mind are important in times of rapid change. Such skills enable pupils to deal more effectively with uncertainty and to initiate, rather than merely respond to, change.

3   Critical thinking
In weighing up information, considering trends and imagining alternatives, pupils will need to exercise reflective and critical thinking. This is often triggered by realising the contradictions between how the world is now and how one would like it to be.

4   Clarifying values
All images of the future are underpinned by differing value assumptions about human nature and society. In a democratic society, pupils need to be able to begin to identify such value judgements before they can themselves make appropriate choices between alternatives.

5   Decision-making
Becoming more aware of trends and events which are likely to influence one's future and investigating the possible consequences of one's actions on others in the future, leads to more thoughtful decision-making in the present.

6   Creative imagination
One faculty that can contribute to, and which is particularly enhanced by, designing alternative futures is that of the creative imagination. Both this and critical thinking are needed to envision a range of preferable futures from the personal to the global.

7   A better world
It is important in a democratic society that young people develop their sense of vision particularly in relation to more just and sustainable futures. Such forward looking thinking is an essential ingredient in both the preserving and improving of society.

8   Responsible citizenship
Critical participation in democratic life leads to the development of political skills and thus more active and responsible citizenship. Future generations are then more likely to benefit, rather than lose, from decisions made today.

9   Stewardship
Understanding the short and long-term consequences of current local and global trends, as well as the action needed to change these, can lead to a sense of stewardship both for the planet now and for those yet to come.

(*Source:* Hicks 1994: 12)

(see also Rawding 2013). To address this, Hicks suggests that that the geography curriculum needs to support pupils' cognitive development (knowledge and understanding) *and* their affective development (feelings, choices and actions) in ways that would help them to interrogate complex problems, and also provide them with a sense that there are real and realistic choices to be made (Hicks 2014: 9). In the context of climate change, he observes:

In the classroom, the time for debates about whether climate change is actually occurring or not is long past. Students need to know about weather and climate but they also need to know how and why it is changing and the possible implications of this for their communities.

(Hicks 2014a: 6)

In order to achieve this, he argues that teachers need to distinguish between what is known and what is yet to be known in order to help young people understand the certainties and the uncertainties of the climate change debate. Teachers' own knowledge is important here.

The known:

- greenhouse gases are warming the planet
- other pollutants are cooling the planet
- the planet is going to get a lot hotter
- sea level is going to rise many metres
- there will be more floods and droughts.

What still needs clarifying is:

- how far greenhouse gas levels will rise
- how great the cooling effects are
- exactly how much hotter things will get
- how the climate will change in specific regions
- how quickly sea level will rise
- how serious a threat global warming is to life
- if and when tipping points will be reached.

(Hicks 2013: 95)

Just as teacher knowledge is important in a futures-orientated curriculum, so is adopting an appropriate curriculum planning framework (see Chapter 2). The framework you adopt is influence by what you want to achieve educationally for your pupils. The headings and definitions in the framework below are deliberately progressive in nature and develop and deepen the futures dimension in the geography curriculum moving from thinking, to imagining, to choosing, to exploring and synthesising.

1   Thinking about the future

This takes pupils into asking questions about the future, exploring images of the future (e.g. in film, adverts) and refining concepts such as continuity, change and consequences. A powerful idea that Hicks develops is that of the '200 year present', which is a fine way to link spatial interdependence with interdependence through time.

An idea that can be used in relation to virtually any thematic and/or place-based topic in geography is to ask pupils to project 'the probable future'. With the help of a *timeline*, what pupils have learnt about recent and current change (in population, or agriculture, or industry, etc.) can be projected into the future, say, at ten-year intervals. The aim is to encourage critical thought about what pupils believe to be aspects of the expected future.

2   Envisioning the future

Imagining the future encourages critical thinking and creative imagination. In contrast to the previous activity concerning probable futures, the core activity here, undertaken in the same manner, with a time line, is to imagine 'the preferable future'. Probable and preferable futures can be considered alongside each other, especially when a key event can be identified (or imagined). Another strategy can be to get pupils to follow through (probable and preferable) impacts arising from various 'what if?' scenarios. As part of the Young Peoples' Geographies project (www.geography.org.uk/projects/youngpeoplesgeographies/) one school devised a 'What if' curriculum: 'What would happen if the oil supply was cut off to our town: in the first 28 seconds . . . 28 minutes . . . 28 hours . . . 28 days . . . 28 months. Pupils had to imagine differ- ent possible future impacts drawing on geographical evidence to support their thinking.

Choosing the future

Activities under this heading are designed to emphasise the concept of choice, and the main technique is to create and compare *alternative* scenarios.

Scenarios are like hypothetical sketches which show the impact of overdevelopment, resource depletion or (conversely) conservation and planning on people and environment; word sketches are also possible. Pupils can produce them or they can be prepared by the teacher for analysis by the pupils; either way, pupils need certain concepts and knowledge to facilitate an intelligent response. Analysis should focus on both the features and the processes.

The following are summaries of four possible scenarios types that pupils could consider (more detailed examples can be found in Hicks, D. (2014) *Educating for Hope in Troubled Times: Climate Change and the Transition to a Post-carbon Future*, Trentham: IOE).

1   **'Business as usual'** emphasises the continued use of fossil fuels and lack of social pre- paredness for 'energy descent'.
2   **'Techno-stability'** emphasises the increase in the use of green technology.
3   **'Energy crash'** emphasises blackouts and social discontent as a result of escalation of the effects of climate change.
4   **Sustainable transition** emphasises social co-operation and adaptation to mitigate against the effect of climate change and build more resilient societies.

(*Source*: Hicks 2014b: 8)

Scenarios such as those above enable pupils to pursue questions of cause and effect, develop their knowledge and understanding of past, present and future actions and speculate on alternative futures. As an approach, these scenarios are useful in prompting debate about alternative futures as they can capture different views and values and present pupils with a range of alternatives to consider for themselves.

Exploring sustainable futures

The thrust here is to synthesise much of the thinking that has taken place hitherto. The key technique is to use a 'case study' approach for the deeper consideration of how a 'sustainable' future can be created. By case study, we include both place exemplar studies (in the traditional sense of case study in geography education) and thematic studies. With reference to sustainable futures, there are two thematic studies of overriding importance: investigating *energy* options and examining *transport* choices. Both require ongoing research for up-to-date information and accurate portrayal; they are both subject to rapid changes in technology, are complex, controversial and go to the heart of any serious consideration of 'sustainability'.

Themes can, and should, be examined on a number of scales (local, regional, national, international). One of the learning outcomes is to see how the scale of analysis influences the kinds of questions investigated, and the kinds of information used to respond to those questions.

Task 9.4 Finding the future (individuals or groups)

1   Examine the text in Table 9.2 (note that it was not compiled solely for geography teachers). To what extent do you agree with the framework? For each item in the list, try to give a concrete example of what the skill, faculty or ability described could look like in a geography classroom. Perhaps you have an example from your own practice, or the observed classroom practice of another teacher, to draw from.

2   Examine the Key Stage 3 curriculum for one school (perhaps one you are working in) and use the criteria in Table 9.2 to evaluate the curriculum. How effectively are aspects of the rationale being implemented in the geography curriculum?

3   Identify a series of lessons you are going to teach and consider in what ways you could draw on the ideas set out in the 'Framework for a Futures Orientation' above to support your planning and teaching.

4   Based upon David Hick's work, you also need to consider the quality of your own subject knowledge in areas such as climate change, peak oil and the limits to growth – how conversant are you with the debates around each of these in order to be able to teach pupils?

Geography and citizenship education

From 2002, 'Citizenship' became a statutory part of the school curriculum. Since then the role and purpose of citizenship education has shifted with the changing political tides. Several significant agendas have had a role to play in the changing profile of citizenship education in England and Wales. The London bombings of July 2005, the return of immigration to the party political agenda in the 2005 general election and the introduction in 2006 of the 'Respect' agenda in the light of perceptions of intergenerational social divides all signalled a degree of nervousness around the alienation of young people and the sense that education had an important role to play in helping young people feel part of and responsible for wider society. In 2006 the Education and Inspections Act reinforced policy makers sense that schools must take responsibility for teaching about and promoting community cohesion.

Since 2010 and the election of the coalition government in England, much has changed: 'in the Big Society, issues around religious and ethnic diversity in communities are neglected and community cohesion will no longer be a focus of Ofsted inspections' (Ajegbo 2011: 46). This discourse shift is reflected in the 2014 Programme of Study for Citizenship. While there is some credence given to the role of citizenship education in enabling pupils to tackle 'political and social issues critically, to weigh evidence, debate and make reasoned arguments' (DfE 2014), the content to be taught places heavy emphasis on democratic governance, the role of parliament, the rule of law, financials management and budgeting and 'the precious liberties enjoyed by the citizens of the United Kingdom' (DfE 2014): there is an undertone of compliance in the content, which invites precious little co-operation with geography other than possibly through reference to community collaboration.

What we can see from the above is how citizenship and citizenship education has been appropriated by politicians and educators of all persuasions to promote local, regional, national and global agendas as well as social, cultural, political or commercial interests. Different approaches to citizenship education place varying degrees of emphasis on civil rights and responsibilities, on compliance with and challenges to authority, and on participation in and critique of dominant practices in society (Lambert and Machon 2001).

A different way to conceptualise citizenship educations is through global citizenship. Table 9.3 shows a helpful framework for supporting the promotion of global citizenship education (Oxfam 2006). There are direct and tangible links here with the geography education that pupils should experience in schools. These would include concepts and themes such as interdependence, sustainability, justice and equity; enquiry-based learning, simulation, active and participatory learning; and skills such as decision-making, argumentation and critical thinking.

Education for global citizenship aims to help pupils develop the knowledge, understanding, skills and values they need to 'participate fully in ensuring their own, and others' wellbeing and to make a positive contribution, both locally and globally' (Oxfam 2006: 1). The goal is to stimulate thinking about the responsibilities of 'global citizens' so that young people can meet the challenges they face now and in the future.

Table 9.3 The key elements of responsible global citizenship

Knowledge and Understanding	Skills	Value and attitudes
Social justice and equity	Critical thinking	Sense of identity and self-esteem
Diversity	Ability to argue effectively	Empathy
Globalisation and interdependence	Ability to challenge injustice and inequalities	Commitment to social justice and equity
Sustainable development	Respect for people and things	Concern for the environment and commitment to sustainable development
Peace and conflict	Co-operation and conflict resolution	Belief that people can make a difference

(*Source*: *The Challenge of Globalisation: A Handbook for Teachers of 11–16 year-olds*, Oxford: Oxfam 2003: 5)

'Thinking geographically' involves exploring the spatial consequences of connections and interconnections between you, your place and other people's places (Jackson 2006). Education for global citizenship should provide pupils with opportunities to develop their critical thinking skills exploring complex and often controversial global issues such as trading systems and globalisation, poverty and inequality, resource development and sustainability. Active and participatory approaches to teaching and learning enable pupils to develop decision-making skills and understand how decisions made by others affect our lives, as well as how our decisions affect the lives of others (see Action Aid 2003)

Priorities for a critical school geography

This chapter has been concerned with how teachers and the geography curriculum can be interpreted to help pupils face the challenges that lie ahead of them more confidently and more knowledgeably: education for the future. On a number of occasions, the overlaps between the chosen headings have been evident. For example, there would be little to be gained in trying artificially to distinguish 'education for conversation' from a moral education. Though the emphasis and precise meanings are different, they are not divisible: they are both concerned and deal with human values.

One thread that runs through the whole chapter is the notion of critical thinking. There are accounts of critical theory which are now fairly accessible (Huckle 1997; Unwin 1992; Morgan and Lambert 2005), and space does not permit a full discussion here. But arising from the notion of a 'critical school geography', aspects of which we believe are helpful in envisioning a geography education for the future, Huckle presents us with a useful list of questions. We quote him at length:

> It would seem important to make more use of critical theory and pedagogy to help young people find their identity and place in the world – to find out how, why, with what, and where they belong, and to develop their sense of longing and belonging within a range of communities and collectivities.
>
> This requires us to develop curricula which help pupils answer the following types of questions:
> - How are people and geography (places, spaces and people – environment relations) being constituted by society?
> - What roles can people and geography play in constituting society?
> - How should people understand and connect with history, the economy, the state, civil society, and the rest of nature as they affect their lives and local and distant geographies?
> - What provides people with their identity, longings, sense of belonging and meaning in life?
> - What social and cultural resources can people use to extend their imaginations, to construct places and communities where they can live sustainably with each other and the rest of nature, and to develop their identities and sense of belonging and meaning in life?
> - What longings and belongings should I develop, and what kinds of society, geography, and community allow me to express my identity and desires?

Addressing such questions through socially critical pedagogy requires inputs of critical knowledge concerning the economy, the state and civil society, contemporary culture, and people-environment relations.

(Huckle 1997: 248)

The questions Huckle raises are useful and may form an element of your self-evaluation of teaching strategies, content selection and the way you planned learning for your pupils. The contents of this chapter will help you interpret the questions and respond to them. But Huckle's final statement is, arguably, the most significant part of the whole passage. Huckle implies that the specialist knowledge you bring into secondary education from your degree studies is vital. Your degree took you close to the frontier, where new knowledge and understandings, of contemporary culture, people – environment relations and such like, are made.

Summary and key points

Most people interpret 'back to basics' in terms of restricted literacies and fundamental skills, the absence of which makes continued learning next to impossible. Good teachers know about the importance of 'the basics' and pupils, too, respond well to teachers (any teachers, including those of geography) who make them into better spellers or better readers at the same time as enthusing them with interesting subject matter.

This chapter is concerned with an even more ambitious vision than making children into competent and confident processors of information. It is concerned with the real basics, by taking seriously the realisation that education has to prepare young people for the changes that will take place over their next 75 years or so. This realisation inevitably takes us into the realm of values. It takes into the consideration of wider educational goals and the need to clarify what is meant by (and what is possible by) a 'moral education'. The most difficult question of all is how to fuse aspects of moral education, those which acknowledge and respect personal autonomy and independence of mind, with an urgent and committed education for sustainability. This is, to coin a phrase, unfinished business.

Further reading

Hicks, D. (2014) Educating for Hope in Troubled Times: Climate change and the transition to a post-carbon future. London: Trentham Books.
This book explores climate change, peak oil and the limits to growth. It offers teachers practical ways to develop their understanding of and engagement with often avoided issues. The underpinning message is one of hope for the future.

Morgan, A. (2011) Morality and Geography Education. In G. Butt (ed) *Geography, Education and the Future*. London: Continuum.
This chapter explores the ethical dilemmas of teaching geography. It poses a significant challenge to all geography educators, namely to consider what we believe to be the moral purpose of geography education. There are no definitive answers, but there are arguments to consider and issues to explore.

10 Professional development

[Teachers] are sustained as active learners by their own sense of moral purposes to do the best they can under all circumstances, and by the sense of common purposes shared with colleagues. Their commitment is to their pupils, and to the subjects and topics they teach.

(Day 2004: 177)

Introduction

There are many important qualities required of teachers. On one level, good interpersonal skills, sound organisation and communication skills and, being academically well-qualified, are all important. However, we would argue that there are two particular qualities that are fundamental: first, and in the context of the discussions in this book, is a love of geography – it would be almost impossible to teach geography with any conviction without a serious commitment to the discipline; the second is respect for young people – teaching would be impossible if you couldn't value and respect for the qualities, capabilities and needs of the children in your classroom. The point here is that it is one thing *entering* the profession with both the basic and fundamental qualities in place: however, the big question is how to *sustain* them when faced with business and busy-ness of being a teacher.

In the education literature, the professional teacher is variously the *activist* professional, the *extended* professional, the *engaged* professional, the *passionate* teacher, the *committed* teacher, and more. These descriptions have much in common in terms of the messages they communicate about what it means to be a teacher. They serve as an important reminder that there is something very 'pro-active' about being a teacher, so this chapter is written in an attempt to show new geography teachers what can be done to keep themselves profession-ally alive; this chapter is intended to speak directly *to* teachers.

By the end of this chapter, you should be able to:

- identify strategies and actions you can take to develop your knowledge and understanding of geography and geography classrooms
- evaluate your progress as a teacher and explain the process of 'reflective practice'
- Understand the rage of opportunities available to support your on-going professional development.

The context of learning to teach

Morgan (2010), writing about 'What makes a "good" geography teacher', reminds us that teaching is politically and socially contextualised and what it meant to 'be a good teacher' 20–30 years ago does not necessarily apply today. Educational provision, he argues, has shifted from a system concerned with welfarist goals of social mobility and equal opportunities to the 'managerial school' focused on image, performance and accountability' (p. 31). The consequence for teaching is that being a 'good teacher' is no longer (or so it seems) about love of subject and love of children, but more about operationalising a technical-rational competency-based model of teaching where 'measurement' of teacher 'performance' is the name of the game. The performance and accountability agenda (referred to by Ball 2003 as the 'Terror of Performativity') is writ large in the professional standards for teachers (encapsulated in the document 'Teachers' Standards' (DfE 2013), and when learning to teach you will be expected to demonstrate that you have met these Standards. To a limited extent, the Standards have had some role in helping teachers analyse and identify particular strengths and weaknesses. They are in some ways ambitious and form a useful code of proficiency, but your professional development – we argue here – cannot be framed entirely in terms of the official Standards.

The Standards are, unavoidably, written at a rather general level. They are strangely 'soulless'. To the enthusiastic geography teacher they may resemble the worst kind of all-purpose guidebook, offering bland all-purpose recipes but taking the heart out of what makes the geography teacher sparkle. In making this statement, we are proposing that the geography teacher can sparkle (that is, do more than express mere competence or even proficiency), and in a different way from the history teacher, physics teacher or PE teacher.

So, 'How to maintain your sparkle?' is the big question.

Maintaining professional motivation

The opening quote to this chapter, from Chris Day's book *A Passion for Teaching*, communicates the key message of this chapter. Namely, that in order to do the best they can for pupils, teachers need to be sustained by a commitment to their own learning – this means continuing to learn about teaching and learning (this never stops), continuing to learn about their subject (here we are talking about geography) and continuing to learn about the context that frames all of their work, that is education and educational processes.

Teaching is a very demanding profession because, as one head teacher says, 'in no other job will you work on a day-by-day, moment-by-moment basis with a 1:30 ratio'.

This suggests an intensity that is possibly unique in the professions, an intensity that is both a pressure and a pleasure. Day (2004) talks about job 'satisfiers' and 'dissatisfiers' in teaching: for teachers in their first decade of teaching the most significant causes of professional *dissatisfaction* were found to be stress, fatigue, uncongenial colleagues and conflict with individuals' principles. Nais (1989, cited in Day 2004), identified professional *satisfaction* to be rooted in:

- a sense of competence
- affective rewards (seeing children progress)
- working with colleagues
- intellectual satisfaction
- feeling autonomous
- continuing personal challenge through the variety and unpredictability in the job.

The list of satisfiers is interesting (and reassuring) because it communicates that the day-to-day intensity of teaching young people does bring a host of rewards. However, maintaining this level of satisfaction is challenging and requires regular, periodic injections of support. The sources of support are varied, and are there to help you with you self-preservation (i.e. coping with the dissatisfactions) and you professional renewal (i.e. bolstering the satisfactions).

Your immediate sources of support will be from with your school – your subject mentor, your school co-ordinator, your colleagues and fellow student teachers/NQTs. In many respects, these 'on the spot' sources will help you deal with the 'dissatisfiers' at the start of your career and also be part of the satisfiers. Regular discussions about your work, regular observation and feedback will all serve to enhance your professional skills and support your ongoing professional development.

However, we would argue that, while invaluable, 'in-school support' runs the risk of being very inward looking, and in order to sustain your professional development you need to look outwards too. This means becoming part of the wider community of geography educators, be it through maintaining your membership of the Geographical Association and attending your local GA branch meetings, being part of online discussion forums, for example via the examination organisations, attending subject sessions at your local university, or staying connected with colleagues in other schools. These wider networks are vital sources of support because they too provide much-needed injections of inspiration for geography and for teaching and they ensure that you develop your professional understanding beyond the confines of one school. Crucially, these opportunities depend upon your initiative and accepting responsibility for your own professional advancement and development.

Developing your subject knowledge

It is very easy, especially during the early stages of a teaching career, to pay so much attention to planning, pedagogy and classroom organisation that issues of subject knowledge become relatively submerged. Often, you can hear some teachers declare, perhaps a touch self-righteously, that they do not 'teach geography', they 'teach children', meaning that their main interest is people, rather than the furtherance of the subject. In the end, it is plain to see that this is not a question of either/or, for no matter how 'child-centred' teachers profess themselves to be, they have to be able to teach the children *something*. And that something cannot just be anything. It needs to be worthwhile, relevant and useful, as well as enjoyable, which is why excellent specialist teachers are highly sought after in schools.

We have seen how geographers have sought to justify the subject in Chapter 1. What is at issue here is the *quality* of the subject knowledge being taught – not only its 'worthwhileness' and 'relevance' but also its accuracy, up-to-dateness and applicability. The process of evaluation at all levels of curriculum-making should ensure that the question of content selection (that is, what we decide to teach, what the key questions are and how best to arrange the main ideas or concepts) is one that is returned to regularly and is properly influenced by developments in the discipline of geography. As recent graduates, many student teachers can exert a significant influence in this respect. Online materials on subject knowledge, including guidance on curriculum-making, can be found at the GA (www.geography.org.uk). Without doubt, membership of the Geographical Association represents remarkable value through its journals and other publications and the annual conference (at Easter time), at which the largest possible collection of published sources is exhibited and is available for your inspection. Here is what one teacher, Stephen Ackeroyd, wrote in a completely unsolicited email to the GA:

> I just wanted to email to say what a fantastic journal *Geography* is, and what a vital role it plays in helping teachers (like me) continue to develop our subject knowledge. As well as developing knowledge and understanding of subject content, it introduces new perspectives on topics we teach in school (such as adaptation and resilience in the articles in Vol 99 by Andrew Kirby), enabling this to be represented in curriculum planning and therefore lessons. As such it is a vital connection between the latest developments in the subject and teaching.
>
> (Email dated 30 August 2014)

In addition, we would suggest that if you have a university local to you, then making contact with the geography department could be valuable. Many university geography departments run public seminars on a wide range of geographies and attending these is another useful way of staying connected with the discipline (and if they don't, then maybe it is worth asking them if they would). This is not because we feel that ideas from a seminar event can then be translated directly into a lesson the following morning, but more because it is an opportunity for *you* to connect with new ideas emerging at the research frontier and also still *feel* like you are a geographer. University departments are increasingly keen to develop their relationships with schools as a means of fulfilling their commitments to their local communities, so you may find university colleagues more than willing to support subject-based initiatives.

Social media can also provide mechanisms for 'staying in touch' with geography. As indicated in Chapter 6 on Resources, the 'WebWatch' pages of *GA News* are full of potential contacts, not just as ideas for teaching, but also ways to stay connected with geography.

Scholarship and teaching

Research has always had a role to play in supporting the professional development of student teachers during their initial teacher education courses. Margaret Roberts' research into geographical education can help us to see things differently and freshly, challenging assumptions and asking critical questions about purposes (Roberts 2000: 293). The role of research in supporting teaching and learning is greater than providing information about 'what works' in the classroom. Roberts (2000: 293) argues that research can 'empower teachers to construct their own understandings, to clarify their own values and to have the professional confidence to make changes in classroom practices'. Through research, geography teachers can learn more about pedagogy and ways of improving practice. Lofthouse and Leat (2006) argue that engaging with new ideas and frameworks, learning socially and getting feedback are fundamental conditions for successful professional development.

With most initial teacher education courses now incorporating elements of Master's level accreditation, student teachers not only need to engage with research but also undertake some small-scale action research as part of coursework assignments. Guidance about undertaking practitioner research as a student teacher can be found in Bartlett and Leask (2005) and for research in geography education in Lofthouse and Leat (2006). Butt (2015) has edited a collection called *MasterClass in Geography Education*, which offers a superb induction to research (and how to do research) in the field. Brooks (2010) has edited a collection of chapters full of advice called *Studying PGCE Geography at M Level*. What is interesting about this publication is that each chapter (on a range of relevant topics such as fieldwork or assessment) discusses both the theoretical and policy arguments relevant to each topic, and then concludes with a summary of a dissertation submitted to the Master's in Geography Education course at the Institute of Education (www.mageoed.webs.com). This illustrates that geography teachers are engaged in their own research and that they have ideas and findings worth disseminating.

So why study for a Master's qualification? Writing about 'the new professionalism' of teachers (a widely used political slogan from approximately the start of the twenty-first century, which seems to value technical competence), Lambert (2010) contends that a Master's qualification has a 'crucial role to play in unlocking teachers' creative potential and that this level of study is important for professional renewal and development' (p. 17). Studying for a Master's degree is, he argues, an antidote or even a form of resistance to the government's more restricted view of professionalism closely linked to performance, outcomes and managerialism. Teachers researching into their own practice are likely to be better informed and have a deep understanding of education and therefore possess a greater capacity to be 'good at what they do' (Brooks 2010). Studying at this level is not a solo venture and huge satisfaction is derived from being a member of a group of colleagues, all curious about teaching, geography and education, who want to read, discuss and think about what they do and why they do it. This kind of engagement helps to inform perspectives, develop understandings and build awareness: this enables those who practice in geography education to do so more thoughtfully and with critically reflective distance. It is these qualities that then enable teachers to participate in meaningful ways in education debates and to question the current ideologically driven orthodoxies of teaching – this is informed resistance and a highly valued aspect of any profession.

Reflecting on practice

Reflection has in some ways become something of a dread word in teacher education and training. The 'R' word is overused and it is often used carelessly, as if it were the theoretical basis for becoming a teacher. Our position is that although 'reflection' can never become a theory for teacher development (let alone training), it is nevertheless a very important activity, especially if focused and undertaken within an enabling – and challenging – framework. We think that few people can improve simply by reflection alone; indeed, we can cite cases of reflection taking on the characteristics of self-serving justification of all kinds of practice, some desirable, but some far less so. Reflection *per se* may even be a dangerous thing therefore: because it can give the illusion of intelligent action, it is in some ways more dangerous than no thought at all!

So when we urge you to be a reflective professional, it is tough thinking we have in mind. Some experts argue that the skilful teacher is one who can adapt and change through a process of reflection *in* action. That is to say, tough-minded thought leading to decisive action *during* a teaching episode. Presumably, this requires thought that occurs at an intuitive level, for classrooms are such busy places there is no time for leisurely pondering about what to do next. Good reflection-in-action results in a teacher's tactics being appropriate and effective. Presumably, reflection-in-action is therefore something that draws from experience: an experienced teacher just 'knows' that certain courses of action with Year 9 are ill-advised on a Thursday afternoon, for example.

But here again there are dangers. For example, 'Oh, you can't do that with the kids I teach' is a phrase often heard. It may be quite correct in the context of the teacher's relationship with the class and the pupils' expectations of the geography classroom – or classrooms in general! But such an attitude can often sound a life-sentence of predictable, undemanding work for the pupils, leading to those very expectations which become so difficult to change once established.

What the situation requires is something more than an immediate response dignified by the quasi-technical term 'reflection-in-action'. It requires a considered response resulting from rigorous and critical reflection *on* action. It probably also requires an attitude of mind not dissimilar to that revealed by a piece of reflective writing from a student teacher, Sophie, who showed that practising lesson observation was a key to deep deliberative thought about classrooms processes. For Sophie, 'classrooms slowly became *less familiar*'. In other words, her application of a framework (she used a model that likened classrooms to ecosystems) enabled her to 'see' things going on in a less taken for granted manner. This deepened her understanding.

Reflection as evaluation

> Evaluation is 'the making of qualitative and quantitative judgements about the value of various curriculum processes'.
>
> (Marsden 1976: 3)

We can pursue the idea of reflection *on* action further with the help of some real overheard snatches of conversation during the PGCE year. What we wish to do with these examples is show that reflection involves mental processes not dissimilar to evaluation – the intent to assess something with a view of coming to a reasonable judgement of its worth.

If we carry in our heads a simple objectives-led model of the curriculum process, then evaluation is something that is assumed to happen at or near the end of the process: you teach a series of lessons, and then you evaluate them. The fundamental flaw with this approach is that the 'judgement of value' that Marsden mentioned stands little chance of having any effect because all the curriculum decisions have already been made. The evaluation is, therefore, in terms of the current teaching and learning experiences, futile: any 'improvement in quality' is not possible – the curriculum horse has bolted!

Evaluation, just like 'formative assessment', needs to be embedded and part and parcel of our work – not something to be tacked on at the end.

Read the following, genuine short exchanges involving student teachers. In different ways, each helps to illustrate the importance of evaluation. Let us examine them, starting with the student teacher and her school mentor.

1   Student Teacher asking her mentor at the end of the lesson:
    ST: How did I do?
    M: Fine.
2   Student Teacher asking a pupil at the end of the lesson:
    ST: 'What did you do in geography today?'
    P: 'We did graphs.'
3   Student Teacher (early on during training):
    'I do not believe in group work.'

Each of these exchanges, in different ways, helps us identify why critical *evaluation* is a key component of reflection and professional development.

Quote 1

The response 'Fine' is of little use and is possibly even misleading, albeit superficially reassuring. Nevertheless, it is a common response to the question asked. Why this should be so is explained in similar terms to the way in which the colloquial 'How are you?' or 'How are you doing?' also attracts (in England) the sometimes downright false response, 'Fine'. In a way, the question is too big – some of us may be tempted to retort, 'Well where would you like me to start?' or 'How long have you got?'

Questions such as 'How did I do?' are in fact not only too broad, but also wholly undefined; to give a meaningful answer requires some criteria to help the mentor and student teacher establish their common territory, to give focus to a conversation. It is precisely this that brings the Teaching Standards to life: they provide a framework for the establishment of criteria on which to base judgement. It soon becomes apparent that in coming to a judgement, the evaluator (whether yourself or someone else, such as your tutor) has to have some kind of evidence. As in research (and evaluation is a form of research), data can be gathered effectively only after a focus has been agreed, such as what exactly is being evaluated?

The mere posing of a question such as this reveals another possible deficiency in the student teacher's wholly understandable and natural question, 'How did I do?' In addition to its need of specification (do *what* exactly?), the question also betrays a particular view of teaching which ignores its essential *relational ethic*. In other words, we not only require specification of 'the what?', but also the 'to whom?'

So, 'How did I do?' is not only vague, it may not even be the right question: a teacher may turn in a wonderful *performance*, but if the pupils fail to learn (or, more likely, we are not quite sure what they have learnt), the teaching may not have been wholly successful. One of the signs that a student teacher is moving beyond a basic level of competence (and beyond an initial focus exclusively on their own needs and their own performance, rather than the needs of their pupils and *their* performance) is a deep and textured knowledge of their pupils, and a willingness to respond to this knowledge. The appropriate question is not 'How did I do?', therefore, but possibly 'How did *they* (the pupils) do?'

Quote 2

We can develop this line of thought further by thinking about the boy's response to the snap question at the classroom door, 'What did you do in geography today?' 'We did graphs' may be wholly accurate and truthful, but disappointing to the teacher. Further probing may well result in a deeper more rounded answer, revealing a knowledge of the kind of graphs used and *what they were used for*, but without such evidence the thoughtful teacher may well conclude that the lesson had in some respects failed: geography is surely more than 'doing graphs'!

On the other hand, there are not many geography teachers who have not experienced the beguiling manner in which 'busywork' (drawing the map; completing the table, using the internet, constructing the graph) can stretch out to fill whole lessons. The problem of course is that such busy work is often mentally undemanding and fails to engage the mind. It does not stretch the intellect; it does not motivate or involve. In fact, it does little to increase pupils' intelligences and is (if repeated too often) a symptom of low expectations: collusion rather than challenge; indulgence rather than guidance.

In making judgements in order to improve quality – that is, in making an evaluation – the teacher has to probe sources of data. But in addition, the teacher needs to apply imaginative insight to the data, for they do not always speak for themselves. This takes enormous practice, and the eyes and ears of another teacher, sometimes referred to as your 'critical friend' can be vital.

Quote 3

But what of the student teacher who 'does not believe in group work'? The statement reminds us of the old Guinness advert with the slogan 'I don't like Guinness because I've never tried it!' It represents an approach to the job which may condemn this teacher to oper-ate with a very limited repertoire of techniques.

While it may be true that belief or intuition can play a significant role in motivating teachers – we need to believe in what we are doing in order to summon the relentless applica-tion that teaching requires – it is probably inappropriate when it comes to practical decisions such as which strategies to adopt in order to teach this or that. The value of evidence-based evaluation is that it invites student teachers to face the question of *choosing* the most apt teaching strategy (from a wide repertoire which they may not yet have acquired) for a given set of objectives. This may be done by trial and error, but what is not a satisfactory option is sim-ply, always, to play safe – not if we have the interests of the pupils as our main focus. Effective evaluation helps us learn what works, in what situations, and with whom. If you 'believe' that group work (or whole-class teaching for that matter) does not work, then the challenge to you as a 'learner teacher' is to *dare* to test this 'belief' – and be willing to be surprised!

Task 10.1 What is your quest?

Read the following examples of various student teachers at work.

A *Sam was a science teacher*. He was teaching the periodic table. He was concerned about the final examination and he wanted to prepare students for it. His notes were prepared on PowerPoint. As he projected them, using the 'striptease' approach, he read them out to the class. He paused occasionally for questions. There were none. I noticed that the pupils also had the notes in front of them, which they were reading. This continued. At the end of the lesson, he reminded them about the test on Friday.

B *Jan was an English teacher*. Teaching *Hamlet*, she wanted the pupils to see the interconnections between the themes of the play and learn skills of textual analysis (or as she put it, 'explication of text'). She also wanted the pupils to understand the power and beauty of the play's language. During the class, she led them through the play word by word, focusing on the themes of linguistic reflexivity and the reflexivity of the play. Among other things, the pupils were asked to do a five-page assignment on a theme in the play, and a test with questions like: Write a well-developed paragraph on the importance of language in *Hamlet*. How does Shakespeare play with language? How are words juxtaposed with actions? How does Hamlet use words to act?

C *Simon was a geography teacher*. Teaching about urban land use models, he wanted the pupils to see the connections between the general patterns and processes developed in the textbook and the knowledge they have of urban environments from their own lives. He wanted to maximise pupils' interest in the topic and geography lessons. He began without even mentioning 'urban land use'. He asked them to draw a map of their 'daily action spaces'. They were not sure, so they had to discuss what this could mean. He had the pupils comparing their maps: What did they show? What didn't they show? What did size of the action space seem to depend on? Then he asked them to analyse the maps – what kinds of spaces did they show? Did the different kinds of spaces form patterns? He then told the pupils that they were going to study the results of a number of similar analyses for whole cities in the next lesson.

1   Which of these teaching approaches 'typifies' secondary teaching, in your view?
2   Which, in your view, is most likely to engage pupils?
3   In what ways are the goals of the teachers different?
4   Is it possible to rank the three according to their effectiveness?

Discussion:

The questions are, partly, trick questions. It is important to understand that one of the objects of your initial education and training is to enable you to move beyond these and other 'templates' and to develop your own ways and means of engaging young minds.

A framework for continuous development

We end this book with reference to some current research and development in geography education which is designed precisely provide a framework for specialist teachers of geography to think creatively and critically about their work.

Geo-capabilities and professional development

The GeoCapabilities project[1] uses capabilities to express the purposes and values of geography as a school subject. The capabilities approach (see Box 10.1) is linked directly to curriculum debates concerning specialist knowledge, introducing and developing Basil Bernstein's ideas of pedagogic rights and Michael Young's notion of 'powerful knowledge' introduced briefly in Chapter 1 (see also Young et al. 2014). One important outcome of geo-capabilities is that those teaching geography have a means to communicate the value of their work in terms of how the development of geographical knowledge and understanding contributes to the educated person.

Key advocates of the geo-capabilities approach take it as axiomatic that young people's geo-capability will be enhanced through formal education. The main reason for this is that the school curriculum provides young people with access to specialised, disciplinary knowledge. Following Basil Bernstein, the capabilities approach to curriculum thinking recognises the power of specialised knowledge enabling individuals and societies to 'think the unthinkable' and 'the not yet thought'.

Thus, the geo-capabilities approach draws from the idea of 'powerful knowledge' as proposed by sociologist Michael Young as a key concept and driver of curriculum thinking and construction. Young argues that 'powerful knowledge' rests upon the distinction between two types of concept – the theoretical (disciplinary) and the everyday or common sense. He elaborates by saying that 'It is everyday concepts which constitute the experience which pupils bring to school. On the other hand, it is the theoretical concepts associated with different subjects that the curriculum can give them access to.' Acquiring 'powerful knowledge' is learning to use these theoretical concepts.

> Schools are places where the world is treated as an 'object of thought' and not as a place of experience. Subjects such as history, geography and physics are the tools that teachers have to help pupils make the step from experience to what the Russian psychologist, Vygotsky, referred to as higher forms of thought. Subjects bring together 'objects of thought' as systematically related sets of 'concepts'.
>
> (Young et al. 2014: 98)

Young and colleagues argue that everyone is entitled to be taught a subject-based curriculum to enable access to 'powerful knowledge'.

The notion of 'powerful knowledge' provides principles to underpin the design and justification of geography in the curriculum. The geo-capabilities approach does this. It takes us beyond knowledge as 'facts' and beyond the 'competences' of a skills-led curriculum.

In summary, the geo-capabilities approach argues that the 'powerful knowledge' offered by geography education consists of a deep descriptive 'world knowledge'; a theoretically informed relational understanding of people and places in the world; and a propensity and disposition to think about alternative social, economic and environmental futures (Solem et al. 2013; Lambert et al. 2015). Geo-capabilities asks teachers to consider the role of geography in helping young people reach their full human potential. Geography does not tell us how to live; but thinking geographically and developing our innate geographical imaginations can provide the intellectual means for visioning ourselves on planet earth.

Capabilities and the role of teachers

'Capabilities' expands and deepens the conceptual language of teaching and curriculum in secondary schools. 'Geo-capabilities', helps connect a progressive form of discipline-oriented teaching to broad and ambitious *educational* aims. It does this through the dialogic space offered by curriculum-making (Lambert and Biddulph 2014; Mitchell and Lambert, forthcoming). We developed the idea of curriculum-making fully in Chapter 2, where we found that powerful knowledge is not enough on its own. Following Margaret Roberts, we saw that it needs to be complemented by 'powerful pedagogies' enabling students to:

- enhance their everyday experiences by extending and modifying their personal geographies
- ask relevant geographical questions
- see the world in a variety of different ways, informed by the academic discipline
- apply what they have learnt to new situations and places
- be critical of sources of geographical information
- analyse conflicting data and different viewpoints
- consider ethical issues implicit in geographical knowledge.

Thus, in a geo-capabilities approach, what is learnt and how it is learnt matters (see also Lambert and Morgan 2010: 64). The teacher can exercise enormous influence through the choices he or she makes over what happens in lessons. The teacher *is* the curriculum-maker. The geo-capabilities approach fully endorses and values this intellectual and practical role of the teacher. It provides a means to conceptualise the process of *curriculum-making*.

For these reasons, we see geo-capabilities as a way to 'frame' the continuous professional development of teachers. Put simply, geography taught well contributes significantly to the development of educated persons. This is what we strive to do. It goes without saying that geography taught poorly may have little to contribute to helping young people develop their potentials as independently minded and autonomous individuals.

Box 10.1 Geo-capability

Geography is an ancient idea, often traced back to Ptolemy and the continuing struggle to describe and make sense of the world as our home: where human relations with the earth is taken as an object of human thought and study. As UK geographer Alastair Bonnet (2012) shows, geography is in this sense always concerned with human survival. Geography is a fundamental idea.

The role of geographical knowledge in primary and secondary education systems around the world does not always reflect this degree of significance. In some jurisdictions, geography is a specialist subject taught by specialist teachers: China, Singapore, England would be examples. In others, geography is less visible: the USA would be an example, where geography is 'hidden' within the social studies. In some, geography is being rediscovered – as in Australia where a national curriculum in geography is being introduced after years of geography being 'lost' to studies of society and environment. In others, the subject is at risk in curriculum reforms driven by notions of 'twenty-first-century skills' and generic competences.

Geo-capabilities is an international approach to articulating the aims, purposes and outcomes of an effective geography curriculum. It is derived from the 'capabilities approach' to human welfare economics, originally espoused by economist Amartya Sen and political philosopher Martha Nussbaum (see Solem et al. 2013; Lambert et al. forthcoming).

Geo-capabilities argues that human capability is deprived without the deep descriptive 'world knowledge' that enables individuals to extend their thinking beyond the immediate 'everyday' experience of their surroundings. Geographical knowledge also enables them to appreciate how places, both near and far, have come to be *and* how they might become. Thus, geographical knowledge is not *only* descriptive. It is also relational, incorporating perspectives that 'hold the world together': place and space, local and global, people and environment, physical and human.

Furthermore, in an increasingly interdependent and globalised world, and a world in which humans seem to have an increasing influence in shaping natural processes, geo-capability enhances an individual's capacity to take responsibility for their lives, to make decisions and act according to what they believe is right. Thus it is argued that 'thinking geographically' contributes to cultural, spiritual, social and moral understanding (Lambert and Morgan 2010: 54) through a comparative and critical appreciation of the world.

Rather than listing discrete skills, capability rests on acquiring and developing a range of 'functionings' that contribute to human autonomy and potential – in thought and action. Thus the 'world knowledge' envisioned by the geo-capabilities approach is not just a collection of memorised facts about locations and places, or a set of competences/skills to be achieved. It is more a way of seeing and understanding the world from multiple perspectives through the 'systematicity' provided by key geographical concepts.

Summary and key points

At the start of your first job, the pressure is on to establish yourself. Quite right too. But you should note Norman Graves's warning as you move through your NQT year, that 'consolidation does not mean stagnation' (Graves 1997: 30). Do not neglect your own professional practice, but continue the process of developing your pedagogic knowledge that you began during your initial teacher education. Professional growth requires attitude, a willingness to be flexible, imaginative and takes risks as much as knowledge, understanding and skills. We have therefore chosen to leave you with the following, timeless advice.

> Past successes pose a danger to person centred education in geography. Once something 'works' we tend to want to use the techniques over again in order to repeat the success . . . If an approach works, rejoice, but then approach the next situation freshly, on its own terms and seek a new perspective. Abandon 'techniques' that get to feel like formulas, and search for freshness as if you have had no past experience. Mistakes? Yes, mistakes must continue to be made if progress is to continue. Failure to make mistakes generally means failure to grow. Teachers must join their students in exploring all possible paths, including what may appear to be dead ends, if better paths into the future are to be found. It is amazing how often a 'safe' path becomes a blind alley and an unlikely, overgrown trail leads to a previously unknown highway.
>
> (Romey and Elberty Jnr 1984: 315)

Further reading

Butt, G. (ed.) (2015) *MasterClass in Geography Education*, London: Bloomsbury.
In some ways, this book is a 'first': the first book in geography education to purposely indict practitioners into how to contextualise, construct and go on and do meaningful research in the field. It is written in a direct and engaging manner – and even includes discussion on the ethics of research and why theory is important – even for extremely busy teachers.

Lambert, D. and Jones, M. (2013) *Debates in Geography Education*. Abingdon: Routledge.
This book, an edited collection, opens up discussions on a range of significant areas in geography education. Covering themes such as the curriculum, geographical enquiry, controversial issues and more, the book provides important and accessible insights into ongoing education debated in the subject.

Brooks, C. (2010) *Studying PGCE Geography at M Level: Reflection, Research and Writing for Professional Development*, Abingdon: Routledge.
As indicated in the chapter, this book provides useful and accessible insights into the importance, viability and processes of engaging in Master's-level thinking as a beginning teacher. The discussions about dissertation ideas and findings provide valuable insights into the myriad ways geography teachers research their work.

www.geography.org.uk/
The website of the Geographical Association, the professional association for geography teachers, with an extensive range of resources and support for professional development.

www.geography.org.uk/projects/gtip
This site has a wealth of material to support the professional development of geography teachers, especially new teachers. A suite of 'think pieces' help to introduce particular aspects of professional concern. It also has an up-to-date bibliography which overviews the current debates in research and professional literature. Finally, there is an online journal *GeogEd* designed for geography educationists – this includes new teachers – who want to develop as writers and researchers. In particular, look out for the electronic 'new teacher network'.

Note

1   GeoCapabilities is an EU Comenius funded project involving partners from Belgium, Greece, Finland, the UK and USA – including the Association of American Geographers (AAG), Eurogeo, the Geographical Association (GA). Find out more from www.geocapabilities.org).

Bibliography

Abbott, J. (1994) *Learning Makes Sense: Re-creating Education for a Changing Future*, Letchworth: Education 2000.

ACAC (1997) 'A local issue: oil spill from the Sea Empress', Key Stage 3 Optional Test and Task Materials, Geography Unit 8. Curriculum and Assessment Authority for Wales.

Adey, P. and Shayer, M. (1994) *Really Raising Standards*, London: Routledge.

Ainscow, M. and Tweedle, D. (1998) *Encouraging Classroom Success*, London: Fulton.

Ajegbo, K. (2011) 'Diversity, citizenship and cohesion', *Teaching Geography* 46-48.

Aldrich-Moodie, B. and Kwong, J. (1997) *Environmental Education*, London: Institute of Economic Affairs.

Alexander, R. (2004) 'Still no pedagogy? Principle, pragmatism and compliance in primary education', *Cambridge Journal of Education*, 3 (1): 7-33.

Alexander, R. (2011) *Towards Dialogic Teaching: Rethinking Classroom Talk* (4th edn). York: Dialogos.

Allen. T. (2011) *Virtual Water: Tackling the Threat to Our Planet's Most Precious Resource*, London: I.B. Tauris and Co.

Allinson, C. W. and Hayes, J. (1996) 'The Cognitive Style Index: a measure of intuition analysis for organisational research, *Journal of Management Studies*, 33 (1): 119-135.

Antonis A., Klanten, R. S., Ehmann, H. and Hellige, H. (2013) *The World According to Illustrators and Storytellers*. Berlin: Gestalten.

Ausubel, D. P. (1968) *Educational Psychology: A Cognitive View*, New York: Holt, Rinehart and Winston.

Author Unknown: *A Tour of the Motherland: the First Geography of the British Isles*, Exeter: A Wheaton and Co. Ltd.

Bailey, P. (1991) *Securing the Place of Geography in the National Curriculum of English and Welsh Schools: A Study in the Politics and Practicalities of Curriculum Reform*, Sheffield: The Geographical Association.

Bailey, P. and Binns, T. (eds) (1987) *A Case for Geography*, Sheffield: The Geographical Association.

Bailey, P. and Fox, P. (1996) *Teaching and Learning with Maps*, in P. Bailey and P. Fox (eds), *Geography Teachers Handbook*, Sheffield: The Geographical Association.

Balderstone, D. (1994) 'An evaluation of the impact of a range of learning experiences on concept acquisition in physical geography', Unpublished MA dissertation, Institute of Education, University of London.

Balderstone, D. (2000) 'Beyond testing: some issues in teacher assessment in geography', in J. Hopkin, S. Telfer and G. Butt (eds), *Assessment Working*, Sheffield: The Geographical Association.

Balderstone, D. (ed.) (2006) *Secondary Geography Handbook*, Sheffield: The Geographical Association.

Balderstone, D. (2006) 'What's the point of learning geography?', Chapter 1 in D. Balderstone (ed.), *Secondary Geography Handbook*, Sheffield: The Geographical Association.

Balderstone, D. and Lambert, D. (1992) *Assessment Matters*, Sheffield: The Geographical Association.

Balderstone, D. and Lambert, D. (2006) 'Sustaining school geography', Chapter 42 in D. Balderstone (ed.) *Secondary Geography Handbook*, Sheffield: The Geographical Association.

Balderstone, D. and Payne, G. (1992) *People and Cities,* Oxford: Heinemann.

Balderstone, D., Dow, M. and Henn, V. (2006) *'Geography and students with EAL',* Chapter 27 in D. Balderstone (ed.) *Secondary Geography Handbook,* Sheffield: The Geographical Association.

Balderstone, D. and King, S. (2004) 'Preparing pupils for public examinations: developing study skills', in S. Capel, R. Heilbronn, M. Leask and Turner, T. (eds), *Starting to Teach in the Secondary School,* London: Routledge.

Bale, J. (1987) *Geography in the Primary School,* London: Routledge and Kegan Paul.

Ball, S. (2003) 'The teacher's soul and the terrors of performativity', *Journal of Education Policy* 18(2): 215-228.

Ball, S. (2012) *Can Education Change Society.* Oxford: Routledge.

Ball, S. (2013) *The Education Debate* (2nd edn) Bristol: Policy Press.

Barlow, A., Potts, R. and Whittle, S. (2010) 'Messy maps and messy spaces', *Primary Geographer* 73(1): 14-15.

Barnes, D. and Todd, F. (1977) *Communication and Learning in Small Groups,* London: Routledge.

Barnes, D., Johnson, G., Jordan, S., Layton, D., Medway, P. and Yeoman, D. (1987) *The TVEI Curriculum 14-16: An Interim Report Based on Case Studies in Twelve Schools,* Leeds: University of Leeds.

Barnes, T. and Duncan, J. (1992) *Writing Worlds,* London: Routledge.

Barnett, M., Kent, A. and Milton, M. (eds) (1995) *Images of earth: A Teacher's Guide to Remote Sensing in Geography,* Sheffield: The Geographical Association.

Barnett, M. and Milton, M. (1995) 'Satellite Images and IT capability', *Teaching Geography* 20(3):142-143.

Barnett, R. (2000) 'Supercomplexity and the curriculum', *Studies in Higher Education,* 25(3): 255-265.

Bartlett, S. and Leask, M. (2005) *'Improving your teaching: An introduction to practitioner research and reflective practice',* unit 5.4 in S. Capel, M. Leask and T. Turner (eds), *Learning to Teach in the Secondary School: A Companion to School Experience,* London: Routledge.

Bates, B. and Wolton, M. (1993) *Guidelines for Secondary Schools for Effective Differentiation in the Classroom,* Essex County Council Education Department.

Battersby, J. (1995) *Teaching Geography at Key Stage 3,* Cambridge: Chris Kington Publishing. Battersby, J. (1997) 'Differentiation in teaching and learning geography', in D. Tilbury and M. Williams (eds), *Teaching and Learning Geography,* London: Routledge.

Battersby, J. and Hornby, N. (2006) *'Inspiring disaffected students',* Chapter 31 in D. Balderstone (ed.), *Secondary Geography Handbook,* Sheffield: The Geographical Association.

Battersby, J., Webster, A. and Younger, M. (1995) *The Case Study in GCSE Geography: Experiences from the Avery Hill Project,* Cardiff: Welsh Joint Education Committee.

Bayliss, T. and Collins, L. (2006) 'Invigorating teaching with interactive whiteboards', *Teaching Geography* 31(3): 133-5.

Bayliss, T. and Collins, L. (2007) 'Invigorating teaching with interactive whiteboards: case studies 3-6', in *Teaching Geography* 32(1).

Bayliss, T. and Collins, L. (2007) 'Invigorating teaching with interactive whiteboards: case studies 7-10', in *Teaching Geography* 32(2).

BBC News (1 July 2014) 'International GCSEs to be axed from school league tables'. Available at www.bbc.co.uk/news/education-28108153 [accessed 19 August 2014).

Beddis, R. (1983) 'Geographical education since 1960: a personal view', in J. Huckle (ed.), *Geographical Education: Reflection and Action,* Oxford: Oxford University Press, pp. 10-19.

Bell, D. (2005) 'The value and importance of geography', *Teaching Geography* 30(1): 12-13.

Bennett, N. (1995) 'Managing learning through group work', in C. Desforges (ed.), *An Introduction to Teaching: Psychological Perspectives,* Oxford: Blackwell.

Bennett, N. (2011) 'Formative assessment: a critical review', *Assessment in Education: Principles, Policy and Practice* 18(1): 5-25.

Bennett, N. and Dunne, E. (1992) *Managing Classroom Groups,* London: Simon and Schuster.

Bennett, R. and Leask, M. (2005) 'Teaching and learning with ICT: an introduction', Unit 1.4 in S. Capel, M. Leask and T. Turner (eds), *Learning to Teach in the Secondary School: A Companion to School Experience*, Abingdon: Routledge.

Bennetts, T. (1995) 'Continuity and progression', *Teaching Geography* 20(2): 75-79.

Bennetts, T. (1996) 'Progression and differentiation', in P. Bailey and P. Fox (eds), *Geography Teachers' Handbook*, Sheffield: The Geographical Association.

Bennetts, T. (2005) 'The links between understanding, progression and assessment in the secondary geography curriculum', *Geography* 90(2): 152-170.

BFI (2000) *Moving Images in the classroom: A Secondary Teacher's Guide to Using Film and Television*, London: British Film Institute.

Biddulph, M. (2013) 'Where is the curriculum created?' in D. Lambert and M. Jones (eds), *Debates in Geography Education*, Abingdon: Routledge.

Biddulph, M. (2014) 'What kind of curriculum do we want?' *Teaching Geography* 39(1): 6-9.

Biddulph, M. and Bright, G. (2003) *Theory into Practice: Dramatically Good Geography*, Sheffield: The Geographical Association.

Biddulph, M. and Clarke, J. (2006) 'Theatrical geography', in D. Balderstone (ed.), *Secondary Geography Handbook*, Sheffield: Geographical Association.

Biddulph, M. and Firth, R. (2009) 'Whose life is it anyway?', in M. Mitchell (ed.), *Living Geographies*, Cambridge: Chris Kington Publishing.

Biggs, J. and Moore, P. (1993) *The Process of Learning*, Sydney: Prentice Hall.

Black, P. (2004) 'Formative assessment: Promises or problems?'

Black, P. and Wiliam, D. (1998a) 'Assessment and Classroom Learning', *Assessment in Education* 5(1):7-74.

Black, P. and Wiliam, D. (1998b) *Inside the Black Box: Raising Standards Through Classroom Assessment*, London: School of Education, Kings College.

Black, P., Harrison, C., Lee, C., Marshall, B. and Wiliam, D. (2002) *Working Inside the Black Box: Assessment for Learning in the Classroom*, London: School of Education, Kings College.

Black, P., Harrison, C., Lee, C., Marshall, B. and Wiliam, D. (2003) *Assessment for Learning: Putting it into Practice*, Milton Keynes: Open University Press.

Bland, K., Chambers, W., Donert, K. and Thomas, T. (1996) 'Fieldwork', in P. Bailey and P. Fox (eds), *Geography Teachers' Handbook*, Sheffield: The Geographical Association.

Bloom's Theory of Learning Domains: Available at www.nwlink.com/~donclark/hrd /bloom.html [accessed 20 August 2014].

Blyth, A., Cooper, H., Derricott, R., Elliot, G., Sumner, H. and Waplington, A. (1976) *Place, Time and Society 8-13: Curriculum Planning in History, Geography and Social Science*, Bristol: Collins-ESL.

Boardman, D. (1983) *Graphicacy and Geography Teaching*, London: Croom Helm.

Boardman, D. (1985) 'Spatial concept development and primary school mapwork', in D. Boardman (ed.), *New Directions in Geographical Education*, London: Falmer Press.

Boardman, D. (ed.) (1985) *New Directions in Geographical Education*, Lewes: Falmer.

Boardman, D. (1986) 'Planning, teaching and learning', in D. Boardman (ed.), *Handbook for Geography Teachers*, Sheffield: The Geographical Association.

Boardman, D. (1987) 'Maps and mapwork', in D. Boardman (ed.) *Handbook for Geography Teachers*, Sheffield: The Geographical Association.

Boardman, D. (1988) *The Impact of a Curriculum Project: Geography for the Young School Leaver*, *Educational Review*, Occasional Publications, Birmingham: University of Birmingham.

Boardman, D. (1989) 'The development of graphicacy: children's understanding of maps', *Geography* 74(4): 321-331.

Boardman, D. (1996) 'Learning with Ordnance Survey maps', in P. Bailey and P. Fox (eds), *The Geography Teachers' Handbook*, Sheffield: The Geographical Association.

Boardman, D. and Towner, E. (1980) 'Problems of correlating air photographs with Ordnance Survey maps', *Teaching Geography*, 6(2): 76-79.

Bonnett, A. (2012) 'Geography: what's the big idea?', *Geography* 97(1): 39-41.

Bradley-Smith, P. (2002) Closing the gender gap in geography: update 2 - invisible girls, *Teaching Geography*, 27 (3): 143-146.

Brooks, Clare (2003) 'Investigating the geography behind the news', *Teaching Geography*, 28(2): 70-74.

Brooks, C. (2006) *'Cracking the code - numeracy and geography'*, Chapter 12 in Balderstone, D.(ed.), *Secondary Geography Handbook*, Sheffield: The Geographical Association.

Brooks, C. (2006) *Geographical Knowledge and Teaching Geography*, Institute of Education, University of London: eprints.ioe.ac.uk/273/1/Brooks2006Geographical353.pdf [accessed 23 July, 2014].

Brooks, C. (2010) 'Introduction', in C. Brooks (ed.), *Studying PGCE Geography at M Level: Reflection, Research and Writing for Professional Development*. Oxford: Routledge.

Brooks, C. (2013) 'Conceptual development in school geography. In D. Lambert and M. Jones (eds) *Debates in Geography Education*, London: Routledge.

Brooks, C. and Morgan, A. (2006) *Theory into Practice: Cases and Places*, Sheffield: TheGeographical Association.

Brooks, J. and Lucas, N. (2004) 'The school sixth form and the growth of vocational qualifications', in Brough, E. (1983) 'Geography through art', in J. Huckle (ed.), *Geographical Education:Reflection and Action*, Oxford: Oxford University Press.

Brundtland Commission, The (1987) *Our Common Future, Report of the World Commission on Environment and Development*, United Nations World Commission on Environment and Development. Published as Annex to General Assembly document A/42/427.

Bruner, J. (1960) *The Process of Education*, Cambridge, MA: Harvard University Press.

Bruner, J. (1966) *Towards a Theory of Instruction*, Boston, MA: Harvard University Press.

Bruner, J. (1996) *The Culture of Education*. Cambridge, MA: Harvard University Press.

Bruner, J. and Haste, H. (1987) *Making Sense*, London: Methuen.

Burn, A. (2005) 'Teaching and learning with digital video', in M. Leask and N. Pachler (eds), *Learning to Teach using ICT in the Secondary School*, London: Routledge.

Burton, D. and Bartlett, S. (2004) *Practitioner Research for Teachers*, London: Paul Chapman Publishing.

Butler, R. (1988) 'Enhancing intrinsic motivation: the effects of task-involving and ego-involving evaluation on interest and performance', *British Journal of Educational Psychology* 58: 1-14.

Butt, G. (1990) 'Political understanding through geography teaching', *Teaching Geography* 15(2): 62-65.

Butt, G. (1991) 'Have we got a video today?', *Teaching Geography* 16(2): 51-55.

Butt, G. (1993) 'The effects of "audience centred" teaching on children's writing in geography', *International Research in Geographical and Environmental Education*, 2(10): 11-24.

Butt, G. (1997) 'Language and learning in geography', in D. Tilbury and M. Williams (eds), *Teaching and Learning in Geography*, London: Routledge.

Butt, G. (2001) *Theory into Practice: Extending Writing Skills*, Sheffield: The Geographical Association.

Butt, G. (2002) *Reflective Teaching of Geography 11-18*, London: Continuum.

Butt, G. (2015) *MasterClass in Geography Education*, London: Bloomsbury.

Butt, G. and Collins, G. (2013) 'Can geography cross the divide?', in D. Lambert and M. Jones (eds),*Debates in Geography Education*, London: Routledge.

Butt, G. and Lambert, D. (1996a) 'Geography assessment and Key Stage 3 textbooks', *Teaching Geography* 22(3): 146-147.

Butt, G. and Lambert, D. (1996b) 'The role of textbooks: an assessment issue?', *Teaching Geography* 21(4): 202-203.

Butt, G. and Lambert, D. (2013) 'International perspectives on the future of geography education: an analysis of national curricula and standards', *International Research in Geographical and Environmental Education*, 23(1): Special Issue.

Butt, G., Bradley-Smith, P. and Wood, P. (2006) 'Gender issues in geography: why do girls perform better than boys?' in D. Balderstone (ed.) *Secondary Geography Handbook*. Sheffield: Geographical Association.

Butt, G., Lambert, D. and Telfer, S. (1995) *Assessment Works*, Sheffield: The Geographical Association

Calder, M. and Smith, R. (1993) 'Introduction to development education', in J. Fien (ed.), *Environmental Education: A Pathway to Sustainability*, Geelong: Deakin University Press.

Cambridge International Examinations (2013) *Syllabus: Cambridge IGCSE: Subject 460*, Cambridge: Cambridge International Examinations.

Capel, S., Heilbronn, R., Leask, M. and Turner, T. (eds) *Starting to Teach in the Secondary School: A Companion for the Newly Qualified Teacher*, London: Routledge.

Capel, S., Leask, M. and Turner, T. (2005) *Learning to Teach in the Secondary School: A Companion to School Experience*, London: Routledge.

Capra, F. (1996) *The Web of Life*, London: HarperCollins.

Carpenter, B., Ashdown, R. and Bovair, K. (1996) *Enabling Access: Effective Teaching and Learning for Pupils with Learning Difficulties*, London: David Fulton.

Carter, R. (ed.) (1991) *Talking about Geography: The Work of the Geography Teachers in the National Oracy Project*, Sheffield: The Geographical Association.

Castree, N., Fuller, D. and Lambert, D. (2007) 'Geography without borders', *Transactions of the Institute of British Geographers* 32(2): 129–132.

Castree, N. (2015) Anthropocene: a primer for geographers, *Geography*, 100, 2.

Catling, S (1978) The child's spatial conception and geographic education, *The Journal of Geography*, 77(1): 24-28.

Caton, D. (2006) '*Real world learning through geographical fieldwork*', Chapter 6 in D. Balderstone (ed.) *Secondary Geography Handbook*, Sheffield: The Geographical Association.

Caton, D. (2006) *Theory into Practice: New Approaches to Fieldwork*, Sheffield: The Geographical Association.

Chambliss, M. and Calfree, R. (1998) *Textbooks for Learning: Nurturing Children's Minds*, Oxford: Blackwell.

Chapman, J. (1998) 'We can save the world!', *Primary Geographer*, 32 (January): 18-19.

Chapman, R. and Digby, B. (2006) '"Gotta get thru this" – GCSE examinations', Chapter 37 in D. Balderstone (ed.), *Secondary Geography Handbook*, Sheffield: The Geographical Association.

Charlton, M., Lapthorn, N., Moncrieff, D. and Turney, A. (2012) 'Changing coastal fieldwork', *Teaching Geography* 37(3): 102–103.

Chorley, R. J. and Haggett, P. (eds) (1965) *Frontiers in Geographical Teaching*, London: Methuen.

Chorley, R. J. and Haggett, P. (1967) *Models in Geography*, London: Methuen.

Christian Aid (1986) *The Trading Game*, London: Christian Aid.

Clark, C. M. and Peterson, P. L. (1986) '*Teachers' thought processes*', in M. Whittrock (ed.), *Handbook of Research on Teaching*, New York: Macmillan, pp. 255-296.

Clemens, R., Parr, K. and Wilkinson, M. (2013) 'Using geographical games to investigate "our place"', *Teaching Geography* 63-65.

Coffield, F., Moseley, D., Hall, E., Ecclestone, K. (2004) *Learning Styles and Pedagogy in Post-16 Learning: A Systematic and Critical Review*, Learning and Skills Research Centre, Trowbridge:Cromwell Press.

Connolly, J. 1993, 'Gender balanced geography: have we got it right yet?', *Teaching Geography* 16(2): 61-64.

Cook, I., Evans, J., Griffiths, H., Mayblin, L., Payne, B., and Roberts, D. (2007) 'Made in . . . ? Appreciating the everyday geographies of connected lives', *Teaching Geography*, 32(2): 80–83.

Corney, G. (1985) *Geography, Schools and Industry*, Sheffield: The Geographical Association.

Corney, G. (1991) *Teaching Economic Understanding Through Geography*, Sheffield: The Geographical Association.

Corney, G. (1992) *Teaching Economic Understanding Through Geography*, Sheffield: The Geographical Association.

Cowie, H. and Ruddock, J. (1988) *Cooperative Group Work: An Overview*, London: BP Educational Service.

Coyle, D. (2007) 'Content and language integrated learning: towards a connected research agenda for CLIL pedagogies', *International Journal of Bilingual Education and Bilingualism* 10(5): 543–562.

Coyle, D., Hood, P. and Marsh, D. (2010) *CLIL: Content and Language Integrated Learning*, Cambridge: Cambridge University Press.

Curtis, P. (2008) Children being failed by progressive teaching, say Tories. *The Guardian newspaper*, 9 May 2008. Available at: http://www.theguardian.com/education/2008/may/09/schools.uk [accessed 2 March 2015].

Daugherty, R. (1996) 'Defining and measuring progression in geographical education', in E. Rawling and R. Daugherty (eds) *Geography in the Twenty-First Century*. Chichester: Wiley.

Davidson, G. (1996) 'Using Ofsted criteria to develop classroom practice', *Teaching Geography* 21(1): 11–14.

Davidson, G. (2006) 'Start at the beginning', *Teaching Geography* 31(3): 105–108.

Davies, P. (1990) *Differentiation in the Classroom and in the Examination Room: Achieving the Impossible?*, Cardiff: Welsh Joint Education Committee.

Davis, A. (1998) *The Limits of Educational Assessment*, Oxford: Blackwell.

Day, C. (2004) *A Passion for Teaching*. Oxford: Routledge Falmer.

Dearing, R. (1995) *Review of 16–19 Qualifications: Interim Report*, London: SCAA.

Dennison, B. and Kirk, R. (1990) *Do, Review, Learn, Apply: A Simple Guide to Experiential Learning*, Oxford: Basil Blackwell.

Derry, J. (2013) *Vygotsky: Philosophy and Education*, Oxford: Wiley-Blackwell.

DES (Department of Education and Science, now DfEE, Department for Education and Employment) (1975) *Language Across the Curriculum* (the Bullock Report), London: HMSO.

DES (1990) *Geography for Ages 5–16: Final Report of the Geography Working Group*, London: HMSO.

DES (1991) *Geography in the National Curriculum (England)*, London: HMSO.

DES/WO (1988) *Task Group on Assessment and Testing: A Report*, London: HMSO.

Desforges, C. (ed.) (1995) *An Introduction to Teaching: Psychological Perspectives*, Oxford: Blackwell.

DfE *National Curriculum in England: framework for key stages 1 to 4. London HMSO.* Available at https://www.gov.uk/government/publications/national-curriculum-in-england-framework-for-key-stages-1-to-4/the-national-curriculum-in-england-framework-for-key-stages-1-to-4 [accessed January 29 2014].

DfE (2010) *The Importance of Teaching: The Schools White Paper*, London: DfE.

DfE (2011) 'Review of the National Curriculum: report on subject breadth in international jurisdictions', Research Report DFE-RR178a. Available at https://www.gov.uk/government/uploads/system/uploads/attachment_data/file/197636/DFE-RR178a.pdf.

DfE/QCA (1999) *The National Curriculum Handbook for Primary/Secondary Teachers in England*, London: HMSO.

DfE (2011, updated 2013) *Teachers' Standards: Guidance for School Leaders, School Staff and Governing Bodies*, London: DfE.

DfE (2013) *Statutory Guidance: National Curriculum in England: Framework for Key Stages 1 to 4*. HMSO. Available at: https://www.gov.uk/government/publications/national-curriculum-in-england-framework-for-key-stages-1-to-4/the-national-curriculum-in-england-framework-for-key-stages-1-to-4 [accessed 29 May 2014].

DfE (2013) *Geography GCSE Subject Content and Assessment Objectives.* Crown Copyright.

DfE (2013) *Teachers' Standards.* London: DfE.

DfE (2014) *GCSE Subject Criteria for Geography.* Crown Copyright. Available at: https://www.gov.uk/government/uploads/system/uploads/attachment_data/file/301253/GCSE_geography.pdf [accessed 4 June 2014].

DfE (2014) *Proposed GCE AS and A Level Subject Content for Geography.* Crown Copyright.

DfE (2014) *Citizenship Programmes of Study: Key Stages 3 and 4 National Curriculum in England,*London: DfE.

DfEE (1995) *Geography in the National Curriculum,* London: HMSO.

DfEE (1998) *Health and safety of Pupils on Educational Visits,* London: DfEE.

DfEE (2000) *Research into Teacher Effectiveness: A model of Teacher Effectiveness,* London: Hay McBer/DfEE.

DfES (2003) *Every Child Matters.* Crown Copyright, London: HMSO.

DfES (2000) *National Numeracy Strategy,* London: DfES.

DfES (2001) *National Literacy Strategy,* London: DfES.

DfES (2001) *National Key Sage 3 Strategy.* London: DfES.

DfES (2002) *Key Stage 3 National Strategy,* London: DfES.

DfES (2002) *Transforming the Way We Learn: A Vision for the Future of ICT in Schools,* London: DfES.

DfES (2002) *Literacy in Geography,* London: DfES.

DfES (2004) *ICT across the Curriculum: ICT in Geography,* Key Stage 3 National Strategy, London: DfES.

DfES (2005) *14-19 Education and Skills (White Paper),* London: DfES.

Dickenson, C. and Wright, J. (1993) *Differentiation: A Practical Handbook of Classroom Strategies,* Coventry: NCET.

Digby, B. (1997) *Global Futures,* London: Heinemann.

Digimap for schools. Available at: http://digimapforschools.edina.ac.uk/cosmo/home?page=login [accessed 26 July 2014].

Dilkes, J. and Nicholls, M. (eds) (1988) *Low Attainers and the Teaching of Geography,* The Geographical Association and the National Association for Remedial Education.

Donaldson, M. (1978) *Children's Minds,* London: HarperCollins.

Dorling, D. and Fairbairn, D. (1997) *Mapping: Ways of Representing the World,* Harlow, Essex: Longman.

Dorling, D. (2011) *Injustice: Why social Inequality Persists.* Bristol: Policy Press.

Dorling, D. (2012) 'Mapping change and changing mapping', *Teaching Geography* 37(3): 94-8.

Dove, J. (1999) 'Immaculate misconceptions', in *Theory into Practice: Professional Development for Geography Teachers,* Sheffield: The Geographical Association.

Dove, J. and Owen, D. (1991) 'Teaching geography through music and sand', *Teaching Geography* 16(1): 3-6.

Dove, J. and Tinney, S. (1992) 'Using classroom display as a record of achievement', *Teaching Geography* 17(2): 57-60.Dowgill, P. (1998) 'Pupils' conceptions of geography and learning in geography', unpublished Ph.D. thesis, University of London Institute of Education.

Dowgill, P. and Lambert, D. (1992) 'Cultural literacy and school geography', *Geography,* 77(2): 143-152.

Downs, R. and DeSouza, A. (2006) *Learning to Think Spatially,* National Research Council (ed.), Washington DC: National Academies Press.

Dowson, J. (1995) The school curriculum', in S. Capel, M. Leask and T. Turner (eds), *Learning to Teach in the Secondary School,* London: Routledge.

Durbin, C. (1995) 'Using televisual resources in geography', *Teaching Geography* 20(3): 118-121.

Durbin, C. (1996) 'Teaching Geography with televisual resources', in P. Bailey and P. Fox (eds), *The Geography Teachers' Handbook,* Sheffield: The Geographical Association.

Durbin, C. (2006) 'Media literacy and geographical imaginations', Chapter 19 in D. Balderstone (ed.),*Secondary Geography Handbook,* Sheffield: The Geographical Association.

Durbin, C. (date unknown) *A Model for Geographical Enquiry.* Available at www.sln.org.uk/geography [accessed 13 August 2014].

Dweck, C. (2000) *Self-Theories: Their Role in Motivation, Personality and Development,* London: Taylor and Francis.

Edwards, G. (1996) 'Alternative speculations on geographical futures: towards a postmodern perspective', *Geography* 81(3): 217–224.

Edwards, R. (1995) 'From the "box" to the classroom', *Teaching Geography* 20(4): 176–178.

Elliott, G. (1975) 'Evaluating classroom games and simulations', *Classroom Geography* October, 3–5.

Elwood, J. and Lundy, L. (2010) 'Revisioning assessment through children's rights approach: implications for policy, process and practice', *Research Papers in Education* 25(3): 335–353.

Enright, N., Flook, A. and Habgood, C. (2006) '*Gifted young geographers*', Chapter 28 in D. Balderstone (ed.), *Secondary Geography Handbook,* Sheffield: The Geographical Association.

Evans, L. and Smith, D. (2006) '*Inclusive geography*', Chapter 26 in D. Balderstone (ed.), *Secondary Geography Handbook,* Sheffield: The Geographical Association.

Everson, J. and Fitzgerald, B. (1969) *Settlement Patterns,* London: Longman.

EXEL (1995) *Writing Frames,* Exeter: University of Exeter School of Education.

Fairgrieve, J. (1926) *Geography in School,* London: University of London Press.

Fargher, M. (2013) 'Geographic information – How could it be used?', in D. Lambert and M. Jones (eds), *Debates in Geography Education,* London: Routledge.

Ferretti, J. (2009) 'Effective use of visual resources in the classroom', *Teaching Geography,* 34(3): 1–8.

Ferretti, J. (2013) 'What ever happened to the enquiry approach', in D. Lambert and M. Jones (eds), *Debates in Geography Education,* London: Routledge.

Field Studies Council (2004) *A Review of Research on Outdoor Learning,* nfer/Kings College, London.

Fielding, M. (1992) 'Descriptions of learning styles', unpublished INSET resource.

Fien, J. (1993) *Education for the Environment: Critical Curriculum Theorizing and Environmental Education,* Geelong: Deakin University Press.

Fien, J. (ed.) (1993) *Environmental Education: A Pathway to Sustainability,* Geelong: Deakin University Press.

Fien, J. and Gerber, R. (1988) *Teaching Geography for a Better World,* Harlow, Essex: Longman

Fien, J., Gerber, R. and Wilson, P. (eds) (1984) *The Geography Teachers' Guide to the Classroom,* Melbourne: Macmillan.

Fien, J. and Slater, F. (1981) 'Four strategies for values education in geography', *Geographical Education* 4(1): 39–52.

Fein, J. and Slater, F. (1985) 'Four strategies for values in education in geography', in D. Boardman (ed.), *New Directions in Geographical Education,* Lewes: Falmer.

Firth, R. (2011) 'Making geography visible as an object of study in the secondary school curriculum', *Curriculum Journal,* 22(3): 289–316.

Firth, R. (2013) 'What constitutes knowledge in geography', in D. Lambert and Jones, M. (eds),*Debates in Geography Education,* London: Routledge.

Firth, R. (2012) 'Disordering the Coalition government's "new" approach to curriculum design and knowledge: the matter of the discipline', *Geograpahy* 97(2): 86–94.

Firth, R. and Biddulph, M. (2009) 'Whose life is it anyway? young people's' geographies', in D. Mitchell (ed.) *Living Geography: exciting futures for teachers and students.* Cambridge: Chris Kington Publishing.

Fisher, S. and Hicks, D. (1985) *World Studies 8-13: A Teacher's Handbook,* Harlow, Essex: Oliver and Boyd.

Fisher, T. (1998) *Developing as a Geography Teacher,* Cambridge: Chris Kington Publishing.

Follow the Things: available at www.followthethings.com/ [accessed 29 August 2014].

Franson, C. (2011) *Bilingualism and Second Language Acquisition*. Available from: National Association for Language Development in the Curriculum (NALDIC). Available at: http://www.naldic.org.uk/eal-initial-teacher-education/resources/ite-archive-bilingualismssed [accessed 5 March 2015].

Freeman, D. (1997) 'Using information technology and new technologies in geography', in D. Tilbury and M. Williams (eds), *Teaching and Learning Geography*, London: Routledge, pp. 202–217.

Freeman, D. (2005) 'GIS in geography teaching and learning', *GTIP Think Pieces*, Sheffield: The Geographical Association. www.geography.org.uk/gtip

Freeman, D. and Hare, C. (2006) 'Collaboration, collaboration, collaboration', Chapter 25 in D. Balderstone (ed.), *Secondary Geography Handbook*, Sheffield: The GeographicalAssociation.

Fry, P. (1987) 'Dealing with political bias through geographical education', unpublished MA dissertation, Institute of Education: University of London.

Fuller, D. and Askins, K. (2010) 'Public geographies II: being organic', *Progress in Human Geography* 34(5): 654–667.

GA (Geographical Association) (2009) 'A different view: world issues survey', Available at: www.geography.org.uk/download/GA_MC_PR_ADifferentView.pdf [accessed 10 August, 2014].

GA/FSC (2005) *Setting the Standards for Safe, Successful Fieldwork for All*, Sheffield: The Geographical Association.

GA/NCET (1992) *Geography, IT and the National Curriculum*, Sheffield: The GeographicalAssociation.

GA. Curriculum Making Artefact. Available at: www.geography.org.uk/cpdevents/curriculum/curriculummaking/artefact/#14155[accessed 13 August 2014].

Gagné, F. (2003) 'Transforming gifts into talents: the DMGT as a developmental theory', in N. Colangelo and G. A. Davis (eds), *Handbook of Gifted Education* (3rd edn), Boston: Allyn and Bacon.

Gagne, R. (1965) *The Conditions of Learning*, New York: Holt, Rinehart and Winston.

George, D. (1992) *The Challenge of the Able Child*, Oxford: David Fulton Publishers.

George, D. (1997) *The Challenge of the Able Child*, 2nd edn, London: David Fulton Publishers.

George, J., Clarke, J., Davies, P. and Durbin, C. (2002) 'Helping students to get better at geographical writing', *Teaching Geography* 27(4): 156–160.

Gerber, R. (1981) 'Young children's understanding of the elements of maps', *Teaching Geography* 6(3): 128–133.

Gerber, R. and Wilson, P. (1984) 'Maps in the geography classroom', in J. Fien, R. Gerberand P. Wilson (eds), *The Geography Teachers Guide to the Classroom*, Melbourne: Macmillan, pp. 146–157.

Gerber, R. (2001) 'The state of geographical education around the world', *International Research in Geographical and Environmental Education* 10(4): 349–362.

Gersmehl, P. and Gersmehl, C. (2006) Wanted: a concise list of neurologically defensible and assessable spatial thinking skills', *Research in Geographic Education* 8: 5-38.

Ghaye, A. and Robinson, E. (1989) 'Concept maps and children's thinking: a constructivist approach', in F. Slater (ed.), *Language and Learning in the Teaching of Geography*, London: Routledge.

Gibran, K. (1926) *The Prophet*, London: Heinemann.

Gilbert, C. (2012) *Towards a Self-Improving System: The Role of School Accountability*, National College for School Leadership.

Ginnis, P. (2002) *The Teacher's Toolkit: Raise Achievement with Strategies for Every Learner*, Carmarthen: Crown House Publishing.

Gipps, C. (1994) *Beyond Testing: Towards a Theory of Educational Assessment*, London: Falmer Press.

Goldstein, G. (1997) *Information Technology in English Schools: A Commentary on Inspection Findings 1995-6*, London: HMSO.

Good, T. L. and Brophy, J. E. (1991) *Looking in Classrooms*, New York: HarperCollins.

Goodchild, M. (2009) 'NeoGeography and the nature of geographic expertise', *Journal of Location Based Services* 3(2): 82–96.

Google earth, *Track Earthquakes in Real time*. Available at: Google earth for Educators. http://sitescontent.google.com/google-earth-for-educators/ [accessed 3 August 2014].

Google Ocean, available at: www.google.co.uk/earth/explore/showcase/ocean.html [accessed 27 July 2014].

Graves, N. (1975) *Geography in Education*, London: Heinemann.

Graves, N. (1979) *Curriculum Planning in Geography*, London: Heinemann.

Graves, N. (1997) 'Geographical education in the 1990s', in D. Tilbury and M. Williams (eds), *Teaching and Learning Geography*, London: Routledge.

Graves, N. J. (ed.) (1982) *The New UNESCO Source Book for Geography Teaching*, London: UNESCO Press.

Grenyer, N. (1985) *Investigating Physical Geography*, Oxford: Oxford University Press.

Grenyer, N. (1986) *Geography for Gifted Pupils*, London: School Curriculum Development Committee.

Gross, P. (2009) 'Betweenlands I-X', in *The Water Table*, High Green: Bloodaxe Books.

Guignard, L. M. (2001) 'Review: *The Atlas of Experience* by Louise van Swaaij, Jean Klare, David Winner', *Geographical Review*, 91(3): 614-616.

Hadyn, T. (2005) 'Assessment for learning', in S. Capel, M. Leask and T. Turner (2005) *Learning to Teach in the Secondary School: A Companion to School Experience*, London: Routledge.

Haggett, P. (1965) *Locational Analysis in Human Geography*, London: Arnold.

Hall, D. (1991) 'Charney revisited', in R. Walford (ed.) *Viewpoints on Geography Teaching*, London: Longman.

Hallam, S. and Ireson, J. (1999) 'Pedagogy in the secondary school', in P. Mortimore (ed.), *Understanding Pedagogy: And Its Impact on Learning*, London: Sage.

Hamilton-Wieler, S. (1989) 'A case study of language and learning in physical geography', in F. Slater(ed.) *Language and Learning in the Teaching of Geography*, London: Routledge.

Harlen, W., Gipps, C., Broadfoot, P. and Nuttall, D. (1992) 'Assessment and the improvement of education', *The Curriculum Journal* 3(3): 215-230.

Harrison, C. (2004) Understanding Reading and Development, London: Sage.

Harrison, C. M. (1986) 'Managing recreational areas; the effects of trampling on an ecosystem', in F. Slater (ed.), *People and Environments: Issues and Enquiries*, London: Collins Educational.

Hart, C. and Thomas, T. (1986) 'Framework fieldwork', in D. Boardman (ed.), *Handbook for Geography Teachers*, Sheffield: The Geographical Association.

Harvey, D. (1969) *Explanation in Geography*, London: Arnold.

Harvey, D. (1973) *Social Justice and the City*, London: Arnold.

Harvey, K. (1991) 'The role and value of A-level geography fieldwork: a case study', unpublished Ph.D. thesis, Department of Geography, Durham University of Geography.

Haubrich, H. (2006) 'Changing philosophies in geography education', in J. Lidstone and M. Williams(eds), *Geographical Education in a Changing World: Past Experiences, Current Trends and Future Challenges*. The Netherlands: Springer, pp. 39-54.

Hawkins, G. (1987) 'From awareness to participation: new directions in the outdoor experience', *Geography*, 72(3): 217-222.

Hawley, D. (2014) 'Looking Into the physical future', *Teaching Geography*, 39(1): 26-29.

Hay, J. (1994) 'Justifying and applying oral presentations in geographical education', *Journal of Geography in Higher Education* 18(1): 43-56.

Heilbronn, R. and Turner, T. (2005) '*Moral development and values*', Unit 4.5 in S. Capel, M. Leask andT. Turner (eds), *Learning to Teach in the Secondary School: A Companion to School Experience*, London: Routledge.

Henning, B. (2010) 'One world, many faces: a brief look at map projections'. Available at: http://www.viewsoftheworld.net/?p=752 [accessed 12 June 2014].

Her Majesty's Inspectorate (HMI) (1980) *A View of a Curriculum*, London: HMSO.

Her Majesty's Inspectorate (HMI) (1985) *Education Observed: Good Teachers*, London: HMSO.

Her Majesty's Inspectorate (HMI) (1986) *Geography from 5-16, Curriculum Matters 7*, London: HMSO.

Her Majesty's Inspectorate (HMI) (1988) *The New Teacher in School*, London: HMSO.

Hewlett, N. (2006) 'Using literacy productively', Chapter 11 in D. Balderstone (ed.), *Secondary Geography Handbook*, Sheffield: The Geographical Association.

Hicks, D. (1981) 'Images of the world: what do geography textbooks actually teach about development?', *Cambridge Journal of Education* 11: 15-35.

Hicks, D. (1993) 'Mapping the future: a geographical contribution', *Teaching Geography* 18(4): 146-149.

Hicks, D. (1994) *Educating for the Future: A Practical Classroom Guide*, Godalming: WWF.

Hicks, D. (2001) *Citizenship for the Future: A Practical Classroom Guide*, Godalming: WWF.

Hicks, D. (2007) *Lessons for the Future: The Missing Dimension in Education*, Oxford: Trafford Publishing.

Hicks, D. (2007) 'Lessons for the future: a geographical contribution', *Geography* 92(3): 179-188.

Hicks, D. (2013) 'Post-carbon geography', *Teaching Geography* 38(3): 94-97.

Hicks, D. (2014a) 'A geography of hope', *Geography* 99(1): 5-12.

Hicks, D. (2014b) *Educating for Hope in Troubled Times: Climate Change and the Transition to a Post-Carbon Future*, Stoke-on-Trent: Trentham/IOE Press.

Hicks, D. and Holden, C. (1996) *Visions of the Future: Why We Need to Teach for Tomorrow*, Stoke-on-Trent: Trentham Books.

Hicks, D. and Steiner, M. (eds) (1989) *Making Global Connections: A World Studies Workbook*, Harlow, Essex: Oliver and Boyd.

Hirsch, E. D. (1987) *Cultural Literacy: What Every American Needs to Know*, Boston: Houghton Mifflin Co.

Hirsch, E. D. (2007) *The Knowledge Deficit*, Boston, MA: Houghton Mifflin Co.

Hirst, P. (1974) *Knowledge and the Curriculum*, London: Routledge and Kegan Paul.

Hollingham, S. (1997) 'Using feature films in geography teaching', *Teaching Geography* 22(3): 111-133.

Holmes, D. and Farbrother, D. (2000) *A-Z Advancing Geography: Fieldwork*, Sheffield: The Geographical Association.

Holmes, D. and Walker, M. (2006) 'Planning geographical fieldwork', Chapter 18 in D. Balderstone (ed.) *Secondary Geography Handbook*, Sheffield: The Geographical Association.

Honey, P. and Mumford, A. (1986) *The Manual of Learning Styles*, Maidenhead: Honey.

Hopwood, N. (2004) 'Pupils conceptions of geography: towards an Improved understanding', *International Research in Geographical and Environmental Education* 13(4): 348-361.

Hopwood, N. (2011) 'Young people's conceptions of geography and education', in G. Butt (ed.),*Geography, Education and the Future*, London: Continuum.

House, D., Lapthorne, N., Moncrieff, D., Owbe-Jones, O. and Turney, A. (2012) 'Risky fieldwork',*Teaching Geography* 37(2): 60-62.

Hopkin, J. and Lambert, D. (2011) *Learning to be Human and the English Baccaluareate: Evidence from the Geographical Association*. Available at: file:///Users/davidlambert/Downloads/GA_AUEBacSelectCommitteeEvidence.pdf [accessed 3 March 2015].

Howes, N. (2006) 'Teacher assessment in geography', Chapter 34 in D. Balderstone (ed.), *Secondary Geography Handbook*, Sheffield: The Geographical Association.

HSGP (American High School Geography Project) (1971) *Geography in an Urban Age*, New York: CollierMacmillan.

Huckle, J. (1981) 'Geography and values education', in R. Walford (ed.), *Signposts for Geography Teaching*, Harlow, Essex: Longman.

Huckle, J. (1983) *Geography Education: Reflection and Action*, Oxford: Oxford University Press.

Huckle, J. (1990) *Environment and Democracy*, Godalming: Richmond Publishing/WWF.

Huckle, J. (1993) 'Environmental education and sustainability: a view from critical theory', inFien, J. (ed.) *Environmental Education: A Pathway to Sustainability*, Geelong: Deakin University Press.

Huckle, J. (1997) 'Towards a critical school geography', in D. Tilbury, and M. Williams (eds), *Teaching and Learning Geography*, London: Routledge.

IAAM (1967) *The Teaching of Geography in Secondary Schools*, 5th edn, Cambridge: Cambridge University Press.

ILEA (1984) *Geography Bulktin* No. 19, London: Inner London Education Authority.

Inman, T. (2006) *'Let's get physical'*, Chapter 22 in D. Balderstone (ed.), *Secondary Geography Handbook*, Sheffield: The Geographical Association.

Intel Teach Programme (2007) 'Designing effective projects: questioning the Socratic questioning technique', Available at www.intel.com/content/dam/www/program/education/us/en/documents/project-design/strategies/dep-question-socratic.pdf [accessed 20 July 2014].

International Baccalaureate: details available at www.ibo.org/diploma/curriculum/core/ [accessed 19 August 2014].

International Geographical Union Commission on Geographical Education (1992) The International Charter on Geographical Education. Available at www.igu-cge.tamu.ed/charters_1.htm [accessed 10 September 2013].

Jackson, P. (1989) *Maps of Meaning*, London: Unwin Hyman.

Jackson, P. (2006) 'Thinking geographically', *Geography* 91(1), Sheffield: The Geographical Association.

Jacobson, D., Eggen, P. and Kauchak, D. (1981) *Methods for Teaching: A Skills Approach*, Columbus, OH: Merrill Publishing.

James, M. (2000) 'Measured lives: The rise of assessment as the engine of change in English schools',*Curriculum Journal* 11(3): 343-364.

Jeans, R. (2006) 'Mapping for the future', Chapter 7 in D. Balderstone (ed.) *Secondary Geography Handbook*, Sheffield: The Geographical Association.

Jenkins, S. (1990) 'Not just about maps', *Times*, 7 June.

Jenkins, S. (1994) 'Rotten to the Core', *Times*, 11 May.

Job, D. (1996) 'Geography and environmental education: an exploration of perspectives and strategies', in A. Kent, D. Lambert, M. Naish and F. Slater (eds), *Geography in Education: Viewpoints on Teaching and Learning*, Cambridge: Cambridge University Press, pp. 22–49.

Job, D. (1997) 'Geography and environmental education', in A. Powell (ed.), *Handbook for Post-16 Geography*, Sheffield: The Geographical Association.

Job, D. (1998) *New Directions in Geographical Fieldwork*, Geography UPDATE Series, Cambridge: Cambridge University Press with Queen Mary and Westfield College, University of London.

Job, D. (2002) 'Towards deeper fieldwork', Chapter 10 in M. Smith (ed.), *Aspects of Teaching Secondary Geography*, London: RoutledgeFalmer.

Job, D. and Buck, A. (1994) 'Learning through models in the laboratory', *Teaching Geography* 19(3): 106–110.

Job, D., Day, C., & Smyth, T. (1999). *Beyond the Bike sheds - Fresh Approaches to Fieldwork in the School Locality*. Sheffield: The Geography Association.

Jones, F. G. (1984) 'Using expository methods well in geography teaching', in J. Fien, R. Gerber and P. Wilson (eds), *The Geography Teachers' Guide to the Classroom*, Melbourne: Macmillan.

Jones, M. and Rycraft, P. (2007) 'Animated discussion in geography', *Teaching Geography* 32(2): 93–6.

Joseph, K. (1985) 'Geography in the school curriculum', *Geography* 70(4): 290-298.

Joyce, B. and Weil, M. (1980) *Models of Teaching, Upper Saddle River, NJ*: Prentice Hall.

Kelly, A. V. (2009) *The Curriculum: Theory and Practice*, Sage: London.

Kent, A. (1996) 'Evaluating the geography curriculum', in A. Kent, D. Lambert, M. Naish and F. Slater (eds), *Geography in Education: Viewpoints on Teaching and Learning*, Cambridge: Cambridge University Press.

Kent, A., Lambert, D., Naish, M. and F. Slater (eds) (1996) *Geography in Education: Viewpoints on Teaching and Learning,* Cambridge: Cambridge University Press.

Kincheloe, J. and Steinberg, S. (1998) *Unauthorized Methods: Strategies for Critical Teaching,* London: Routledge.

Kinder, A. (2007) 'Planning a revised Key Stage 3 Curriculum', *Teaching Geography* 32 (3): 133.

Kinder, A. (2013) 'Keeping up with curriculum change', *Teaching Geography* 38(2): 56–59.

King, S. and Taylor, E. (2006) *'Using ICT to enhance learning in geography'*, Chapter 17 in D. Balderstone (ed.) *Secondary Geography Handbook,* Sheffield: The Geographical Association.

Kohlberg, L. (1976) *Recent Research in Moral Development,* New York: Holt, Reinhart and Winston.

Kolb, D. (1976) *Learning Style Inventory: Technical Manual,* Boston: McBer and Company.

Kyriacou, C. (1986) *Effective Teaching in Schools: Theory and Practice,* Oxford: Basil Blackwell.

Kyriacou, C. (1991) *Essential Teaching Skills,* Oxford: Basil Blackwell.

Kyriacou, C. (1997) *Essential Teaching Skills,* 2nd edn, Cheltenham: Stanley Thornes.

Lambert, D. (1991) *Geography Assessment,* Cambridge: Cambridge University Press.

Lambert, D. (1996) 'Assessing pupil attainment', in A. Kent, D. Lambert, M. Naish and F. Slater (eds), *Geography in Education: Viewpoints on Teaching and Learning,* Cambridge: Cambridge University Press.

Lambert, D. (1997a) 'Teacher assessment in the National Curriculum', in D. Tilbury and M. Williams (eds), *Teaching and Learning Geography,* London: Routledge.

Lambert, D. (1997b) 'Geography education and citizenship: identity and intercultural communication', in F. Slater and J. Bale (eds), *Reporting Research in Geography Education,* no. 5, London: University of London Institute of Education, pp. 1–13.

Lambert, D. (1997c) 'Opening minds', in F. Slater, D. Lambert and D. Lines (eds), *Education Environment and Economy: Reporting Research in a New Academic Grouping,* London: Bedford Way Papers, University of London Institute of Education, pp. 9–36.

Lambert, D. (1999) 'Geography and moral education in a super complex world: the significance of values education and some remaining dilemmas', *Philosophy and Geography* 2(1): 5–18.

Lambert, D. (2003) 'Effective approaches to curriculum development', in R. Gerber (ed.), International Handbook on Geographical Education. Netherlands: Kluwer Academic Publishers.

Lambert, D. (2004) Learning To Be Human: Why School Geography Matters',Lambert, D. (2004) 'Geography', in J. White (ed.), *Rethinking the School Curriculum: Values, Aims and Purposes,* London: RoutledgeFalmer.

Lambert, D. (2005) 'An axis to grind', *Times Educational Supplement,* 4 March 2005.

Lambert. D. (2007) 'What to teach', *The Guardian,* 13 September 2007. Available at: www.theguardian. com/education/2010/sep/14/curriculum-private-schools [accessed 15 February 2013].

Lambert, D. (2010) 'On being a professional geography teacher', in C. Brooks (ed.), *Studying PGCE Geography at M Level: Reflection, Research and Writing for Professional Development.* Abingdon: Routledge.

Lambert, D. (2014) *Think Piece: Issues in Geography Education: Session 8: 'Progression'.* Available at: file:///C:/Users/user/Downloads/GA_PRMGHProgressionThinkPiece.pdf [accessed 28 May 2014].

Lambert, D. and Balderstone, D. (2010) *Learning to Teach Geography in the Secondary School.* London: Routledge.

Lambert, D. and Biddulph, M. (2014) 'The dialogic space offered by curriculum making in the process of learning to teach, and the creation of a progressive knowledge led curriculum', *Asia-Pacific Journal of Teacher Education.* Published online 15 July 2014:DOI:10.1080/1359866X.2014.934197.

Lambert, D. and Butt, G. (1996) 'The role of textbooks: an assessment issue?', *Teaching Geography* 21(4): 202–3.

Lambert, D. and Jones, M. (2013) 'Introduction', in D. Lambert and Jones, M. (eds), *Debates in Geography Education,* London: Routledge.

Lambert, D. and Lines, D. (2000) *Understanding Assessment: Purposes, Perception and Practice*, London: RoutledgeFalmer.

Lambert, D. and Machon, P. (2001) *Citizenship through Secondary Geography*, London: RoutledgeFalmer.

Lambert, D. and Matthews, H. (1996) 'The contribution of geography to personal and social education', in E. Rawlings and R. Daugherty (eds), *Geography into the Twenty-first Century*, Chichester: John Wiley.

Lambert, D. and Morgan, J. (2010) 'What does it mean to be a teacher of geography', in *Teaching Geography 11–18: A Conceptual Approach.* Maidenhead: Open University Press.

Lambert, D. and Morgan, J. (2011) 'Geography and development: development education in schools and the part played by geography teachers', Centre for Development Education, Research Paper 3. London: Development Education Research Centre, Institute of Education.

Lambert, D. and Reiss, M. (2014) *The Place of Fieldwork in Geography and Science Qualifications.* London: Institute of Education, University of London.

Lambert, D. and Widdowson, J. (2006) 'Using geography textbooks', in D. Balderstone (ed.), *Secondary Geography Handbook,* Sheffield: Geographical Association.

Lambert, D., Morgan, A. and Swift, D. (2004) *Geography: The Global Dimension. Learning Skills for a Global Society,* London: DEA.

Lambert, D., Solem, M. and Tani, S. (2015) 'Achieving human potential through geography education: a capabilities approach to curriculum making in schools', *Annals of the Association of American Geography,* http://dx.doi.org/10.1080/00045608.2015.1022128.

Laws, K. (1984) 'Teaching the gifted student in geography', in J. Fien, R. Gerber and P. Wilson (eds), *The Geography Teachers Guide to the Classroom,* Melbourne: Macmillan, pp. 226–234.

Leask, M. and Pachler, N. (2005) *Learning to Teach using ICT in the Secondary School: A Companion to School Experience,* London: Routledge.

Leat, D. (1996) 'Raising attainment in geography', in M. Williams (ed.), *Understanding Geographical and Environmental Education: The Role of Research,* London: Cassell Education.

Leat, D. (1997) 'Cognitive acceleration in geographical education', in D. Tilbury and M. Williams (eds), *Teaching and Learning Geography,* London: Routledge.

Leat, D. (ed.) (1998) *Thinking Through Geography,* Cambridge: Chris Kington Publishing.

Leat, D. and Chandler, S. (1996) 'Using concept mapping in geography teaching', *Teaching Geography* 21(3): 108–112.

Leat, D. and McAleavy, T. (1998) 'Critical thinking in the humanities', *Teaching Geography* 23(3): 112–114.

Lederer, N. (2013) 'How to evaluate a movie', Video, or Film Clip. Available at: http://lib.colostate.edu/howto/evalmovie.html [accessed 6 August 2014].

Lewis, L. (2005) 'GTIP think piece - geography and literacy'. Available at: http://www.geography.org.uk/gtip/thinkpieces/geographyandliteracy/ [accessed 17 June 2014].

Lewis, M. W. (2012) 'Global warming and Siberia: blessing or curse?' Available at: www.geocurrents.info/place/russia-ukraine-and-caucasus/siberia/global-warming-and-siberia-blessing-or-curse#ixzz309ZVaP5A

Lofthouse, R. and Leat, D. (2006) 'Research in geographical education', Chapter 41 in D. Balderstone (ed.) *Secondary Geography Handbook,* Sheffield: The Geographical Association.

Long, M. and Roberson, B. S. (1966) *Teaching Geography,* London: Heinemann Educational.

Lunnon, A. (1969) 'The understanding of certain geographical concepts by primary school children',Unpublished M.Ed. thesis, University of Birmingham.

Lunzer, E. and Gardner, K. (1979) *The Effective Use of Reading,* London: Heinemann Educational Books for the Schools Council.

Lyle, S. and Sterling, S. (1992) *The Global Environment,* London: BBC/Longman/IBT.

Mackinder, H. J. (1911) 'The teaching of geography from an imperial point of view and the use which could and should be made of visual instruction', *Geographical Teacher* 6(30): 79–80.

Macleod, H. (1993) 'Teaching for ecologically sustainable development', in J. Fien (ed.), *Teaching for a Sustainable World*, Brisbane: Australian Association for Environmental Education.

Manning, A. (2014) 'Gersmehl and Gersmehl's "Wanted: a concise list of . . . spatial thinking skills"',*Geography* 99(20): 108–110.

Marland, M. (1993) *The Craft of the Classroom*, London: Heinemann.

Marsden, B. (1997) 'On taking the geography out of geography education: some historical pointers', *Geography* 82(3): 241–252.

Marsden, W. (1992) 'Cartoon geography: the new stereotyping?', *Teaching Geography* 17(3): 128–130.

Marsden, W. E. (1976) *Evaluating the Geography Curriculum*, Edinburgh: Oliver and Boyd

Marsden, W. E. (1989) '"All in a good cause": geography, history and the politicization of the curriculum in nineteenth and twentieth century England', *Journal of Curriculum Studies* 21(6): 509–526.

Marsden, W. E. (1995) *Geography 11–16: Rekindling Good Practice*, London: David Fulton.

Marsden, W. E. (2001) *The School Textbook: Geography, History, and Social Studies*, London: Psychology Press.

Martin, F. (2006) *e-geography: Using ICT in quality geography*, Sheffield: The Geographical Association.

Martin, F. (2006) *'Using ICT to create better maps'*, Chapter 10 in D. Balderstone (ed.), *Secondary Geography Handbook*, Sheffield: The Geographical Association.

Martin, F. (2011) 'Global ethics, sustainability and partnership', in G. Butt (ed.), *Geography, Education and the Future.* London: Continuum.

Marton, F. and Saljo, R. (1976) 'On qualitative differences in learning – 1: Outcome and process', *British Journal of Educational Psychology* 46: 4–11.

Massey, D. (2007) *For Space*, London: SAGE publications.

Matthews, H. (1998) 'Using the Internet for meaningful research', *Journal of the Geography Teachers Association of Victoria* 26(1): 15–19.

Matthews, M. (1984) 'Environmental cognition of young children: images of journey to school and home area', *Transactions of the Institute of British Geographers* 9: 89–105.

May, S. and Richardson, P. (2005) *Managing Safe and Successful Fieldwork*, Sheffield: The Geographical Association/Field Studies Council.

Maye, B. (1984) 'Developing valuing and decision-making skills in the geography classroom', in J. Fien, G. Gerber and P. Wilson (eds), *The Geography Teacher's Guide to the Classroom*, Melbourne: Macmillan.

McCormick, J. and Leask, M. (2005) 'Teaching styles', in S. Capel, M. Leask and T. Turner (eds),*Learning to Teach in the Secondary School: A Companion to School Experience*, London: Routledge.

McDowell, L. (1994) 'The transformation of cultural geography', in D. Gregory, R. Martin and G. Smith (eds), *Human Geography: Society, Space, and Social Science*, London: Macmillan.

McElroy, B. (1988) 'Learning geography: a route to political literacy', in J. Fien and R. Gerber (eds), *Teaching Geography for a Better World.*, Harlow, Essex: Longman.

McLaughlin, H. (1969) 'SMOG grading – a new readability formula', *Journal of Reading* 12(8): 639–646.

McPartland, M. (2001) *Theory into Practice:Moral Dilemmas*, Sheffield: The Geographical Association.

McPartland, M. (2006) 'Strategies for approaching values education', Chapter 15 in D. Balderstone(ed.), *Secondary Geography Handbook*, Sheffield: The Geographical Association.

Mitchell, D. (2008) *ICT in School Geography: More Than Motivation*, Sheffield: The Geographical Association.

Mitchell, D. (2007) *Getting Started with GIS . . . on the Internet . . . for Free*, Sheffield: The Geographical Association.

Mitchell, D. (2008) *Getting Started with GIS . . . Online . . . GIS in the World of Work*, Sheffield: The Geographical Association.

Mitchell, D. (2013) 'How do we deal with controversial issues?', in D. Lambert and M. Jones (eds), *Debates in Geography Education.* London: Routledge.

Mitchell, D. and Lambert, D. (forthcoming) 'Subject knowledge and teacher preparation in English secondary schools: the case of geography', *Journal of Teacher Development*.

Morgan, A. (2006) 'Teaching geography for a sustainable future', Chapter 23 in D. Balderstone (ed.),*Secondary Geography Handbook*, Sheffield: The Geographical Association.

Morgan, A. (2011) 'Sustaining ESD in geography', *Teaching Geography*, 36(1): 6–8.

Morgan, J. (2003) *'Cultural studies goes to school'*, Geography 88(3): 217–224.

Morgan, J. (2008) 'Curriculum development in new times', *Geography* 93(1): 17–24.

Morgan, J. (2010) 'What makes a good geography teacher?', in C. Brooks (ed.), *Studying PGCE Geography at M Level: reflection, research and writing for professional development*,Abingdon: Routledge.

Morgan, J. (2011) *Teaching Secondary Geography as if the Planet Matters*, London: Routledge.

Morgan, J. (2013) 'What do we mean by thinking *geographically*?' in D. Lambert and M. Jones (eds),*Debates in Geography Education*, Abingdon: Routledge

Morgan, J. and Lambert, D. (2005) *Teaching School Subjects 11–19: Geography*, London: Routledge.

Morris, J. (ed.) (1997) *Climate Change: Challenging the Conventional Wisdom*, London: Institute of Economic Affairs.

Myerson, G. and Rydin, Y. (1996) *The Language of Environment: The New Rhetoric*, London: University of London Press.

Naish, M. (1988) 'Teaching styles in geographical education', in R. Gerber and J. Lidstone (eds), *Developing Skills in Geographical Education*, Brisbane: International Geographical Union Commission on Geographical Education and the Jacaranda Press, pp. 11–19.

Naish, M. (1997) 'The scope of school geography: a medium of education', in D. Tilbury and M. Williams (eds), *Teaching and Learning Geography*, London: Routledge.

Naish, M., Rawling, E. and Hart, C. (1987) *Geography 16–19. The Contribution of a Curriculum Project to 16–19 Education*, Harlow, Essex: Longman. National Oracy Project (1990).

Naish, M. C. (1982) 'Mental development and the learning of geography', in N. J. Graves (ed.) *The New UNESCO Source Book for Geography Teaching*, London: UNESCO Press.

Nash, P. (1997) 'Card sorting activities in the geography classroom', *Teaching Geography* 22(1): 22–25.

National Oracy Project, Carter, R. (ed.) (1990) *Talking about Geography: The Work of Geography Teachers in the National Oracy Project*, Sheffield: The Geographical Association.

Natt, K. (1996) 'An example of pupil evaluation developed by a student teacher', inA. Kent et al. (eds), *Geography in Education*, Cambridge: Cambridge University Press.

NCET/GA (1997) *Geography: A Pupil's Entitlement for IT*, Sheffield: The Geographical Association.

NCGE (2014) 'Geography for Life: National Geography Standards', 2nd edn, Washington, DC: National Council for Geography Education.

Nicholls, A. (1996) 'Who's to blame for sharpe point flats?' *Northumberland 'Thinking Skills' in the Humanities Project: A Report on the First Year 1995–96*, Northumberland Advisory/Inspection Division.Nicholls, A. with Kinninment, D. (2001) *More Thinking Through Geography*, Cambridge: Chris Kington Publishing.

Nichols, A. (2006) 'Thinking skills and the role of debriefing', in D. Balderstone (ed.), *The Secondary Geography Handbook*. Sheffield: Geographical Association.

Norman, R. (2014) 'Creating crazy questions', *Teaching Geography*, Spring edition, 24–25.

Northumberland 'Thinking Skills' in Humanities Group (1996) *Northumberland 'Thinking Skills' in the Humanities Project: A Report on the First Year 1995–96*, Northumberland Advisory/Inspection Division.

Novak, J. and Gowin, D. (1984) *Learning How to Learn*, Cambridge: Cambridge University Press.

O'Connor, P. (2008) *GIS for A-level Geography*, Sheffield: The Geographical Association.

Oates, T. (2010) *Could Do Better: Using International Comparisons to Refine the National Curriculum in England*, Cambridge: Cambridge Assessment.

Oates, T. (2011) 'Could do better: using international comparisons to refine the national curriculum in England', *Curriculum Journal* 22(2): 121-150.

Oates, T. (2014) 'National Curriculum' (YouTube video), available at https://www.youtube.com/watch?v=-q5vrBXFpmO [accessed 5 March 2015].

Obrist, H. U. and McCarthy, T. (2014) *Mapping It Out: An Alternative Atlas of Contemporary Cartographies*, London: Thames and Hudson.

Ofsted (1993) *Geography: Key Stages 1, 2 and 3. First Year 1991-92. The Implementation of the Curricular Requirements of the Education Reform Act*, London: HMSO.

Ofsted (1994) *The Handbook for the Inspection of Schools*, London: The Stationery Office (TSO, formerly HMSO).

Ofsted (1995) *Geography: A Review of Inspection Findings 1993/4*, London: TSO.

Ofsted (2003) *Geography in Secondary Schools: Ofsted Subject Report Series 2001/02*, London: Ofsted.

Ofsted (2008) *Geography in Schools - Changing Practice*, London: Ofsted.

Ofsted (2011) *Learning to Make a World of Difference*, London: Ofsted.

Ofsted (2013) *Unseen Children: Access and Achievement 20 Years On - Evidence Report*, Crown Copyright.

Ofsted (2014) *School Inspection Handbook*, Crown Copyright 2015. Available at: https://www.gov.uk/government/publications/school-inspection-handbook [accessed 5 March 2015].

Orr, D. (1992) *Ecological Literacy: Education and the Transition to a Post-modern World*, Albany: State University of New York Press.

Oxfam (2003) *The Challenge of Globalisation: A Handbook for Teachers of 11-16 Year Olds*, Oxford: Oxfam.

Oxfam (2006) *Teaching Controversial Issues, Global Citizenship Guides*, Oxford: Oxfam.

Oxfam (2006) *Education for Global Citizenship: A Guide for Schools*, Oxford: Oxfam.

di Palma, M. T. (2009) 'Teaching geography using films: a proposal', *Journal of Geography*, 108(2): 47-56.

Palot, I. (1999) *Going Places: A Geography Careers Resource Pack*, Sheffield: The Geographical Association.

Parkinson, A. (2004) 'Have you met Geo Blogs?', *Teaching Geography* 29(3).

Parkinson, A. (2009) 'Think inside the box: miniature landscapes', *Teaching Geography* 34(3): 120-121.

Parkinson, A. (2013) 'How has technology impacted on the teaching of geography and geography teachers?', in D. Lambert and M. Jones (eds), *Debates in Geography Education*, London: Routledge.

Parkinson, A. and Vannet, V. (2008) 'Using digital learning resources in geography teaching', *Teaching Geography* 33(1).

Parnell, E. (2007) 'Geography is all about location, location, location', *Teaching Geography* 32(2): 91-2.

Payne, C. and Featherstone, R. (1983) 'Fieldwork in the classroom: How to make and use a stream table', *Teaching Geography* 8(4): 162-164.

Peacey (2005) *An introduction to Inclusion, Special Educational Needs and Disability*, in S. Capel, M. Leask and T. Turner (eds), *Learning to Teach in the Secondary School: A Companion to School Experience*, London: Routledge.

Perkins, D. (1996) *Outsmarting IQ: The Emerging Science of Learnable Intelligence*, Cambridge, MA: Harvard University Press.

Peters, R. S. (1965) *Education as Initiation*, Inaugural Lecture, London: ULIE.

Pike, G. and Selby, D. (1988) *Global Teacher Global Learner*, London: Hodder and Stoughton.

Pike, G. and Selby, D. (1995) *Reconnecting: From National to Global Curriculum*, Godalming: WWF.

Pomeroy, J. (1991) 'The press conference: a way of using visiting speakers effectively', *Teaching Geography* 16(2): 56-58.

Porter, A. (1986) 'Political bias and political education', *Teaching Politics*, September, 371-384.

Postman, N. and Weingartner, C. (1971) *Teaching as a Subversive Activity*, Harmondsworth: Penguin.

Powell, A. (ed.) *Handbook for Post-16 Geography*, Sheffield: The Geographical Association.

Price, J. (2003) *'Get Global!'*, London: Action Aid.

QCA (1997) *The Promotion of Pupils' Spiritual, Moral, Social and Cultural Development Draft Guidance for Pilot Work - November 1991*, London: Qualifications and Curriculum Authority.

QCA (2001) *Citizenship: A scheme of work for key stage 3, Teachers' Guide*, London: QCA.

QCA (2006) *GCE AS and A level subject criteria for geography*, London: QCA.

QCA (2007) *The National Curriculum for Geography*, London: QCA.

QCA (2008) *The National Curriculum for Information and Communication Technology*, London: QCA.

Ranger, G. (1995) 'Choosing places', *Teaching Geography* 20(2): 67-68.

Raths, J. (1967) 'Worthwhile Activities', in J. Raths, J. R. Pancella, and J. S. Van Ness (eds), *Studying Teaching*, Hemel Hempstead: Prentice Hall.

Raven-Ellison, D. (2005) 'Using digital video in geography', Geography PGCE workshop, Institute of Education, University of London.

Rawding, C. (2007) *Theory into Practice: Understanding Place as a Process*, Sheffield: The Geographical Association.

Rawding, C. (2013) *Effective Innovation in the Geography Curriculum: A Practical Guide*. Oxford: Routledge.

Rawding, C. (2014) 'The Importance of teaching 'Holistic' Geographies', *Teaching Geography* 39(2): 10-13.

Rawling, E. (1986) 'Approaches to teaching and learning in the classroom', in D. Boardman (ed.),*Handbook for Geography Teachers*, Sheffield: The Geographical Association, pp. 56-67.

Rawling, E. (1987) 'Geography 11-16: criteria for geographical content in the secondary school curriculum', in P. Bailey and T. Binns (eds), *A Case for Geography*, Sheffield: The Geographical Association.

Rawling, E. (1991) 'Making the most of the National Curriculum', *Teaching Geography* 16(3): 130-1.

Rawling, E. (1996) 'The impact of the National Curriculum on school based curriculum development in geography', in A. Kent, D. Lambert, M. Naish and F. Slater (eds), *Geography in Education: Viewpoints on Teaching and Learning*, Cambridge: Cambridge University Press, pp. 100-32.

Rawling, E. (1997) 'Geography and vocationalism: opportunity or threat?', *Geography* 82(2): 167-178.

Rawling, E. (2001) *Changing the Subject: The Impact of National Policy on School Geography 1980-2000*, Sheffield: The Geographical Association.

Rawling, E. (2003) 'Connecting Policy and Practice: Research in geography education', A Professional User Review of Educational Research undertaken for the British Educational Research Association (BERA).Rawling, E. (2004) 'Introduction: school geography around the world', in A. Kent, E. Rawling and R. Robinson (eds), *Geographical Education: Expanding Horizons in a Shrinking World*. Symposium of the Commission on Geographical Education (CGE), Glasgow: International Geographical Union - Commission on Geographical Education (IGU-CGE) in association with the Scottish Association of Geography Teachers.

Rawling, E. (2007) *Planning your Key Stage 3 Geography Curriculum*, Sheffield: The Geographical Association.

Rawling, E. (2008) *Planning your Key Stage 3 Geography Curriculum*, Sheffield: Geographical Association.

Rawling, E. (2010) '"The Severn was brown, and the Severn was blue" - a place for poetry in school geography? *Teaching Geography*, Autumn.

Rawling, E. and Westaway, J. (1996) 'Progression and assessment in geography at Key Stage 3', *Teaching Geography* 21(3): 123-129.

Ray, A. and O'Brien, R. (1990) 'South American housing crisis: a role-playing exercise based on urban issues in developing countries', *Teaching Geography* 15(1): 34-35.

Reay, D. and Wiliam, D. (2006) '"I'll be a nothing": structure and agency and the construction of identity through assessment', *British Journal of Educational Research* 25(3): 343-354.

Reid, A. (1996) 'Exploring values in sustainable development', *Teaching Geography* 21(4): 168-171.

Reigeluth, C. M. (1979) 'In search of a better way to organize instruction: the elaboration theory', *Journal of Instructional Development* 2(3): 8-15.

RGS-IBG (2007) 'Analysis of the 2007 Examination Results and the Current Status of Geography in England and Wales, Northern Ireland and Scotland'.

Rhodes, B. (1994) 'Learning curves . . . and map contours', *Teaching Geography* 19(3): 111-115.

Rice, G. (1994) 'The global AIDS pandemic: a diffusion simulation', *Teaching Geography* 19(3): 124-125.

Richardson, R. (1983) *Daring to Be a Teacher: Essays, Stories and Memoranda*, Stoke-on-Trent: Trentham Books.

Roberts, M. (1986) 'Talking, reading and writing', in D. Boardman (ed.), *Handbook for Geography Teachers*, Sheffield: The Geographical Association, pp. 68-78.

Roberts, M. (1987) 'Using video cassettes', *Teaching Geography* 12 (3): 114-117.

Roberts, M. (1995) 'Interpretations of the Geography National Curriculum: a common curriculum for all?', *The Journal of Curriculum Studies* 27(2): 187-205.

Roberts, M. (1996) 'Teaching styles and strategies', in A. Kent, D. Lambert, M. Naish and F. Slater (eds) *Geography in Education: Viewpoints on Teaching and Learning*, Cambridge: Cambridge University Press, pp. 231-259.

Roberts, M. (1997) 'Curriculum planning and course development: a matter of professional judgement', in D. Tilbury and M. Williams (eds), *Teaching and Learning Geography*, London: Routledge.

Roberts, M. (1997) 'Teaching styles and strategies', in A. Kent, D. Lamber, M. Naish, and F. Slater (eds), *Geography in Education: Viewpoints on Teaching and Learning*, Cambridge: Cambridge University Press.

Roberts, M. (2000) 'The role of research in supporting teaching and learning', in A. Kent (ed.), *Reflective Practice in Geography Teaching*, London: Paul Chapman.

Roberts, M. (2003) *Learning through Enquiry: Making Sense of Geography in the Key Stage 3 Classroom*, Sheffield: The Geographical Association.

Roberts, M. (2006) 'Geographical enquiry', Chapter 9 in D. Balderstone (ed.), *Secondary Geography Handbook*, Sheffield: The Geographical Association.

Roberts, M. (2010) 'Where's the geography? Reflections on being an external examiner', *Teaching Geography* 35 (3): 112-113.

Roberts, M. (2013) *Geography through Enquiry: Approaches to Teaching and Learning in the Secondary School*, Sheffield: Geographical Association.

Roberts, M. (2014) 'Powerful knowledge and geographical education', *Curriculum Journal* 25(2): 187-209.

Robinson, R. (1987) 'Discussing photographs', in D. Boardman (ed.), *Handbook for Geography Teachers*, Sheffield: The Geographical Association.

Robinson, R. (1995) 'Enquiry and connections', *Teaching Geography* 20(2): 71-73.

Robinson, R. and Serf, J. (1997) *Global Geography: Learning Through Development Education at Key Stage 3*, The Geographical Association/Birmingham Development Education Centre.

Rokeach, M. (1973) *The Nature of Human Values*, London: Free Press.

Romey, W. and Elberty, Jr., W. (1984) 'On being a geography teacher in the 1980s and beyond', in J. Fien, R. Gerber and P. Wilson (eds), *The Geography Teachers Guide to the Classroom*, Melbourne: Macmillan of Australia, pp. 306-316.

Rose, G. (1993) *Feminism and Geography*, London: Polity.

Ross, S. (1991) 'Cartoons in the classroom', *Teaching Geography* 16(3): 116-117.

Rubins, L. (1985) *Artistry and Teaching*, New York: Random House.

Sadler, R. (1989) 'Formative assessment and the design of instructional systems', *Instructional Science* 18: 119-144.

Saint Exupéry, A. de (1945) *The Little Prince*, London: Heinemann.

St. John, P. and Richardson, D. (1997) *Methods of Presenting Fieldwork Data*, Sheffield: Geographical Association.

St. John, P. and Richardson, D. (1996) *Methods of Analysing Fieldwork Data*, Sheffield: Geographical Association.

SCAA (1995) *Spiritual and Moral Development*, London: SCAA.

SCAA (1996b) *Consistency in Teacher Assessment: Exemplification of standards*, London: SCAA.

SCAA (1997) *Curriculum, Culture and Society*, London: SCAA.

Schaefer, F. W. (1953) 'Exceptionalism in geography: a methodological examination', *AAAG* 43: 226-249.

Schools Council (1973) *Teachers' Guide; Starting from Rocks; Starting from Maps; Case Studies*, Environmental Studies 5-13 Project, London: Hart-Davies Educational.

Shulman, L. S. (1986) 'Those who understand: knowledge growth in teaching', *Educational Researcher* 15(2): 4-14.

Sidall, S. (2009) *Landscape and Literature*. Cambridge: Cambridge University Press.

Simon, F. and Wright, I. (1974) 'Moral education: problem solving and survival', *Journal of Moral Education* 3(3): 241-248.

Slater, F. (1970) *The Relationship between Levels of Learning in Geography, Piaget's Theory of Intellectual Development and Bruner's Teaching Hypothesis*, Australia: Geographical Education AGTA.

Slater, F. (1982) *Learning through Geography*, London: Heinemann.

Slater, F. (1986) 'Steps in planning', in D. Boardman (ed.), *Handbook for Geography Teachers*, Sheffield: The Geographical Association, pp. 41-55.

Slater, F. (1988) 'Teaching style? A case study of post graduate teaching students observed', in R. Gerber and J. Lidstone (eds), *Developing Skills in Geography Education*, Brisbane: IGU Commission on Geographical Education/Jacaranda Press.

Slater, F. (1989) (ed.) *Language and Learning in the Teaching of Geography*, London: Routledge.

Slater, F. (1991) *Societies, Choices and Environments*, London: Collins Educational.

Slater, F. (1992) ' . . . to travel with a different view', in M. Naish (ed.), *Geography and Education: National and International Perspectives*, London: Kogan Page/ULIE.

Slater, F. (1993) *Learning through Geography, Washington, DC:* The National Council for Geographic Education.

Slater, F. (1996) 'Values: mapping their locations in a geography education', in A. Kent, D. Lambert, M. Naish and F. Slater (eds), *Geography in Education: Viewpoints on Teaching and Learning*, Cambridge: Cambridge University Press, pp. 200-230.

Slinger, Jonathan (2011) *Threshold Concepts in Secondary Geography Education*, Research report presented at The Geographical Association Annual Conference, University of Surrey, 16 April 2011.

Smith, D. M. (1977) *Human Geography: A Welfare Approach*, London: Arnold.

Smith, M. K. (1996) 'Curriculum theory and practice', *The Encyclopaedia of Informal Education*, Available at: www.infed.org/biblio/b-curric.htm [accessed 20 January 2014].

Smith, P. (1997) 'Standards achieved: a review of geography in secondary schools in England, 1995-96', *Teaching Geography* 22(3): 123-124.

Smith, M. K. (2000) 'Curriculum theory and practice', *The Encyclopaedia of Informal Education*, Available at: www.infed.org/biblio/b-curric.htm [accessed 5 March 2015].

Smith, M. K. (2012) 'What is pedagogy?' *The Encyclopaedia of Informal Education*. Available at: http://infed.org/mobi/what-is-pedagogy/ [accessed 16 July 2014].

Smith, M. (2013) 'How does ESD relate to geography education', in D. Lambert and M. Jones (eds), *Debates in Geography Education*, London: Routledge.

Smithers, A. and Robinson, P. (2012) *Educating the Highly Able*, Sutton Trust.

Soja, E. (1989) *Post Modern Geographies: The Reassertion of Space in Critical Social Theory*, New York: Verso.

Solem, M., D. Lambert and Tani, S. (2013) 'Geocapabilities: toward an international framework for research-ing the purposes and values of geography education', *Review of International Geographical Education Online (RIGEO)* 3, 3: 214-229. Available at: www.rigeo.org/2013-volume-3/number-3-winter.html.

Spencer, H. (2014) 'The sweatshop production game', *Teaching Geography,* Summer: 68-69.

Stenhouse, L. (1975) *An introduction to Curriculum Research and Development,* London: Heinemann.

Standish, A. (2009) *Global Perspectives in the Geography Curriculum: Reviewing the Moral Case for Geography,* London: Routledge.

Standish, A. (2012) *The False Promise of Global Learning: Why Education Needs Boundaries,* London: Continuum.

Standish, A. (2013) *The False Promise of Global Learning: Why Education Needs Boundaries,* New York: Continuum. Steiner, M. (ed.) (1996) *Developing the Global Teacher: Theory and Practice in Initial Teacher Education,* Stoke-on-Trent: Trentham Books.

Stembridge, J. H. (1936) *The Worldwide Geographies Series, Book IV: The World We Live In,* Oxford: Oxford University Press.

Sterling, S. (2001) *Sustaining Education: Revisioning Learning and Change,* Shumacher Briefings 6, Dartington: Green Books.

Stevens, S. (2001) 'Fieldwork as commitment', *The Geographical Review* 91: 66-73.

Stimpson, P. (1994) 'Making the most of discussion', *Teaching Geography* 19(4): 154-157.

Stott, P. (1997) 'Teaching lies', lecture given at the Geographical Association Annual Conference, London: Institute of Education, April.

Stradling, R., Noctor, M. and Bains, B. (1984) *Teaching Controversial Issues,* London: Arnold.

Sutton, R. (1995) *Assessment for Learning,* Salford: RS Publications.

Swain, Ashok (2001) 'Water wars: fact or fiction?' *Futures* 22(8-9): 769-781.

Swift, D. (2005) *Meeting SEN in the Curriculum: Geography,* London: David Fulton/The Geographical Association.

Taylor, D. (1997) 'The role of inspection in initial teacher training', in A. Hudson and D. Lambert (eds), *Exploring Futures in Initial Teacher Education: Changing Key for Changing Times,* London: Institute of Education Bedford Way Papers.

Taylor, E. (2001) 'Using presentation packages for collaborative work', *Teaching Geography,* 26(1): 43-45.

Taylor, E. (2004) *Re-presenting Geography,* Cambridge: Chris Kington Publishing.

Taylor, E. (2008) 'Key concepts and medium term planning', *Teaching Geography* 33(2): 50-54.

Taylor, E. (2009) *GTIP Think Piece – Concepts in Geography.* Geographical Association. Available at: www.geography.org.uk/gtip/thinkpieces/concepts/ [accessed 25 April 14].

Taylor, L. (2013) 'What do we know about concept formation and making progress in learning geogra-phy', in D. Lambert and M. Jones (eds), *Debates in Geography Education,* London: Routledge.

Thomas, S. and McGahan, H. (1997) 'Geography – it makes you think', *Teaching Geography* 22(3): 114-118.

Thompson, L. (2006) 'Target setting and target getting in geography', Chapter 33 in D. Balderstone (ed.), *Secondary Geography Handbook,* Sheffield: The Geographical Association.

Thompson, L., Roberts, D., Kinder, A. and Apicella, P. (2001) 'Raising literacy standards in geography lessons', *Teaching Geography* 26(4): 169-174.

Thompson, P. (2002) *Schooling the Rustbelt Kids: Making the Difference in Changing Times,* London: Trentham Books.

Thomson, P. and Hall, C. (2008) 'Opportunities missed and/or thwarted? Funds of knowledge meet the English national curriculum', *Curriculum Journal* 19(2): 87-103.

Tilbury, D. (1997) 'Cross-curricular concerns in geography: citizenship and economic and industrial under-standing', in D. Tilbury and M. Williams (eds), *Teaching and Learning Geography,* London: Routledge.

Tilbury, D. and Williams, M. (1997) *Teaching and Learning Geography*, London: Routledge.

Times Educational Supplement (TES) (1996) 'Historians want to curb the growth of GCSE rival', 13 September.

Tolley, H., Biddulph, M. and Fisher, T. (1996) *Beginning Initial Teacher Training*, Cambridge: Chris Kington Publishing.

Tolley, H. and Reynolds, J. B. (1977) *Geography 14–18. A Handbook for School-based Curriculum Development*, Basingstoke: Macmillan Education.

Totterdell, M. and Lambert, D. (1997) 'Designing teachers' futures: the quest for a new professional climate', in A. Hudson and D. Lambert (eds), *Exploring Futures in Initial Teacher Education: Changing Key for Changing Times*, London: University of London Institute of Education Bedford Way Papers, pp. 178–202.

UNESCO (1965) *Source Book for Geography Teaching*, London: Longman.

University of Newcastle School of Education (1995) *Improving Students' Performance: Guide to Thinking Skills in Education and Training*, Newcastle upon Tyne: Tyneside TEC.

Unwin. T. (1992) *The Place of Geography*, Harlow: Longman.

Urban earth: Mexico City. Available at: http://urbanearth.ning.com/video/urban-earth-mexico-city [accessed 4 August 2014].

Usher, R. and Edwards, R. (1994) *Postmodernism and Education*, London: Routledge.

van Matre, S. (1979) 'Sunship earth: An acclimatization programme for outdoor learning', Martinsville, IN: American Camping Association.

van Swaaig, L., Klare, J., and Winner, D. (2000) *The Atlas of Experience*. Oxford: Bloomsbury.

Vygotsky, L. S. (1978) *Mind in Society: The Development of Higher Psychological Processes*, Cambridge, MA: Harvard University Press.

Walpert, D. (2010) 'High-tech maps: Education or 'eye-candy?' Available at: www.learnnc.org/lp/editions/mapping/6408 [accessed July 28 2014].

Walford, R. (1969) *Games in Geography*, London: Longman.

Walford, R. (1984) Geography and the Future, *Geography*, 69(3): 193–208.

Walford, R. (1987) 'Games and simulations', in D. Boardman (ed.), *Handbook for Geography Teachers*, Sheffield: The Geographical Association.

Walford, R. (1991) *Viewpoints on Geography Teaching*, London: Longman.

Walford, R. (1995a) 'Fieldwork on parade', *Teaching Geography* 20(3): 112–117.

Walford, R. (1995b) 'Geographical textbooks 1930–1990: the strange case of the disappearing text', *Paradigm* 18: 1–11.

Walford, R. (1996) 'The simplicity of simulation', in P. Bailey and P. Fox (eds), *Geography Teachers' Handbook*, Sheffield: The Geographical Association.

Walford, R. (1998) 'Geography: the way ahead', *Teaching Geography* 23(2): 61–64.

Walford, R. and Haggett, P. (1995) 'Geography and geographical education: some speculations for the twenty-first century', *Geography* 80(1): 3–13.

Warn, S. (2006) *'Preparing for public examinations'*, Chapter 36 in D. Balderstone (ed.) *Secondary Geography Handbook*, Sheffield: The Geographical Association.

Warn, S. (2012) 'Teaching about conflicts at post-16', *Teaching Geography* 37(2): 57–59.

Water Footprint Network. Available at http://www.waterfootprint.org/?page=cal/ WaterFootprintCalculator [Accessed 11 June 2014].

Waterhouse, P. (1990) *Classroom Management*, Stafford: Network Educational Press.

Waters, A. (1995) 'Differentiation and classroom practice', *Teaching Geography* 20(2): 81–84.

Watkins, C. and Mortimore, P. (1999) 'Pedagogy: What do we know?', in P. Mortimore (ed.), *Understanding Pedagogy: And Its Impact on Learning*, London: Sage.

Watkins, C., Carnell, E., Lodge, C. and Whalley, C. (1996) *Effective Learning*, School Improvement Network, Research Matters: Institute of Education, University of London.

Waugh, D. and Bushell, T. (1992) *Key Geography Connections*, Cheltenham: Stanley Thornes.

Webb, M. (2005) 'ICT and classroom management', in M. Leask and N. Pachler (eds), *Learning to Teach Using ICT in the Secondary School*, London: Routledge.

Webb, N. M. (1989) 'Peer interaction and learning in small groups', *International Journal of Educational Research* 13, 21–39.

Webb, N. M. and Kenderski, C. M. (1985) 'Gender differences in small group interaction and achievement in high and low achieving classes', in L. C. Wilkinson and C. B. Marrett (eds), *Gender Differences in Classroom Interaction*, New York: Academic Press.

Weeden, P. (1997) 'Learning through maps', in D. Tilbury and M. Williams (eds), *Teaching and Learning Geography*, London: Routledge.

Weeden, P. (2005) 'Feedback in the classroom: developing the use of assessment for learning', *Teaching Geography* 30 (3): 161-163.

Weeden, P. (2013) 'How do we link assessment to making progress in geography?', in D. Lambert and M. Jones (eds) *Debates in Geography Education*, London: Routledge.

Weeden, P. and Butt, G. (2009) *Assessing Progress in Your Key Stage 3 Geography Curriculum*, Sheffield: The Geographical Association.

Weeden, P. and Hopkin, J. (2006) 'Assessment for learning in geography', Chapter 32 in D. Balderstone (ed.), *Secondary Geography Handbook*, Sheffield: The Geographical Association.

Weeden, P. and Lambert, D. (2006) *Geography Inside the Black Box: Assessment for Learning in the Geography Classroom*, London: nferNelson.

Weeden, P. and Lambert, D. (2010) 'Unequal access: why some young people don't do geography', *Teaching Geography* 35 (2): 74-75.

Weeden, P., Winter, J. and Broadfoot, P. (2002) *Assessment: What's in It for schools?* London: RoutledgeFalmer.

Wellsted, E. (2006) '*Understanding "distant places"*', Chapter 14 in D. Balderstone (ed.), *Secondary Geography Handbook*, Sheffield: The Geographical Association.

Wheelahan, L. (2009) *The Problem with CBT (& Why Constructivism Makes Things Worse)*. Griffith University, Australia. Available at: www98.griffith.edu.au/dspace/bitstream/handle/10072/28513/56421_1.pdf?sequence=1 [accessed 26 August 2014].

Whitaker, M. (1995) *Managing to Learn: Aspects of Reflective and Experiential Learning in Schools*, London: Cassell.

White, J. (1997) 'Quest for new moral givens', *Times Educational Supplement*, 10 January.

White, J. (ed., 2004) *Rethinking the School Curriculum: Values, Aims and Purposes*. London: Routledge Falmer.

Widdowson, J. and Lambert, D. (2006) '*Using geography textbooks*', Chapter 13 in D. Balderstone (ed.), *Secondary Geography Handbook*, Sheffield: The Geographical Association.

Wideen, M. and Grimmett, P. (1997) 'Exploring futures in initial teacher education: the landscape and the quest', in A. Hudson and D. Lambert (eds), *Exploring Futures in Initial Teacher Education: Changing Key for Changing Times*, London: University of London Institute of Education Bedford Way Papers, pp. 3–42.

Widdowson, J. and Lambert, D. (2006) 'Using geography textbooks', in D. Balderstone (ed.) *Secondary Geography Handbook*, Sheffield: Geographical Association.

Wiegand, P. (1996) 'Learning with atlases and globes', in P. Bailey and P. Fox (eds), *Geography Teachers' Handbook*, Sheffield: The Geographical Association.

Wilce, H. (1998) 'Timewasting is only a keystroke away', *Times Educational Supplment*, 30 January: 44.

Wiliam, D. (2006) *Excellence in Assessment: Assessment for Learning.* A supplement to the Cambridge Assessment Network Assessment for Learning Seminar held on 15 September 2006 in Cambridge, UK.

Wiliam, D and Black, P. (2002) 'Feedback is the best nourishment', *TES*, 4 October, 2002, Available online at https://www.tes.co.uk/article.aspx?storycode=369889 [accessed 5 March 2015].

Wilkinson, L. C. and Marrett, C. B. (eds) (1985) *Gender Differences in Classroom Interaction*, New York: Academic Press.

Williams, M. (1981) *Language Teaching and Learning in Geography*, London: Ward Lock.

Williams, M. (1997) *'Progression and transition'*, in D. Tilbury and M. Williams (eds), *Teaching and Learning Geography*, London: Routledge.

Wilson, P. (1971) 'An investigation into the understanding of certain geomorphological concepts of first year college of education students', unpublished MA dissertation, London: University of London Institute of Education.

Winchester, H., Kong, L. and Dunn, K. (2003) *Landscapes: Ways of Imagining the World*, Harlow, Essex: Pearson Education.

Winter, C. (1997) 'Ethnocentric bias in geography textbooks: a framework for reconstruction', in D. Tilbury and M. Williams (eds), *Teaching and Learning Geography*, London: Routledge.

Winter, C. (1997) 'Reconstructing curricular and pedagogical knowledge about places and people inthe geography classroom', in F. Slater and J. Bale (eds), *Reporting Research in Geography Education: Monograph Number 5*, London: Institute of Education.

Witt, S. (2013) 'Chance encounter of the playful kind: exploring places', *Teaching Geography* 38(3): 114–115.

Wood, P. (2002) 'Closing the gender gap in geography: update 1', *Teaching Geography*, 27 (1) , 41-43.

Wood, P. (2008) 'GTIP think piece – questioning', Geographical Association. Available at: www.geography.org.uk/gtip/thinkpieces/questioning [accessed 20 July, 2014].

Wray, D. and Lewis, M. (1997) *Extending Literacy: Children Reading and Writing Non-Fiction*, London: Routledge.

Wright, D. (1985) 'In black and white: racist bias in textbooks', *Geographical Education* 5, 13–17.

Wright, D. (2000) *Maps with Latitude*, Sheffield: Geographical Association.

WWF (1991) *The Decade of Destruction*, Godalming: Worldwide Fund for Nature UK.

WWF (1995) *Reaching Out, Godalming*: Worldwide Fund for Nature UK.

Yorkshire Dales National Park Committee (1989) *Landscapes for Tomorrow*, Skipton: YDNPC.

Youens, B. (2005) 'External Assessment and Examinations', in S. Capel, M. Leask and T. Turner (eds), *Learning to Teach in the Secondary School: A Companion to School Experience*, London: Routledge.

Young, M. (2008) *Bringing Knowledge Back In: From Social Constructivism to Social Realism in the Sociology of Education*, London and New York: Routledge.

Young, M. and Lambert, D. with Roberts, C. and Roberts, M. (2014) *Knowledge and the Future School: Curriculum and Social Justice*, London: Bloomsbury.

Young, M. and Muller, J. (2010) Three educational scenarios for the future: lessons from the sociology of knowledge, *European Journal of Education* 45(1): 11-27.

Young Peoples' Geographies Project. Available at www.geography.org.uk/projects/youngpeoplesgeographies/ [accessed 29 August 2014].

Younie, S. and Moore, T. (2005) 'Using ICT for professional purposes', Chapter 2 in M. Leask and N. Pachler (2005) *Learning to Teach Using ICT in the Secondary School: A Companion to School Experience*, London: Routledge.

Yoxall, W. (1989) 'A regional laboratory for earth science instruction – a rationale for using regional laboratories for practical work in the earth science component of physical geography', *Teaching Geography* 14(4): 169-172.

Index